SCHOOLING AND SOCIETY

EDITED BY

Lawrence Stone

SCHOOLING
AND
SOCIETY

Studies
in the History of
Education

THE JOHNS HOPKINS UNIVERSITY PRESS

Baltimore and London

Published under the auspices
of the Shelby Cullom Davis Center for Historical Studies,
Princeton University.

The Johns Hopkins University Press, Baltimore, Maryland 21218
The Johns Hopkins Press Ltd., London

Originally published, 1976
Second printing, 1978

Library of Congress Catalog Card Number 76–15005
ISBN 0–8018–1749–8
Library of Congress Cataloging in Publication data will be
found on the last printed page of this book.

CONTENTS

TABLES

CONTRIBUTORS

C. Arnold Anderson
Comparative Education Center
The University of Chicago
5835 Kimbark Ave.
Chicago, Illinois 60637

Mary Jean Bowman
Professor Emeritus of Economics
    and Education
The University of Chicago
5835 Kimbark Ave.
Chicago, Illinois 60637

Peter Clark
Economic History Department
Leicester University
University Road
Leicester, England

Patrick J. Harrigan
Department of History
University of Waterloo
Waterloo, Ontario N2L 3G1
Canada

Carl F. Kaestle
Department of Educational Policy Studies
School of Education
The University of Wisconsin
Madison, Wisconsin 53706

Thomas W. Laqueur
Department of History
University of California
Berkeley, California 94720

Peter Lundgreen
University of Bielefeld
USP Wissenschaftsforschung
4800 Bielefeld 1
Kurt-Schumacher-Str. 6
West Germany

Charles E. McClelland
Department of History
University of New Mexico
Albuquerque, New Mexico 87131

Howard Miller
Department of History
University of Texas
Austin, Texas 78712

Gerald Strauss
Department of History
Indiana University
Ballantine Hall
Bloomington, Indiana 47401

Selwyn K. Troen
Department of History
Ben Gurion University of the Negev
Beersheva, Israel

Arthur Zilversmit
Department of History
Lake Forest College
Sheridan and College Roads
Lake Forest, Illinois 60045

INTRODUCTION

This is the second, and last, volume of essays on the history of education to be sponsored by the Shelby Cullom Davis Center for Historical Studies. It is the product of papers produced by fellows and visitors to the center in the last two years of its concentration on the history of education, before it turned its attention to another theme.[1]

As with the first volume, the central concept behind all the articles here is to study the interaction between the formal institutions of education and the society within which they were set and on behalf of which they were supposed to function. Again, it becomes apparent that no clear relationship emerges from which a general theory can be constructed. The nearest approach to such a model is that provided by Professors Anderson and Bowman in the first article in the volume, in which they survey the whole field of educational history and relate it to theories of economic growth as applied to backward societies. They argue that literacy has certainly been a necessary, but not a sufficient, cause of economic growth in the West; that decisions about investment in education have been based on economic cost-benefit considerations, however crudely defined and imperfectly understood; and that the key educational sector for economic growth has been neither literacy nor the traditional literary high culture, but the development and transmission of specific technological and organizational skills. These are most likely to be fruitful if the social structure is open and fluid rather than closed; if there exist rapid communication networks and the presence of a critical intellectual mass which will generate an accelerator effect; if there is freedom for the import of human capital and skills; and if there is a tradition of practical administrative and technical expertise upon which to draw.

Professor Lundgreen uses nineteenth-century Germany as a test case for these theories about the relationship of education to economic growth. Using highly sophisticated computerized statistical models, he tries to determine definitively the exact degree to which economic growth was a result of education, independent of all other factors. His data consist of enrollment figures in educational institutions related to population size, and of money invested in education on the one hand, and statistics of output of capital and labor on the other. Given these variables, the problem is how to measure the importance of changes in the quality of labor, assuming that this is a function of the amount of schooling. Another test is measurement of earning differentials, which are taken to be partly due to differences in marginal productivity, themselves caused by changes in the amount of education. The third test is that of educational expenditure per capita in real as opposed to nominal terms. The gloomy conclusion of all three tests, based on very elaborate statistical calculations, is that in Germany between 1864 and 1911 and again in the 1950s "very little of the impressive rate of growth appears directly attributable to the growth of education." This challenging case study, which casts doubt on many traditional assumptions, is certain to start a vigorous controversy.

Part II is concerned with the ideas behind the startling expansion of education in Protestant Europe in the sixteenth century and with its practical consequences. It has long been known that the early Lutherans embarked on the first crusade for mass education that the West has ever seen, and Professor Strauss uses new sources to reveal the assumptions and methods of the first advocates of this revolutionary program. Not surprisingly, their ideas came not from nature, not from a prior examination of children and of the learning process, but from books, running all the way from Plato to Erasmus. Professor Strauss shows that the reformers had to choose between two contradictory theories of human nature, the first optimistic—that the child is born apt and eager for learning—and the second pessimistic—that the child is born with original sin, which it is the function of education so far as possible to bring under control. The reformers tended to the pessimistic position, which was the cause of much subsequent human misery. They did, however, have a clear view of the stages of growth and recognized that adolescence was a period of particular psychological stress. The learning process was thought to rely heavily on the memory, so that repeated exercises and an orderly system of instruction were seen as the keys to successful pedagogy. The chief inducements to learning were thought to be the desire for pleasure and the aversion to pain. Despite the warnings of the reformers, the latter was rapidly twisted by lazy schoolmasters into an excuse for the massive brutality that was to prevail in grammar schools for many centuries. The other inducement was the competitive instinct, every incentive for which was to be provided. Religious and moral indoctrination through the installation of fixed habits were taken for granted as the prime purposes of education, the child being regarded as plastic and easily and properly molded to whatever shape the educator considered desirable.

The prime purposes of this vast new educational enterprise were, first, the training of the good citizen, his socialization to accept the values of his culture; and second, indoctrination in the desired sectarian form of Christian piety. Self-fulfillment came a bad third, although the reformers did take over the humanists' insistence on the importance of a classical education for the elite. One can conclude that the sixteenth-century Protestant pedagogues approached their new task with a set of values and presuppositions which ensured that the methods would be authoritarian and the objectives repressive. They hoped by such means to create a virtuous and holy society—and inevitably they failed.

Mr. Clark looks at the outcome of the educational expansion of the sixteenth century by examining the social distribution and the type of books owned by members of the urban communities in southeast England between 1560 and 1640. He tackles what is—surprisingly enough—a relatively new problem in the historiography of education, namely, just what effect schooling had on the subsequent lives of ordinary people. He does this by asking the question, Who owned what books? He finds evidence that very substantial libraries were collected by a number of the wealthier members of the community, the books ranging all the way from religious tracts to the latest news sheets. The obsessive book collector had already appeared on the English provincial scene. More astonishing still is the growth of book ownership among that very substantial section of the urban population who made wills: by the 1630s almost half owned books. Professional men—lawyers, clerics, and schoolmasters—inevitably had the largest collections, but ownership was now spread widely down the social and occupational ladder to victuallers, textile workers, butchers, and even some laborers. By far the most widely owned book was the Bible, and religious works make up the bulk of all books specifically mentioned. Books dealing with the more secular aspects of middle-class culture of the time—whether plays or technical manuals or hand-books on conduct—are conspicuously absent.

This remarkable growth of book ownership was the product of a variety of forces: the rising standard of living, the Protestant drive for literacy to read the Bible, the provision of educational facilities and book stores in the towns. But of all the factors, Puritanism seems to have been the most important. The main driving force behind the educational revolution in England was religion.

Part III is concerned with explaining why at least two universities escaped the general decay, both in numbers and in intellectual vitality, that affected most of the institutions of higher education in the West in the eighteenth century. In England, Spain, Italy, France, and most of Germany and Austria, the decay was all too visible. In the American colonies, however—as in Scotland—most universities flourished; and Professor Miller uses both statistical and literary evidence to show how in at least one case—that of Princeton College—the driving force was the evangelical religious revival that characterized the time and place. Each college in the colonies represented a particular sectarian position and was designed primarily to produce ministers loyal to that sect, who would go out and proselytize on its behalf. Each college also enjoyed a local monopoly, in the sense that there was no competitor within the boundaries of the state within which it was situated. The colleges were also the training grounds for a fairly wide spectrum of the propertied classes, certainly far wider than was the case in England. Professor Miller shows how closely the fortunes of each college were dependent on the response of its constituency, and how any failure to respond to consumer demand was liable to prove almost fatal—for example, President Clapp of Yale's defiance of the new religious party known as "New Lights."

It was the alienation of these New Lights from Yale which provided the stimulation for the founding of the College of New Jersey. The frustrated energies of the revivalist movement were poured into making a success of the new college, which finally settled in the village of Princeton. Princeton from the start thus benefited from the revived Presbyterian enthusiasm of the age, and in turn spawned a far-flung evangelical empire through its alumni, who then fed students back into the college which had shaped them. Professor Miller shows how Princeton catered to three distinct groups: the sons of the secular commercial and landed elite, who were demanding no more than a pious, strict, and sound education for their children, who were destined for secular professions and offices, although a few were diverted into the ministry; the sons of the clergy, previously educated at Presbyterian schools and already destined for the ministry; and the sons

of small farmers, businessmen, and artisans, to whom higher education was a
means of upward social mobility by access to the ministry.

Professor McClelland tackles, again with the use of both literary and statistical
materials, another exception to the rule of decay, namely, Göttingen, which was
one of the two reformed universities in eighteenth-century Germany. Just as
Princeton catered to the evangelical revival and the needs of the middle-class elite,
so Halle and Göttingen catered to the need of the German nobility for a different
type of education which would fit them for service to the state. Göttingen,
therefore, enjoyed both state support and planning and a guarantee of consumer
demand. The state of Hanover wanted to enhance its prestige and to obtain the civil
servants it needed, but it realized that to survive, the university would have to
attract nobility from other states. It therefore deliberately designed a university that
served the wealthy nobility. It carefully avoided religious sectarianism (unlike
Princeton), it was staffed by the most famous professors in Europe that it could
attract, and it laid most emphasis on the two faculties of law and philosophy
(meaning history, languages, and mathematics). It thus offered a highly modern
and rationalistic curriculum, a broad but dilettantish survey of useful knowledge,
which was taught by the most distinguished of scholars. This was just what the
German nobility wanted in order to equip themselves for state service. Professor
McClelland's statistical evidence shows that the university succeeded in its objectives and did indeed attract a disproportionate number of nobles, especially to the
faculty of law. By tying admission and promotion in the civil service to academic
qualifications, the state of Hanover assured the success of Göttingen with the
nobility, while Göttingen's modern and practical curriculum in "philosophy"
had a wide appeal to the middle classes.

The stories of Princeton and Göttingen in the eighteenth century show how
universities could succeed even in a period of general stagnation and decay if they
were prepared to offer a curriculum carefully geared to the needs of a specific elite
and also attractive to other social groups.

Part IV takes up the unsolved problem of the motives behind the thrust towards
mass education in the late eighteenth and early nineteenth centuries on both sides
of the Atlantic. Professor Kaestle looks at the problem from the point of view of
supply, Professor Laqueur from the point of view of demand. The first question is,
What did the proponents of mass education hope to achieve? Was mass education a
middle-class device for social control over the brutalized urban proletariat of the
cities, to imbue them with middle-class values, the Puritan ethic, and a respect for
free-enterprise capitalism? Or was it a birthright freely conferred on all as a mere
act of humanitarian justice, the provision of individual opportunity for maximum
self-development?

In England in the early nineteenth century both views existed, and there was also
strong support for a more conservative position, that the education of the poor was
a dangerous step likely to lead to subversion, and possibly even revolution.
Professor Kaestle argues that very slowly the advocates of reform prevailed, but
largely by using the conservative argument of social control.

In America, on the other hand, the extreme conservative position had few if any advocates, largely because of the absence of the social basis—a formal nobility and a state church—for creating a Tory opposition to limited social mobility. As a result, the arguments on both sides of the Atlantic were similar, but the thrust in America was far more tolerant of social mobility than in England. The only area where the Tory argument prevailed was in the teaching of slaves, which was generally agreed to be a most dangerous and imprudent step. This peculiar openness of the Americans to the promotion of mass education stems, according to Professor Kaestle, from four factors: the higher level of literacy in America in the eighteenth century; the lower level of industrialization and urbanization, which dampened the fears of the elite; the egalitarian ideology inherited by America from its revolutionary origins; and the obvious need for acculturation and socialization of the constant stream of immigrants. The result was a system of education which in fact served collective needs, while professing individualistic goals.

Professor Laqueur turns the argument upside down and looks at the problem as it affected England in terms of popular demand rather than of elite supply. He points out that although the proportion of children in school doubled between 1818 and 1851, yet a very large proportion remained in private, fee-paying schools, under very informal, undisciplined methods of instruction, taught by amateur, unqualified teachers. The rationalized, disciplined, professional public institution of the modern school was not created until the middle and late nineteenth century.

Professor Laqueur rejects the argument that the lag in the development of a publicly supported system was due to the quarrel of the elite, the dispute between Anglicans and Dissenters for control over the system. He points out that the growth of other levels of schooling—grammar schools and public schools, for example—is explained in terms of consumer demand and argues that the same is true of elementary education. Even when free public schools were available, the poor preferred private fee-paying schools, partly because they belonged to their own culture and made no attempt to impose middle-class standards upon their children, partly because they offered a broader curriculum, and partly because they were more adaptable to the rhythms of working-class life. Since the private system satisfied the consumers, it maintained its share of the market in elementary education up to the 1830s.

Professor Harrigan tackles another open question about nineteenth-century education: Whether secondary education in France encouraged social mobility or deliberately obstructed it. It is a debate which can be solved only by the use of hard statistical data, and the essay is based on the records of a nationwide questionnaire issued in 1864–65. Professor Harrigan finds that the pattern of recruitment effectively excluded the children of unskilled rural or even urban workers, but that no less than one-third of the students came from the lower middle classes. The system thus provided a ladder of upward mobility for the petite bourgeoisie and helped to unify all classes from the lower middle class up, but in doing so it isolated the working class even more than ever. Although the *lycées* were attended mainly by children of the higher professions, they too were not impermeable to lower classes.

In terms of career realities (as opposed to aspirations, which were often disappointed), secondary education was clearly a road to upward mobility and to new careers, especially in medicine, teaching, and the army. On the other hand, the alumni of the lycées had a far better chance of entry into the professions than alumni of the *collèges communaux,* and to that extent the difference between the high bourgeoisie and the lower middle class was maintained. Occupational mobility existed to a greater extent than has previously been suspected, but it was limited by the existing social structure. What secondary education did offer, however, even to those who merely moved sideways, was a clear increase in status, which marked its alumni off from those whose education terminated at the elementary level.

Part V tackles some key problems concerning educational reform in twentieth-century America. Professor Troen asks why educators began to worry about the proportion of high school dropouts and to institute measures to reduce it by the use of the carrot—a more vocational curriculum—and the stick—measures of legal compulsion. The traditional explanation is that this movement was a humanitarian response to new awareness of the peculiar problems of adolescence, made popular by the writings of G. Stanley Hall. Professor Troen takes a more economic determinist view, concluding that the driving force was the need to prepare a larger labor force as future workers in the expanding urban technological society. He points to the extraordinarily high attrition rate of attendance between elementary and secondary education in St. Louis in 1898, and demonstrates educators' lack of concern about this problem, largely because there was no demand for higher levels of skill in the current labor market. He shows how during the next twenty years trained personnel using more complex machinery were displacing the unskilled teenage labor force in many urban occupations. At the same time, the apprentice system of on-the-job training declined, thus forcing the schools to take over the task of vocational education in many areas. The result was a dramatic increase in the number of high school students, especially in the new curriculum. This shift of secondary education from being oriented primarily to preparation for college to being also a preparation for a skilled occupation in a more technological society fundamentally transformed the character of the American high school.

Professor Zilversmit picks up the story where Professor Troen leaves off and looks at the practical effects of the "progressive" educational reforms from 1920 to 1940. "Progressive" means a curriculum oriented around the individual child and the elimination of both rote learning and a subject-centered curriculum. He shows how, despite the great publicity that attended these reforms and the attention paid to them by educational historians, the results, in practical statistical terms of the number of children affected, were in fact minimal. Insofar as their impact on American education in general is concerned, the reforms were a resounding failure. The application of statistical tests—such as the educational level of the teachers, the use of mobile rather than bolted-down classroom furniture, and the presence of child psychologists and social workers—corrects previous generalizations based on too easy acceptance of the rhetoric of the reformers themselves.

Professor Zilversmit attributes the failure of the reforms partly to the depression of the 1930s and partly to the shortage of teachers committed to the new ideology.

The problems studied by the authors of these essays range widely over time and space. But they are all asking similar questions, about the relationship of ideas and religion on the one hand and economic and social realities on the other to the formation of educational institutions and curriculum. Whenever possible and relevant, they try to answer these questions by the use of statistical evidence. Where such methods are not suitable, they employ the traditional technique of a close examination of literary sources. But whatever the methods employed, all the essayists are determined to relate the peculiar character of the specific educational institutions to the peculiar demands—intellectual, religious, social, or economic—of the particular clientele which they served.

Lawrence Stone

NOTE

1. The first volume was *The University in Society,* ed. L. Stone (Princeton: Princeton University Press, 1974). The next theme to be taken up by the Davis Center is popular religion and popular culture.

PART I

Education and Economic Growth

CHAPTER 1

Education and Economic Modernization in Historical Perspective

BY C. ARNOLD ANDERSON

AND MARY JEAN BOWMAN

The proposition that education is requisite for economic "growth" is today virtually a platitude. Attempts to explain in general terms how education becomes combined with other factors to bring about such growth are being pushed vigorously by representatives of all the social sciences.[1] To show also how education has played now a leading and now a secondary part in the waxing and waning of forward economic surges in a given society must be a task for our scholarly heirs.[2]

There are many sorts and many loci of education: in the home, at work, in schools; formal and informal; variously spaced over individuals' lifespans. These many aspects of education or learning are in various ways and degrees complementary to and substitutes for each other. Separately and in combination they come to be linked diversely with other aspects of economic activity and institutional evolution as successive phases of growth unfold. "Human capital" is a multifaceted resource, and no simple formula for human capital as a single aggregative variable can carry us beyond the essential first awareness of how crucial human competencies are for economic development. By the same token, partisans of schooling as a key factor in change must acknowledge the independent and associated effects on change of other components in human resources, of physical capital formation, and of social and political institutions. Nevertheless, to seek to trace the mutual connection of education (whether narrowly or broadly defined) with "political" or "social" as well as with economic aspects of societal change presents problems so difficult and concepts so elusive that we can as yet barely sketch these influences. One route into this complex matrix is to start with economic models and then to move out to a broader nexus of potential causes and effects.

Over the past two decades there has been a cumulation of research efforts to construct economic models of long-term change or growth that assign an explicit place to education and to measure the place of education in growth. As models are

This is a revised and shortened version of a paper originally presented at the 1968 meetings of the International Economic History Association.

made more complex, however, more and more must be borrowed from sociologists or historians who may have little interest in economic analysis. At the same time, the applicability of today's economic-decision theories to explaining families' choices of education or training in fourteenth-century Flanders or sixteenth-century England and to evolution of apprenticeship rules becomes more obviously useful.[3]

Ranging into other disciplines will more thoroughly convince us that no school "system" is fitted closely to the environing society. The formation of capabilities and the transmission of attitudes and information are functions of interaction among schooling and other educational agencies, experiences, and influences.

The exposition below has three parts: (1) We trace connections between early industrialization in the West and literacy. We conclude that literacy was more essential than usually has been acknowledged. (Japanese developments, to which we give only passing mention, would support our conclusions.) On the other hand, although a moderate spread of literacy was necessary, literacy alone could not initiate or sustain economic advance. (2) We argue that explicit decisions based on economic considerations guided the spread of training and of schooling. Even if one finds conclusions about the impact of education unconvincing, the dissemination of education tangibly reflects a balancing of benefits and costs to identifiable sets of families and enterprises. Moreover—though we do not treat this topic— "practical" forms of education were especially responsive to economic decisions, and such training was salient among the educational influences upon economic development. (3) The development and transmission of know-how, or practical ingenuity, and of intellectual skills are at the heart of economic development. These qualities are especially important for men who adapt to and participate in the implementation of technological and organizational change—in contrast to those who carry on routine practices. Arrangements for the shaping of men to participate in change include schooling but go beyond it; they include diverse sorts of learning at work and the diffusion of know-how by migration.[4]

LITERACY IN EARLY MODERNIZATION

Invention of crops and new methods of tillage that laid the agricultural foundation for modern industrial revolutions owed little to literate men.[5] Neither the invention of the horse collar nor improved rigging of sails stemmed from the reading of books. But the emergence of sustained industrial advance, with its special integration of many threads of technical skill and of organization, cannot so confidently be viewed as independent of recorded lore and intellectual broadening. How widespread did literacy have to be to consolidate fifteenth- or seventeenth-century impulses to growth? Does our earlier Western experience yield any guidelines for the aspiring societies of today?

The prevalent view of recent books on economic history is that the initial industrial revolution was carried through by an English population in which few men except clergy and the leading merchants could read. Indeed, it would seem that, in contrast to economic historians, historians interested mainly in noneconomic events have been most ready to accept the proposition that a broad distribution of literacy and of schooling underlay the emergence of the modern European economy.[6]

Since much of this evidence has been summarized in the sources cited, only main threads in the interrelated educational developments need be identified here.[7] Numerous programs for education have been pinpointed over northwestern Europe beginning with the thirteenth century, and there is evidence for the growing literacy of laymen during the succeeding couple of centuries. A large proportion of London merchants were literate by the mid-fourteenth century. Various documents, including bills for services of laborers, suggest that there were substantial proportions of literate artisans; this proportion rose steadily as we move into the seventeenth century, at least in England. Before the middle of the nineteenth century more than half the males in England and in French cities had some competence in reading and writing.[8] In France the percentages of grooms unable to sign their names declined from seven in ten in the late seventeenth century, to one-half in the late eighteenth century, and to one in five by the 1870s; for brides, the corresponding proportions were five in six, three in four, and one in three.[9] The spectacular economic expansion of the United States during the nineteenth century surely reflected the near-universal white male literacy of the northern sections even before we became a nation.

Only a few bits of the indirect evidence that economic historians may use need be mentioned. For example, in England men striving for reform wrote in the vernacular even in the fifteenth century, and during the political controversies of the sixteenth century handbills in English were scattered in the streets. Contemporary efforts by the Crown to interdict the reading of the Bible by ordinary men could hardly succeed. There is a long history of legal efforts by the clergy to keep tight control over teachers—and often for quite nonreligious motives. For example, in Gloucester in 1410 there was a protest because private-venture teachers had cut tuition from forty to twelve pence per quarter.

A cross-sectional analysis of the world's nations in the 1950s yielded a conclusion that seems also to reflect the historical evidence: a male literacy rate of about 40 percent is required (but alone will not suffice) to support sustained economic growth.[10] More diffuse literacy (or the equivalent rate of elementary enrollment) will bring little further economic advancement until literacy rates of around 70 to 80 percent are achieved. Using data spanning only a short generation in the middle of this century, we concluded that earlier levels of national per capita income predicted primary schooling of the 1950s better than 1955 incomes could be predicted from primary enrollments a generation earlier.[11]

The governments in today's less-developed countries are forcing the pace of expansion in education, principally of formal schooling. Hence, countries that today reach intermediate or higher levels of income will have higher literacy or schooling levels than did the bellwether nations at a corresponding point in their history. Widespread schooling has become an end in itself to a degree not true in most of the earlier-developing countries. But modern productive organizations are built upon more complex structures for compiling, storing, and communicating information. Although higher levels of trained intelligence are required for adopting and adapting our technology, only by means of a complex auxiliary and complementary culture resembling that of the pace-setting societies will higher levels of schooling yield prompt or impressive economic results.[12]

The historical data permit us to conclude that various modalities of literacy become essential for economic advance prior to the appearance of "scientific" technology. The more historical confirmations of that generalization we possess, the more urgent it becomes that we find out just *how* education fosters economic progress. Numerous new studies are identifying the importance of human capital for the manifold aspects of modern production.[13] But, as set forth above, education played a key part in earlier commercial and technological revolutions. The following three speculative paragraphs lay out some inquiries we would like to see historians undertake into the way education enters the "process" of development.

1. Not uncommonly, a historian will remark that "there was a demand for people to keep accounts and to conduct commercial correspondence." But would this demand have added up to even a third of the work force? How many literate men, if any, came to be needed as manufacture grew in importance? Perhaps the needed initial increase in the proportion of literate men (among nonpeasant workers) was not large in those countries first to industrialize. The increment may be larger, however, for countries now striving to build on new technology for economic growth. Does the size of this incremental demand for literacy reflect the comparative weight of "collectivized" direction over the economy? The important element may indeed be more organizational than technological. But the organizational transformations are of several kinds. While reorganization of production, transportation, and trade both foster and presuppose literacy, the total number employed as scribes and bookkeepers may tell us more about political bureaucratization than about innovative progress in the organization of economic life.

2. A second set of hypotheses arises when we focus more upon diffusion of reading ability than on ability to write and to cipher. Where ability to read is widespread, diversification of channels and media for communication ensues. As economic transactions ramify and accompanying organizations become more extended, the volume of depersonalized transmission of information expands.[14] Literacy facilitates the storage of information in many forms accessible to ever larger proportions of a population. Practical handbooks were prominent among the early products of printing. Less often noticed by economic historians, pamphlets and books about strange and different places (often imaginary) found ready sale. The wearing away of provincialism through reading about life in exotic circumstances surely strengthened orientations toward the nonlocal aspects of economic affairs that constitute a vital part of any commercial revolution. For some countries one must emphasize religious motives for becoming literate; a map of vernacular versions of the Bible resembles a map of early modern centers of trade.

3. Almost every effect of literacy includes an element of change in men's perceptions of the alternatives in action that are open to them. Literacy contributes awareness of nonconventional and nontraditional possibilities—of ways to do things—including other kinds of jobs or careers than kin or neighbors have followed. Even old lines of work become changed because literacy (and other components of the basic three Rs) brings accessibility to the storehouse of how-to-do-it handbooks. In tracing out any of these effects from education one need not try to determine whether literacy was "required" for the job. Even meager schooling can affect the kinds of job a man seeks, and it can encourage him to innovate in his work. Literacy fosters, but is not essential to, adaptability to changes introduced by employers or by innovative competitors. Undeniably, these change-fostering traits are displayed only weakly by most literate men, just as most university graduates do only a modest amount of hard reading in leisure hours. But elementary (and, in due course, secondary) schooling enlarges the number of individuals who can play at least a corporal's role in economic development. Perhaps in the early stages of an economic transformation these alert individuals are aroused in numbers greater than are recruits to literacy. But the stimuli to innovation and capability for adaptation operate in due course at successively higher levels of schooling; these successive levels are generated by and are required to cope with the rising complexity in content of written materials used in daily life.

The correlation between the amount or quality of an individual's education and the kind of work he does is not one-to-one in any society.[15] The better-educated men (at whatever level) typically precede others in decoding new information and in adopting innovations. Where these changes are highly visible and face-to-face, communication is well developed, and early innovators may be imitated quickly by men with little or no schooling. Recent studies of relationships between schooling and agricultural progress in a community bring this out clearly. It is not clear, however, to what extent this was true historically, in periods of less rapid advance in agricultural technology.[16] Nevertheless, however tight or tenuous the association between education and economic performance, schooling does tend everywhere to become linked to distinctive contrasts in ways of living, ways that represent functionally different contributions to an economy that is undergoing transformation. This pattern has been depicted for certain sets of nonwhites in South Africa, as follows:

The illiterate in the community tend to form a group with mutual interests and conservative outlook. As boys, they will have played and fought together while herding stock, at a time when many of their contemporaries are attending school. As youths, they are recruited from the village, in groups, by the Native Recruiting Corporation for work in the gold mines, and, not having had their awareness developed by education, their experiences while away on tours of work do little to alter their conservatism. . . . On the other hand, the people with some education prefer to seek employment in industries rather than the mines and, having had their perceptibilities sharpened by education, they are usually greatly influenced by the experiences of town life.[17]

Yet, however stable such contrasts in ways of life may be, the economic payoff from schooling for individuals is an imprecise index to the aggregative effects of education upon economic development. Income differentials for sets of individuals possessing different amounts of schooling may either overestimate or underestimate societal benefits from education, even in a single sphere such as the economic. In societies that are elitist or rigid, the power of men in positions of privilege blocks many contributions of education to growth, even as they magnify gains from observed differentials between the more and the less educated. In a more open society, on the other hand, the potential economic contributions of education will be realized more fully; by the same process, artificially maintained diseconomic disparities in incomes will be worn away. The importance of education, accordingly, is overestimated just where rigidities subvert its potentials. By the same logic, underrating the income differentials associated with disparities in education leads to understating societal returns just where open opportunity allows schooling to make its maximum contribution to change.

ECONOMIC CHOICE AND THE DIFFUSION OF SCHOOLING

Some patterns of relationship between schooling and economic development have been delineated in the preceding section. To a degree it has been possible to identify the ways in which the specific capabilities induced by schooling or training become part of forward-thrusting economic changes. In the present section we will argue that anticipations of demands for skill and capability such as are produced by education also influence individuals' decisions to obtain education. Economic considerations are important, though never all-determining, influences upon the rate at which education diffuses and the social groups or networks through which aspirations for it spread. Studies providing evidence concerning determinants of diffusion of education are uncommon even for contemporary societies. Presentations of historical evidence are rare indeed, though presumably a model that was useful in present-day investigations for the less-developed countries would also be applicable in investigations by historians.

Conceptual models for these investigations must allow us to explore contrasting patterns in diffusion of education within and among key subpopulations. Cross-section data by areas or population categories provide a basis for initial tests, but observations in actual historical sequences will be needed to establish firm generalizations. Hägerstrand's diffusion models[18] can be combined with economists' theories about decisions to invest in human resources.[19] Economists posit that investment will be made in education so long as the present value of a future stream of earnings from added training exceeds the present value of the costs of qualifying to obtain those earnings. This model does resemble actual behavior in procuring education.

A tautological model would not be helpful; that is, it would not be enlightening to say that people desire the amount and kind of education that they do in fact absorb.[20] The economic investment model by intent does not take account of attitudes toward education "as a value in itself."[21] This constraint is an advantage in empirical studies, for it allows us to ascertain the extent to which group differentials in schooling or rising levels of schooling over time may be attributed explicitly to economic considerations.[22]

Let us consider what proportion of an age cohort of some stated subpopulation will acquire a given increment of schooling. There are four categories of explanatory factors:

$C:$ costs of schooling the stated subpopulation;

$R:$ expected or perceived returns (earnings or occupational advantages) to be obtained from the intended increment of schooling;

$B:$ anticipated noneconomic benefits, such as more leisure or greater prestige (but not including pleasures of the schooling "in itself");

$A:$ total resources within the subpopulation to pay for the added schooling of their youth.

C *(costs).* There are (a) direct costs and (b) earnings given up while in school or under apprenticeship. In situations familiar to us public subsidies absorb much of direct costs. Indeed, the fashion of today to assign these costs to the state blinds us to the frequency with which, in the past, payment for schools was made by the group whose offspring received the instruction.[23] In some developing countries today direct fees are added to local taxes, leaving only a modest share of costs for the larger public.

It would surely prove rewarding if economic historians were to search in the records of medieval church schools to find out which people paid the costs and who supplied the pupils. Surely it is possible to trace how guild support of instruction in reading or ciphering reflected the sources from which apprentices came. When guilds made literacy a prerequisite to apprenticeship rather than a part of it, a shift in bearing of costs followed. So far as we can find out, no one has gone very far in explaining the financing of the English charity schools. As a related question, for which sorts of children were charity schools a process of "searching out talent" that could be directed toward the schools of higher quality (which perhaps demanded supplementary fees from parents)? English historians have pointed out how community support of community schools led to broader educational opportunities: since the school was viewed as a collective service, boys and even girls from humble families of the town were admitted as normal pupils.

That children's usefulness in parental business affects levels of attendance in school was not first discovered in the industrial cities of the nineteenth century. Insuring flexibility in the school calendar parallels Heaton's story of how shops were closed in the early wool towns to get all possible hands into the harvest fields. Such adaptation to circumstances affects the total input of resources into a child's year of schooling.[24] One can still see crop seasons reflected in school attendance among farm populations in industrial countries. In urban jobs seasonal labor demands rarely induce a parallel rise and fall in foregone earnings per school day.

Urban enrollments, however, are affected by wage rates at the margin for those year-round jobs that are open to juveniles. Standard histories of education in Britain recount how eighteenth- (and even nineteenth-) century Sunday schools offered several hours of secular instruction on the Sabbath. And the more canny working-class parents patronized those Sunday schools that provided a superior instruction (often for a fee) because pupils from those schools were reputed to get better jobs. These effects of urban working and living conditions upon patronage of schools are now receiving more attention from historians.[25] Parallel explorations of how changed farming practices affect the schooling of rural children are not numerous.[26]

R (earnings and occupational gains). The economic effects of education include not only income yielded from investment in human capital but also job satisfactions over and beyond earnings. Historical data will rarely permit us to compute even monetary rates of return, though burrowing in the archives has hardly begun. We may expect that information will accumulate on how people in the past calculated what they might gain from spending more time in school or training. Crucial evidence is found in data that reveal the "supply responsiveness" of private-venture instruction. Occupations requiring more than the average preparation sometimes brought only modest advantages in earnings, but the attractiveness of such occupations could be reflected in the multiplication of programs of "teaching for hire." Increased access to such occupations also in turn strengthens emulation and fosters mobility. Response to emerging opportunities could take many forms. If we include "job satisfactions," we can envisage a multidimensional perception of opportunities.

Presumably, returns to schooling reflect existing and anticipated differentials in occupational status and income. A dynamic interpretation calls for evidence as to how relevant and how visible such opportunities were for specified subpopulations. Could children of nonpropertied peasants, for example, see a way out of rural poverty by means of schooling?[27] The economists' decision model will be more powerful if it includes sociological evidence about social mobility alongside the human geographer's analyses of how information and attitudes spread in geographic space and among or within social strata. Surely aspirations for and utilization of education diffuse in accordance with visibility of opportunities. New perceptions of gains to be realized from education will follow the looser rather than the more rigid segments of the social structure. In turn, education normally loosens that structure; rarely can benefits of expanded formal instruction be narrowly held within small elites or ethnic subpopulations.

The Russian peasants in the eighteenth century who had the most urban contacts were the most likely to get some schooling and to enter industrial jobs, as Kahan shows.[28] Goldblatt found that literacy and school enrollments in rapidly growing cities of contemporary Mexico are less buoyant than one would expect; presumably, the hordes of new migrants into these cities retain limited horizons despite the visibility of the high returns of schooling among their more assimilated neighbors.[29] Among Mexican states, strong demand for employment of young children is negatively associated with rural enrollments. Yet this variation in opportunity costs of attendance seems to be unimportant for explanation of locational differences in urban enrollments. Gaps in information fields and lags in closing those gaps appear to have been more important than differential opportunities for child employment in explaining the spread of primary schooling among urban residents.

Growth nodes and spatial mutipliers are familiar concepts for describing the ecological disparities in economic growth. In dynamic centers there are stronger incentives for acquiring useful training. In such places there is also more disposable income to support nonuseful or "consumption" education. Thus, a century ago, those English counties with highest literacy had less early marriage and fewer employed in agriculture but larger savings per capita. These kinds of geographic disparities in economic level are very persistent; for example, literacy contrasts among French departments did not change greatly from the late seventeenth to the mid-nineteenth century.[30]

In writing prescriptions for third-world educational policy today, one would be imprudent to specify hastily what kinds of education will prove to be most "practical." If we have rich historical data, it is somewhat easier to avoid unfounded conclusions on that point. Throughout Western history "literary" schooling has been highly useful, and not only for the clergy, who were its main early supporters. Not every historian takes care to point out how zealously merchants fostered literacy and auxiliary skills ranging from knowledge of foreign languages to navigation. The example of leading merchants was copied in due course by traders, by artisans, and by many sorts of apprentices. That a large part of the earliest printed material consisted of how-to-do-it manuals speaks to the tangible incentives for active men to learn what was in those books—or even to write one.

The users, sponsors, and founders of schools often had quite similar social backgrounds, as Jordan showed in his study of bequests in England.[31] If, as has been said, boys went up to university from about 850 English secondary schools during the first half of the seventeenth century, that is evidence both of widespread interest in education and of a vigorous economic life supporting those schools and scholars. The thickening network of localities in which English boys (and sometimes girls) could prepare for postsecondary study can be mapped; a diligent search in the archives of other European countries no doubt would yield similar maps.[32]

Economic historians find it more congenial to trace developments across geographic rather than through social space, though the latter is no less important. Vulgarization of sociologists' investigations into stratification has led to the erroneous conclusion that in past centuries school places (beyond primary grades) were preempted by children from upper-strata homes. But even when opportunities were scantiest, they seem to have varied greatly and erratically as to accessibility. At the end of the fourteenth century, the right of English villeins' children to attend school was proclaimed; in 1541 there was again explicit refusal to bar poor boys. Local allegiance among school patrons, as already indicated, could favor local poor boys over those in better families but residing where no school has been opened. The social background of Oxford and Cambridge students had not been consistently aristocratic.[33] Even today, and not only in England, workers' children do not hold their proportion of places after the end of the age for compulsory attendance. Yet in all periods the small elite and upper-middle strata have received steady infusions of rising men. At all times, and continuing today, there are exhortations to prevent civic injury through allowing commoners to use education to aspire above their station. Fears of flooding the white-collar job market were not heard first in our day nor even first in the nineteenth century.

Incentives and channels for the spread of primary schooling and of literacy were duplicated later for secondary and higher education. This diffusion has been more sluggish in some societies, and in some, the ideological resistance to a widening of opportunities has been stiffer. The balance between intrusive thrust by aspirants and benevolent opening of opportunities by the already successful has not been the same everywhere. In broadest outline, among Western nations these processes have been similar, nevertheless, and economic development can be expected to bring convergence on many (but by no means all) educational responses.

B (intangible benefits). Even those writers who most emphasize the economic elements in demand for schooling will add that "there are also consumption returns." In which subpopulations are these returns largest? Are they mainly a camouflage for economic motives? Do these returns usually vary directly in amount to the "material" incentives? Do intangible benefits become relatively larger or less important as economic development proceeds?

Throughout Europe in early modern centuries and later, educational programs designed to cultivate "gentlemen" flourished. Looking backward from our present nonclassical mood, doubtless we exaggerate the element of sheer adornment. The schools founded and maintained avowedly from motives of status preservation also enrolled youth who conceived a more utilitarian use for what they were learning. And even among the already privileged students, motives were mixed.

Status-reinforcing schools were not confined to Europe; early Tokugawa schools also had dual aims. Likewise, the use of religious motives to foster literacy and learning occurs in many societies, supported with varying fidelity by the leading secular groups. As in other patronage relationships, the clergy's motives in fostering and guiding instruction found at most only distorted reflections in the incentives responded to by their pupils. Where schools are both foreign in pattern and religious in management, as in much of Africa for several generations, the discrepancy in viewpoints between sponsors and users can be dramatic. Not even in colonial New England was the freeing of men from "bonds of ignorance" attempted solely out of piety.

Perhaps the salience of religious aims in school policy is measured by the degree to which reading was separated from other subjects. Indeed, a minor theme in educational history relates to the varying inclusion of writing and of arithmetic with reading in elementary instruction. The former two were often taught only to pupils who had part of their instruction in a separate school or upon payment of special fees. Closely related is the division of subjects by sex of pupils; sometimes girls were allowed only to learn to read. We have no comprehensive mapping of how subjects were distributed among schools and types of pupils. Nor do we know how to link such information with economic analysis of either demand for instruction or its effects on productivity.

"Popular" schooling almost everywhere contains a large moral element. The aim, often quite avowedly, is to produce a work force that is disciplined—and to reduce abject poverty. The utilitarian virtues to which rising elites attribute their success they often seek also to instill in their apprentices and workmen and especially in the children of the poor. We are familiar with the prominence of this theme in controversies about the British charity schools. In modified variants the moral theme appears again as part of the debate of the 1960s in the United States over how best to infuse "effective" vocational education into antipoverty programs and into schooling for youth in central cities.

Among the many noneconomic motives or perceived benefits of education in addition to the status, religious, and moralistic themes already discussed is one that deserves special mention: sheer curiosity. Does economic change stimulate and diffuse curiosity? Or is curiosity nourished by schooling and then made use of in progressively more dynamic economic relationships?

A (ability to pay).   Whatever the actual or perceived advantages of schooling (and of other sorts of investments in formation of human resources) may be, the extent of such investments will depend also on ability to pay their costs, collectively and by various subpopulations. Studies within modern industrialized nations have shown demand for schooling to be relatively "income elastic," both in cross-section for individuals and in the aggregate by areas and over time. Historical data amenable to similar analysis are scarce, but even crude estimates could be informative.

Rising incomes in a society give more scope for noneconomic inducements to spend on education. On the other hand, economic development has generated greater demand for competencies acquired through schooling—partly because of the forms taken by technological change, partly because of the very occurrence of change, which calls for continuous adaptation and further learning among members of the labor force. How are these various conjunctures of situations reflected in the availability and price of education (both in school and at work) for various groups? Did "price rationing" of schooling become more or less important during the nineteenth century in Britain? What about access to opportunities for training and learning during the working years? How do shifting balances between anticipated returns, costs, and ability to pay alter the social status patterning of human-resource development?[34]

But this topic has many ramifications. Is the emergence of new technologies, industries, and occupations accompanied by an initial rise in opportunity costs of attending school?[35] If so, is the relative size of this effect larger for the upper- or the lower-income families? Major economic transformations are accompanied by new segmentalizations of education, formal and nonformal. Thus, two centuries ago in Britain separate educational programs were launched by workers, but these and later "workingmen's institutes" came to enroll mainly clerks. Yet workers did continue to purchase schooling beyond that supplied by public agencies, as West's studies show. How closely were British events paralleled elsewhere? Whatever the answers to particular queries, not every educational change was "progressive," even if we can root it in a broad current of economic development.

Agencies for training or instruction emerge and are changed by interactions among traditional pedagogic practices, labor market structures, social status attitudes, and private economic calculations of ability to pay balanced against prospective gain. In analyzing institutions for development of human resources, at least four main aspects need to be kept in mind:

1. How separate is responsibility for making certain that children are educated from actual provision of the education?
2. How specialized is the training agency, not only among occupations but among the component skills of an occupation?
3. What kind of economic attachment (claims and obligations) does the learner have to the supplier of his training, and for how extended a period of time?
4. What part of the costs of training are paid by third parties (e.g., "the public")?

But to pursue these features of educational relationships with economic change would unduly lengthen this presentation.

Until the many questions about distributions of benefits and burdens and ability to bear the burdens are explored in diverse historical and educational settings, each incidental example seems insubstantial. Feedback processes link different types of education and different kinds of pupils to one or another economic activity. Most of the subtle facilitating and inhibiting conditions remain to be traced out, however. Evidence already known to us suffices mainly to demonstrate how productive further investigations by economic historians could be.

COMMUNICATION, KNOW-HOW, AND THE SHAPING OF MEN FOR CHANGE

Any meaningful examination of interrelationships between economic development and the formation of human resources is of necessity a study of both institutional stabilities and social change. Central questions are then concerned with what induces, sustains, or dampens social change and in what ways. The pace of change, measured in units of a man's working life, is reflected in changing ways of forming human skills. The specific arrangements for training can take many forms: in school or at work, formal lessons, or the incidental learning by doing that accompanies most economic activities. There is more learning by doing when men are faced in their work with repeated injections of new techniques, each presenting new problems for decision. Economic development follows more than one path, but certain basic kinds of questions about the forming of human capabilities occur in each path. Our aim in this section is to delineate in broad terms how in different historical conjunctures mixtures of human resources and modes of their formation evolve from socioeconomic structures and in time reshape those structures. Moreover, particular educational arrangements can accelerate or retard the pace of social change. Despite diversity in details across societies, we hypothesize that certain key features in arrangements for forming human skills are found only where growth is rapid (whether as cause or as effect). Some attributes of educational systems may survive only in situations of economic stagnation. These hypotheses will not bear much resemblance to the battles over "vocational" education or nonformal versus formal education and so on that have been successive slogans among many would-be educational planners in recent years. We propose four broad generalizations.

First, development of human resources is more likely to go on vigorously, and those resources will be used more productively, when the social structure of a society is open. Such a structure facilitates the development of information fields or communication networks that attenuate geographic and social status isolation. Nevertheless, agencies for communication will function weakly and will not reinforce the extending of education unless the recipients of a communication perceive meaning and utility in the new ideas. But this last condition affects the rate and direction of communication itself, in addition to affecting its utilization. Perhaps well-integrated rather than segmentalized information fields may exist even amidst unfavorable institutional constraints: this is a question of historical and contemporary fact. A parallel question relates to the role of education in social mobility. Such mobility may be less variable among societies or historical periods than we conventionally assume. Contrast may lie more in the means than in the rate of mobility. In particular, education may be considerably more important, relative to other means of mobility, in some periods or in certain types of society than in others.

Second, there are scale and agglomeration effects upon economic growth flowing from expansion of a society's stock of human capital; moreover, these growth effects may further stimulate a rapid pace and high level of further human-capital formation. Such a pattern of events is embedded also in communication networks that foster initiation and more rapid spread of innovations. By "agglomeration effects" we refer to the enchancement of innovation resulting from the emergence of a critical mass of innovators and enterprisers who are actively in communication. Some of these effects were mentioned in discussing the diffusion of literacy and schooling. There can be face-to-face inventive stimulation among men who are on the forefront of change even though they are not marked off by possession of superior schooling. Neither Passin's "portents of modernity" in Tokugawa Japan nor the coffeehouse circles of eighteenth-century England[36] would have been possible without intimacy among knowledgeable men who shared in the excitement of change. The importance of "critical mass" in educational programs is often recognized today, as in arguments for building "programs of excellence" in African universities. The same issues underlay recent wrangles over what to do about "brain drain."[37] One of the most debated issues for both advanced and less-developed societies concerns the minimum effective scale of operation of agricultural research institutes and the case for concentration of resources in a few large research centers or spread of resources over many agricultural institutes.[38]

Third, major economic change cannot occur without large migrations of human capital that bring skills and know-how from other societies. The first industrializing country, England, was a heavy debtor in this respect. The Japanese Meiji reforms dealt with this situation in a unique array of policies. However autarchic Soviet industrialization appeared to be, it rested on enormous inflows of foreign skills.

Fourth, a dynamic economy can be launched and sustained only through the efforts of men at all social levels who embody both conventional learning and technical-manipulative skills—including specifically skills in the decoding of instructions and the "debugging" of new processes. A complex economy rests on widely diffused tools for communication, storage, and retrieval of knowledge. But it depends no less on the unrecorded know-how that grows out of experience in practical affairs, knowledge that spreads only among men with technical "feel." We refer not to empty demands that "youth must be taught to value manual work." It is Schumpeter's "innovative entrepreneurship" that we have in mind; this, he insisted, was linked mainly to processing and technical rather than to commercial activities.[39]

NOTES

1. A comprehensive outline of some of the principal interrelationships between education and aspects of the environing society can be found in C. Arnold Anderson, "Education and Society," *International Encyclopedia of the Social Sciences* 4:517–25.

2. The asymmetry of biases in the mix of physical and human capital and the importance of disequilibria have been discussed by Mary Jean Bowman in lectures over the past decade. The most recent discussion is in "Postschool Learning and Human Resource Accounting," *Review of Income and Wealth,* Income and Wealth Series 20, no. 4 (December 1974). T. W. Schultz emphasized the importance of education of farmers in facilitating adjustment to change in the modernization of agriculture in his *Transforming Traditional Agriculture* (New Haven: Yale University Press, 1964). More recently, he has put increasing stress on the disequilibrium theme: see his "The Value of the Ability to Deal with Disequilibria," *Journal of Economic Literature* 12, no. 3 (September 1975).

3. E. A. J. Johnson discussed early views on the development and diffusion of human skills as a means to economic progress in his "The Place of Learning, Science, Vocational Training, and 'Art' in Pre-Smithian Economic Thought," *Journal of Economic History* 24 (1964): 129–44 (reprinted in UNESCO, *Readings in the Economics of Education* [1968]).

4. Analysis of the use of technical assistance to circumvent deficiencies in local human capital within contemporary underdeveloped countries suggests that much of the Western historical evidence can be viewed also in terms of intercountry diffusion of education and skills. Italian and Dutch manuals were translated into English, English lads were apprenticed into Italian workshops, Flemish weavers were enticed into England and Huguenot refugees were welcomed there. If nothing else, these illustrations reemphasize that a commercial preceded an industrial revolution. This many-faceted process is discussed in R. E. Cameron, *France and the Economic Development of Europe, 1800–1914* (Princeton: Princeton University Press, 1961), pp. 41–54. See also M. J. Bowman, "From Guilds to Infant Training Industries," in *Education and Economic Development,* ed. C. A. Anderson and M. J. Bowman (Chicago: Aldine, 1965).

5. B. H. Slicher van Bath, *Agrarian History of Western Europe, 500–1850* (London: Arnold, 1963).

6. See C. A. Anderson (chap. 18), H. Passin (chap. 21), A. Kahan (chaps. 14 and 15), and R. A. Easterlin (chap. 22) in Anderson and Bowman, *Education and Economic Development*. See also R. Dore, *Education in Tokugawa Japan* (Berkeley: University of California Press, 1966); J. C. Toutain, *La Population de la France de 1700 a 1959* (Paris, 1963), chap. 4; M. C. Cipolla, *Literacy and Development in the West* (Baltimore: Penguin, 1969).

7. Comments relating education to economic development (or to political or to broad "social" developments) are rarely included in histories of education.

8. The evidence presented by E. G. West in *Education and the State* (London: Institute of Economic Affairs, 1965) and in a subsequent study, *Education and the Industrial Revolution* (London: Batsford, 1975), suggests that the date for mass possession of these skills may have to be put a few decades earlier.

9. C. A. Anderson, in Anderson and Bowman, *Education and Economic Development*, chap. 18.

10. M. J. Bowman and C. A. Anderson, "Concerning the Role of Education in Development," in *Old Societies and New States*, ed. C. Geertz (Glencoe: Free Press, 1963), pp. 247–79.

11. Both the literacy rate and the proportion with at least primary schooling describe diffusion of minimal education. But the distributions of amount of schooling or degrees of literacy also need to be considered. In European distributions during the last century of compulsory education—but surely not in earlier periods—there is a concentration of years of schooling around the stipulated completion level. In the United States (and perhaps Canada) "completion norms" were less formal, and dispersion of attained schooling was large. The degree to which particular completion norms constituted sharp breaking points in the rates of school continuation, the processes of shift from lower to higher modal norms, and some of the implications of these patterns were discussed by C. A. Anderson and M. J. Bowman, "Educational Distributions and Attainment Norms in the United States," *Proceedings: World Population Congress, 1954,* 4:931–41. Historically, legal specifications of compulsory ages for attendance have tended to be made after most of a population have reached the stated norm. The promulgation of what turn out to be fictional norms for school attendance where facilities are largely inadequate for implementation is a new phenomenon, common among the less-developed countries of our day.

12. In highly industrialized societies, with their built-in impulses toward organizational and technological change, the complementarity between schooling and postschool learning becomes evident. A rich technical literature has appeared recently dealing with postschool investments in the formation of human resources; for a summary and assessment of these lines of investigation see Mary Jean Bowman, "Learning and Earning in the Post-School Years," in *Review of Research in Education,* ed. Fred N. Kerlinger and John B. Carroll, vol. 2 (Itasca, Ill.: F. E. Peacock, 1974).

13. These include analyses of efficiency in consumption and of the family contribution to formation of human resources. For an overview see T. W. Schultz's editorial introductions to two symposia: "Investment in Education: the Equity-Efficiency Quandry" and "New Economic Approaches to Fertility," *Journal of Political Economy,* supplements to the issues of May/June 1972 and March/April 1973, respectively. There is also a recent "backlash" literature stressing how schools serve as screening agencies; as a result, it is argued, the private benefits from education may substantially exceed the societal returns in the advanced industrial nations.

14. Even today, however, its mediation through face-to-face interaction remains essential.

15. Scattered data for a few less-developed countries indicate that the associations between literacy and jobs are by no means tight. Usually there is an association between literacy and rural–urban migration, though the independent effect of literacy after other influences are controlled is probably modest. For one of the earlier discussions on the job-education correlation, see C. A. Anderson, "The Impact of the Educational System on Technological Change and Modernization," in *Industrialization and Society,* ed. B. F. Hoselitz and W. E. Moore (Paris: UNESCO, 1963), pp. 259–78.

16. An impressive array of evidence is appearing that highlights how literacy or schooling (along with other investments in human capital, such as agricultural extension programs) contribute to transforming agriculture. But one must draw conclusions cautiously, for under favorable conditions illiterate peasants can rapidly expand output even with little technological change. B. H. Slicher van Bath's *Samenleving onder Spanning* (1967), pp. 151–57, gives some eighteenth-century evidence for the Netherlands that suggests that increased production came mainly from areas with more numerous educational influences. A very general discussion is presented by C. A. Anderson, "Education for Agriculture," in *World Yearbook of Education,* ed. Philip Foster and James Sheffield (London: Evans, 1974). In the same volume B. Harker compares the effects of schooling on communication, innovation, and productivity in contemporary Japanese and Indian agriculture, and R. Evenson summarizes some of his recent work on the conditions that underlie effective agricultural extension

programs. Taking states as units, F. Welch has shown that high levels of schooling among farmers in the United States affect productivity most where there has been intensive agricultural research and development activity, giving rise to innovative behavior on the farm; see his "Education in Production," *Journal of Political Economy* 78 (1970): 35–59.

17. M. Wilson et al., *Keiskammahoek Rural Survey* (1952), 8: 155–57.

18. T. Hägerstrand, *Innovation Diffusion as a Spatial Process* (Chicago: University of Chicago Press, 1967; original Swedish edition, 1953).

19. For a short discussion of empirical research that has combined Hägerstrand's work on information fields with economic decision theory, see M. J. Bowman, "The Economics of Education," in a methodology issue of *Review of Educational Research* 39 (1969): 641–70.

20. The model presents an economic explanation of what often is called social demand in writings by European manpower planners. In fact, "social demand" as they conceive it is *private*. The adjective "social" was appended out of a belief that the educational decisions of individuals were noneconomic and even economically irrational.

21. This latter attitude is close to, though distinct from, the historic religious motive for literacy. A balancing of educational and other motives is presented in Lawrence Stone's "The Educational Revolution in England, 1560–1640," *Past and Present*, no. 28(1964), pp. 41–80.

22. In conventional applications of the economic decision model, disparities in information are typically ignored; it is assumed that individuals possess accurate knowledge of the alternatives open to them or that errors in this respect are unbiased. But education is one of the goods or services the purchase of which may be especially sensitive to disparities among subpopulations in knowledge of the outcomes of different choices. The simplest way of taking such disparities into account is to specify the model in the first place in terms of expected or perceived returns and benefits, as we do here.

23. T. W. Schultz (in conversation) has pointed out that the local responsibility for schools in America during the nineteenth century entailed a very close match between the public paying for a particular school and the families using it. Parallel examples can be found in Britain in earlier centuries.

24. Lewis Solmon gave explicit attention to this question in his research on investments in schooling in the United States during the latter nineteenth century; see "Capital Formation by Expenditure on Formal Education, 1880 and 1890" (Ph.D. diss., University of Chicago, 1968).

25. A detailed chronicle of motivations for schooling in response to outside opportunities for employment can be found in R. Thabault, *Education and Change in a Village Community: Mazières-en Gâtine, 1848–1914*, trans. P. Tregear (London: Routledge and Kegan Paul, 1971; original French ed., 1945).

26. See Solmon, "Capital Formation," and A. Fishlow, "Levels of Nineteenth-Century American Investment in Education," *Journal of Economic History* 26 (1966): 218–36.

27. Recent studies of "substitutability between quantity and quality of children" are relevant here. As schooling comes to be seen as more important for children, there may be a tendency to reduce family size while devoting more resources to the rearing of each child. This new line of research on fertility is well represented in the March/April 1973 issue of the symposium edited by T. W. Schultz (*Journal of Political Economy*). See also C. Tilly, "Population and Pedagogy in France," *History of Education Quarterly* 13 (1973): 113–28, for an account of converging lines of work by historians.

28. A. Kahan, chaps. 14 and 15, in Anderson and Bowman, *Education and Economic Development*.

29. P. Goldblatt, "The Geography of Youth Employment and School Enrollment in Mexico," in *Schools in Transition*, ed. A. M. Kazamias and E. H. Epstein (Boston: Allyn and Bacon, 1968), pp. 280–94.

30. See the graphical presentation on pp. 331–40 of Anderson and Bowman, *Education and Economic Development*.

31. W. K. Jordan, *Philanthropy in England, 1480–1660* (London: Allen and Unwin, 1959), and related volumes by him.

32. Japanese parallels are startling; there were close links also between religious and commercial interests, as in the use of temples for courses on the abacus.

33. The series of papers by Lawrence Stone in *Past and Present* provide much evidence. See also M. Schnaper and C. A. Anderson, *School and Society in England: Social Backgrounds of Oxford and Cambridge Students* (Washington: Annals of American Research, 1952). There are reasons to conclude that Swedish postprimary schools contained a distinctively large representation from peasant families. A fresh analysis of status profiles of university students for several countries (especially Sweden), using more refined techniques, can be found in C. Arnold Anderson, "Expanding Educational Opportunities: Conceptualization and Measurement," *Higher Education* 4, no. 4 (1975): 1–16.

34. For a discussion of relationships between generally rising incomes and schooling decisions among relatively rich and relatively poor subpopulations, see T. W. Schultz's editorial introduction to the May/June 1972 issue of *Journal of Political Economy*.

35. In the most fundamental sense, all real costs are opportunity costs; they are what is given up or sacrificed in making a particular choice. The reference to ''opportunity costs'' here is to the value in its best alternative use of the time devoted by the individual to schooling. On opportunity cost in formation of human resources, see M. J. Bowman, ''The Costing of Human Resource Formation,'' in *The Economics of Education,* ed. E. A. G. Robinson and J. E. Vaizey (London: Macmillan, 1966), chap. 14.

36. See chap. 21, by H. Passin, and chap. 20, by W. H. G. Armytage, in Anderson and Bowman, *Education and Economic Development*.

37. R. G. Myers, *Education and Emigration: Study Abroad and the Migration of Human Resources* (New York: McKay, 1972).

38. R. Evenson has demonstrated the importance of critical mass in widely dispersed agricultural institutions in adapting basic research for application in diverse agronomic environments; see his chapter in Foster and Sheffield, *World Year Book of Education*.

39. Much of what has been said here about economic development holds equally for political and civic relationships, but that is a topic for another essay.

CHAPTER 2

Educational Expansion and Economic Growth in Nineteenth-Century Germany: A Quantitative Study

BY PETER LUNDGREEN

WITH A CONTRIBUTION BY

A. P. THIRLWALL

The relations between education and the economy are manifold and have been discussed by economists and educators since at least the eighteenth century. But it is only recently that education has been treated as a quantifiable factor contributing to economic growth. The basic question in this regard is, How much economic growth can be attributed to the growth of education? This sort of question implies that a high level of education, if remaining constant over time, does not "explain" any economic growth, although it may be an important factor in keeping the rate of growth from falling. In other words, education may have an unmeasured impact upon measured growth; its measured impact refers only to the increase of education over time.

Obviously, the data needed for the kind of question raised must be time series, and one may ask what data history provides for our purpose. There are basically two categories of data that can be used for measuring educational expansion over time, enrollment figures and money expenditures. For the twentieth century several studies have been made which rely on various possible specifications of both enrollment and expenditure data. The general picture of a long trend in educational expansion and its fairly close correlation with measures of economic growth is quite impressive.[1] On the other hand, correlations do not establish cause-and-effect relationships, nor do they quantify precisely the contribution of education to growth. There are other studies, however, which aim at this goal, and it is mainly their methods whose applicability to history will be probed in this paper.

Are there the necessary time-series data available for the nineteenth century? Thanks to the painstaking work of Walther Hoffmann, we have, for Germany, series for the growth of output (as well as of labor and capital) from 1850 onwards.[2] He also provides, on the basis of Prussian and Bavarian statistics, a series for public expenditures on education going back to 1861.[3] As far as enrollment figures are concerned it is necessary to resort to the original published sources of the German states. This has been done with respect to Prussia only and thereby limits any generalization, although I am not aware of grave differences between Prussia and the other German states. I propose here to deal with enrollment and expenditures separately, first, by indicating the expansion over time, and secondly, by answering the "master question," How much of economic growth can be attributed to the increase of education? It is this question which makes us try three different ways of relating education to economic growth: (1) Denison's approach of adjusting labor input for quality changes; (2) Schultz's approach of estimating returns to the investments gone into the educational stock; and (3) a production function approach (taken by Thirlwall) where a measure of education along with labor and capital is included and directly enters the production function.

THE AMOUNT OF SCHOOLING

1. Our first concern is the amount of schooling and its increase over time with respect to type of education and population growth. This information can be obtained from the enrollment figures, broken down for the various institutions of learning, as summarized in Tables 2.1–3.[4] Together with Table 2A.1 (in the Appendix to this chapter) these tables essentially comprise the data available and indicate the underlying time trends. The differentiation between the sexes is justified on three grounds: first, there may be a higher enrollment of males than females, and if so this is important to know since the working population consists mainly of males; secondly, the breakdown of the data is much more detailed for males at secondary schools, whereas females seem to have been offered an extended secondary education only in the very late nineteenth century; thirdly, there are only rare bits of information about the sex composition of the student body at the university and professional/vocational school level, but it seems safe to assume that virtually all students were males. It was hence decided to base the argument of this section on male students' enrollment only.

Another basic fact which is immediately obvious from Table 2.1 is the structure of the educational system. Many of the institutions of learning were competitive rather than successive, in the sense that their students belonged to the same "typical age" and had to make a choice whether to serve their compulsory years of schooling at this or that institution. This so-called bifurcated system of educational institutions is a widespread European experience and contrasts sharply with the American comprehensive school system. Without discussing the merits of the respective systems, one procedural consequence for our investigation was the need to draw a sharp line between compulsory and voluntary education. Mainly, this meant splitting the enrollment figures for secondary education into those within the compulsory age range and those beyond it (Tables 2.2 and 2.3, respectively). This

TABLE 2.1

Enrollment of Males in Prussia, 1822–1911, by Types of Institutions and Typical Ages of Students

Year	Elementary (6–14 yrs.)		Middle (6–14/15 yrs.)		Secondary (6/8–16/19 yrs.)	University (19–23 yrs.)	Teacher training		Vocational/professional schools		
	Public	Private	Public	Private			Preparatory (14–17 yrs.)	Seminary (17–20 yrs.)	(14–16 yrs.)	(16–19 yrs.)	(19–22 yrs.)
1822	743,207	(14,470)	47,598	(5,788)	24,344	4,072	(1,800)	(1,800)	(400)	(150)	(450)
1828	925,438	(15,816)	59,533	(6,326)	25,819	6,125	(2,100)	(2,100)	(600)	(150)	(450)
1837	1,108,015	(17,598)	40,772	(7,039)	37,074	4,508	(2,583)	2,583	(700)	(150)	(450)
1846	1,235,448	(20,116)	43,315	(8,046)	45,548	4,378	(2,179)	2,179	(800)	(300)	(600)
1855	1,322,747	(21,443)	44,786	(8,577)	61,802	4,725	(2,595)	2,595	(900)	(450)	(750)
1864	1,427,191	25,286	43,730	8,420	77,136	6,050	(3,610)	3,610	1,040	653	922
1873	(1,925,438)	(25,167)	(69,712)		127,045	7,384	(6,000)	6,000	60	1,280	3,745
1882	2,182,883	(18,002)	(80,315)		152,828	12,557	(9,955)	9,955	250	560	2,026
1891	2,467,558	10,839	(49,752)	(18,126)	156,796	13,000	(10,836)	10,836	618	942	3,690
1901	2,839,569	6,700	73,453	13,498	200,167	17,500	(15,000)	12,138	1,594	2,061	8,018
1911	3,292,877	0	98,196	18,020	267,134	26,550	(21,779)	18,571	1,853	3,707	7,995

Note: Figures given in parentheses in the body of this table and of subsequent tables are explained in the Appendix to Chapter 2.

TABLE 2.2
Enrollment of Males in Prussia, 1822–1911, by Types of Institutions:
Compulsory Education

a: number of students enrolled
b: students as percentage of male population
c: students as percentage of total students enrolled

Year		All institutions	Elementary		Middle		Secondary	
			Public	Private	Public	Private	Preparatory	VI to lower III
1822	a	829,796	743,207	(14,470)	47,598	(5,788)	(3,164)	15,569
	b	14.33	12.84	(0.25)	0.82	(0.10)	0.05	0.27
	c	100	89.56	1.74	5.74	0.70	0.38	1.88
1828		1,024,622	925,438	(15,816)	59,533	(6,326)	(3,356)	14,153
		16.19	14.63	(0.25)	0.94	(0.10)	0.05	0.22
		100	90.32	1.54	5.81	0.61	0.33	1.38
1837		1,201,958	1,108,015	(17,598)	40,772	(7,039)	(4,819)	23,715
		17.08	15.74	(0.25)	0.58	(0.10)	0.07	0.34
		100	92.18	1.46	3.39	0.58	0.40	1.97
1846		1,341,632	1,235,448	(20,116)	43,315	(8,046)	(5,921)	28,786
		16.67	15.35	(0.25)	0.54	(0.10)	0.07	0.36
		100	92.08	1.50	3.23	0.60	0.44	2.14
1855		1,444,341	1,322,747	(21,443)	44,786	(8,577)	(8,034)	38,754
		16.83	15.42	(0.25)	0.52	(0.10)	0.09	0.45
		100	91.58	1.48	3.10	0.59	0.56	2.68
1864		1,560,229	1,427,191	25,286	43,730	8,420	8,730	46,872
		16.27	14.89	0.26	0.45	0.09	0.09	0.49
		100	91.47	1.62	2.80	0.54	0.56	3.00
1873		2,111,711	(1,925,438)	(25,167)	(69,712)		18,666	72,728
		17.02	15.52	0.20	0.56		0.15	0.59
		100	91.18	1.19	3.30		0.88	3.44
1882		2,386,806	2,182,883	(18,002)	(80,315)		21,667	83,939
		17.54	16.04	0.13	0.59		0.16	0.62
		100	91.46	0.75	3.36		0.91	3.52
1891		2,654,793	2,467,558	10,839	(49,752)	(18,126)	20,762	87,756
		17.82	16.57	0.07	0.33	0.12	0.14	0.58
		100	92.95	0.41	1.87	0.68	0.78	3.31
1901		3,069,207	2,839,569	6,700	73,453	13,498	25,700	110,287
		17.78	16.45	0.04	0.42	0.08	0.15	0.64
		100	92.51	0.22	2.39	0.44	0.84	3.59
1911		3,589,248	3,292,877	0.00	98,196	18,020	34,442	145,713
		18.02	16.53	0.00	0.49	0.09	0.17	0.73
		100	91.74	0.00	2.74	0.50	0.96	4.06

TABLE 2.3
Enrollment of Males in Prussia, 1822–1911, by Types of Institutions:
Voluntary Full-Time Education

a: number of students enrolled
b: students as percentage of male population
c: students as percentage of total students enrolled

Year		All institutions	Secondary				Teacher training	Vocational/ professional schools
			Upper III to upper I	Upper III to lower II	Upper II to upper I	University		
1822	a	14,283	5,611	3,310	· 2,301	4,072	(3,600)	(1,000)
	b	0.25	0.10	0.06	0.04	0.07	0.06	0.02
	c	100	39.28	23.17	16.11	28.51	25.20	7.00
1828		19,835	8,310	4,112	4,198	6,125	(4,200)	(1,200)
		0.31	0.13	0.06	0.07	0.10	0.07	0.02
		100	41.90	20.73	21.16	30.88	21.17	6.05
1837		19,514	8,540	5,049	3,491	4,508	5,166	(1,300)
		0.27	0.12	0.07	0.05	0.06	0.07	0.02
		100	43.77	25.87	17.89	23.10	26.47	6.66
1846		21,277	10,841	6,450	4,391	4,378	4,358	(1,700)
		0.26	0.13	0.08	0.05	0.05	0.05	0.02
		100	50.95	30.31	20.64	20.58	20.48	7.99
1855		27,029	15,014	9,141	5,873	4,725	5,190	(2,100)
		0.31	0.17	0.11	0.06	0.06	0.06	0.02
		100	55.55	33.82	21.73	17.48	19.20	7.77
1864		37,419	21,534	12,942	8,592	6,050	7,220	2,615
		0.39	0.22	0.14	0.08	0.06	0.07	0.03
		100	57.55	34.59	22.96	16.17	19.29	6.99
1873		60,120	35,651	22,361	13,290	7,384	12,000	5,085
		0.48	0.29	0.18	0.11	0.06	0.10	0.04
		100	59.30	37.19	22.10	12.28	19.96	8.46
1882		82,525	47,222	29,060	18,162	12,557	19,910	2,836
		0.61	0.35	0.21	0.14	0.09	0.15	0.02
		100	57.22	35.21	22.01	15.22	24.13	3.44
1891		88,200	48,278	30,928	17,350	13,000	21,672	5,250
		0.59	0.32	0.21	0.11	0.09	0.15	0.04
		100	54.74	35.07	19.67	14.74	24.57	5.95
1901		120,491	64,180	39,779	24,401	17,500	27,138	11,673
		0.70	0.37	0.23	0.14	0.10	0.16	0.07
		100	53.27	33.01	20.25	14.52	22.52	9.69
1911		167,434	86,979	53,803	33,176	26,550	40,350	13,555
		0.84	0.44	0.27	0.17	0.13	0.20	0.07
		100	51.95	32.13	19.81	15.86	24.10	8.10

procedure was necessary for purposes to be dealt with later in the paper, but it yields results at least as meaningful as if one compares total primary vs. total secondary students. For there is now a common denominator for all institutions given in Table 2.2: they comprise eight age cohorts, and the grand total is equivalent to the number of students in the age of compulsory school attendance who were actually enrolled.

This number, broken down with respect to institutions, is certainly an important indicator of educational expansion, but allowance has to be made for population growth. The common procedure is to express enrollment figures as percentages of the respective age groups. This may be necessary if the age structure of the population changes significantly over time. For Germany, as far as we know, the age structure remained virtually constant during the nineteenth century (Table 2A.6). In this case it does not matter whether we calculate the enrollment figures as percentages of the male population or of those males 6–14 years old. The latter method is adopted later on when we want to know how many males were not enrolled at all. Tables 2.2 and 2.3 follow the former approach, however, and give the enrollment figures as percentages of the total male population. There is a practical reason advising us to do so: if one has a common denominator for all different enrollment figures (comprising different numbers of age cohorts and hence referring to different age groups for recruitment), then the percentages can be added and subtracted in all desired combinations. In addition, the argument has been advanced that it makes good sense on general grounds to take the percentages from the population rather than from age groups if our interest is focused on the possible importance of many school children for a future working population (and ultimately for the economy) rather than on high enrollment ratios among certain age groups whose share in the population may vary.[5] It may be added that the age groups which should be taken are by no means self-evident, and international comparisons may be barred by differing educational systems applying to different "typical" age groups.

If, then, educational expansion is measured by numbers of students enrolled as percentages of the male population, we are now in a position to describe the trends between 1822 and 1911. The total enrolled in compulsory education (Table 2.2, col. 1) increased from 14.33 percent to 18.02 percent of the population, or by 25.75 percent over the ninety years under consideration. Most remarkable in terms of comparative history is the early achievement of a very high level of enrollment of the respective age cohorts (6–14 years old), which constituted about 17.50 percent of the population. Among those institutions offering schooling for pupils of this age, the public elementary school clearly and persistently dominated, although it is noticeable that during the whole period covered some 10 percent of the pupils attended other institutions. Among these institutions, the private elementary and the public and private middle schools show a relatively declining enrollment. Secondary schools, on the other hand, increased their share in the total student body of the compulsory age (Table 2.2, lines c). At the same time, the increase of the enrolled students as a percentage of the male population (Table 2.2, lines b) was tremendous: 240 percent for the preparatory grades (if the figures for the earlier times are valid) and 170 percent for the four lower grades of secondary schools proper.

The impressive rise in secondary school enrollment, relative to population growth, can be followed up if we turn to voluntary education (Table 2.3). The five upper grades of all secondary schools (Table 2.3, col. 2) comprise considerably fewer students than the four lower ones (Table 2.2, col. 7), but the increase of enrolled students as a percentage of the male population goes up by 340 percent between 1822 and 1911. This figure is even higher (350 percent) for two grades at the lower end (upper III and lower II), whereas it is somewhat lower (325 percent) for the three uppermost grades. These two subcategories have been held separately, since it is of interest to distinguish between students aiming at the leaving certificate of the lower II (providing the privilege of one year's military service instead of three years) and students striving for the leaving certificate of the upper I (providing the prerequisite for studying at university). Of course, Table 2.3 can indicate only roughly the relationship between these two categories of students, the former ones being much more numerous and, as has been seen, increasing more over time. More precise information about this point may be obtained from Table 2A.3 in the Appendix.

Enrollment at secondary schools, even if confined to grades beyond the age range of compulsory schooling, makes up the largest single share in the total voluntary enrollment. University attendance follows a rather peculiar development. Starting at a very high level, it drops both in absolute and relative terms, only to regain its 1828 level of students, as a percentage of the male population, by the turn of the century. Consequently, the rate of growth (Table 2.3, lines b) is first negative, then constant, and positive only in the latter decades of the nineteenth century. The share of university students in the total of voluntarily enrolled students never again reaches its size of the early decades; this has to be ascribed to the rising importance of other institutions for education and training of graduates from both primary and secondary schools. Unfortunately, this part of the available statistical information is the most diffuse and weak. In general, it was decided to exclude all institutions which did not require a full-time attendance of their students and to make conservative assumptions wherever necessary. If the orders of magnitude arrived at are taken as valid, the outstanding result is that vocational/professional schools played a perhaps astonishingly small part within voluntary education,[6] whereas teacher training held a quite sizeable share (Table 2.3, lines c). Yet the growth rates of the number of students at these two kinds of institutions, taken as percentages of the male population, are very high and approach the size of those of voluntary secondary education.

The conclusion to be drawn with respect to educational expansion seems dependent on whether we take rates of increase for specific institutions singled out or whether we look at the significance of small minorities in the aggregate, no matter how dramatically they grow over time. This is clear if we notice that the total voluntary enrollment (Table 2.3, col. 1) increases by 236 percent from 1822 to 1911, but that its absolute size adds only tiny fractions to those enrolled within the compulsory age range. The rate of increase of the number of students as a percentage of the male population was 25.75 percent over ninety years for compulsory enrollment. The inclusion of the voluntarily enrolled students brings this figure up to 29.34 percent (Tables 2.2 and 2.3, cols. 1, lines b). One may tend to evaluate this increase as a rather small one which can be explained by an early achievement of high enrollment within the compulsory age range. After all, the limit in this regard is a 100 percent enforcement of compulsory schooling. Every additional enrollment has then to be by voluntary education, and great numbers are needed if voluntary education is to make itself felt in the aggregate. The *increase* of the amount of schooling, however, and not its attained *level,* is wanted if the contribution of education to economic growth is to be measured. No matter whether we think the recorded increase of education in nineteenth-century Germany was small or remarkable, the question now arises how to relate it to economic growth.

2.   Economic growth can be operationalized, within the theory of production, as the growth of output dependent upon the growth of inputs. The two classical factors of input are, of course, capital and labor; but it is well known that output grows faster than the weighted average of inputs of labor and capital, a phenomenon sometimes referred to as the growth of total factor productivity. The size of this "technical progress," to give another name often used, is usually obtained as a residual—that is to say, as the difference between the growth rate of output and of weighted inputs. There is now a considerable literature concerned with dissecting the residual, attacking the omnibus category of "technical progress."[7] One can label this endeavor as the search for the sources of economic growth, and it is precisely this title which was chosen by Edward F. Denison for his celebrated book on the U.S. economy of the twentieth century.[8] Denison distinguishes between some twenty sources of economic growth which either affect the inputs or the growth of output per unit of inputs (i.e., total productivity).

Capital and labor inputs, thereby, are no longer taken at face value, i.e., as conventionally measured. Especially with regard to labor the point is that a mere adding of man-hours assumes a constant quality distribution over time which is equal to counting empty "bodies" without allowing for changes in the quality of labor. Again it is clear that a high (or low) but *constant* quality of labor would not affect the calculation of measured growth. It is the *increase* of the quality of labor which makes a difference and can be regarded as contributing to economic growth. The underlying assumption is that of neoclassical marginal productivity theory: labor is paid according to its marginal product, and income differentials do essentially reflect variations in the marginal product which are caused by variations in the quality of labor. If this is true, then an increase in the average quality of labor contributes to the growth of output.

How can changes in the quality of labor be assessed? Denison and his camp followers propose to take the amount of schooling embodied in the labor force as

TABLE 2.4

Enrollment of Males in Prussia, 1822–1911, by Attendance of the 8th, 9th, 10th,..., 17th Year of School

Version a: all full-time institutions
Version b: only primary and secondary education and university

Year	Compulsory		Voluntary								
	8th		9th	10th	11th	12th	13th	14th	15th and 16th, each	17th
1822	103,724	a	2,692	2,218	1,451	1,451	1,349 (+473)	1,768	1,168	1,018
		b	1,892	1,418	801	801	699 (+473)	1,018	1,018	1,018
1828	128,077		3,305	2,807	2,188	2,155	2,105 (+611)	2,381	1,681	1,531
			2,305	1,807	1,438	1,405	1,355 (+611)	1,531	1,531	1,531
1837	150,244		4,093	3,378	2,123	2,074	2,027 (+111)	2,138	1,277	1,127
			2,882	2,167	1,212	1,163	1,116 (+111)	1,127	1,127	1,127

Year									
1846	167,704	4,809	3,893	2,472	2,305	1,992 (+ 83)	2,020	1,294	1,094
		3,683	2,767	1,646	1,579	1,166 (+ 82)	1,094	1,094	1,094
1855	180,542	6,553	5,218	3,160	3,084	2,674	2,296	1,431	1,181
		5,238	3,903	2,145	2,069	1,659	1,181	1,181	1,181
1864	195,028	8,777	7,611	4,866	4,395	3,591	3,022	1,819	1,512
		7,054	5,888	3,446	2,975	2,171	1,512	1,512	1,512
1873	263,963	14,173	12,248	8,010	6,929	5,629	5,094	3,094	1,846
		12,143	10,218	5,584	4,503	3,203	1,846	1,846	1,846
1882	298,350	18,372	17,574	10,848	9,818	8,008	7,132	3,814	3,139
		14,929	14,131	7,344	6,314	4,504	3,139	3,139	3,139
1891	331,849	20,092	18,678	11,435	9,541	8,152	8,092	4,480	3,250
		16,171	14,757	7,509	5,615	4,226	3,250	3,250	3,250
1901	383,650	26,867	24,506	15,207	12,486	11,231	11,093	7,047	4,375
		21,070	18,709	10,150	7,753	6,498	4,375	4,375	4,375
1911	448,656	36,726	33,447	22,622	17,799	16,099	15,492	9,302	6,637
		28,541	25,262	14,128	10,374	8,674	6,637	6,637	6,637

an indicator of quality. After all, it is a well-established fact that better educated people generally obtain higher incomes, although the earnings differentials associated with additional education are not necessarily entirely due to it. But let us first try to measure the amount of schooling embodied in the working population of nineteenth-century Germany. What we need to know is the percentage distribution of the labor force by years of school completed. These data are clearly different from the enrollment data discussed above, and the easiest way to obtain them is by a census. Unfortunately, the relevant question was asked for the first time in Germany only in 1964.[9] Therefore we are forced to see whether there is a way to transform enrollment data (for students) into the percentage distribution of the population (labor force) by years of school embodied.

Ironically, the first thing we have to do in order to construct a quality index for labor is to neglect the quality of education (by types of institution and by time of enrollment). We want to know the *amount* of schooling, i.e., the number of years of school completed. The enrollment figures given in Tables 2.2 and 2.3 (and Tables 2A.3 and 2A.4) are hence reorganized (Table 2.4) by asking, How many male students were enrolled for a specific year of their schooling if the overall enrollment from the eighth through the seventeenth years is broken down by attendance of the 8th, 9th, 10th, . . . , 17th year of school, regardless of institution attended? The assumptions made to answer this question are given in the Appendix to this chapter. The main step taken from Tables 2.2 and 2.3 to Table 2.4 is that we are now dealing separately with students for each additional year of school, though still with enrollment figures. The major problem ahead is to transform the number of enrolled students into the number of graduates (with a given number of years of school embodied); in other words, we want to know how many male students have completed 8, 9, 10, . . . , 17 years of school only. This is essentially to ask for the distribution of male age cohorts by years of school.[10] If this question can be answered satisfactorily, then it should be easy to construct the distribution, by years of school, of a population composed of age cohorts whose distribution is known.

Age cohorts could be followed up with respect to how many stop going to school and how many continue for another year if enrollment figures were available for every single year. Lacking this information, one can interpolate the enrollment figures for the years in between the census years and follow the age cohorts one by one. This tedious exercise has been done by a computer, and the results are given in Table 2A.7.[11] Since they differ remarkably little from my own final results, I consider it worthwhile to indicate my procedure as a rule of thumb which relies on the same set of assumptions but avoids excessive calculations. Instead of following specific age cohorts I tried to assess the distribution, by years of school, of typical age cohorts (generations) representative of the decade between two census years. Starting from Table 2.4, it was decided that the total voluntary enrollment of *one* age cohort (Table 2.5, col. 1) is (1) a subtotal of this age cohort compulsorily enrolled (Table 2.4, col. 1); and (2) that the total voluntary enrollment of one age cohort comprises students whose *differing* amounts of schooling can be guessed at

TABLE 2.5
Distribution of Voluntarily Enrolled Male Students in Prussia, 1822–1911,
by Years of School Completed

Version a: all full-time institutions
Version b: only secondary and university education

Year		Total (enrollment in 9th year)	9	10	11	12	13	14	15	16	17
		Distribution by years of school completed									
1822	a	2,692 (+473)	474	767	0	102	54	600	0	150	1,018
	b	1,892 (+473)	474	617	0	102	154	0	0	0	1,018
1828		3,305 (+611)	498	619	33	50	335	700	0	150	1,531
		2,305 (+611)	498	369	33	50	435	0	0	0	1,531
1837		4,093 (+111)	715	1,255	49	47	0	800	0	150	1,127
		2,882 (+111)	715	955	49	47	100	0	0	0	1,127
1846		4,809 (+ 83)	916	1,421	67	413	55	900	0	200	1,094
		3,683 (+ 83)	916	1,121	67	413	155	0	0	0	1,094
1855		6,553	1,335	2,058	76	410	378	1,000	0	250	1,181
		5,238	1,335	1,758	76	410	478	0	0	0	1,181
1864		8,777	1,166	2,745	471	804	569	1,200	0	307	1,512
		7,054	1,166	2,442	471	804	659	0	0	0	1,512
1873		14,173	1,925	4,238	1,081	1,300	535	2,000	0	1,248	1,846
		12,143	1,925	4,634	1,081	1,300	1,357	0	0	0	1,846
1882		18,372	798	6,726	1,030	1,810	876	3,318	0	675	3,139
		14,929	798	6,787	1,030	1,810	1,365	0	0	0	3,139
1891		20,092	1,414	7,243	1,894	1,389	60	3,612	0	1,230	3,250
		16,171	1,414	7,248	1,894	1,389	976	0	0	0	3,250
1901		26,867	2,361	9,285	2,721	1,255	138	4,046	0	2,672	4,375
		21,070	2,361	8,559	2,397	1,255	2,123	0	0	0	4,375
1911		36,726	3,279	10,845	4,823	1,700	607	6,190	0	2,665	6,637
		28,541	3,279	11,134	3,754	1,700	2,037	0	0	0	6,637

by subtracting those enrolled in their tenth year from those in their ninth, those in their eleventh from those in their tenth year, etc. In other words, the assumption is that all voluntarily enrolled students have a ninth year, but some only a ninth year; the rest continue for a tenth year, after which some again stop; and so on. This procedure leads to Table 2.5, which may be interpreted as a breakdown of the entire voluntary enrollment of a given age cohort into students with different amounts of additional schooling. These students, then, can be taken as graduates, of a typical age cohort, if their numbers are converted into percentages.

The construction of such typical age cohorts (generations), distributed by years of school, has been undertaken in Table 2.6 and is explained in the Appendix. We are now in a position to see how the amount of schooling embodied in male age cohorts varies from generation to generation. The general picture is bound to be very similar to the one obtained by looking into the educational expansion via enrollment figures (Tables 2.2 and 2.3): a very high and early enforcement of compulsory schooling, which remains somewhere at the 90 percent level, and a far-flung range of tiny minorities having some additional schooling. These minorities increase over time, except for the typical slope of the university students' distribution curve (seventeen years of schooling) referred to earlier; the shift to more voluntary education in later times cannot yet be expected to raise the average amount of schooling per capita significantly, since all movements occur within a 10 percent range of the aggregate.

It is now possible, however, to calculate averages and thus to arrive at a precise measurement of the increase of embodied education. Averages could be taken for every generation (Table 2.6), but the quality of a given labor force is still in question. The task then is to build up, somehow, the distribution by years of school of a labor force which after all consists of certain age cohorts. It is proposed to take the male population of working age, i.e., 14–64 years old, as the labor force. The actual labor force consisted of roughly 75 percent males and 25 percent females in nineteenth-century Germany.[12] Strictly, a table similar to 2.6 should be constructed for females, but to judge from the enrollment data (Table 2A.1) there was virtually no voluntary education for females in Prussia until the very end of the century. This in turn would yield a comparatively higher concentration of female age cohorts in the categories "no schooling" and "8 years of school." If we take the male age cohorts (Table 2.6) as the basis for our construction of the labor force, this consequently results in an overestimation of the quality of labor but does not affect its increase over time.

We can now proceed to our final step: to build up male populations, 14–64 years old, for two points in time, namely 1864 and 1911. Demographic statistics show the age structure of those two populations (Table 2A.6). If we break down the working population into five age groups (14–24, 25–34, 35–44, 45–54, 55–64), these categories correspond to the range covered by our typical age cohorts of Table 2.6, and we simply pick up as large a percentage of each generation as are alive in the working populations of 1864 and 1911, respectively. Thus we finally arrive at Table 2.7, which gives the information we are looking for: the percentage distribution of the male population, 14–64 years of age, by years of school completed.[13] If we bear in mind the reservations with regard to female members of the labor force, the results are directly comparable to those of the microcensus of 1964 for the Federal Republic of Germany. This means we can follow the changes in the amount of schooling embodied over one hundred years.

The pattern of distribution looks extraordinarily stable, and the increase of the

TABLE 2.6

Percentage Distribution of Male Age Cohorts in Prussia, 1822–1911, by Years of School Embodied

Compulsory enrollment:	1806–23	1816–33	1826–43	1835–53	1846–64	1853–70	1863–80	1873–90	1883–1900	1893–1911
Years of school	Age cohorts: 1800–1809	1810–19	1820–29	1830–39	1840–50	1847–56	1857–66	1867–76	1877–86	1887–97
0	18.08	7.24	2.43	4.73	3.80	6.97	2.72	0.00	0.00	0.00
8	78.83	89.77	94.28	91.47	91.52	87.51	90.51	93.27	91.88	90.42
9	0.39	0.52	0.59	0.76	0.62	0.75	0.29	0.47	0.71	0.86
10	0.49	0.91	0.92	1.17	1.46	1.68	2.48	2.43	2.81	2.83
11	0.03	0.04	0.04	0.04	0.25	0.41	0.38	0.63	0.82	1.26
12	0.04	0.03	0.27	0.23	0.43	0.51	0.67	0.47	0.38	0.44
13	0.26	0.00	0.04	0.21	0.30	0.20	0.32	0.01	0.05	0.15
14	0.55	0.58	0.58	0.57	0.64	0.78	1.22	1.21	1.22	1.62
15	0.00	0.00	0.00	0.00	0.00	0.00	0.00	0.00	0.00	0.00
16	0.12	0.11	0.13	0.14	0.16	0.47	0.25	0.43	0.81	0.70
17	1.21	0.81	0.71	0.67	0.81	0.72	1.16	1.09	1.32	1.73
	100.00	100.00	100.00	100.00	100.00	100.00	100.00	100.00	100.00	100.00

TABLE 2.7
Percentage Distribution of Male Population or Labor Force,
14–64 Years of Age, in Prussia, 1864 and 1911, and in Germany, 1964,
by Years of School Embodied and Weighted Averages
of This Embodied Education

Years of school	Population			Weights	
	1864	1911	1964 (labor force)	Years of schooling	Earnings differentials
0	5.69	1.03	0.0	0	0.70
8	90.41	90.88	82.5	8	1.00
9	0.61	0.65	0.0	9	1.07
10	1.10	2.59	7.6	10	1.18
11	0.11	0.83	0.5	11	1.29
12	0.25	0.48	2.9	12	1.39
13	0.19	0.13	2.5	13	1.50
14	0.59	1.30	0.3	14	1.60
15	0.0	0.0	0.2	15	1.70
16	0.13	0.59	0.1	16	1.80
17	0.79	1.33	3.4	17	2.10
	100.00	100.00	100.00		

Weighted averages					
Years of schooling	7.70	8.25	8.75		
Earnings differentials	99.94	103.23	108.04		

Increase of the averages

Years of schooling	1864–1911:	7.19%	Earnings differentials	1864–1911:	3.29%
	1911–64:	6.03%		1911–64:	4.66%
	1864–1964:	13.65%		1864–1964:	8.10%

average amount of schooling embodied is therefore very small. Averages can be obtained by applying weights to the percentages, which are then added. One weight which comes to mind at once is the amount of schooling we are talking about. Its application yields the average amount of schooling embodied per capita; this figure rises from 7.70 years in 1864 to 8.25 years in 1911, or by 7.19 percent. A similar increase is recorded for the following half century. We may call this development educational expansion, but its dimensions are, as measured, rather limited. This leads to the inevitable conclusion that the quality of labor, if measured solely by years of school embodied, did not increase very much over time and thus cannot have contributed significantly to economic growth.

We are not justified, however, in relating a measure of the quality of labor, whose average has been obtained by using years of school as weights, to the growth rate of output. For this would imply that educational differences match directly differences in the marginal product of labor—that, for instance, labor with no schooling does not contribute to output at all. Accordingly, some other weights have to be used, and they are to be found in the realm of marginal productivity theory, which assumes that labor's marginal product equals labor's income. Earnings differentials are thereby due to differences in marginal product and are partly caused by better (or lower) quality of labor; quality of labor, in turn, is indicated by education. Empirically, earnings differentials with respect to the educational background of labor are hard to come by, especially for earlier periods of time. For the twentieth century Denison constructed two scales, one for the United States, one for northwest Europe, both adjusted for factors other than education influencing earnings differentials.[14]

For nineteenth-century Germany/Prussia, there is no information on earnings differentials associated with educational differences, so, as a first approach, we have applied Denison's northwest-European scale, knowing that this is not the reality. But it is probably not far off the reality either. Most likely, earnings differentials with respect to educational differences were greater in nineteenth-century Prussia. This seems plausible if only small minorities occupied the better jobs, and it seems to be corroborated by other findings referred to in a later section of this paper. But any arbitrary assignment of even higher weights than in Denison's scale to the upper echelons of education would not yield remarkably different results. In any case, the rate of increase of the averages would probably remain below the level indicated by applying years of school instead of earnings differentials as weights. Taking Denison's weights results in an increase of the quality of labor by 3.29 percent between 1864 and 1911, clearly a very small change over time but consistent with our earlier judgment about a rather modest educational expansion in the aggregate.

In order to complete the analysis of how much additional education (measured as amount of schooling) contributed to economic growth, some final remarks have to be added. First, the increase of the quality of labor over 47 years (3.29 percent) has to be converted into an annual rate of growth, which amounts to 0.07 percent. Secondly, this annual growth rate has to be weighted with the labor share in national income, because labor, whose earning capacity is assumed to be related to its quality, receives only some 75 percent of the national income. Hence the growth rate of labor's quality is equal to 0.052 percentage points (= 75 percent of 0.07) of the growth rate of output (or national income). In short, 0.052 percentage points of the annual growth rate of output between 1864 and 1911 can be "explained" by, or "attributed" to, an increase of labor's quality (or to education). If the German economy grew, as Hoffmann claims, at an annual rate of growth of 2.6 percent before 1913, and if Prussian labor quality is representative of the German one, those 0.052 percentage points equal 2.0 percent of the growth rate of output. In other words, if we assume that all factors contributing to the growth of the German economy operated at their actual level of effectiveness, but assume that education as measured by years of school per capita remained constant at the 1864 level, then the rate of growth of output would have been smaller by only 2.0 percent.[15]

This is small by any standard, although Denison had to record that European countries, even in the period after World War II, do not compare with the United

States with respect to educational expansion over time.[16] It should be repeated that the question goes for the increase rather than the attained level of education. Since Prussia apparently introduced very early a high level of compulsory education, an additional educational expansion was bound to be rather limited. Of course, the picture would change if we only could break down the large 90 percent bloc of compulsory education and could allow for such things as variations in school attendance (days of schooling per year), the shift from ungraded schools (all age cohorts in one classroom) to graded schools, the shift from rural to urban schools, and the like. For the moment, at least, any endeavor in this direction has to be given up. Indirectly, the developments just referred to, which we might call quality changes of education and which are not reflected in the enrollment figures, may be captured by turning to the second category of time-series data for educational expansion: expenditures for education.

THE EXPENDITURES FOR EDUCATION

1.   The pattern of educational expansion, as outlined with respect to the enrollment of students into various institutions of learning, should be paralleled by the expansion and distribution of expenditures for education. Walther Hoffmann has summarized the available information in a series covering the years 1861–1913 (Table 2A.8, col. 1). This series, which indicates an enormous increase in expenditures over time, is based on Prussian and Bavarian statistics and extrapolated for Germany via the population shares. If we reverse this procedure we get the total public expenditures for education in Prussia (Table 2.8, line 1). The confinement to *public* expenditures must not worry us too much, since private enrollment was never of major significance (cf. Tables 2.1–3). Our major interest, first of all, relates to the distribution of the educational expenditures by types of institution. Unfortunately, the respective information is rather scattered and covers some 80 percent of Hoffmann's totals from 1891 onwards only (Table 2.8). Fortunately, on the other hand, the complex bifurcated educational system, where competitive institutions catered for identical age groups, does not impose problems this time. For it is precisely the differences in costs of education, no matter which age is concerned, which we want to know and which constitute varying degrees of freedom of choice as to who goes to which school.

The general trend of rising expenditures for education, derived from the Hoffmann figures, holds true for every single institution within the educational system (Table 2.8, lines a). Of interest, however, are the expenditures per student by the respective institutions. For a meaningful comparison over time the figures should be converted into constant prices, but since only twenty years are sufficiently covered by census data there was not much left for studies of time trends. Nevertheless, for secondary schools at least we have enough information, and the per student expenditures (Table 2.8, lines d) rose from 176 marks in 1864, to 340 marks in 1911, as measured in 1913 prices (cf. Table 2A.8 for inflation index). Such a development indicates that the rising expenditures for education reflect not only the rising enrollment of students as a percentage of the population (cf. Tables 2.2–3) but also the rising costs per unit. In other words, it was more expensive (in constant prices) to provide one year of school for one student in the very late nineteenth century than it was in earlier decades. There are two familiar reasons for rising costs of education: (1) a decline of the student-teacher ratio; (2) an increase of teachers' salaries relatively faster than the increase of average labor earnings. Both factors were present in nineteenth-century Germany and may be termed "quality changes" of educational services.[17]

If we combine both quality improvement of education (as reflected by rising costs per unit) and quantitative expansion of education (as expressed in rising enrollment relative to population growth), we can take the total expenditures for education at constant prices and per head of the population (Table 2.8, last line) as an indicator of the "true" educational expansion. These data show a steady increase until, in the early twentieth century, there is nearly an explosion, a steep surge of the curve. On the other hand, the relative shares of the major educational institutions in the overall expenses for education are remarkably stable (Table 2.8, lines c): elementary schools, which accounted for some 90 percent of all students enrolled, were allotted some 55 percent of all public expenditures for education; the second largest share, of some 13 percent but slightly declining over time, went to secondary schools; middle schools (including girls' high schools) and universities made up some 5 percent each. These shares, however, do not mean very much by themselves, and we have to return, for a moment, to the expenditures per student.

For even if the relevant data limit intrainstitutional comparisons over time, the interinstitutional proportions of public and private expenses per student are of major interest. To be sure, one would expect one year of higher education to be much more expensive (per student) than, say, one year of either primary or secondary education. And indeed, the order of magnitude involved is quite different between the costs of general education and that of any kind of postsecondary education (Table 2.8, lines b). Within higher education, mining and forestry academies are relatively most expensive, perhaps because of their small student body. Universities and technical colleges require more money per student than the other professional and vocational schools, except that those for the textile industry seem to have cost exceptionally much. The corresponding tuition fees for the institutions just mentioned (Table 2.9, lines b) vary considerably; yet there seem to have been institutions which were markedly more expensive (technical colleges, mining and forestry academies, and schools for textile industry) than others.

University enrollment comprises the bulk of postsecondary education. There are two traits noteworthy with regard to its costs. (1) The proportion of the expenditures for universities covered by tuition fees is the smallest, compared to other institutions, except, of course, elementary schools (Table 2.9, lines c). In other words, most of the costs per university student were paid by the public. (2) The absolute amount of the tuition fees per student is relatively moderate if compared to the seemingly high tuition fees per student at the preceding level of education,

TABLE 2.8

Public Expenditures for Education in Prussia, 1864–1911, by Types of Institutions

a: total (in thousands of marks, at current prices)
b: per student (marks, at current prices)
c: as percentage of total expenditure for education
d: per student (marks, at 1913 prices)

Institution		1864	1873	1882	1891	1901	1911
Total expenditures	a	55,000	114,000	176,000	238,000	424,000	759,000
	c	100	100	100	100	100	100
Public elementary school	a	33,000	—	—	129,000	227,620	420,890
	b	11.7	—	—	26.2	40.1	64
	c	60	—	—	54.2	53.7	55.5
	d	20.7	—	—	32	44.6	65
Public middle and girls high school	a	—	—	—	12,000	20,900	49,320
	b	—	—	—	91.4	111	169.8
	c	—	—	—	5	4.9	6.5
	d	—	—	—	111.7	123.5	171
Secondary school (boys)	a	7,700	20,400	25,500	30,920	54,000	90,000
	b	99.8	160.6	166.8	197.2	269.8	336.9
	c	14	17.9	14.5	13	12.7	11.9
	d	176.3	219	203.9	241.1	300.1	340
Teacher training (seminar)	a	—	2,400	—	4,950	8,000	14,500
	b	—	400	—	456	659	780
	c	—	2.1	—	2.1	1.9	1.9
	d	—	545.7	—	557.4	733	788

		1	2	3	4	5	6
University	a	—	6,770	7,820	13,540	17,260	23,435
	b	—	919	622	1,041	986	849
	c	—	5.9	4.4	5.7	4.1	3.1
	d	—	1,253.7	760.4	1,272.6	1,096.8	857
Technical college	a	—	—	—	1,600	2,700	5,105
	b	—	—	—	837	502	1,145
	c	—	—	—	0.7	0.6	0.7
Mining and forestry academies	a	—	—	—	535	960	880
	b	—	—	—	1,988	1,811	2,000
	c	—	—	—	0.2	0.2	0.1
Agricultural and veterinary colleges	a	—	—	—	620	900	1,580
	b	—	—	—	511	562	658
	c	—	—	—	0.3	0.2	0.2
School for engineering	a	—	—	—	230	1,405	2,075
	b	—	—	—	366	669	751
	c	—	—	—	0.1	0.3	0.3
School for textile industry	a	—	—	—	290	775	1,070
	b	—	—	—	747	1,183	1,070
	c	—	—	—	0.1	0.2	0.1
Total per capita at 1913 prices (marks)		5.04	6.16	7.76	9.06	13.44	18.91

TABLE 2.9
Tuition Fees for Public Education in Prussia, 1864–1911, by Types of Institutions

a: total (in thousands of marks, at current prices)
b: per student (marks, at current prices)
c: as percentage of total public expenditure for the institution (or tuition per student as percentage of expenditure per student)

Institution		1864	1873	1882	1891	1901	1911
Public elementary							
school	a	7,500	—	—	1,380	825	1,155
	b	2.6	—	—	0.3		
	c	22.7	—	—	1	0.4	0.3
Public middle and girls							
high school	a	—	—	—	5,550	10,205	23,765
	b	—	—	—	42.3	54.2	81.8
	c	—	—	—	46.2	48.8	48.2
Secondary school							
(boys)	a	3,600		12,100	14,330	20,500	35,460
	b	46.7		79.2	91.4	102.4	132.7
	c	46.8		47.5	46.3	37.9	39.4
Teacher training							
(seminar)	a	—	—	—	1,290	1,500	1,700
	b	—	—	—	119	123	91
	c	—	—	—	26	18.7	11.7
University	a	—	500	730	1,660	2,565	4,650
	b	—	67	58	127	146	169
	c	—	7.4	9.3	12.3	14.9	15.6
Technical college	a	—	—	—	260	1,285	1,235
	b	—	—	—	136	239	277
	c	—	—	—	16.3	47.6	24.2
Mining and forestry							
academies	a	—	—	—	—	135	105
	b	—	—	—	—	254	238
	c	—	—	—	—	14	11.9
Agricultural and							
veterinary colleges	a	—	—	—	110	250	400
	b	—	—	—	90	156	166
	c	—	—	—	17.7	27.8	25.3
School for							
engineering	a	—	—	—	75	300	305
	b	—	—	—	119	142	110
	c	—	—	—	32.5	21.4	14.7
School for textile							
industry	a	—	—	—	100	150	280
	b	—	—	—	257	229	280
	c	—	—	—	34.5	19.4	26.2

secondary schools. At the same time it has to be noticed that the proportion of total costs covered by tuition fees is nowhere near as high as for secondary (and middle) schools. Under these circumstances, it is almost impossible to resist the conclusion that the bifurcated educational system had strong roots in the way schools were financed and public resources allotted to them, a way which led to the well-known combination of "education and property."[18]

2.   Having outlined the major trends of educational expansion as measured in expenditures, we face now a problem similar to the one we encountered when dealing with the expansion of enrollment: how to aggregate the figures, and how to measure the increase. One way of indicating the increase of educational expenditures by a single series of data has already been alluded to: the per capita expenditures at constant prices (Table 2.8, last line). This figure captures both quality improvements (rising costs per unit) and quantitative changes (rising numbers of units per head of population). Use of this kind of data as an input factor into a production function will be made in a final section of this paper.

Another way of measuring the increase of educational expenditures, more in line with the first part of this paper, is to tie expenditures to the amount of education embodied. If each year of school at the various institutions has its costs (Table 2.8), and if the distribution of the amount of schooling among the population is known (Table 2.7), then it should be possible to estimate the educational stock at costs carried by different populations (labor forces) and to measure the increase. The rationale for asking for the educational stock at costs is that investment in human capital (via education) is expected to yield a return which means a relatively larger earning to each individual. Such additional earnings, supposedly due to more and better education (i.e., returns to investments in education), eventually add up to a portion of that part of labor's income which cannot be "explained" by the increase of sheer physical labor.

This application of so-called cost-benefit analysis to aggregative national income accounting is the way T. W. Schultz tried to measure the contribution of education to economic growth.[19] Obviously, for both Schultz and Denison, earnings differentials associated with educational differences are decisive, and so is the marginal productivity theory as a common underlying framework. But whereas Denison asked for the increase of the quality of labor (notwithstanding its costs) as an input which contributed to the output, Schultz is concerned with the resources entering into the production of the quality of labor and considers the returns to this productive investment a contribution to output. The question of the appropriate rate of return raises difficult problems on both theoretical and empirical grounds.[20] But the educational stock at costs is a meaningful measure of educational expansion.

If only we had enough information about costs (Table 2.8) we could easily calculate the human capital formation by education at historic costs, which then would have to be converted into constant prices. Strangely enough, Schultz, in his article covering the twentieth century for the United States, takes the 1956 prices for one year of primary, secondary, or higher education and applies them constantly to the varying distribution of this schooling among the population over time. Thereby he neglects rising costs per unit, a matter which played a major role (to judge from Table 2.8). In order to calculate the educational stock at historic costs for the Prussian populations of 1864 and 1911, data on current costs of education, by types of institution, would be required for the time from 1800 onwards. The earliest census year for which I have an approximately complete set of data on costs, however, is 1891 (Table 2.8). Therefore, I propose to follow an alternative course of estimating the educational stock at costs before we rejoin Schultz's reasoning about possible returns to human capital.

The annual expenditures for education represent a flow of resources entering the stock of human capital which adds to its value. The stock of human capital is made up of the sum of annual flows of the preceding years. These annual flows, however, do not depreciate annually, as physical capital does, but lose value abruptly insofar as individual carriers have died or ceased to be members of the labor force. Consequently, the annual expenditures for education have to be depreciated along the lines of the life expectancy profile of the educated; and the depreciated annual outlays make up, if added, the educational stock at costs of the time under consideration. This approach of estimating the educational stock at costs is followed, for nineteenth-century Germany, by two authors. Walther Hoffmann confines his study to public expenditures only (cf. his series in Table 2A.8).[21] W. Krug includes not only public and private school inputs in his figures for annual resource costs of education, but also the so-called opportunity costs, or earnings foregone.[22] Thereby he accounts for the same components of education's costs as Schultz does, and we take the Krug figures for further consideration.

First of all, the time series on annual flows of educational outlays has to be converted into the annual stock of human capital. For this purpose Krug develops an order of depreciation based on the life expectancy of those being educated and allowing for a complete depreciation of one year's educational expenditures within fifty years. Applied to the time series on annual resource costs of education, and starting with a stock of human capital in the base year as estimated by Hoffmann, Krug arrives at his series of annual stock figures, i.e., the stock enlarged by annual additions but depreciated over time. Thus, between 1870 and 1913, the educational stock at costs, or human capital, rose in Germany from 7.2 to 32.1 billion marks (in 1913 prices).[23] In order to obtain the educational stock at costs of the labor force (in contrast to that of the population) we calculate the human capital per capita, which, when multiplied by the number of persons employed, yields the human capital as embodied in labor. Its rise over time is partly due to rising employment (educational widening) and partly due to an additional increase of human capital per member of the labor force (educational deepening). And it is to be expected that an increased human capital per head yields returns which are part of labor's income and which are otherwise unexplained.

Returns to education, however, are a tricky matter to deal with. Considerable work has been done within the framework of cost-benefit analysis. Most studies have two traits in common: they relate to microunits such as individuals, social groups, business enterprises; and they are based on empirical data of the present time. Thus it is possible to control for age, experience, sex, and intelligence, which may also influence earnings differentials associated with educational differences. But the range of rates of return to education found so far is rather wide and inconclusive.[24] If we turn to the nineteenth century, things get worse, although witnesses such as Horace Mann, for Massachusetts, and Ernst Engel, for Prussia, tried to estimate returns to education.[25] Their calculations have too many flaws to be taken seriously; but even if we could rely upon them, we would know, at best, the rate of return to specific educational levels which made a specific expense necessary.

Schultz, however, wants to add up, in a sense, the returns to each laborer's educational investments and to treat this "national" return to an increase of the educational stock as the contribution of education to national income growth. Applied to the German economy his argument runs like this: From 1870 to 1913 national income rose by 34.3 billion marks (= 100 percent), and labor, which shares some 75 percent of national income, increased its income by 25.7 billion marks (Table 2.10). If the earning capacity of labor had remained constant at the 1870 level, the rising employment of labor of the same quality would have raised labor's income by 8.5 billion marks, explaining 25 percent of national income growth. An additional 17.2 billion mark labor income (50 percent of national income growth) remains "unexplained" by rising employment. But labor may have improved its quality, and quality changes may be indicated by the increase of the educational stock at costs over time. If allowance is made for rising employment, the additional increase of human capital embodied in the labor force (educational deepening, or quality changes of labor) amounts to 10.9 billion marks between 1870 and 1913 (Table 2.10). Clearly, some of the "unexplained" labor income (and hence "unexplained" national income) should be attributed to quality changes of labor.

At this point Schultz quits the framework of aggregative national income accounting and introduces cost-benefit analysis (as an application of decision theory to investment choices). This procedure has been attacked as inappropriate on methodological grounds.[26] In addition, it encounters the empirical difficulty of choosing the right rate of return. After all, there are, if any, only rates of return to specific educational investments. Schultz, in his article on the American economy, offers three possible alternatives: two different estimates of rates of return to college education and one rate of return composed of weighted averages of rates of return for specific educational levels.[27] Since we do not have any rates of return to education for the nineteenth century, one thing we might do is treat alike human and physical capital. For physical capital (invested in industry) Hoffmann gives 6.68 percent as a rate of return before 1913.[28] If applied to the 10.9 billion mark increase of the educational stock (deepening above the 1870 level per member), this rate of return yields an income of 728 million marks, which would "explain" 2.12 percent of national income growth.

TABLE 2.10
National Income and Educational Stock at Costs in Germany,
1870 and 1913 (In Billions of Marks, at 1913 Prices)

	1870	1913	increase
National income	14.2	48.5	34.3
Labor income (= 75% of national income)	10.6	36.3	25.7
"Explained" by rising employment	10.6	19.1	8.5
"Unexplained"			17.2
Educational stock of population at costs	7.2	32.1	24.9
Educational stock of labor at costs	3.6	17.4	13.8
"Explained" by rising employment (educational widening)	3.6	6.5	2.9
Additional increase (educational deepening)			10.9

The contribution of additional education to economic growth, if measured along the lines of Schultz's approach, conveys a numerical value which accords, in the German case, precisely with the one obtained by using Denison's approach. The same congruence of results had been recorded when the two approaches were originally applied to the U.S. economy of the twentieth century, although the order of magnitude involved was quite different—i.e., some 20 percent as compared to 2 percent for Germany. It looks as if we are held to discount the role usually ascribed to education as a factor contributing to German economic performance. Premature as this conclusion may appear, it is corroborated by a third effort to measure education's contribution to economic growth, which consists of including educational expenditures, along with labor and capital, as an argument in a production function.

3. To begin with it should be noted that both Denison and Schultz argue essentially along the lines of a production function approach, namely, to ask how much of output can be explained by the increase of inputs. But neither Denison's years of school embodied in labor nor Schultz's educational stock at costs directly enter any production function describing the functional relation between output and inputs of the factors of production. Rather, both authors use their respective data on educational expansion to adjust the labor input series in a basic two-factor production function. If education is a positive, growth-inducing force, however, a measure of the growth of education *added* to the basic production function might be expected to add to the proportion of the variance in output growth explained by the growth of physical inputs, labor and capital, except to the extent that the growth of education is collinear with the growth of factor inputs. But in any case, we should expect the marginal product of education to be positive. The drawback of the Denison-type approach is that the education-income correlations used for

adjusting the labor input series may be spurious. Using the production function approach, on the other hand, it is possible to make direct estimates of the education-income relation rather than simply to infer it. There have been some experiments with this approach in recent years, notably by Griliches,[29] but using mainly cross-section data, which introduce fewer complications into statistical estimation procedures than time-series data which we must work with here.

The basic production function extended to include education as a productive input may be written:

$$O_t = A_t \, L_t^\alpha \, K_t^\beta \, E_t^\tau \tag{1}$$

where O is real output

       A is the level of technology

       L is a measure of labor input (preferably man-hours worked)

       K is a measure of capital input (preferably capital services)

       E is a measure of educational expenditure in real terms

       α is the elasticity of output with respect to labor

       β is the elasticity of output with respect to capital

       γ is the elasticity of output with respect to education, and

       t is a time subscript.

There are several ways of obtaining estimates of the parameters α, β, and γ,[30] and of calculating the contribution of education to growth. The method adopted here is to take logarithms of the variables and to estimate the parameters freely by ordinary least squares regression techniques.[31] In estimating form equation (1) becomes

$$\log O_t = \log A_t + \alpha \log L_t + \beta \log K_t + \gamma \log E_t \tag{2}$$

The parameters α, β, and γ are the regression coefficients of equation (2) when equation (2) is fitted to the data by ordinary least squares. The parameters are to be interpreted as partial elasticities—that is, they give the effect on output of 1 percent change in the variables they are attached to, holding all other variables constant. Then, if we know the average growth of capital, labor, and education over time, the relative contribution of inputs to output can be estimated. In particular, the contribution of education to growth can be calculated, and an estimate can also be made of the social rate of return.

Before discussing the results of adopting this procedure, we must turn to the question which naturally arises, of the measure of the growth of education to be used in the function. The measure decided on was a measure of educational deepening, defined as the amount of educational expenditure in excess of that required to keep educational expenditure per head constant in real terms.[32] This seemed sensible on two counts. First, it makes the study most directly comparable with studies which estimate the contribution of education to growth by taking education-income profiles on the assumption that a certain percentage of differences in income of people of the same age are due to differences in the quantity of education embodied in them. Secondly, since the interest is in education and growth, a closer relation is to be expected between increases in educational expenditure per head and the growth of output than simply the growth of educational expenditure itself, a large proportion of which is necessary to keep the quantity of education per head constant. By neglecting educational widening we are, in a sense, underestimating the contribution of education to growth, but we have taken this risk in an attempt to make estimates comparable with other studies.

We are now in a position to discuss the analysis and results. Fitting the basic production function, $O_t = A_t L_t^\alpha K_t^\beta$, to the Hoffmann series on output, man-hours, and capital stock for the period 1861 to 1913 yielded the following result:[33]

$$O_t = 0.051 L_t^{0.085} K_t^{0.902} \qquad r^2 = 0.9971$$

Judging by the high coefficient of determination (r^2) the function fits the data almost perfectly.[34] Notice, however, that the size of the elasticities attaching to labor and capital are the reverse of what one might have expected on the basis of factor shares. Clearly, the use of these coefficients will give estimates of the contribution of capital and labor to growth very different from those given by the use of factor shares, which is what Hoffmann uses. Notice also, that the two coefficients sum virtually to unity, indicating constant returns to scale.

When our measure of educational deepening (E) was added to the basic production function as an additional explanatory variable, the following results were obtained:

$$O_t = 0.0232 L_t^{0.082} K_t^{0.884} E_t^{0.0053} \qquad r^2 = 0.9972$$

The elasticities of output with respect to labor and capital stay roughly the same as before. The elasticity of output with respect to the educational deepening variable is 0.0053. Applying this figure to the mean rate of growth of educational deepening expenditure over the period under review, namely 11.5 percent, we find that the contribution of our measure of educational expansion to the growth of output has been $0.0053 \times 11.5 = 0.061$ percentage points. Given an average annual rate of growth of output of 3.2 percent[35] over the period, the estimated contribution of education to growth is 2 percent. This is clearly a very small contribution, but is very much in line with estimates by Denison for northwest Europe in more recent times, and accords precisely both with the estimate for Germany for the period 1950 to 1962[36] and with our own findings for nineteenth-century Germany discussed in previous sections of this paper. On the other hand, the implied social return to educational deepening is quite high. The marginal product of educational deepening expenditure may be expressed as

$$\frac{\Delta O}{\Delta E} = \frac{\Delta O}{O} \bigg/ \frac{\Delta E}{E} \times \frac{O}{E},$$

where $\dfrac{\Delta O}{O} \bigg/ \dfrac{\Delta E}{E}$ is the elasticity of output with respect to education

and O/E is the ratio of the mean level of output to the mean level of educational deepening expenditure.

From our data,

$$\frac{\Delta O}{\Delta E} = 0.0053 \times \frac{25,000 \text{ mill marks}}{312 \text{ mill marks}}$$

$$= 0.4 \text{ mark of output per year for each additional mark of educational deepening expenditure.}$$

This calculation implies the relatively high gross rate of return of approximately 40 percent. The contrast between the small contribution of educational deepening to the growth of output in the aggregate and the apparent high social return to expenditure on educational deepening in no way presents a paradox. There is no necessary relation between the size of the percentage contribution of education to growth and the social return to education. If anything, the relation may be inverse if the contribution of education to growth depends on the quantity of education and the rate of return depends on the ability of individuals to reap monopoly rents.

Altogether, the results of using the production function approach to the measurement of the contribution of education to growth are encouraging. They lend support to the results of the more ad hoc approach discussed earlier and are consistent with estimates for more recent times. The general conclusion must be that in Germany in the nineteenth century, as in the postwar period 1950–62, very little of the impressive rate of growth of output appears directly attributable to the growth of education.

NOTES

1. See Friedrich Edding, *Internationale Tendenzen in der Entwicklung der Ausgaben für Schulen und Hochschulen* (Kiel, 1958); M. C. Kaser, "Education and Economic Progress: Experience in Industrialized Market Economies. A Preliminary Approach to a Statistical Examination," in *The Economics of Education: Proceedings of a Conference Held by the International Economic Association,* ed. E. A. G. Robinson and J. E. Vaizey (London and New York, 1966), pp. 89ff.

2. Walther G. Hoffmann, *Das Wachstum der deutschen Wirtschaft seit der Mitte des 19. Jahrhunderts* (Berlin, Heidelberg, and New York, 1965).

3. Hoffmann, *Wachstum der deutschen Wirtschaft,* pp. 726ff.; cf. Walther G. Hoffmann, "Erziehungs- und Forschungsausgaben im wirtschaftlichen Wachstumsprozess," in *Eine Freundesgabe der Wissenschaft für Ernst Hellmut Vits,* ed. G. Hess (Frankfurt am Main, 1963), pp. 101ff.

4. The detailed derivation of the tables is given in the Appendix to this chapter.

5. Kaser, "Education and Economic Progress," pp. 98, 109.

6. Since the number of students enrolled in vocational/professional schools was apparently rather small, it seems safe to assume that the lack of statistical information and errors in the extrapolations do not significantly affect the overall totals.

7. Charles Kennedy and A. P. Thirlwall, "Surveys in Applied Economics, 3: Technical Progress," *Economic Journal* 82 (1972): 11ff.

8. Edward F. Denison, *The Sources of Economic Growth in the United States and the Alternatives before Us,* Committee for Economic Development Supplementary Paper no. 13 (New York, 1962).

9. "Erwerbstätigkeit und berufliche Ausbildung: Ergebnis des Mikrozensus April 1964," *Wirtschaft und Statistik,* 1966, no. 3, pp. 177ff.

10. The relations between enrollment in single grades, graduation from single grades, and age cohorts are discussed in the explanations of Tables 2.4 and 2.5 in the Appendix.

11. See the Appendix, where Table 2A.7 is discussed and the work is acknowledged.

12. Hoffmann, *Wachstum der deutschen Wirtschaft,* pp. 204ff., 209f.

13. Compare the computer results (Table 2A.7), referred to in n. 11.

48 Peter Lundgreen

14. Edward F. Denison, assisted by Jean-Pierre Poullier, *Why Growth Rates Differ: Postwar Experience in Nine Western Countries,* The Brookings Institution (Washington, D.C., 1967), p. 85.

15. Another attempt has been made to calculate the growth rate of labor's quality and its impact upon productivity for Germany before the First World War: see Doris André, *Indikatoren des technischen Fortschritts: Eine Analyse der Wirtschaftsentwicklung in Deutschland von 1850 bis 1913,* Weltwirtschaftliche Studien 16 (Göttingen, 1971). The author declares, however, that a construction of the percentage distribution of a given labor force by years of schooling is virtually impossible. Instead, she starts out with the annual increase of school years in excess of a constant per capita ratio. Unfortunately (and unnecessarily) the number of school years is grossly overestimated, since it is not taken directly from enrollment statistics but inferred from educational expenditures divided by outlays per student. In addition, only elementary school students are taken into consideration. The neglect of secondary and higher education leads unavoidably to an overestimation of "school years" allegedly financed per year, which, according to enrollment statistics, amounts to some 60 percent. This misspecification has harmful effects on all further steps of André's reasoning. For it is not the growth rate but the annual absolute size of the "educational deepening" that enters the quality index of labor (ibid., pp. 108ff.). The (overestimated) quality change of labor is treated as a fictitious (and overestimated) addition of quantity to labor input; it conveys an annual growth rate of 0.2 percent (ibid., p. 115), which implies a "contribution" to national income by 5.8 percent if weighted with the labor share in national income. Nevertheless, this result, though considerably higher than my own calculation, remains within the same order of magnitude if compared with the twentieth-century U.S. experience, which exceeds 20 percent. Cf. Denison, *Sources of Economic Growth,* p. 73.

16. Denison, *Why Growth Rates Differ,* pp. 78ff.

17. Hoffmann, "Erziehungs- und Forschungsausgaben," pp. 120f., 124f.

18. Cf. Knut Borchardt, "Zum Problem der Erziehungs- und Ausbildungsinvestitionen im 19. Jahrhundert," in *Beiträge zur Wirtschafts- und Stadtgeschichte: Festschrift für Hektor Ammann,* ed. Hermann Aubin (Wiesbaden, 1965), pp. 388f. (with reference to Ernst Engel).

19. Theodore W. Schultz, "Education and Economic Growth," in *Social Forces Influencing American Education: The Sixtieth Yearbook of the National Society for the Study of Education,* pt. 2, ed. Nelson B. Henry (Chicago, 1961), pp. 46ff.

20. Ibid., pp. 73ff.; Mary Jean Bowman, "Schultz, Denison, and the Contribution of 'Eds' to National Income Growth," *Journal of Political Economy* 72 (1964): 450ff.

21. Hoffmann, "Erziehungs- und Forschungsausgaben," pp. 125ff.

22. Walter Krug, "Quantitative Beziehungen zwischen materiellem und immateriellem Kapital," *Jahrbücher für Nationalökonomie und Statistik* 180 (1967): 43ff.; cf. Walter Krug, "Erfassung des durch Ausbildung entgangenen Einkommens," *Schmollers Jahrbuch für Gesetzgebung, Verwaltung und Volkswirtschaft* 86 (1966): 561ff.

23. Krug, "Quantitative Beziehungen," pp. 56f.

24. Fritz Machlup, *Education and Economic Growth* (Lincoln, Neb., 1970), pp. 43ff., and the literature summarized there.

25. Maris A. Vinovskis, "Horace Mann on the Economic Productivity of Education" *New England Quarterly* 43 (1970): 481ff.; Borchardt, "Zum Problem der Erziehungs- und Ausbildungsinvestitionen," pp. 381ff.

26. Bowman, "Schultz, Denison," pp. 453, 460.

27. Schultz, "Education and Economic Growth," pp. 80f.

28. Hoffmann, "Wachstum der deutschen Wirtschaft," p. 502.

29. Z. Griliches, "The Sources of Measured Productivity Growth: United States Agriculture, 1940–1960," *Journal of Political Economy* 71 (1963): 331ff.; idem, "Research Expenditures, Education, and the Aggregate Agricultural Production Function," *American Economic Review* 54 (1964): 961ff.

30. See Kennedy and Thirlwall, "Surveys in Applied Economics, 3," pp. 14ff., 39ff.

31. This was the original approach of Charles Cobb and Paul Douglas, who gave their names to the now-celebrated Cobb-Douglas production function $O_t = A_t L_t^\alpha K_t^\beta$. Ordinary least squares regression is a statistical technique designed to obtain the parameters of a function which minimize the sum of squared differences between actual observations of the dependent variable and the predicted values of the dependent variable, in terms of the explanatory variables, when the estimated function is applied to the data. In other words, it seeks to estimate a function which best "explains" variations in the dependent variable in terms of variations in the explanatory variables.

An alternative procedure to the one adopted here is to regress the first differences of the log of output on the first differences of the logs of the explanatory variables (i.e., to work with the rates of growth of the variables rather than their levels). With this approach it can be shown that under the perfectly competitive assumption that factors of production are paid the value of their marginal products, the exponents of the basic production function will equal labor and capital's share of the national income. Indeed, it is often the case in growth studies that the parameters of the basic production function are not estimated directly but inferred on the basis of the shares of national income received by the factors of production in question (e.g., in Denison's calculations). Even if legitimate, which is doubtful, this approach is out of place here because we require an estimate of γ as well as of α and β.

Hoffmann, "Wachstum der deutschen Wirtschaft," mentions in a footnote (p. 27) that he experimented with estimating the production function for Germany directly by taking first differences of the logarithms of the variables (i.e., their rates of growth) but found the results economically meaningless and therefore resorted to the factor shares approach. We also experimented in the way Hoffmann describes, including various measures of education growth in the production function. We also confirm that the basic production function, estimated by taking first differences of the logs of the variables, makes very little economic sense, although a measure of the growth of educational deepening proved to be a statistically significant explanatory variable. One reason for the odd results obtained by Hoffmann and ourselves may be that taking first differences of the logs of the variables assumes that first order serial correlation of the residuals from the equation is unity. This may be a serious misspecification. Taking the Cobb-Douglas approach, as we have done, avoids this extreme assumption. Some adjustment has been made for serial correlation, however, which otherwise would give inefficient estimates, by using the Cochrane-Orcutt iterative technique when estimating the function by ordinary least squares.

32. See the discussion of Table 2A.8 in the Appendix.

33. The data are to be found in Hoffmann, "Wachstum des deutschen Wirtschaft," pp. 454f. (output); pp. 204f. (labor force); pp. 213f. (hours worked per week); pp. 253f. (capital stock). The Hoffmann series on output, labor, and capital stock run from 1850. The analysis here starts from 1861 because this is the earliest date for which public expenditure on education is available. The years 1876–80, inclusive, and 1901 and 1903 have been excluded from the time series on the grounds that changes in output in these years seemed to bear no relation to inputs. All the data are measured in real terms (i.e., at constant prices in the case of output and capital).

34. This close fit is not due to the passage of time. The introduction of an exponential time trend produced an insignificant negative coefficient on the time variable.

35. This is higher than the Hoffmann average because of the exclusion of the years mentioned in n. 33.

36. Denison, *Why Growth Rates Differ,* p. 309.

APPENDIX: THE DERIVATION OF THE TABLES
AND SUPPLEMENTARY TABLES

The principal sources for the tables, by census years, are as follows:

1822–64 Ernst Engel, "Beiträge zur Geschichte und Statistik des Unterrichts, insbesondere des Volksschul-Unterrichts, im preussischen Staate, I," in *Zeitschrift des Königlich Preussischen Statistischen Bureaus* 9 (1869): 99ff.

1873 *Jahrbuch für die amtliche Statistik des preussischen Staats,* 4, pt. 2 (Berlin, 1876): 1ff.

1882 *Jahrbuch für die amtliche Statistik des preussischen Staats,* 5 (Berlin, 1883): 539ff.

1891 *Statistisches Handbuch für den preussischen Staat,* 2 (Berlin, 1893): 453ff.

1901 *Statistisches Jahrbuch für den preussischen Staat,* 1904 (Berlin, 1905): 123ff.

1911 *Statistisches Jahrbuch für den preussischen Staat,* 1913 (Berlin, 1914): 388ff.

Additional information was obtained from the following sources:
Jahrbuch für die amtliche Statistik des preussischen Staats, 1 (Berlin, 1863).

Statistisches Handbuch für den preussischen Staat, 1 (Berlin, 1888).

L. Wiese, *Das höhere Schulwesen in Preussen: Historisch-statistische Darstellung*, vol. 1 (Berlin, 1864).

W. Lexis, *A General View of the History and Organization of Public Education in the German Empire* (Berlin, 1904).

In the body of the tables, all figures which cannot be found directly in the sources are given in parentheses and explained in this Appendix.

The basic information on enrollment of males and females is summarized in Tables 2.1 and 2A.1. Females are excluded from the analysis for the reasons given in the text, but some remarks with regard to the data available are perhaps in order.

Table 2A.1

col. 1: The figure for 1873 had to be interpolated, since there was no strict distinction, in the Prussian statistical assessment of the time, between elementary and middle schools (*Statistisches Handbuch*, 2 [1893]: 453).

col. 2: The first data available for private elementary (and middle) schools are from 1858. The figures for 1873 and 1882 are interpolated.

cols. 3–6: It seems a fair assumption that secondary education for females branched off from female middle schools rather than that there are simply no data for secondary schools in the earlier decades.

cols. 3–4: The figures for 1873 and 1882 are interpolated by taking the given figures for secondary education in these years (cols. 5–6) into account.

col. 3: For 1891 it was necessary to divide the number of boys and girls of the coeducational middle schools; this was done according to the proportion of the sexes in 1896 (*Statistisches Jahrbuch* [1904], p. 140).

cols. 4 and 6: For 1891 it was necessary to divide boys and girls according to the 1896 relationship (*Statistisches Jahrbuch* [1904], p. 143); in addition, middle and secondary girls' schools had to be separated, and this was done according to the relationship of 1901. For 1901 the girls' middle and secondary schools are given separately in *Preussische Statistik*, 176, pt. 2: 392–93, 408.

cols. 5–6: The figures for 1873 and 1882 are based on the figures for 1874 and 1881, given in the sources.

A comparison of Table 2A.1 with Table 2.2 reveals that the enrollment of females in public elementary schools, as a percentage of the female population, was also already very high in the early nineteenth century but lagged behind the male enrollment by 0.5 to 1.0 percent of the respective populations. Furthermore, middle schools seem to have functioned as a substitute for secondary schools for females until girls' high schools emerged. As late as 1894 these girls' high schools regularly comprised only nine grades and differed from the middle schools mainly in offering a second foreign language in their curriculum (Lexis, *Public Education*, p. 81).

Tables 2.1–3 contain the basic information available for male enrollment in Prussia. As mentioned earlier it is assumed that the students at universities, teacher training institutes, vocational schools, and professional colleges are virtually all males. What are the implications if this assumption is not valid? Either those females who underwent any kind of full-time higher (tertiary) training joined the labor force, in which case they are included in my estimation of the "quality" of labor; or else they abstained from working, in which case my estimation is slightly biased, and the "increase" of the quality of labor would have to be reduced—which means even less of a contribution of education to economic growth.

TABLE 2A.1
Enrollment of Females in Prussia, 1822–1911, by Types of Institutions and Typical Ages of Students

Year	Elementary (6–14 yrs.) Public	Elementary Private	Middle (6–14/15 yrs.) Public	Middle Private	Secondary (6–15/16 or 19 yrs.) Public	Secondary Private
1822 a b	683,838 11.64	— —	34,194 0.58	— —	— —	— —
1828	866,265 13.54	— —	47,221 0.74	— —	— —	— —
1837	1,061,232 15.03	— —	42,540 0.60	— —	— —	— —
1846	1,197,885 14.85	— —	48,302 0.60	— —	— —	— —
1855	1,292,635 14.99	— —	52,123 0.60	— —	— —	— —
1864	1,398,131 14.45	27,406 0.28	47,170 0.49	27,590 0.28	— —	— —
1873	(1,887,312) 14.79	(25,166) 0.20	(58,638) 0.46		(42,783) 0.33	
1882	2,156,846 15.31	(18,001) 0.13	(60,929) 0.43		(54,835) 0.39	
1891	2,448,918 15.85	10,839 0.07	(52,816) 0.34	(12,912) 0.08	28,702 0.18	(49,830) 0.32
1901	2,831,301 15.92	6,264 0.03	61,192 0.34	11,813 0.07	53,480 0.30	73,440 0.41
1911	3,279,263 15.93	— —	95,171 0.46	44,140 0.21	97,046 0.47	60,494 0.29

Table 2.1

The main purpose of this table is to indicate the range of age cohorts comprised by the enrollment figures for the various institutions. The table requires the breakdown by the following tables.

Table 2.2

Similar procedures were necessary as with regard to Table 2A.1, cols. 1–4. In particular:

col. 2: The figure for 1873 had to be interpolated.

col. 3: For 1822–55 I had to make an extrapolation, which I did by applying a constant percentage of the male population. The figures for 1873 and 1882 are interpolated.

cols. 4–5: The figures for 1873 and 1882 are interpolated, with the information for 1886 as a given assistance. For 1891 cf. the discussion of Table 2A.1, cols. 4 and 6.

col. 5: Here again, an extrapolation done on the basis of a constant percentage of the male population was necessary for 1822–55. The figure for 1901 is from *Preussische Statistik,* 176, pt. 2: 392–93.

col. 6: Engel's figures for secondary school enrollment for 1822–64 do include the students of the preparatory grades, as can be seen by comparison with Wiese's figures. In the second half of the century, the percentage of preparatory students among the total secondary school students was 13 percent on the average; this breaks down, for 1864, into 10.5 percent for the *Gymnasien,* 6.0 percent for the *Progymnasien,* and 18.0 percent for the *Realschulen.* These percentages have been taken constantly from the Engel figures for 1822–55 and are given in Table 2.2, col. 6.

col. 7: These figures are the residuals if one subtracts the grand total of Table 2A.3 from the total of Table 2A.2. See the derivation of these tables.

col. 1: To arrive at col. 1, the total of cols. 2–7, is the purpose of Table 2.2. It is only this figure which indicates, in a bifurcated educational system, the level of enforcement of compulsory schooling.

Table 2.3

col. 2: See the grand total of Table 2A.3.

cols. 3–4: These are subtotals of col. 2; they are indicative of the benchmark constituted by the one year's military service privilege connected with the "maturity" for the upper II of many secondary schools. A complete breakdown by single grades is given in Table 2A.3.

col. 5: Statistics about university students are usually easily available. Unfortunately, we do not know how the students were distributed by years of study.

col. 6: Teacher training was carried on in two stages: preparatory institutions and teachers' seminars. Until 1901 the statistics refer to the latter only. It has been assumed, for the earlier years, that there were an equal number of candidates enrolled in preparatory institutions (cf. Table 2.1, col. 7). For 1822 and 1828 the figures had to be extrapolated.

col. 7: Statistical knowledge about vocational and professional training is very incomplete; the information is scattered and diffuse. My own trial on this ground is given in Table 2A.4 and thence cautiously extrapolated backwards (cf. Table 2.1, cols. 8–10).

Summing up the "original" information given in Tables 2.1–3, probably at least the orders of magnitude are valid, since the weak points, and especially the extrapolations, refer to institutions of learning whose enrollment was relatively small and does not therefore significantly affect the overall proportions as indicated by these tables. The outstanding though by no means astonishing difference, of course, is that between compulsory (Table 2.2, col. 1) and voluntary (Table 2.3, col. 1) education; the latter seems to defy a meaningful quantitative treatment, and consequently, the figures may grossly misrepresent the importance of this group, which consisted of social elites and highly qualified man-power.

Table 2.4

This table reorganizes the information of Tables 2.2 and 2.3, with the help of Tables 2A.3 and 2A.4, into enrollment figures for students (supposedly, as we argue later on, of a single age cohort) for each additional year of school. In other words, the question asked is, How many students, of those enrolled at a given time, are enrolled for the 1st, 2nd, 3rd, . . . , 16th, 17th year of schooling? The age range of the various institutions of learning is given in Table 2.1.

col. 1: Compulsory education (Table 2.2, col. 1) comprised eight years of schooling; assuming an equal distribution, we arrive at the enrollment figure for the 1st, 2nd, or 8th year by taking one-eighth of the total compulsory enrollment (Table 2.4, col. 1). The assumption of equal distribution over 8 years is not strong if one concerns oneself only with the rising number of children of the respective age within eight years; this effect averages out by aiming at typical age cohorts for every decade and their distribution by years of school. The assumption of equal distribution of compulsory schooling over eight years is strong, however, if, and insofar as, it implies that every child who enrolled did stay in school for the full eight years at least. Actually, the figures for compulsory enrollment (Table 2.2, col. 1) may comprise, especially for the earlier decades, relatively more students who finish with six or seven than with eight years. Unfortunately, there seems no way to assess this distribution; equal distribution hence has to be regarded as a nonconserva-tive assumption which probably overestimates the amount of schooling for the early nineteenth century but which leads, consequently, to an underestimation of the *increase* of the amount of schooling embodied.

cols. 2–6, lines b: The distribution of secondary school students by grades is derived in Table 2A.3 and given as the totals for the upper III to the upper I. Fortunately, it was possible to assess the actual distribution by additional years of school, at least for the students at secondary schools, who composed some 50 percent of the total voluntary enrollment (Table 3, col. 2); it is clear how misleading an assumption of equal distribution would have been.

col. 6: The leaving certificate of the Gymnasium (''Abitur'') entitled its holder to access to university. Yet this ''maturity'' was not only to be obtained by passing regularly through a Gymnasium but also by private studies (or elsewhere). Hence we encounter the so-called external *maturi* who applied for the Abitur and had to pass the equivalent examination. For the earlier decades these external maturi comprise a considerable portion of all students eligible for university studies; they had consequently to be added (Wiese, *Das höhere Schulwesen*, pp. 512ff.). Otherwise the high numbers for students would not be understand-able.

cols. 7–9, lines b: We know the number of university students enrolled in the various faculties, but not the number enrolled for the 1st, 2nd, 3rd, or 4th year of studies. Neither do we know what the average length of study was, or how many students dropped out or did not even aim at a degree. I have made the very optimistic assumption that all students completed a four-year course of studies. Most certainly this results in an overestimation of voluntary enrollment, but does not necessarily invalidate my calculation. For if there was a fairly constant distribution between dropouts and degree-holders over time, then it does not matter which distribution we assume so long as our main interest is to know the *increase* of the amount of schooling embodied.

cols. 2–8, lines a: Similar reasoning applies if we add teacher training and vocational/ professional training (Table 2.1, cols 7–10). The assumptions are: (1) Teacher candidates are equally distributed over three years in the preparatory and again in the seminars' grades; every student finished his six years, which leads to a high concentration of graduates at the level of fourteen years of school (Table 2.4, col. 7). (2) Most complicated are the circumstances with respect to vocational/professional training. To take the qualification for admission as indicator for the ages involved (Table 2A.4) is debatable since many, and especially the lower, schools required, besides graduation from an institution of general education, a practical training (like an apprenticeship) as an additional qualification. I have neglected this factor, which means that someone who finished elementary school at the age of 14, became an apprentice and wound up as a journeyman at the age of 17, and then resumed formal training by attending a full-time vocational school (which, then, was his ninth year of school) is treated the same as someone who continued school attendance without interruption and hence might be 14 years old when starting his ninth year. Yet the procedure seems to be legitimate if we ask for the number of years of formal schooling embodied in the population (or age cohorts). Besides the problem of interrupting and resuming studies, the other assumptions are by now familiar: The courses were assumed to last two years for the lower vocational schools, and three years for both the higher ones and the colleges; and every student was supposed to have finished his course, which means to assume equal distribution of the enrollment figures by grades of school.

Thus, Table 2.4 involves a number of assumptions. But any variations in the distribution of voluntarily enrolled students by years of school, as a result of better information or different assumptions, would not change the orders of magnitude in the aggregate as much as a variation with respect to compulsory enrollment would do. Since we have probably overestimated compulsory education by assigning eight years of school to everybody as a minimum, it is perhaps justifiable to make similar optimistic assumptions for voluntary education. But because the data on secondary schools are better than the data for the other training institutions beyond compulsory education, Tables 2.4, 2.5, and 2A.7 offer version a and version b separately.

Table 2.5

Table 2.4 is meant to give help in answering the question, How many students graduated with 8, 9, 10, . . . , 17 years of school completed? The gradual decline of the enrollment figure with rising additional schooling (Table 2.4) indicates that at every turn of the year some students finished their studies (or dropped out) while others continued. Table 2.5 takes this at face value and simply subtracts, on the basis of Table 2.4, the following column from the preceding one each time. Thus we arrive from enrollment figures for students at distribution figures for graduates.

There are obviously two assumptions inherent in this. (1) The students of, say, 1822 who are enrolled for the ninth year of their schooling (Table 2.4, col. 2) should be compared with the students of 1823, and of the then tenth year of schooling, if the graduates with nine years of school completed are to be calculated. Since my whole procedure did not calculate the interpolations necessary for this follow-up but rather aimed at "typical" distributions, there is a slight overestimation in my graduate figures in Table 2.5. This is because the numbers for the upper grades refer to older age cohorts and are hence slightly smaller; the arithmetical differences between two consecutive columns of Table 2.4 thus become slightly larger. The resulting error of measurement is probably very small but does not in any case affect our calculation of the *increase* of education embodied. (2) Both the enrollment figures (Table 2.4) and the figures for graduates (Table 2.5), although given for single grades of the institutions of learning, do not necessarily comprise students always of one age cohort only. In fact, there are, within a single grade, considerable age ranges; the distribution, however, peaks at a "typical" age. For the further calculations it is assumed that *all* students of a specific grade (Table 2.4) are of the typical age and hence belong to a single age cohort. This assumption appears stronger than it is. First, there is a considerable averaging out if the assumption is upheld for each grade. Secondly, if someone who repeats a grade is counted as an additional student of the first year in this grade, this slightly increases the overall number of students of an alleged single age cohort who enroll voluntarily, and thus is in line with our general tendency to estimate the voluntary enrollment optimistically.

The reason for the assumption just mentioned, which practically leads to equating enrollment by grades with age cohorts, is the following one: The distribution of graduates by years of school, if to be given in relative terms, needs a denominator. The only meaningful denominators are the age cohorts. Out of each age cohort (of a living population) a very high percentage passes through compulsory education, but only a small proportion attends an additional ninth year of school (Table 2.5, col. 1). This fraction, then, continually diminishes because of the loss of graduates in the various upper grades until the university students finish their seventeenth year of school (Table 2.5, cols. 2–10). The two main assumptions thus yield the distribution pattern, by voluntary years of school, for typical age cohorts.

Table 6

The denominator for the percentage distribution of male age cohorts by years of school must be the absolute number of males in each cohort. This information is demographical, but the relevant statistics do not exist for most of the period under consideration. On the other hand, the existing data suggest that the age structure of the Prussian population did not change significantly over time (cf. Table 2A.6). Therefore, a constant percentage was applied to the populations of the census years, namely 17.5 percent, standing for the eight age cohorts of compulsory schooling. The slightly higher percentages for 1882–1911 (Table 2.2, col. 1) may be considered a result of a population which slowly increases the relative proportion of its younger age brackets. As a consequence of the 17.5 percent assumption, defiance of compulsory schooling fades out from 1882 onwards. Differing assumptions would have led to different percentage distributions for the male age cohorts but would be irrelevant with respect to the *increase* of education embodied over time.

Dividing the 17.5 percentages of the populations by eight yields, then, single age cohorts. These typical single male age cohorts have to be related to the actual compulsory enrollment in the respective census years (Table 2.4, col. 1). The comparison allows us to estimate the number of pupils who, although of the compulsory school age, did not attend school. This relationship is typical, however, for all eight age cohorts which are included in the original enrollment data. Since the voluntary schooling stretches, at maximum, over another nine years, some allowance for the passing time should be made. This was done by relating the distribution pattern of graduates with voluntary education (Table 2.5) to one age cohort of the *preceding* census year as a basis. The procedure of lagging assignments is illustrated, with an example included, in Table 2A.5.

Table 2.7

cols. 1–2: The number of members of the typical age cohorts (Table 2.6) who were part of the working populations in 1864 and 1911 can be obtained from Table 2A.6. If the respective percentages are taken from each relevant typical age cohort, simple addition gives the distribution, by years of school, of two working populations. The underlying assumption is, this time, a very minor one: that below 64 years of age there is no systematic relationship between men of different educational levels and their life expectancy.

col. 3: The distribution of the labor force by years of school was assessed directly for the first time in 1964 ("Erwerbstätigkeit und berufliche Ausbildung: Ergebnis des Mikrozensus April 1964," *Wirtschaft und Statistik,* 1966, no. 3, pp. 178, 167*). These figures have been used by Edward F. Denison in his comparative study *Why Growth Rates Differ: Postwar Experience in Nine Western Countries,* The Brookings Institution (Washington, D.C., 1967), pp. 389ff. As Denison notes (p. 390) the correspondence between the two tables of the 1964 microcensus is difficult to establish: the table on p. 178 refers to general education only, and therefore it is directly comparable to my Table 2A.7, version b; the table on p. 167* gives the information on vocational/professional training. Denison, in his combination of the two tables, treats the students of all full-time training institutions below the higher education level as subdivisions of the *Volksschule* graduates. This is most likely not true in reality, and my own assignments give much more weight to secondary school students. The differences are, however, not that large and do virtually vanish if compared with the persistent distribution pattern which gives little weight to any kind of voluntary education above the compulsory level.

Table 2.8
Totals (first and last lines): Walther G. Hoffmann, *Das Wachstum der deutschen Wirtschaft seit der Mitte des 19. Jahrhunderts* (Berlin, Heidelberg, and New York, 1965), p. 728. Hoffmann gives the public expenditures for education for Germany, but his figures are extrapolated from Prussian and Bavarian statistics. The totals of Table 2.8 are reversely extrapolated (via the population shares) to Prussian figures. In order to allow for inflation the total expenditures per capita were converted into 1913 prices by using Hoffmann's price index for public expenditures (ibid., p. 599, col. 12). The same price index was used in order to convert the expenditures per student (lines b) into 1913 prices (lines d).

Tables 2.8 and 2.9
col. 1, 1864: Ernst Engel, "Beiträge zur Geschichte . . . , II," in *Zeitschrift des Königlich Preussischen Statistischen Bureaus* 9 (1869): 178; Wiese, *Das höhere Schulwesen,* 1:607.
cols. 2–6, 1873ff.: *Jahrbücher,* 1876–1914.
lines b: Male and female students had to be added in order to obtain expenditures per student.

Table 2.10
line 1, National income: Hoffmann, *Wachstum der deutschen Wirtschaft,* pp. 454ff.
line 2, Labor's share in national income tends to oscillate around 75 percent in many economies; for Germany see Hoffmann, p. 87.
line 3, rising employment: Hoffmann, pp. 204ff. The figure for 1913 refers to an assumed constant income per head of the labor force.
line 5, educational stock of population: Krug, "Quantitative Beziehungen zwischen materiellem und immateriellem Kapital," *Jahrbücher für Nationalökonomie und Statistik* 180 (1967): 57.
line 6, educational stock of labor: Calculated from the educational stock (line 5) per head of population (6 years of age and older). Hoffmann, pp. 173ff., gives figures for the population and its age structure.
line 7, rising employment: See the explanation for line 3.

Apart from the supplementary information about female enrollment (Table 2A.1) discussed earlier, the A-tables contain some detailed data which are important for specific points of the text Tables 2.1–3. Some other A-tables offer additional material, illustration, and results.

Table 2A.2

One important requirement for our purposes was to know the distribution of the secondary school student body by years of school. First, the history of the institutions had to be clarified; this was done on the basis of the studies by Wiese and Lexis cited at the beginning of the Appendix and yielded the pattern apparent from Table 2A.2. For 1822 and 1828 Engel gives no breakdown of the enrollment figures into the three then existing types of secondary schools; consequently, I applied the percentages of 1837 to the figures for the two preceding census years. Secondly, enrollment figures for preparatory grades had to be separated, where necessary (1822–55), from the overall enrollment; this was done as indicated in the remark to Table 2.2, col. 6. Table 2A.2 comprises therefore the secondary school enrollment figures from grade VI onwards, broken down by types of institution. (The breakdown for 1855 between the *Realschule* and the *höhere Bürgerschule* was done by extrapolation from 1864.)

Table 2A.3

The various types of secondary schools offered curricula which, starting with grade VI, stretched over either six, seven, or nine grades (Table 2A.3, col. headed "typical age"). We wanted to know (1) how many students of those given in Table 2A.2 attended secondary schools beyond the compulsory age range, i.e., from grade upper III onwards; and (2) how were these voluntary secondary students distributed over the grades from upper III to upper I. Lexis gives, mostly for the years 1860–1900, the enrollment figures for secondary school students by types of institutions and by grades. The percentage shares of the grades in the whole enrollment of secondary school students were calculated on this basis and are given in Table 2A.3, lines b. These percentages were then applied to the enrollment figures of Table 2A.2 (because Lexis gives enrollment figures for slightly different years). For the years 1822–64 and 1911 the percentages had to be extrapolated, with a few exceptions; every extrapolation is indicated by parentheses. Fortunately, there is more information for the Gymnasien, the institutions which were responsible for by far the largest portion of secondary schooling in the early years. In addition, the results based on the Lexis percentages could be checked against and improved by similar data provided by Wiese, and by the *Jahrbuch* 5 (Berlin, 1883). Addition of the enrollment figures of equivalent grades yielded the totals for the five upper grades, which, together, make up for the grand total of voluntary secondary schooling. We can see from Table 2A.3 that only a relatively small fraction of the secondary school students proceeded until the Abitur level. If we take the Gymnasien only, an equal distribution of the student body among nine grades would yield 11.1 percent of the students for each grade; grade upper I, however, shows an average share of some 5.0 percent.

Table 2A.4

As has been pointed out earlier, there is nowhere as little knowledge in the realm of enrollment for the existing institutions of learning as with respect to vocational schools and professional colleges. This is partly due to the fact that practical training can be given or undergone in various ways: on-the-job training; apprenticeship; part-time schooling (evening, Sunday, or continuation schools); full-time schooling. In order to add units compara-

TABLE 2A.2
Enrollment of Males in Secondary Schools (Excluding Preparatory Grades) in Prussia, 1822–1911, by Types of Schools

Type of school	1822	1828	1837	1846	1855	1864	1873	1882	1891	1902	1911
Gymnasium	(13,767)	(14,376)	(20,917)	(24,968)	(31,336)	44,114	63,207	78,126	74,907	92,465	103,702
Progymnasium	(1,059)	(1,349)	(1,656)	(1,848)	(2,879)	2,463	3,269	4,087	4,512	5,209	4,015
Realgymnasium								26,725	25,017	24,012	48,160
Realschule 1. Ordnung[a]						16,491	26,187				
Realschule 2. Ordnung						2,618	4,745				
Oberrealschule								4,120	3,970	17,202	40,664
Realschule (1832 type)	(6,354)	(6,738)	(9,682)	(12,811)	(14,000)						
Höhere Bürgerschule					(5,553)	2,720	10,971	4,514	12,259		
Realschule (1882 type)								4,161	6,883	33,992	32,248
Realprogymnasium								9,428	8,486	1,587	3,903
All schools	(21,180)	(22,463)	(32,255)	(39,627)	(53,768)	68,406	108,379	131,161	136,034	174,467	232,692

[a]Includes those Realschule 2. Ordnung having nine grades.

Enrollment of Grades within the Voluntary Age Range in Secondary Schools in Prussia, 1822–1911, by Types of Schools and Grades

a: numbers of students enrolled
b: students as percentage of total students enrolled (excluding preparatory grades)

Institutions, by grades	Typical age		1822	1828	1837	1846	1855	1864	1873	1882	1891	1902	1911
Gymnasium													
Upper III	14–15	a	1,170	1,521	1,777	2,247	3,039	4,587	7,015	9,218	8,969	11,188	12,651
		b	(8.5)	(10.6)	8.5	(9.0)	9.7	10.4	11.1	11.8	12.1	12.1	(12.2)
Lower II	15–16		1,151	1,507	1,757	2,247	3,102	4,102	6,320	8,350	8,524	10,356	11,614
			(8.4)	(10.5)	8.4	(9.0)	9.9	9.3	10.0	10.7	11.5	11.2	(11.2)
Upper II	16–17		775	1,405	1,171	1,598	2,068	2,735	4,234	5,588	5,855	7,582	8,607
			(5.6)	(9.8)	5.6	(6.4)	6.6	6.2	6.7	7.1	7.9	8.2	8.3
Lower I	17–18		801	1,405	1,163	1,579	2,069	2,646	3,666	5,086	4,818	6,195	7,051
			(5.8)	(9.8)	5.6	(6.3)	6.6	6.0	5.8	6.5	6.5	6.7	(6.8)
Upper I	18–19		699	1,355	1,116	1,166	1,659	1,941	2,654	3,693	3,632	5,270	6,014
			(5.1)	(9.4)	5.3	(4.7)	5.3	4.4	4.2	4.7	4.9	5.7	(5.8)
Progymnasium													
Upper III	14–15		87	111	137	155	244	214	300	416	545	640	497
			(8.3)	(8.3)	(8.3)	(8.4)	(8.5)	8.7	9.2	10.2	12.1	12.3	(12.4)
Lower II	15–16		77	98	120	136	215	187	254	396	527	557	429
			(7.3)	(7.3)	(7.3)	(7.4)	(7.5)	7.6	7.8	9.7	11.7	10.7	(10.7)
Upper II	16–17		26	33	41	48	77	68	94	142	198		
			(2.5)	(2.5)	(2.5)	(2.6)	(2.7)	2.8	2.9	3.5	4.4		
Realgymnasium													
Realschule 10.													
Upper III	14–15							1,715	2,880	3,153	3,202	3,169	6,405
								10.4	11.0	11.8	12.8	13.2	(13.3)
Lower II	15–16							1,418	2,749	3,119	2,901	2,761	5,538
								8.6	10.5	11.7	11.6	11.5	(11.5)
Upper II	16–17							643	1,256	1,397	1,175	1,536	3,082
								3.9	4.8	5.2	4.7	6.4	(6.4)
Lower I	17–18							329	837	1,110	750	1,008	2,022
								2.0	3.2	4.2	3.0	4.2	(4.2)
Upper I	18–19							230	549	738	575	816	1,685
								1.4	2.1	2.8	2.3	3.4	(3.5)

(Table continues)

TABLE 2A.3 (continued)

Institutions, by grades	Typical age	1822	1828	1837	1846	1855	1864	1873	1882	1891	1902	1911
Oberrealschule												
Upper III	14–15								498	484	2,047	4,839
									12.1	12.2	11.9	(11.9)
Lower II	15–16								488	400	1,823	4,351
									11.8	10.1	10.6	(10.7)
Upper II	16–17								102	95	1,032	2,439
									2.5	2.4	6.0	(6.0)
Lower I	17–18								118	47	550	1,301
									2.9	1.2	3.2	(3.2)
Upper I	18–19								73	19	412	975
									1.8	0.5	2.4	(2.4)
Realschule[a]												
Upper III	14–15	635	673	968	1,281	1,955	538	1,948	843	1,894	3,807	3,611
		(10.0)	(10.0)	(10.0)	(10.0)	(10.0)	10.1	12.4	9.7	9.9	11.2	(11.2)
Lower II	15–16	190	202	290	384	586	181	895	605	1,472	3,025	2,870
		(3.0)	(3.0)	(3.0)	(3.0)	(3.0)	3.4	5.7	7.0	7.7	8.9	(8.9)
Realprogymnasium												
Upper III	14–15								801	1,077	219	538
									8.5	12.7	13.8	(13.8)
Lower II	15–16								1,173	933	187	460
									12.4	11.0	11.8	(11.8)
Upper II	16–17								115	186		
									1.2	2.2		
Totals												
Upper III	14–15	1,892	2,305	2,882	3,683	5,238	7,054	12,143	14,929	16,171	21,070	28,541
Lower II	15–16	1,418	1,807	2,167	2,767	3,903	5,888	10,218	14,131	14,757	18,709	25,262
Upper II	16–17	801	1,438	1,212	1,646	2,145	3,446	5,584	7,344	7,509	10,150	14,128
Lower I	17–18	801	1,405	1,163	1,579	2,069	2,975	4,503	6,314	5,615	7,753	10,374
Upper I	18–19	699	1,355	1,116	1,166	1,659	2,171	3,203	4,504	4,226	6,498	8,674
Grand total	14–19	5,611	8,310	8,540	10,841	15,014	21,534	35,651	47,222	48,278	64,180	86,979

[a]Includes 1832 and 1882 types, 2. Ordnung, and the höhere Bürgerschule.

TABLE 2A.4
Enrollment of Students at Vocational and Professional Schools or Colleges
in Prussia, 1864–1911 (Excluding Part-Time Institutions)

Institution	1864	1873	1882	1891	1901	1911
1. Qualification for admission: graduation from elementary school (age: 14)						
Provincial trade schools	(1,000)					
Lower schools for textile industry	(40)	60	(50)	44	141	200
Lower schools for engineering			(200)	574	1,453	1,653
2. Qualification for admission: eligibility, by secondary education, for one year's military service (typical age: 16)						
Polytechnic institute	353					
Provincial trade schools		(1,000)				
Higher schools for engineering			(50)	54	647	1,107
Higher schools for textile industry			(50)	344	514	800
Agricultural colleges	200	130	150	544	900	1,800
Veterinary schools	(100)	150	310			
3. Qualification for admission: leaving certificate after nine grades of secondary education (typical age: 19)						
Academy of architecture	432 ⎫	2,930	976	1,910	5,368	4,455
Technical colleges	⎭					
Mining academies	(80)	125	125	245	420	300
Forestry academies	60	170	325	124	110	140
Veterinary colleges				667	700	600
Commercial colleges					700	1,600
Academies of fine arts	(200)	(300)	(350)	445	400	500
Academies of music	(150)	220	(250)	299	320	400

ble with regard to the amount of schooling as per years of school, only full-time institutions of learning were included in this study. Thereby, not only did we have to neglect the large numbers of students attending continuation schools, but also some doubtful cases such as agricultural or building trade schools where students probably studied during the winters only. One set of institutions which perhaps ought to have been included but which had to be omitted because of lack of information were military schools, especially the technical military schools and/or colleges. On the other hand, the principle of taking only full-time institutions naturally led to a relatively large representation, among the students at vocational/professional schools (Table 2.3, col. 7), of those students who attended professional colleges (Table 2.1, col. 10). These professional colleges are somewhat better known and provide some statistical information as guidelines for the time before 1864; on the whole, however, this time period had to be reconstructed by pure guesswork, as shown in Table 2.1, cols. 8–10. Fortunately, the numbers involved are small enough that even misspecifications would not affect significantly the larger proportions.

For the late nineteenth century, Lexis gives comprehensive information about enrollment figures, curricula, and admission requirements. For Table 2A.4, however, we had to rely on a wide range of scattered information, as follows:

1. Provincial trade schools (*Provinzial-Gewerbeschulen*): G. Holzmüller, "Das technische Schulwesen," in *Geschichte der Erziehung vom Anfang an bis auf unsere Zeit*, ed. K. A. Schmid, 5, pt. 3 (Berlin, 1902): 292ff. Holzmüller provides enrollment figures for 1854 (p. 299) and 1877 (p. 305), both times excluding preparatory grades. After 1878/79 the provincial trade schools were functionally succeeded by the lower and higher schools for the engineering and textile industries.

2. Lower/higher schools for textile industry (*Textilfachschulen*): The information for 1864 was extrapolated from 1873; that for 1873 was derived from *Jahrbuch* 4 (Berlin, 1876); that for 1882 was interpolated and divided into lower and higher schools; for 1891ff., see Lexis, *Public Education*, p. 175, and the respective *Jahrbücher*.

3. Lower/higher schools for engineering (*Maschinenbauschulen*): The data for 1882 were extrapolated from 1891 and divided into lower and higher schools; 1891 and following years are derived from Lexis, p. 170, and the respective *Jahrbücher*.

4. Polytechnic institute (*Gewerbe-Institut*): F. W. Nottebohm, *Chronik der Königlichen Gewerbe-Akademie zu Berlin* (Berlin, 1871), p. 82.

5. Academy of architecture (*Bauakademie*): For 1864, Lexis, pp. 134ff., gives the enrollment figures for the Berlin Technische Hochschule by combining, for the time before 1879, those of the academy of architecture and of the polytechnic institute. If Nottebohm's figure, cited under item 4 above, is subtracted, we have the enrollment for the academy of architecture.

6. Technical colleges (*Technische Hochschulen*): For 1873ff., the respective *Jahrbücher*. By 1873, the academy of architecture and the Berlin polytechnic academy can be dealt with jointly since the qualification for admission is identical.

7. Agricultural colleges (*Landwirtschaftliche Hochschulen*): For 1864ff., the respective *Jahrbücher*. These colleges do not appear to have demanded the Abitur as a prerequisite for admission; cf. Lexis, p. 157.

8. Veterinary schools/colleges (*Tierarznei-Schulen*, and after 1887, *Tierärztliche Hochschulen*): 1864 is extrapolated from 1873; for 1873ff., see the *Jahrbücher*.

9. Mining academies (*Bergakademien*): 1864 is extrapolated from 1873; 1873ff. are derived from the *Jahrbücher*.

10. Forestry academies (*Forstakademien*): 1864ff. are derived from the *Jahrbücher*.

11. Commercial colleges (*Handelshochschulen*): For 1901, Lexis, pp. 160f.; for 1911, the *Jahrbuch*.

12. Academies of fine arts (*Kunstakademien*): 1864–82 are extrapolated from 1891; 1891ff. are derived from the *Jahrbücher*.

13. Academies of music (*Musikhochschulen*): 1864 is extrapolated from 1873; 1882 is interpolated; 1873 and 1891ff. come from the *Jahrbücher*.

Table 2A.5

Part A of this table illustrates the procedure employed for the construction of Table 2.6. The main point is that the distribution pattern of voluntary education relates to an age cohort which was compulsorily enrolled during the preceding decade. This lagging assignment of two census years to each typical cohort brought about, in one case, a small difficulty. If the census years of 1864 and 1873 are assigned to the typical age cohort of 1847–56, some allowance has to be made for the changing territorial basis. The figures for voluntary enrollment in 1873 were therefore proportionately related to the population of 1873 within

TABLE 2A.5

**Construction of Typical Male Age Cohorts with Respect to Their Percentage
Distribution by Years of School Embodied**

A.   Scheme

| Age cohorts | Compulsory enrollment | | Voluntary enrollment | |
	Years	Census year assigned	Years	Census year assigned
1800–1809	1806/14–1815/23	1822	1814/23–1823/32	1828
1810–1819	1816/24–1825/33	1828	1824/33–1833/42	1837
1847–1856	1853/61–1862/70	1864	1861/70–1870/79	1873
1857–1866	1863/71–1872/80	1873	1871/80–1880/89	1882

B.   Example. One cohort typical of the age cohorts of 1857–66 (version a)

Category of students	Number	Percent	Source
1. All boys, 14 years old	271,344	100.0	17.5% of 1873 male population divided by 8
2. All students, 14 years old, actually enrolled	263,963		Table 2.4, col. 1
3. All boys, 14 years old, never enrolled	7,381	2.72	Line 1 minus line 2
4. Students enrolled for 8 years only	245,591	90.51	Line 2 minus total voluntary enrollment of 1882 (Table 2.5, col. 1)
5. Students with 9 years	798	0.29	Table 2.5, col. 2 (1882)
6. Students with 10 years	6,726	2.48	ibid., col. 3
7. Students with 11 years	1,030	0.38	ibid., col. 4
8. Students with 12 years	1,810	0.67	ibid., col. 5
9. Students with 13 years	876	0.32	ibid., col. 6
10. Students with 14 years	3,318	1.22	ibid., col. 7
11. Students with 15 years	0	0	ibid., col. 8
12. Students with 16 years	675	0.43	ibid., col. 9
13. Students with 17 years	3,129	1.09	ibid., col. 10
Total of lines 3–13	271,344	100.0	

the old boundaries prior to the political gain of 1867. Part B of Table 2A.5 simply gives an example of the procedure described above, with "version a" referring to the data of Tables 2.4 and 2.5.

Table 2A.6

Information for part A of Table 2A.6 is directly available for 1911 (*Jahrbuch*, 1913 [Berlin, 1914], pp. 12f.). For 1864 I applied the distribution by age, given for 1871 in *Jahrbuch* 4 (Berlin, 1876), p. 60; but even for 1871 the breakdown is only into groups of ten age cohorts. The data given in part B of the table are provided by the various *Jahrbücher*.

Table 2A.7

David Hunter, doctoral candidate in the Department of Statistics, Princeton University, calculated these percentage distributions of male populations, 25–64 years old, by years of school. In doing so he relied on the material summarized in Tables 2.4 and 2.5; that is to say, the same assumptions which went into these tables and their interpretation (see above, remarks on Tables 2.4 and 2.5) are also inherent in Table 2A.7. The procedures applied in order to build up the distribution, by years of school, of given populations differ, however. Whereas I aimed at constructing typical age cohorts for every decade, which then had to be mixed according to the age structure, Mr. Hunter interpolated, for the years in between the census years, the missing data. By following up the individual age cohorts, he thus arrived at the distribution, by years of school, for every single (''real'') age cohort from 1800 to 1886. Finally, the age profile of a given population (1864 and 1911, respectively) had to be applied to these cohorts, which then added up to the percentage distributions given in Table 2A.7. For the weights applied, see the discussion of Table 2.7 in the text of the chapter.

I gratefully acknowledge both Mr. Hunter's painstaking work and the computer assistance of the Department of Statistics, Princeton University. Although I am pleased that Tables 2A.7 and 2.7 convey highly similar results, I must admit in candor that this may be due to the common underlying assumptions. These assumptions are mine, and Mr. Hunter bears no responsibility for the validity of Table 2A.7 except for its arithmetical aspect.

TABLE 2A.6
Population in Prussia, 1822–1911, by Age and Sex

A. Age structure of male population, 14–64 years old, in Prussia, 1864 and 1911

		1864			1911	
		Percent of			Percent of	
Age	Age cohorts	Whole population	Population 14–64 years old	Age cohorts	Whole population	Population 14–64 years old
14–24	1840–50	20.3	32.6	1887–97	21.2	33.1
25–34	1830–39	14.6	23.5	1877–86	15.4	24.1
35–44	1820–29	11.8	19.0	1867–76	12.3	19.2
45–54	1810–19	9.2	14.8	1857–66	9.1	14.2
55–64	1800–09	6.2	10.0	1847–56	5.9	9.2
14–64	1800–50	62.1	100.0	1847–97	63.9	100.0

B. Population in Prussia, 1822–1911, by sex

Year	Males	Females
1822	5,788,322	5,875,811
1828	6,326,763	6,399,347
1837	7,039,223	7,058,902
1846	8,046,771	8,066,167
1855	8,577,568	8,625,263
1864	9,583,367	9,671,772
1873	12,404,330	12,762,340
1882	13,606,362	14,088,492
1891	14,891,572	15,445,346
1901	17,256,921	17,779,751
1911	19,914,725	20,585,555

TABLE 2A.7
**Percentage Distribution of Male Population 25–64 years old in Prussia,
1864 and 1911, by Years of School Embodied**

Years of school	Version a[a]		Version b[a]	
	1864	1911	1864	1911
0	6.44	1.97	6.44	1.97
8	90.45	91.51	91.25	92.25
9	0.50	0.49	0.50	0.49
10	0.81	2.10	0.64	2.08
11	0.03	0.52	0.03	0.50
12	0.15	0.46	0.15	0.46
13	0.10	0.13	0.17	0.46
14	0.57	1.10	0	0
15	0	0	0	0
16	0.13	0.53	0	0
17	0.82	1.19	0.82	1.19
Total	100.0	100.0	100.0	100.0
Weighted averages				
Years of schooling	7.64	8.14	7.79	8.04
Earnings differentials	99.71	102.60	99.26	101.67
Increase of the averages				
Years of schooling, 1864–1911	6.54%		2.90%	
Earnings differentials, 1864–1911	5.93%		2.43%	

[a]See Tables 2.4 and 2.5.

Table 2A.8

col. 1: Hoffmann, *Wachstum der deutschen Wirtschaft,* p. 728.

col. 2: This is a conversion of col. 1 into 1913 prices by using Hoffmann's price index for public expenditures (ibid., p. 599, col. 12).

col. 3: The 1861 level of expenditures per capita at constant prices is held constant; educational widening thus allows only for population growth.

col. 4: This is the difference between cols. 2 and 3.

TABLE 2A.8
Public Expenditures for Education in Germany, 1861–1913 (In Millions of Marks)

Year	In current prices	In 1913 prices Total	In 1913 prices Widening	In 1913 prices Deepening	Year	In current prices	In 1913 prices Total	In 1913 prices Widening	In 1913 prices Deepening
1861	97	173			1890	376	429	224	205
2	102	182	174	8	1	390	450	226	224
3	107	189	176	13	2	407	468	228	240
4	112	197	178	19	3	426	488	230	258
5	116	203	180	23	4	444	512	233	279
6	121	176	181	−5	5	463	535	236	299
7	125	178	182	−4	6	481	554	240	314
8	131	198	183	15	7	519	599	243	356
9	136	201	184	17	8	561	646	247	399
1870	143	199	185	14	9	599	687	251	436
1	152	210	186	24	1900	641	721	255	466
2	173	235	187	48	1	688	765	258	507
3	189	257	189	68	2	710	803	262	541
4	211	270	191	79	3	762	859	266	593
5	233	271	193	78	4	794	887	270	617
6	238	288	196	92	5	827	920	274	646
7	251	305	198	107	6	854	947	278	669
8	273	337	200	137	7	931	1,000	282	718
9	277	340	203	137	8	975	1,049	286	763
1880	281	346	205	141	9	1,062	1,141	289	852
1	285	349	206	143	1910	1,144	1,190	293	897
2	291	355	208	147	1	1,114	1,136	297	939
3	298	361	209	152	2	1,289	1,294	300	994
4	304	365	211	154	3	1,378	1,378	304	1,074
5	312	374	212	162					
6	318	380	214	166					
7	331	393	216	177					
8	347	393	219	175					
9	362	418	221	197					

PART II

Protestant Education in Sixteenth-Century Europe

CHAPTER 3

The State of Pedagogical Theory c.1530: What Protestant Reformers Knew About Education

BY GERALD STRAUSS

The urge to persuade, present in us all, is most active in reformers. In the 1520s Lutherans seized the opportunities offered by pulpit and press to propagate their faith, releasing an unprecedented flood of spoken and written words to a society ill trained to receive them. Fearful of their movement's prospects, they resolved to prepare the ground for a more understanding response in the future. A great educational enterprise was launched and plans made for the systematic indoctrination—in no pejorative sense of that word—of the young.

The decision to embark on an experiment in mass education was heavy with difficulties, not the least of which arose from ambiguities inherent in the Lutheran creed then taking shape. When men were invited to join in the excitement of eschatological expectations imminently to be realized, what was the use of building for the future? When Luther's theology made it clear that mortals cannot enlighten themselves, much less each other, by their own efforts, why make elaborate designs for schools and teachers?[1] Most likely these inconsistencies are more apparent to us now than they were to the first generation of Protestants. In any case, they vanish as impediments when set against the opportunities for educational organization present in the intimate alliance with political authorities to which the emerging Lutheran churches owed their structures and their strength. Backed by the legal and financial power of territorial and municipal states, the reformers could plan an education system equipped with all the features they thought desirable, the absence of which from medieval schools they had deplored: order, control, clearly perceived and pursued objectives, a coherent pedagogy, uniform curricula, skilled teachers with professional qualifications, above all a sense of religious purpose to give meaning to the endeavor.

After 1525 needs and opportunities converged in a crisis mood. The unhappy events of the early 1520s convinced the reformers that they must lose no time in taking steps to gain some measure of control over the minds of men and, thus, over their actions.[2] Deploring the general indifference to learning and the decrepit state of schools, and highly sensitive to charges that the disturbances following the appearance of the Lutheran movement were accelerating the distressing decline in intellectual culture,[3] the reformers turned emphatically to matters of education. Beginning in 1528, wherever Lutherans were in authority, they produced a host of school ordinances establishing school systems in cities and territories.[4] Consisting of concrete, specific provisions for curriculum and instruction framed in statements of general purpose, these ordinances set the pattern for school organizations for centuries to come. While only moderately important to the development of German universities, they are of quite extraordinary significance in the history of secondary and elementary schooling, in both its Latin and its vernacular streams. In an attempt to reach the masses, and to reach them at an impressionable age, school ordinances (which were nearly always parts of church constitutions imposing ecclesiastical organization on a region or a city) established networks of popular schools and provided for religious teaching through catechism instruction. Notwithstanding his serious doubts concerning the wisdom of allowing formal schools to cater to popular interests,[5] Luther concluded that the decades ahead offered no grounds for hope if attempts were not made to exert some influence on the young. As early as 1517 he had told his parishioners that "if the Church is ever to flourish again, we must make a beginning by teaching our children." After 1525 the need to make a beginning had become all the more urgent.[6]

In view of the magnitude of this undertaking, it is interesting to ask, What did these men know about education and about those to be educated? It will not come as a surprise to anyone familiar with the sixteenth century to learn that what they knew was what they had read. Not that interest in real-life youngsters was lacking. Luther himself can be quoted for a great number of acute, and often very touching, observations on his own and other people's children,[7] and it would not be difficult to cull from contemporary autobiographical and other writings the evidence to show that adults regarded children with concern and affection.[8] The growing corpus of pediatric books also suggests that the young were being studied with something like the care which we feel they deserve.[9] Empirical attention given to children was never systematized, however. It remained fragmentary, occasional, and—except for medical writings—subjective. The literary tradition, on the other hand, supplied a ready-made and coherent set of assumptions about the nature of children and young people. It also offered apparently reliable predictors of their behavior and responses in each stage of development. Given the receptive attitude of sixteenth-century intellectuals to written authority, it is not surprising to see them turn to literature for their general ideas about the young, for clues to the possibilities and the limits of education, and for tangible suggestions on how to train them to good purposes. A rich and prolific body of writings on education reaching back to Plato carried a cumulative weight of conviction which was hard to resist, even where written dicta could not easily be reconciled with observed or sensed reality. In any case, in the context of their culture it was an obvious move for the reformers to depend on the distant and recent past for usable answers to their many conceptual and technical questions concerning the education of the young.[10]

In order to answer our question, What did sixteenth-century reformers know about education? let us assume that they were familiar with the entire body of pedagogical literature from Plato to Vives and Erasmus. This is not as absurd a supposition as might appear at first glance. The sixteenth-century intellectual was a voracious reader. He took pleasure in fullness and reiteration. He had a professional interest in the study of books on special subjects. He kept himself informed of the appearance of new editions of the works of distinguished authors. He knew that the subject of education had occupied most of the great minds of pagan and Christian antiquity and of the philosophical schools of the Middle Ages. He also knew—and here we come perhaps closer to the realm of the feasible—that older writers had, for their part, drawn inspiration from books available to them, much as he proposed to do now. When he read Vincent of Beauvais he also came to know Hugh of St. Victor, Jerome, and Quintilian. In Wimpheling's *Adolescentia* he could find a veritable mosaic of educational bits and pieces gathered from earlier writers.[11] Otto Brunfels' *Catechesis puerorum* of 1529 made an effortless introduction to Quintilian, Cicero, Plutarch, and a wide assortment of fifteenth-century Italian writers. Our reformer could also, if he wished, obtain anthologies of educational classics which would give him a speaking acquaintance with the pedagogical tradition,[12] an acquaintance often indistinguishable to the modern reader from familiarity with the true sources. No one in the sixteenth century needed to be ignorant of what the great thinkers had said on the subject of education. For browsers there was plenty to read in digests, and for the scholar who wished to go back to the sources there were convenient editions, and innumerable references to them.

In any case, the men charged with the awesome task of consolidating the tentative gains and reversing the incipient failures of the Lutheran movement in Germany had a deep interest in educational questions. Sustaining this interest was an implicit trust in the power of education to achieve desired ends. This confidence could not have arisen from Luther's faith, which permitted scant hope of men's ability to mend their ways. Nor could it have been drawn from observed reality, for reformers tended to be inveterate pessimists when it came to judging the behavior of their fellow men. Confidence in the ability of some to teach and others to learn could have come only from the many writers who in the previous millennium and a half had speculated on some of the great questions now occupying the reformers. These lessons from the past were by no means unambiguous. The pedagogical tradition did not speak with one voice. It was not a program to be adopted but a critical discussion to be confronted. But on two points, at least, there was substantial agreement among the authors: that men could and should be taught, and that one must begin with the young. It was a matter of common knowledge among the reformers that their own generation was too far gone for help. But in the young there was still hope. "Don't bother with the older generation; they are a waste of time. Instead let us, with God's help, try it with children."[13] Or, "When we have begun to train our foolish, tender youth to Christian doctrine and discipline we may expect to see a beneficial evangelical change among us and a better Christian society. This is our only hope for restoring corrupt Christendom."[14] Such expressions of trust abound in the prefaces to the catechisms and schoolbooks of early Lutheranism.

It follows that reformers lacked neither incentive nor opportunity to steep themselves in the literature of the pedagogical tradition. Let us now examine this literature in order to discover what principles men could extract from it and to what actions they were likely to be moved.

II

At the root of all that was said and done on the subject of education lay two contradictory sets of convictions about the child's essential nature. The affirmation of human instincts, and their adoption as effective and beneficial impulses to learning, was most attractively summarized by Quintilian, whose observations on children and their upbringing exerted a lasting but not unequivocal influence on sixteenth-century pedagogues. "Nature brought us into the world that we might attain to all excellence of mind"[15] can stand as the motto of the optimistic school, which accepted the fundamental soundness of human nature, at least to the point of denying its inescapable corruption. Most children are intelligent by endowment and eager to learn by instinct.[16] The function of education is to deepen and extend this promise.

An equally eloquent opposing view rejected nature as a basis of trust and severely limited expectations and scope of education. Corrupt from birth, or corrupted within a few years of it, human impulses exist only to be restrained, not to be aroused and encouraged to unfold. This pessimistic view, firmly anchored in the Old Testament (Genesis 8:21: "because [man's] heart contrives evil from infancy"), was given powerful momentum by the compelling assertions of Augustine on the subject of infants and children and by a large assemblage of pedagogical writers from Gerson to Wimpheling and Vives who had fallen under Augustine's spell. Their position is epitomized by Augustine's introspections on the motives underlying the childish pranks and petty deceptions of his own childhood. "Is this childish innocence?" he asks. "It is not, Lord, it is not. . . . These are the same things, the very same, which as our years go on . . . are done with regard to kings and governors, business and profit."[17] Among the Protestant reformers this pessimistic strain struck a lasting echo. In a large part of the pedagogical literature of Lutheranism it is the dominant theme.

Augustine's position is far from simple. Quite apart from the polemical purpose of much of his writing (of which his sixteenth-century readers need not have been aware), and from the serious internal inconsistencies which have often been pointed out, the Bishop of Hippo harbored ambivalent and shifting attitudes toward the early stages of life and their influence on adult behavior. For the purposes of our inquiry, however, it is not so important to discover what he really meant—this question has been meticulously examined[18]—as to know how he was read in the sixteenth century.

Looking back from the literature written for children in that age we can see

Augustine looming as the apostle of unmitigated pessimism. From his *On the Merits and Forgiveness of Sins and on the Baptism of Infants* later readers could, if they wished, extract passages to prove the rottenness of the babe in his cradle: "Seeing that the soul of an infant fresh from its mother's womb is still the soul of a human being, . . . I ask why, or when, or whence it was plunged into that thick darkness of ignorance in which it lies? If it is man's nature thus to begin, and that nature is not already corrupt, then why was not Adam created thus? Whereas [the infant], although he is ignorant where he is, what he is, by whom created . . . is already guilty of offense."[19] Augustine is here at pains to prove against the Pelagians that original sin is inherited and that baptism makes no sense without assuming this, and that sin does not have to be committed; it is our human heritage. In the *Confessions* the same point emerges, sharpened by the author's self-portrait as a natural sinner: "It is the physical weakness of a baby that makes it seem 'innocent,' not the quality of its inner life. I myself have seen a baby jealous: it was too young to speak but it was livid with anger as it watched another baby at the breast."[20] Augustine shows that the young child, the infant even, displays the signs of human depravity, greed, envy, lust, the insistent will, and the *amor sui* which is the heart of sin. Without grace the infant remains in the "thick darkness of ignorance," incapable out of his own powers to surmount his animallike condition. He is all instinct, and his behavior reveals the direction of his infantile drives.[21]

But Augustine does not have to be read quite so dismally. Jean Gerson, whose influence on the religious strain of early modern educational thought almost equaled the Bishop of Hippo's,[22] while also rejecting the innocence of infants as a Pelagian heresy and pointing to evidence of *concupiscentia* as proof, insisted on a basic natural goodness in the child which, he says, renders him capable of yielding to influence and instruction. Gerson denied that every human instinct was depraved, preferring to speak of an inclination, or a susceptibility, to concupiscence, a tendency which could be counteracted.[23] As a pedagogue—which he was with a passion—Gerson built on the existence of germs of goodness and reason in the child which, with careful cultivation and protection by a "wall of discipline," could grow into virtues.[24] Gerson believed in restraint, particularly in matters relating to the senses, and he worked out rules for exerting beneficent influences on children.[25] His writings show that the Augustinian position on inherited sin did not necessarily lead to total educational pessimism. His arguments persuaded many who found Augustine himself too hard to take. Jacob Wimpheling, who was much influenced by his older French colleague, worked up Gerson's suggestions into a comprehensive (though incoherent and not very profound) theory of pedagogy.[26] Although the young are full of undesirable inclinations, Wimpheling states, four means exist for reaching the residue of virtue in each child, and these make training possible. They are the efficacy of divine grace, the influence of intelligent parents, good examples, and direct appeals to mind and character. Small children, being least corrupted by life, offer the best chance of success through restrictive, if necessarily coercive, action on the part of educators charged with creating favorable conditions around the child, conditions in which every influence tends toward the desired end.[27] Only within this all-enclosing pedagogical environment, Wimpheling suggests, can the slender shoots of virtue prevail against the proliferating weeds of the natural vices.

In the Reformation the Augustinian position was most often cited as an argument for the systematic use of severe restriction and enforced conditioning in the education of the young. One naturally wonders whether this was a case of theology leading to educational ideas or, conversely, an empirically based feeling seeking a principle on which to rest a determination that the young must be kept down. No matter. The fact is that the question of the natural innocence or natural depravity of children, remote though it seems from the everyday world of practical teaching, had a profound impact on the form and content of religious and secular instruction in the sixteenth century. Arguments were available to show that the young would inevitably misuse even the slightest extension of freedom to give in to the self-destructive urges in which concupiscence manifests itself in all men. The only correctives were restraint and control.

Other arguments existed, however, to supply a different set of guiding principles. Little was made of theological affirmations of the natural innocence of infants and young children,[28] nor of the exceedingly positive appreciation of the child implied in Jesus' injunction (Matthew 18: 1–6) to "become as little children." Childlike qualities exalted in these and many other passages[29] were invoked as correctives to adult proclivities—constantly in sermons, frequently in pedagogical writings—but they supplied nothing in the way of concrete suggestions for educating the young. Much more promising as a starting point was the idea of "crude matter," which pictured the infant at birth as a neutral entity and placed on the educator the burden of fashioning the raw substance into something good and useful. Taken from Quintilian into the sixteenth century, and acquiring in the passage a mildly Augustinian overtone, the *rudis massa* concept is prominent in the educational thought of Erasmus, especially in his *De pueris instituendis,* his pedagogical best seller which was first published in 1529 and had great influence on Reformation pedagogy. "Nature" was to Erasmus simply the ability to be taught. It does not incline children to wickedness. Men accuse "nature," he says, when they should blame themselves "for ruining the minds of children by allowing faults to be acquired before directing them to the good."[30] This position explains Erasmus's emphatic insistence on early childhood training which is the chief purpose of his treatise. Education molds the unformed mass into the shape of a man ("in hominis speciem"). Left to itself the substance would turn "naturally" into the image of a beast.[31] Erasmus is not free of latent pessimism. But he has confidence in the power of instruction. As dogs are born for hunting and birds for flying, man is put on earth for the recognition of truth and virtue. Every creature is capable of learning that for which it is born. The human child, when properly taught with purpose and industry, is quick to acquire good discipline. Without such teaching he is speedily corrupted, for humans are always readier to choose the bad than aim at the good.

It is easy to see how Erasmus failed to give a satisfactory answer to the contradiction posed by his classical and Christian sources. While rejecting—often indignantly—rigorous Augustinianism, he was enough of a pessimist to agree that education should be more than helping natural abilities to unfold. Unremitting vigilance is indicated, for the young are driven by desires, not by judgment. "Indeed, the good is more quickly forgotten than the bad, which we remember much longer."[32] The fact that children succumb instantly to corruption from external influences had been unquestioningly accepted since antiquity. It was, moreover, common knowledge that the young were an unruly, naturally rebellious, shiftless, and fickle lot. There was no disagreement with Plato on this ("Of all the animals the boy is the most unmanageable, since the fountain of reason in him is not yet regulated"), nor with his corrective: "When he gets away from mothers and nurses, he must be under the management of tutors."[33] This conclusion could be buttressed with comments from Augustine to the effect that the young were naturally lazy and irresponsible, capable of effort only when placed under constraint.[34]

Such basic convictions about human nature tended to be applied indiscriminately across the age span from infancy to adolescence. But this does not mean that authors failed to make distinctions among the obvious stages of biological development. Divisions of childhood and youth into the periods of *infantia, pueritia,* and *adolescentia* were ancient. Pagan as well as Judeo-Christian sources could be consulted on this tripartite division, as well as on finer discriminations, based upon observed behavior within each phase.[35] Thus Augustine distinguishes between the nursing and the learning-to-speak phases of infancy, and between the *puer loquens,* who has just emerged from childish helplessness, and a later condition of *pueritia,* just preceding puberty, when reason begins to be active.[36] Far from being periods of mere physical growth, the stages of youth leave profound and lasting experiences in the psyche. With the development of memory in infancy comes the retention of impressions. Augustine maintains that all early impressions are stored and become the formative experience which shape the adult man.[37] When the power of will first asserts itself, also in infancy, the child begins to notice the outside world, but sees it as an object of resistance to his instinctive wishes. Taking his will to be a command, he responds violently if denied. Thus the will is established early on as the driving faculty it is in adulthood.[38] Augustine's psychological perspicacity is unusual among the sources of the pedagogical tradition, but the importance he attributes to development itself is a matter of general agreement. Human life was lived in stages, the onset of each of which signaled an important physical and mental transformation.[39]

There was no doubt about the significance of one such stage, adolescence, coming at age fourteen.[40] It would be difficult to improve upon the picture of the inner storms and pressures, the restless longing and seeking for something not clearly perceived which is conveyed by Augustine in his *Confessions* (II, 2 and III, 1). A similar impression, though a much cruder one, emerges from the books of Vincent of Beauvais and Aegidius Romanus on the education of young princes, where the adolescent's rampant pride, arrogance, and rebelliousness are stressed.[41] All authors clearly identify the source of these tensions and excesses as sexual. Unrestrained by experience of consequences and with no care about the future,[42] adolescents, in the first flush of their physical powers, are driven to "natural" vices: lying, blaspheming, violence and cruelty, theft, disobedience of parents and disrespect toward their elders, idleness, gambling, recklessness and lack of shame, and—to come to the point—"voluptuous desires which consume the body and mind," namely masturbation and sexual advances ("contactus sui ipsius in locis abstrusis aut aliorum eiusdem sexus"). Catalogues of this sort were frequent in the pedagogical literature. The one just cited comes from Wimpheling's *Adolescentia,* [43] but Wimpheling takes it mainly from Gerson who, as is well known, was fixated on the apparently irrepressible sexual proclivities of adolescent boys, the gravest peril to their souls, as he saw it.[44] Sensuality had to be suppressed to the extent it was possible to do so by influencing youthful minds. No sexual stimulus was permitted in the seeing and hearing of young boys; Gerson never ceased to plead with secular and religious authorities for help in guarding the young from corruption. At the very least, he thought, these safeguards would delay sexual maturity until the boy had acquired some self-control.[45] All authors agreed that a more or less rigorous system of control was needed to keep boys of from fourteen to sixteen from destroying themselves for life. Even those who, like Erasmus in his *Colloquies,* make no attempt to conceal the unabashed sexuality which seems to have existed among the young in the early modern period deplore the effects of it on character and fortitude. Few writers, incidentally, addressed themselves more than cursorily to the problems of female adolescence, although when Vives, writing on the education of girls, quotes Jerome's "neither the burning of Etna, nor the country of Vulcan . . . boils with such heat as the bodies of young folk inflamed with wine and delicate meats,"[46] it is clear to everyone what he is saying.

All that was written on adolescence, then, pointed to the conclusion that in this, as well as in the earlier, even more impressionable phases of young life, nothing beneficial to the individual and to society could be achieved through any means other than restrictive ones. All authors advocated kindness and understanding. But the idea that the young might be allowed to develop with a minimum, rather than a maximum, of coercive authority was—if discussed at all—declared to be abhorrent. In any case, childhood and adolescence were seen as stages to be transcended, as a segment of life the sooner surmounted the better. Early life was obviously important to the educator. But it was understood as a period of privation, a stage leading, if correct educational means were employed, to something better. Child into man was a passage from imperfection to—if not perfection[47]—then at least to something less imperfect. Adulthood, or the change in status from *adolescens* to *iuvenis,* signified success in having learned to overcome the traits of childishness rooted in the instinctive, untaught, unrefined nature of man. To be a child meant saying whatever came into one's head, craving none but frivolous things, giving thought only to the cares of the moment, being unclean and enjoying it, being unreliable and fickle, reacting to the world with superstition and fear, desiring everything one saw and wanting it all at once, showing lack of consideration for others, and being thoughtless and self-centered.[48] Such enumerations of childish traits were common in the literature. No one idealized the young.[49]

Everything said so far relates to the *nature* of the young—that is to say, to the instinctual, emotional, and biological drives which equip the basic human personality with its natural impulses and impetus. Against nature, seen in this way, was set mind, intellect, *ingenium,* the seat of intelligence and reasoning power. Nature was force, mind was retraint, holding the reins and, if resourceful and skilled, able to guide impulses and control drives. The training of the mind is the first important task of the educator, for (to quote Augustine in a less pessimistic vein) in the child "reason and intelligence somehow slumber, as if non-existent, but ready to be roused and developed with the increase of age, so as to become capable of knowledge and learning. . . . Thanks to these faculties it may imbibe wisdom and be endowed with the virtues so as to struggle . . . against errors and the other inborn vices and conquer them."[50]

What enables the mind to know? The question may be narrowed at once. Pedagogues had mundane concerns. They worked toward the inculcation of practical disciplines the possession of which defined the useful member of church and society. True knowledge, knowledge of metaphysical and religious truth, did not enter their province, for they generally accepted Augustine's distinction between two kinds of knowing or, rather, two levels of knowing: the grasping of essential truth, which is a matter of illumination and not available to all, and ordinary knowledge, useful information. The distinction does not affect the work of practical teaching through which the usual disciplines are communicated by means of language and other "signs."[51] Sixteenth-century pedagogues were for obvious reasons unable to adopt the ideal tutoring situation portrayed by Augustine in his book on the teacher, a situation—in the sixteenth-century context a Utopian idyll—where mentors guided and suggested while pupils "consider within themselves whether what has been said is true . . . by gazing attentively at that interior truth, so far as they are able."[52] In the 1530s practical teaching faced different problems. But the educators of this period must have shared Erasmus's conviction that "there is no branch of learning for which the human mind is not receptive," for without embracing this innate capability as a starting point of their endeavors, they would at the very outset have reduced themselves to mere drillmasters (a task many did, in fact, accept later on when disappointing results cast a shadow on earlier expectations). Erasmus added a proviso to this optimistic assessment of the mind: "As long as we do not fail to supply instruction and practice."[53] This, indeed, was the province of the pedagogue. Instruction and practice "depend entirely on our industry," Erasmus said.[54] Here solid work could be done.

Nearly all authors agreed that three elements were necessary to effective learning: natural endowment ("the ability to grasp easily what they hear and to retain firmly what they grasp"),[55] practice (usually called *exercitium* or *exercitatio*), and discipline. If learning was the development of potentiality into actuality, as suggested by the useful scholastic model,[56] practice and discipline were the means by which the transition was effected. The teacher himself was the efficient cause of the knowledge engendered in the pupil. Thomas Aquinas saw the mind working naturally by the method of "discovery" (*inventio*). Good instruction imitates this method: "Natural reason by itself reaches knowledge of unknown things; this way is called 'discovery.' In the other way someone else aids the learner's natural reason, and this is called 'learning by instruction,' [*disciplina*]. . . . For the teacher leads the pupil to knowledge of things he does not know in the same way that one directs himself: through the process of discovering something he does not know."[57] Natural learning proceeds by turning into concrete and particular knowledge concepts at first only indistinctly grasped ("by sense we judge of the more common before the less common"). In the same way, teaching moves from the general to the particular, aiming at orderly arrangement.

What was learned was stored up in memory through an activity sometimes called "gathering" (*colligere*). Thomas, who was not very much interested in practical educational questions, said nothing about this, but other writers told how it was accomplished: "Reducing to a brief and compendious outline things which have been written and discussed at some length."[58] The faculty of memory had since antiquity been regarded as a prime indicator of the ability of a mind to learn easily and well. Quintilian said so, and what he said was restated by nearly every educational writer who came after him.[59] The capacity of the human mind which so excited Quintilian—"so swift and nimble and versatile that it cannot be restricted to doing one thing only"[60]—depended in the first instance on memory. In Augustine's persuasive presentation (*De Trinitate,* books 9–14) memory is pictured as the scene where thought takes place; understanding (*intelligentia*) works with the materials found there and subjects them to imagination and reasoning; the will acts as catalyst, gets the thought process under way, and gives it direction and purpose.[61] Memory, intelligence, and will, while affected in their qualities by inborn endowment, are subject to training. Innumerable mnemotechnic manuals and devices attest to the conviction present throughout medieval and early modern history that a good memory was, at least in large part, the result of practice. With memory trained and subject matter well arranged, learning was not much of a problem. Only occasions had to be provided, and able instructors, and some form of compulsion to overcome inertia.

Some authors went very far in their efforts to present the activity of learning as an orderly and essentially simple procedure. Rudolf Agricola, for example, a widely read humanist and pedagogical writer whose *De formando studio* was written in 1484 and first printed in 1518, having asked rhetorically, What distinguishes the scholar's mind from the books he reads? replies, There is very little difference, except that the human mind is more efficient and—if equipped with a keen memory—quicker in its operation than a book, even a well-designed commonplace book. Able minds have swift recall. More important, the mind can use the stored material for new purposes not originally foreseen when information was placed in the memory. Unlike books, the mind works with general governing concepts to which facts are related as we learn them. These enable us to have new thoughts.[62]

This kind of reductionism, which pictured the mind as an efficient engine with discrete parts and a tidy division of mechanical operations, simplified matters enormously for pedagogues. While nothing could be done about the pupil's *natura*, his talent, much might be accomplished by working on *ratio*, his thinking faculty, and *exercitatio*, the practiced discipline with which he employed it. (The Latin words are Erasmus's; terms differ slightly among the various authors but refer to the same faculties.) Teaching procedures and materials in the sixteenth century reflect this prevailing model of the mind and its operations. Intellectual differences among children were recognized, of course,[63] and the gifted were quickly spotted and advanced to special schools. But there was also the conviction, and a sense of rightness in holding it, that instruction can, to a considerable extent, level the gifts unequally bestowed by nature.[64] Erasmus enjoyed telling Plutarch's story about Lycurgus and the two puppies, one a highly bred but ill-trained animal, the other a mongrel but carefully drilled. Not surprisingly, Lycurgus discovered that the latter performed better. "Nature can do much," comments Erasmus, "but instruction is superior because it can do more" ("efficax res est natura, sed hanc vincit efficacior institutio").[65] Education was mainly training, and every child could be trained. The modest expectations held by Reformation pedagogues for all but their brightest pupils were thought to be attainable by all minds in good working order.

This conviction was supported by another set of assumptions about the pupil's responses to learning situations. It was believed that the human being exhibits certain basic psychological impulses affecting his interaction with his fellow men. If presented in the form of appeals to these impulses, learning is not simply a possible result, but a highly likely one.

At the most rudimentary level there was the pleasure-pain principle. Plato had written that this was responsible for the initial impetus to all actions,[66] and educators made use of this principle in many ways. Erasmus argued at length that learning should be fun to the young child—make it a game, he said[67]—but he was only restating what had often been said before. It was, after all, mere common sense, verified by experience, that children always seek delight and avoid pain.[68] Hence the many injunctions to "make play a road for learning" and to offer frequent rewards "so that [the child] may love what [he] is forced to do, and it be not work but pleasure, not a matter of necessity but one of free will."[69]

Sterner pedagogues could draw from the same principle a more rigorous physiological interpretation and employ it to create situations where positive and negative reinforcement techniques produced desired responses. Plutarch's popular treatise on the education of children suggested how this might be done. Counseling against the use of corporal punishment as unfit for freeborn youngsters, Plutarch recommended instead the use of methodical praise and rebuke: "It is well to choose some time when children are full of confidence to put them to shame by rebuke, and then in turn to cheer them up by praises, and to imitate the nurses who, when they have made their babies cry, in turn offer them the breast for comfort.'' He concludes: "These two things—hope of reward and fear of punishment—are, as it were, the elements of virtue.''[70] There were other ways, too, some not so gentle as Plutarch's. In view of generally prevailing notions that early educational thought was a set of variations on the theme of corporal punishment, it should be said at once that the weight of traditional authority was emphatically against this device. Quintilian, Plutarch, Maffeo Vegio, Battista Guarino, Wimpheling, and Erasmus were quoted in condemnation of this inhuman practice,[71] and explicit rules against it in the school ordinances of the sixteenth century show that this advice was accepted. On the other hand there existed in many minds an irrepressible, nagging suspicion that natural wickedness required unnatural punishment. The Old Testament supplied a wealth of vivid passages to prove that punishment administered by parents and educators was a good and godly thing; indeed, it has been pointed out that the very word for education in Hebrew came from the term for chastisement.[72] These passages exerted a certain influence on sixteenth-century teachers. There is, however, hardly an educational writer of the medieval and early modern periods who fails to point out that severe and frequent punishment is counterproductive. Vives, for example, who tended to disagree with the rejection on principle of all corporal punishment, regarded corrective blows as effective only if held in abeyance, as a threat. In any case, as with pleasure-oriented stimuli, the use of the human inclination to avoid pain suggested itself by way of common sense and observation. But if authorities were consulted on this point, the arguments against harsh punishment as a stimulus to learning were not only more eloquent, but also more practical than those arguments recommending it.[73]

Beyond simple reactions to pleasure and pain—but of course not independent of them—there was the innate urge to compete for success. Appeals to this impulse were highly recommended in the literature, but for Reformation pedagogues the principle of competitiveness was a two-edged weapon, as easily turned against their best efforts as it was likely to advance them. Their image of the desirable man, the new man, was of a being freed from the ultimately self-destructive ego drives of ambition. Nevertheless they recognized competition as a fact of life and made use of it for—they hoped—good purposes.

The principle of competition was said to depend on the instinctive operation of two urges, the positive desire to excel, to win fame and honor, and the equally pronounced negative wish to avert disgrace and avoid shame. The possibility of appealing to these desires had, of course, long been recognized. The literature furnished abundant proofs of their effectiveness and many illustrations of their use in practical teaching. Writers who, as Christians, deplored the persistence of the deadly sins among men nevertheless endorsed the sense of pride as a beneficial impetus to good scholastic performance. Jerome was often quoted: "Let her [the girl Paula about whom he was writing] have companions in her lessons, so that she may seek to rival them and be stimulated by any praise they win. . . . Let her be glad when she is first and sorry when she falls behind.''[74]

The writers of the Italian Renaissance supplied most of the arguments for using the urge to excel as the psychological ground of successful teaching. Battista Guarino denied even the possibility of teaching where the desire to excel is lacking. This, he says, was recognized by his famous father Guarino da Verona and made the starting point of his practice.[75] Maffeo Vegio suggests a number of devices for awakening feelings of honor and ambition in young boys.[76] The judicious and sparing bestowal of praise, he says, produces a "noble contest" among pupils. Boys may be seated in ranked order, each according to his performance. Let the brightest boys always display their attainments before the whole group. Never hesitate to give preferential treatment to achievers; this will not fail to spur the rest to greater efforts, which is a good thing not only for performance, but for character as well. Few writers troubled to explain the inconsistency between their adoption of the principle of competitive ambition on the one hand and their Christian values on the other; some, indeed, made the incongruity obvious. Thus Wimpheling says that the signs of a good disposition in the young are the striving for praise and the desire for honor and fame ("studio laudis excitari incendique amore gloriae").[77] This he takes from Piero Paolo Vergerio's *De ingenuis moribus,* where it is asserted that a sound nature is one that is stimulated by praise. Upon this stimulus rests emulation, "which may be defined as rivalry without malice."[78] On the other hand Wimpheling concludes his treatise with a set of cautionary maxims taken from Petrarch (alphabetized for ready reference), prominent among which is the reminder that fame is an empty bubble: "Fama ventus est, fumus est, umbra est, nihil est."[79] Wimpheling may never have reflected on the incongruity between the two attitudes demanded by these contrasting pieces of advice. He was not much of a thinker. But he was a useful purveyor of wisdom gathered from others. And the received wisdom accepted ambition, and relied on it. Only Vives among early modern pedagogues was consistent to his religious values in rejecting ambition. But Vives looked at the world with a much colder eye, and he had seen too much havoc done by the search for fame and glory to accept it as a guiding principle for the education of the young.

As effective as the wish to be praised was the fear of being put to shame. Most pedagogical authors advise reliance on this as an alternative to physical punishment. Inflicting pain and humiliation is not needed where the dread of failure and the sense of shame are utilized.[80] These fears are innate in human nature; it is the teacher's job to bring them into the pupil's consciousness and establish them as impulses to action. The teacher who does this well is a good teacher.[81] A visible manifestation of the sense of shame is the tendency to blush. Boys who blush readily reveal their susceptibility to this appeal.[82] *Pudor,* the "fear of deserved censure," is an effective internal control and obviates the use of the rod in all but desperate cases.[83]

By playing on the child's inborn senses and feelings the knowing teacher could thus begin to shape his pupil's mind and mold his personality. He had every confidence that instruction early in life would determine the entire direction of an individual's existence. The pedagogical tradition sustained him in this conviction.

Plato's system of compulsory training, prescribed and supervised by a board of philosophers in accordance with fixed norms and rules, was too distant from recognizable reality to be of specific use, but it did make available a powerful argument for systematic indoctrination in the service of an idea. Where the ideal mandated a renovation of the human personality—as it certainly did in the Reformation—Plato's *Republic* was a relevant text. But the entire pedagogical tradition could be summoned to supply evidence that such renovation could really be done, that the child, at a young and tender age, could in fact "be molded to take the impression one wishes to stamp on it."[84]

The extreme position on this point is given by Plutarch's lapidary "character is habit long continued."[85] Christian writers ought not to have accepted this assertion in principle. They should have known too much about sin and its effects to be tempted into regarding the moral character as a neutral substance shaped by habit. But Plutarch's observation is never explicitly challenged, and it is very often repeated. In its weakened form—"youth is impressionable and plastic, and while such minds are still tender, lessons are infused deeply into them"[86]—it is certainly unexceptionable. A more moderate and feasible position on early childhood education therefore expected of the teacher nothing more than the successful inculcation of right ideas, sound purposes, and good habits which, even if the child's nature tended to wickedness, would set him on a straight path. Thus, Aegidius Romanus advocates religious indoctrination for all children at an early age. Since the Christian faith cannot be proven by reason, he says, and is best accepted in a spirit of simple credulity, it is most efficaciously imbued in childhood.[87] This is true also of habits of civility and morality. Let children be trained "not to see" objects catering to base instincts. For what they absorb early in life they will remember always.[88] Jean Gerson, as has been seen, spent much effort in arguing that children should never be subjected to sense impressions that would make them lifelong slaves to passion.[89] More important, he had practical suggestions on how to shape the little ones into good Christians. The confessional, he thought, offered the best means of sound indoctrination. He speaks of rooting the habit of confession in children. But public instruction and preaching are also vital to the creation of the proper environment.[90] In a social setting very different from the one Gerson had in mind, Maffeo Vegio proposed the creation of a complete environment for the young child, in which he might develop a forceful character, a good disposition, and habits appropriate to the pursuit of worthwhile aims.[91]

Like all writers, Maffeo used the plastic argument. You can make the child what you wish. It is like soft wax. Bend the twig and the tree will incline as you wish. Even more revealing of how pedagogical writers imagined the process of molding is the constantly drawn analogy to the training of animals.[92] Erasmus has the most to say on this, and he says it very divertingly in his little book on early education. You train a puppy from birth; why not a child?[93] He multiplies examples from the animal kingdom until he has covered it from parrots to elephants. His *declamatio* is, in fact, of all pedagogical treatises the most emphatic on beginning the conditioning process in infancy, almost from the moment of birth, not only the indoctrination of behavior, but of learning too. To fail to do this is to waste the most receptive years and to miss the best chance of making a lasting impression. Without the shaping hand of the educator, Erasmus says, the child will grow into a wild creature, not a man. Teaching is everything. The crude mass of life must be molded to shape. There is no use deploring the effects of sin. This is empty posturing. It is we who are at fault if a child turns out badly, for we have allowed him to take on faults before directing him to the good. It is impossible to unlearn bad habits, but easy to be trained in good ones, so long as training comes early in life.[94] Basic nature may be impervious to mutation; but the evil to which man is inclined may, as Vives writes, "be amended by education" ("disciplina emendatur").[95]

It would be otiose to quote passages from the literature to show that Erasmus's and Vives's arguments for early conditioning were the received wisdom. Pedagogical writers spoke with one voice on this, and they prove the contention by citing the young child's pliability, his innocence and trusting openness, and the facility with which he absorbs and remembers what he is taught.[96] In any case, early learning is mere rote work, for which the child, even the infant, is especially well suited.[97]

How does one get him started? There was agreement on this point too: Utilize the child's natural love of imitation to get his physiological and psychological impulses under way. The *imitandi libido* exists even in infants. You may see it, says Erasmus, in the signs of joy they give when they have succeeded in imitating something. They are like monkeys. It is this eagerness to imitate which makes children "docile," ready to be taught.[98] The knowing educator will use this readiness methodically, moving from imitation of simple acts and words to emulation of complex ones. As Quintilian said, "Repeated imitation passes into habit" ("frequens imitatio transit in mores").[99] Quintilian is at pains to point out that no more than a learning technique is suggested here. Imitation is not enough. The object of study is not rote imitation. It is to reach inventiveness and independent judgment.[100] But it remains a rule of life that "it is expedient to imitate whatever has been invented with success."[101] For the first years of life this is the cardinal rule. It shapes the personality. Directed imitation passes by frequent repetition into habit, and—as we have seen—"character is habit long continued."[102]

"If one were to call the virtues of character the virtues of habit," Plutarch continues, "he would not seem to go far astray."[103] This generally accepted assertion gave educators much confidence in their labors. Over habits they had some measure of control. If, in his actions and reactions, the finished person was indeed the sum of the habits instilled in him, they had some hope of success in their attempts to shape him to conform to their standards. Plutarch's dictum did not need to be taken literally for educators to devote the most careful attention to that part of their activity which dealt with the formation of habits.

The fundamental importance of habit training had been pointed out by Aristotle when he cautioned against establishing in the young person behavior and thought patterns uninformed by reason and good purpose. Once firmly set, habit was all but ineradicable. "It is possible for man to be wrongly trained through the habits," he warned; we can prevent this only "if the most perfect harmony [is created] between reason and habit." Since the body develops before the soul, habituation must precede the training of understanding.[104] Man shares with all animals the propensity for modifying his nature by means of acquired habit (an argument favored by Christian writers confronting rigorous Augustinian pessimism).[105] Understood as a way of acting and thinking with sufficient frequency and regularity to have become unconscious, habit turns into a kind of second nature. "Consuetudo est quasi altera natura" was a commonplace among medieval and early modern educational writers.[106] If bad habits learned early in life are inextinguishable,[107] good habits may be as firmly rooted. It takes practice and endless repetition. Stoic philosophy reinforced the point: the mind, Seneca said, can "by practice make mercy its own" ("usu suam faciat").[108] Seneca was speaking of adults, who knew what they were doing, and why. But the method worked even better with the young. Accustom the child to do and think by rote habit what reason tells you he should do. Don't confuse him with explanations and justifications. Unpremeditated response is enough at this stage of life. Understanding will come later and with it his acceptance, as right and good, of rules the compliance with which has already become automatic.[109]

Extravagant claims were sometimes made in the sixteenth century for the power of habit. Vives encouraged mothers to think that their intimate control over young children's lives empowered them "to form [their] disposition. For she may make them what she will—good or bad."[110] Supporting evidence could be found in pediatric literature from Galen[111] to the medical popularizers of the sixteenth century, who asserted that good habits, inculcated early on, were capable even of changing a child's "complexion."[112] Few words turn up with greater frequency in the educational regulations of the Reformation than "habituation" (*Gewöhnung, consuetudo, usus*). No other pedagogical idea is more confidently accepted as a good thing and more insistently applied as the only way. It was hoped, of course, that comprehension would come later, and with it internalization of rules and doctrines first imposed by drill: "For the young cannot grasp our teachings unless they are first habituated to them by means of verbatim repetition."[113] Events would show that this was a vain hope. Little or no understanding seemed to come to most men. But in the end educators could at least console themselves with the thought that as long as habits stuck, their work had not been entirely futile.

III

Nature, impulses, responses, habits—the pedagogical literature had much to say on these. It had accumulated a large body of pedagogical assertions and reflections which—profound or not, empirically verifiable or not—generated confidence by showing agreement on many important problems, and by frequent reiteration of arguments advanced by writers of unassailable authority.

To what general educational purpose were pedagogical ideas harnessed? What specific goals of education were implicitly assumed and explicitly advocated in the literature? Let us first state some underlying propositions about educational activity itself. It was generally agreed that education must proceed in accordance with a governing purpose. The definition of this ideal was not, of course, the function of educators; but unless they accepted it, they labored without purpose. Secondly, education cannot limit itself to one part of the human personality or to one side of life; it must instruct the young in religion, in the arts, and in civility, and it must instruct them in these simultaneously. Finally, educational activity must be not only high minded, but also competent. The pedagogical literature set high standards for the teaching profession; it also furnished some practical directives on techniques. But all this was rudimentary, and it hardly needs to be said that a wide gap separated expectations from the ability of educators to fulfill them.

Specific educational goals were various, but not often clearly defined, at least not clearly enough to permit tidy classification. There seem to have been three groups of objectives. The first describes educational goals as an aspect of civic well-being, society being the general object of education, the citizen's place in society its particular goal. As its most grandiose the end is the creation of the ideal state, or the rigorous reform of an existing less-than-ideal one, by means of the education of its citizens. More modestly considered, education aims at the inculcation in the individual of a code of civic ethics likely to make him a useful member of the commonwealth.

Plato's state—the ideal state of the *Republic* and the model state of the *Laws*—was a compelling instance of the harmony of education and politics.[114] In the sixteenth-century context Plato's propositions had no practical application, but Lutheran theologians and pedagogues would have been well advised to mind Plato's demonstration of how an ethos established as the guiding principle of a society may be transmitted by means of education to the new generations who are to uphold and practice it in the future. There is no doubt that many of the leading proponents of the Reformation hoped that this could now be done. At the very least they recognized the relationship between religious and civic virtues and advocated early indoctrination in both. It was a truism to say—and nearly every writer in the pedagogical tradition did say it—that the commonwealth flourished only while its citizens accepted its principles as their own, or at least acted as if they did. The culture of the community defines the normative values of the individual. It must determine the pattern of his education. Education therefore was a public concern, and nearly every writer from Plato and Quintilian to the Renaissance said so.[115] Few Lutheran pedagogues evinced much interest in the particular civic virtues on which the educators of the Italian Renaissance placed such emphasis.[116] But they knew that peace and prosperity in the community depended on the good behavior of its members, and they quoted the "Christian" humanists on the important place to be given in pedagogy to civic education.[117]

A second objective was predominantly religious. At the maximum it sought to create in the individual person, insofar as it could be done by human effort, those dispositions which were the preconditions of salvation. The moral and religious restoration of Christendom was to be the aggregate result of this effort in individual reform. Augustine defined the problems and indicated the possibilities of this endeavor. The origin of sin lies in man's natural pride (*superbia*). Pride is expressed in thoughts and acts of egotism (*amor sui*). Only grace can deliver man from this condition, but hope of grace is open only to those who have faced up to their predicament and entered the state of humility in which they come to recognize themselves as sinners, as a *massa peccati*.[118] This image of man and his condition defines the role of education: Destroy the "old man," the "old Adam," and raise the "new man." Augustine states the aim of Christian education most explicitly in *De vera religione* (which argues that Christianity grasps fully what Platonism had seen but dimly). He passes before us the ages of man: infancy and the purely nutritive existence; childhood, when memories are stored; adolescence and the onset of sexual power; manhood with its responsibilities; and lastly the calm of old age. "This," he concludes the review, "is the life of man so far as he lives in the body. . . . This is the 'old man,' the 'exterior or earthly man.' " Among these old men some are reborn: "With their spiritual strength and increase of wisdom they overcome the 'old man' and put him to death and bring him into subjection to the celestial laws. This is 'the new man,' 'the inward and heavenly man.' "[119] The aim of all education, then, is to augment the qualities necessary to the inward creation of the new man. With the *humilitas Christi* as his paradigm, the educator selects specific goals and procedures toward the restructuring of the sinner's personality, insofar as it is amenable to human manipulation. Augustine did not raise very much hope on that score. But he did reject passivity and resignation, encouraging men instead to be energetic in the endeavor to supplant the self-seeking impulses of the old man with the humility and charity of the new man.

Obviously, Augustine's design is too schematic to be a prescription for teaching anyone or anything. His ideal types are as abstract as are Plato's concepts. They are about Man, not men. They can be usefully tested only as theology. Still, the enormous religious and moral force pulsating in his phrases exercised a strong hold upon sixteenth-century theologians and pedagogues, who succeeded in bringing Augustine down to earth by translating the abstract qualities that defined his old and new men into concrete vices and virtues, recognizable to every observer of the human scene and largely congruous with the traits enumerated by secular-minded pedagogues as the attributes of citizenship. The overwhelming majority of Christian writers on pedagogy described their desired objective, the product of right education, as a young man exhibiting habits of obedience, humility, modesty, submissiveness, a bland passivity of behavior, and lifelong docility.[120] Vives thought that human faculties could stand a bit of blunting. Not that he wanted boys made dull or stupid; but at the end of their education they ought to be simpler, more honest, less cunning, above all less self-seeking persons than the "natural" creatures they had been at the beginning.[121] This product was a long way from the exuberance and precocious self-confidence of Quintilian's ideal youngster, who "runs riot in the luxuriance of his growth."[122] Christianity is not the only explanation of the distance between the two types. It was also that the Christian writers of the early modern period saw the violence and tensions of their age as being in large part the result of the indifference and permissiveness with which parents, as well as society as a whole, allowed the young to develop and give free play to their natural impulses. In the days of antiquity, Erasmus notes shrewdly, pedagogues could count on the homogeneity of their culture to do their educating for them. Alas, such conditions prevail no longer.[123] The young must be taken in hand. They cannot be left to themselves, or to society at large. They must be taught. There is no other way to individual reform, nor to social renovation.

The third group of educational writers concerned themselves less with social objectives than with the individual person's drive to self-fulfillment. It will be obvious that this group had least to say to sixteenth-century reformers, who lacked sympathy with the implicit assumptions of Renaissance humanism. On the other hand, the liberal and often very eloquent pleas on behalf of the intellectually, emotionally, and physically growing young person could be taken as a corrective to the many suppressive tendencies in Lutheran education. To enlarge the mind,[124] to direct the growing person toward "virtus et gloria" as the only worthwhile pursuits,[125] to create in him resources for becoming the "vir probus atque perfectus" or the "homo virtuoso,"[126] to build a foundation for self-respect by encouraging methodical examination of conscience[127]—these were noble objectives. They were beyond the reach of all but the select few for whom pedagogical writers in the classical tradition had always written.[128] They related to a social and political setting increasingly alien to the conditions for which Reformation theologians were legislating. Above all, they offered no concrete suggestions for solving the most vexing of the problems facing reformers in the 1530s. But as reminders of a humane tradition they never lost their force. As sentences from the works of the great authorities they continued to command respect. And in Erasmus's eloquent and reasonable fusion of these ideals with the cause of religious reform, Lutheran pedagogues could, if they wished, find justification for tempering their theoretical and empirical pessimism with the benign gentility of classical humanism.[129] Erasmus's goal of a "sapiens et eloquens pietas" could be cultivated as common ground. It was, in fact, an attainable goal for that part of Reformation pegagogy which concentrated on the training of a professional elite. But Lutheran pedagogues also wished to cast a wider net. And to the purposes of mass indoctrination in the rudiments of religion and in the minimum requirements of useful and peaceful citizenship, the humanist ideal had no practical contribution to make.

IV

The Pedagogical literature spoke not only on fundamental questions relating to guiding purposes and methods. It also offered suggestions on a host of corollary issues on which sixteenth-century reformers ill prepared by experience to make decisions sought the counsel of tradition. Is education best accomplished in public institutions or in the home? This question answered itself in the 1530s, but it was comforting to know that the pedagogical tradition spoke overwhelmingly with the reformers in urging the creation of a system of public schools. Who has authority to establish and control such schools? Again, the answer was clear: the lawgiver, the state. Erasmus's uncompromising phrase "opportet scholam aut nullam esse aut publicam"[130] epitomizes the discussion reaching back to Quintilian and brings it up to date with an excoriation of teaching by monks and unskilled privateers. Should learning and teaching be rigidly structured, or should they be informal? Arguments existed on each side of this question, but writers whose concerns coincided most closely with those of Lutheran reformers recommended formalized curricula and instruction. These were adopted. The role of the family in education was an important consideration for the reformers, specifically the training given in infancy and the responsibilities of fathers and mothers toward their children's formal schooling. On these points, too, the tradition was informative, as also on questions concerning the education of girls—whether or not, how much, to what end. The literature abounded with detailed suggestions on practical methods and instructional devices. Curricula were, of course, entirely conventional in the sixteenth century. Only the introduction of the catechism as an instrument of mass education offered opportunities for new departures. These were very rarely grasped, however; and innovational teaching, in the sense of experimenting with methods not recommended in the classical and medieval literature, was unknown. Persuasive arguments existed for setting standards of professional skill for teachers; indeed teacher training, to the extent that this could be carried out in the sixteenth century, owes something to the idea that formal education should be so systematically organized that, as Quintilian wrote, if anyone fails to learn, "The fault will lie not with the method but with the individual."[131] To these and other concerns the pedagogical literature made solid contributions.

In general the pedagogical literature gave powerful support to ideas and assumptions already firmly lodged in the reformers' thoughts. Few pedagogues could have approached the problems of education with an open mind. They came to them with their guiding concepts intact. The literature supplied pedagogues with a battery of arguments to present their case for a reorganization of the educational structure according to the principles of the Reformation. It convinced them that the learning process was a simple mechanism which could, without great difficulty, be set in motion and given momentum. It lent them the confidence of knowing that behind their own efforts stood an ancient and intellectually unimpugnable tradition. And this tradition sustained them in their sense of being engaged in a profoundly important enterprise on whose success or failure rested the shape of the future.

Less fortunately, the literature encouraged them in their unwillingness or inability to consider educational questions from the point of view of the child. Granted, this is a criticism of doubtful historical validity. But one is almost forced to make it by the insuppressible and, to us, irritating inclination of pedagogical authors to discourse upon the nature and behavior of children without giving much evidence of having studied them. It has already been said that there was no lack of interest in children. Nor is a certain warmth and sympathy absent from the literature about the young. Many passages could be quoted to convey the human feelings aroused by their subject in most authors. But these natural responses to the affective appeal of the theme of education did not prompt writers to increase their familiarity with real children. They did not ask what flesh-and-blood, true-to-life children were like, what their needs were, what it felt like to be subjected to educational methods drawn from their theories.

In the end, what mattered to the reformers, as it had mattered to older pedagogical writers, was the objective result obtained by their procedures. The Lutheran theologian cared for the faith he preached and for the religious disposition of the society which did or did not live by this faith. Similarly, Erasmus and Vives showed genuine concern only for the fate of the learned disciplines they loved, not for the child who was expected to acquire them. Few if any authors were much interested in the individual youth, except as the recipient of their ideas and the respondent to them. Sixteenth-century educators thought in abstractions. The "natural" child was one such abstraction; a second was the finished, educated product seen as a model conceived on the lines of a biblical Tobias, an Isaac, or a Joseph. The good society peopled by such types was a third.

To say all this is merely to repeat a well-known fact. But it is one which goes a long way toward explaining another fact not so well known. The educational enterprise of the Lutheran reformers was a failure when judged by their own aims. It was a grand failure, perhaps even a tragic one. But a failure it was, nonetheless, and as such an important historical factor. The disappointing outcome of their fervently pursued educational endeavor affected the ways in which reformers understood and judged themselves. It forced them to reappraise their efforts and their talents. It gave them second thoughts about their mission. It may even have led them to doubt their cause. But this is a different story, which need not be told here.

NOTES

1. The sense of living at the end of time was implicit in much that was said and done by the first generation of the Reformation. On Luther's complex views concerning the possibilities and limits of education, see the stimulating discussion by Ivar Asheim, *Glaube und Erziehung bei Luther* (Heidelberg, 1961), esp. pp. 88ff. Also interesting is Edgar Reimers, *Recht und Grenzen einer Berufung auf Luther in den neueren Bemühungen um eine evangelische Erziehung* (Weinheim, 1958).

2. For a particularly striking account of the impact of the religious and political troubles of the 1520s on a reformer's mind, see Wilhelm Maurer, *Der junge Melanchthon*, 2 vols. (Göttingen, 1967–69), esp. vol. 2.

3. These arguments are acknowledged and met in Luther's *An die Ratsherren aller Städte . . . dass sie christliche Schulen aufrichten und halten sollen* (1524), W[eimar] A[usgabe] XV, pp. 9–53.

4. For a convenient list of these ordinances, in chronological order, see Georg Mertz, *Das Schulwesen der deutschen Reformation* (Heidelberg, 1902), pp. 162–65. Mertz prints the texts of many of these ordinances. Others are printed by Emil Sehling, ed., *Die evangelischen Kirchenordnungen des 16. Jahrhunderts*, 5 vols. (Leipzig, 1902–13).

5. See the warning against teaching in the German language in the *Unterricht der Visitatoren* (1528), WA XXVI, p. 236. At that time Luther was concerned mainly with ensuring the church of an adequate supply of trained ministers.

6. From *Decem praecepta Wittenbergensi praedicata populo* (1528), WA I, p. 494, comments on the sixth commandment. The sermons were given in late 1516 and early 1517.

7. See the many references to *Kinder* in the index to Luther's Table Talk, WA *Tischreden* VI, pp. 595–96.

8. For one example among many, see *Das Buch Weinsberg,* ed. Johann Jakob Hässlin (Munich, 1961), which contains childhood memories suggesting that parents and children were closely involved with each other.

9. A survey of sixteenth-century medical literature shows that from about 1520 physicians devoted more attention to the diseases of babies and children. A growing number of special treatises on pediatrics were published beginning c. 1540.

10. Very few of the innumerable general histories of education and of educational thought are of much use to the historian. Two exceptions: Josef Dolch, *Lehrplan des Abendlandes: Zweieinhalb Jahrtausende seiner Geschichte* (Ratingen, 1965); Karl Schmidt, *Geschichte der Pädagogik, dargestellt in weltgeschichtlicher Entwicklung,* 4 vols. (Cöthen, 1890), which is encyclopedic. There are, of course, numerous excellent works dealing with particular periods.

11. See Otto Herding's elaborate identification of Jacob Wimpheling's sources in his edition of Wimpheling's *Adolescentia (Jacobi Wimpfelingi opera selecta,* 1 [Munich, 1965]: 31–151).

12. For example, Antonio Mancinelli, *De parentum cura in liberos . . .* (Milan, 1504), a compilation of choice classical and patristic thought on education. Mancinelli gives a chapter each to Plutarch, Quintilian, Plato, Aristotle, Aulus Gellius, Xenophon, Cicero, Diogenes Laertius, the Plinys, the Book of Proverbs, St. Paul, Augustine, Jerome, Isidore of Seville, and Vergerio.

13. Johann Agricola, *Hundert und dreyssig gemeyner Fragestücke für die jungen kinder . . .* (Wittenberg, 1528), preface, Aii verso.

14. Johann Bader, *Ein Gesprächbüchlein vom Anfangk des christlichen Lebens mit dem jungen Volk zu Landaw* (Landau, 1526), quoted in J. P. Gelbert, *Magister Johann Baders Leben und Schriften* (Neustadt, 1968), p. 123. Bader's was one of the earliest Protestant catechisms.

15. Quintilian, *Institutio oratoria* XII, 11, 12. I use the Loeb Classical Library edition with the English translation by H. E. Butler. The *editio princeps* of Quintilian was Rome, 1470.

16. *Ibid.* I, 1, 1f.

17. Augustine, *Confessions* I, 19. Cf. II, 4, on the famous incident of robbing the pear tree. I use the Loeb Classical Library edition with the English translation of William Watts of 1631.

18. Joseph Hogger, *Die Kinderpsychologie Augustins* (Munich, 1937).

19. *De peccatorum meritis et remissione,* in *A Select Library of the Nicene and Post-Nicene Fathers of the Christian Church,* vol. 5, *Augustine's Anti-Pelagian Writings* (New York, 1887), chap. 67. For a particularly strong view of infant sinfulness and a colorful description of its symptoms, see Andreas Osiander, *Catechismus oder kinder Predig . . .* (Nuremberg, 1533), also printed in Johann Michael, Reu, *Quellen zur Geschichte des kirchlichen Unterrichts . . . ,* 1 (Gütersloh, 1904): 542–564, esp. 545–46, 556.

20. *Confessions* I, 7, 11. Here I use the translation by Peter Brown, who quotes this passage on pp. 28–29 of his *Augustine of Hippo* (Berkeley, 1967).

21. Hogger, *Die Kinderpsychologie Augustins,* p. 48, remarks shrewdly about Augustine's explanations of his own childhood that "from a hoard of stored-up psychological knowledge he laid bare only such items as would carry a conscious or unconscious conflict into his philosophy of life."

22. See Klaus Petzold, *Die Grundlagen der Erziehungslehre im Spätmittelalter und bei Luther* (Heidelberg, 1969), chap. 2. The first of many editions of Gerson's works was published in Cologne in 1483–84. The Strassburg edition of 1502 was partly edited by Wimpheling.

23. Jean Gerson, *De innocentia puerili,* in *Opera omnia* (Antwerp, 1706), 3: 293–96.

24. For an excellent discussion of this, see Petzold, *Die Grundlagen,* chap. 2.

25. *Tractatus de parvulis trahendis ad Christum,* in *Opera omnia,* 3: 277–91, esp. 283.

26. The first edition of Wimpheling's *Adolescentia* was printed in Strassburg in 1500. Many others followed within a few years. I use the critical edition by Otto Herding (see n. 11 above). For Wimpheling's debt to Gerson, see Herding's introduction (pp. 110–32).

27. *Adolescentia,* Herding ed., pp. 206–40.

28. As advanced, for example, by Clement of Alexandria, *Paedagogus,* ed. H. I. Marrou and Marguerite Harl, 4 vols. (Paris, 1960–70), 1: 19–21.

29. For these, for an excellent discussion of the whole problem, and for a large bibliography, see Werner Jentsch, *Urchristliches Erziehungsdenken: Die Paideia Kyriu im Rahmen der hellenisch-jüdischen Umwelt* (Gütersloh, 1951), particularly pt. 2.

30. *De pueris instituendis,* in the critical edition by J. C. Margolin, *Opera omnia Desiderii Erasmi,* I, 2 (Amsterdam, 1971): 39–40.

31. Ibid., p. 33.

32. Ibid., p. 50.

33. *Laws* 808d.

34. *Confessions* I, 9–10, 12–13.

35. For the immense literature on the subject of the ages of human life see Franz Boll, "Die Lebensalter: Ein Beitrag zur antiken Ethologie und zur Geschichte der Zahlen," *Neue Jahrbücher für das klassische Altertum, Geschichte und deutsche Literatur* 16 (1913): 89–154; and Adolf Hofmeister, "Puer, iuvenis, senex . . . ," in Albert Brockmann, ed., *Papsttum und Kaisertum . . . Paul Kehr zum 65. Geburtstag dargebracht* (Munich, 1926), pp. 287–316. Boll stresses the numerological sources and significance of the division of the life span into three, four, six, or seven stages.

36. For passages, mostly from the *Confessions* and *De peccatorum meritis et remissione et de baptismo parvulorum,* see Hogger, *Die Kinderpsychologie Augustins,* pp. 63–165.

37. Augustine further distinguishes between the merely nutritive stage of early infancy, when all impressions are quickly forgotten, and the memory stage, when they are retained.

38. Hogger, *Die Kinderpsychologie Augustins,* pp. 88–89. Pedagogical material exists in astonishing profusion in Augustine's works, but it is scattered, some of it in his early writings, much in his late works. While the sixteenth-century reader could not have drawn a coherent system of educational thought from Augustine, he would certainly have been profoundly impressed by the acuteness and psychological force of many of his observations.

39. See Hofmeister, "Puer, iuvenis, senex," for examples from Varro, Isidore of Seville, and others whose writings might have influenced sixteenth-century readers.

40. The legal literature agreed with this: e.g., Ulrich Tengler, *Layenspiegel: Von rechtmässigen ordnungen inn bürgerlichen und peinlichen Regimenten . . .* (Strassburg, 1544), x recto; Justin Göbler, *Handbuch . . . kayserlicher und bürgerlicher Rechten . . .* (Frankfurt am Main, 1564), I, title 12.

41. Vincent of Beauvais, *De eruditione filiorum nobilium,* ed. Arpad Steiner (Cambridge, Mass., 1938), chap. 35. The book was printed in 1477 and 1481. Egidio Colonna (Aegidius Romanus), *De regimine principum,* ed. S. P. Molenaer (New York, 1899), pp. 220–24 (the thirteenth-century French version). This work was printed frequently after 1473.

42. Maffeo Vegio, *De educatione liberorum,* written 1444, printed frequently from 1491. I use the German translation by K. A. Kopp in Bibliothek der katholischen Pädagogik, vol. 2 (Freiburg i.B., 1889), p. 121.

43. Herding ed., pp. 198–99, 242.

44. Jean Gerson, *Doctrina pro pueris ecclesiae Parisiensis,* in *Opera omnia,* 3: 717–20; *Expostulatio ad potestates publicas adversus corruptionem juventutis per lascivas imagines,* in ibid., 3: 291–92; *Tractatus de pollutione diurna,* in ibid., 3: 335–45.

45. Gerson may have been on the right track. Hans Heinrich Muchow, in an interesting study *Jugendgeneration im Wandel der Zeit: Beiträge zur Geschichte der Jugend* (Vienna, 1964), argues that while the onset of biological sexuality occurs at about the same age in all periods and among all peoples in history, "psychic-sexual maturity," the psychic acceptance of sexuality and the readiness to employ it, comes later. The length of this lag is determined by cultural and social factors. Repression means a longer lag. See esp. p. 26.

46. Vives, *De institutione feminae christianae,* bk. I, chap. 7, in *Joannis Ludovivi Vivis . . . opera omnia,* vol. 4 (Valencia, 1783).

47. This scholastic argument was presented by Aegidius Romanus in *De regimine principum* (see n. 41 above).

48. *De eruditione principum,* in *Sancti Thomae Aquinatis . . . opera omnia,* vol. 16 (New York, 1950; reprint of the 1852–73 Parma ed.), opusculum 37, bk. V, chap. 48. This anonymous book was attributed to St. Thomas throughout the late Middle Ages and the early modern period. On the authorship question see Wilhelm Berges, *Die Fürstenspiegel des hohen und späten Mittelalters* (Leipzig, 1938), pp. 309–13.

49. I leave out of consideration here the matter of eugenics, although a number of early modern writers stressed it, notably Vegio, *De educatione liberorum,* Kopp trans., p. 37 ("The physical and moral condition of the father at the moment of conception is transmitted directly and inexpungeably to the body and mind of the offspring"), and Erasmus, *De pueris instituendis,* Margolin ed., p. 43. Most authors did not advise eugenic practices consonant with those in plato's *Republic* but confined themselves to counseling continence and abstemiousness before intercourse. In any case, such advice did not enter the province of the sixteenth-century pedagogue.

50. *City of God* XXII, 24.

51. *De magistro*, 45, in *Saint Augustine, The Teacher* . . . , trans. R. P. Russell, The Fathers of the Church: A New Translation, vol. 59 (Washington, D.C., 1968).

52. Ibid.

53. *De pueris instituendis*, Margolin ed., p. 45.

54. Ibid., p. 46.

55. Hugh of St. Victor, *Didascalicon* III, 6. I use the critical edition by Charles Henry Buttimer, *Hugonis de Sancto Victore, Didascalicon* . . . (Washington, D.C., 1939). The translation is by Jerome Taylor, *The Didascalicon of Hugh of St. Victor* (New York, 1961).

56. Thomas Aquinas, *De magistro*, Article 1, Reply (Quaestio XI of *Quaestiones disputatae de Veritate*, trans. James V. McGlynn as *The Disputed Questions on Truth*, 2 vols. [Chicago, 1952–54], 2: 77–101). Cf. John W. Donohue, *St. Thomas Aquinas and Education* (New York, 1968); Mary Helen Mayer, *The Philosophy of Teaching of St. Thomas Aquinas* (New York, 1929). In this treatise Thomas seeks to prove that man *can* teach, against the view, ascribed by him to Augustine, that only God teaches.

57. *De magistro*, Article 1, Reply.

58. Hugh of St. Victor, *Didascalicon* III, 11: "Opportet ergo ut, quae discendo divisimus, commendanda memoriae colligamus. Colligere est ea de quibus prolixius vel scriptum vel disputatum est ad brevem quandam et compendiosam summam redigere." The translation in the text is that of Jerome Taylor.

59. Quintilian I, 3, 1: a good memory has two characteristics; it is "quick to take in and faithful to retain." Cf. Augustine, *Confessions* X, 8–19, where Augustine gives voice to his delight at the workings of the mind, particularly of memory. For another example see Vives, *De disciplinis* (1531). I use the German translation by Rudolf Heine, *Johann Ludwig Vives: Ausgewählte pädagogische Schriften* (Leipzig, n.d.), pp. 55–56.

60. Quintilian I, 12, 8.

61. *De Trinitate* X, 10–11 (*A Select Library of the Nicene and Post-Nicene Fathers* . . . , vol. 3 [Buffalo, 1887]). On this see the comments by Charles Trinkaus, *In Our Image and Likeness: Humanity and Divinity in Italian Humanist Thought* (Chicago, 1970), vol. 1, pt. 2, chap. 4.

62. *De formando studio* (Freiburg, 1539), pp. 75–90.

63. The pedagogical tradition speaks with one voice on this point. From Quintilian and Augustine to Vegio, Vergerio, Wimpheling, and Erasmus, authors maintained that intellects differ in natural endowment.

64. E.g., Erasmus, *De pueris instituendis*, Margolin ed., p. 45.

65. Ibid., p. 29. Cf. Plutarch, *De liberis educandis*, 4.

66. For the clearest statement see *Laws*, bk. V, 732e–734e. See also R. C. Lodge, *Plato's Theory of Education* (London, 1947), pp. 193ff.

67. *De pueris instituendis*, Margolin ed., p. 53 and passim. Also *De ratione studii*, in Margolin, ed., *Opera omnia* I, 2: 111–151 passim, with reference to Quintilian I, 1, 20.

68. Aegidius Romanus, *De regimine principum*, Molenaer ed., pp. 195–96.

69. These quotations from Jerome, Ep. 107 and 128, respectively (*Select Letters of St. Jerome*, ed. and trans. F. A. Wright [London, 1933], pp. 347 and 469).

70. Plutarch, *De liberis educandis*, 12; 16. Plutarch is probably not the author of this treatise, but throughout the early modern period it was attributed to him. On the authorship question see Daniel Wyttenbach in his edition of Plutarch's *Moralia*, vol. 6, *Animadversiones* (Oxford, 1810), pp. 29–64. Many Latin translations of this work were published in the fifteenth century, including one by Guarino da Verona.

71. Quintilian I, 3, 13–18; Plutarch, *De liberis educandis*, 12; Maffeo Vegio, *De educatione liberorum*, Kopp trans., pp. 52–56; Battista Guarino, *De ordine docendi et studendi*, in *Vittorino da Feltre and Other Humanist Educators*, trans. William Harrison Woodward (New York, 1963), pp. 162–63; Wimpheling, *Isidoneus Germanicus*, in *Jakob Wimphelings pädagogische Schriften* . . . , trans. Joseph Freundgen (Paderborn, 1898), p. 170; Erasmus, *De pueris instituendis*, Margolin ed., p. 61.

72. For this, and for references to passages advocating corporal punishment, see Jentsch, *Urchristliches Erziehungsdenken*, pp. 85–139.

73. For an especially eloquent, as well as sensible, argument against harsh punishment see Erasmus, *De pueris instituendis*, Margolin ed., pp. 61–62.

74. Ep. 107, Wright ed., p. 347.

75. *De ordine docendi et studendi,* Woodward trans., p. 162. His treatise, says Battista, "represents the doctrine of my father Guarino Veronese; so much so that you may suppose him to be writing to you by my pen" (ibid., p. 161). Battista's treatise was first printed in Heidelberg in 1489 and reprinted several times thereafter.

76. Vegio, *De educatione liberorum,* Kopp trans., pp. 78–82.

77. *Adolescentia,* Herding ed., pp. 194–95.

78. Pietro Paolo Vergerio, *De ingenuis moribus* (edition in Princeton University Library, n.p., n.d., but probably 1472), 3 verso–4 recto. Vergerio's treatise had twenty or more editions before 1500.

79. *Adolescentia,* p. 368.

80. Guarino, *De ordine docendi et studendi,* Woodward trans., p. 163.

81. Vegio, *De educatione liberorum,* p. 78.

82. Wimpheling, *Adolescentia,* p. 195, taken from Vergerio.

83. Erasmus, *De pueris instituendis,* Margolin ed., pp. 62–63.

84. *Republic,* bk. II, 377b.

85. *De liberis educandis,* 3A (F. C. Babbitt, trans. Loeb Classical Library). A more accurate translation of Plutarch's ἠθικὰς ἀρετὰς would be "moral virtue." Latin translations of the Greek phrase usually read "cum mores ipsi Graeco sermone nihil sint quam assuefactio diuturna" (*Plutarchi . . . moralia . . .* , trans. Guilielmus Xylander [Basel, 1572], p. 4). Plutarch's phrase is a Peripatetic commonplace; see the references by Stobaeus in his Anthology (*Ioannis Stobaei Anthologii libri duo priores,* ed. Curt Wachsmuth II [Berlin, 1884]), pp. 116–17).

86. *Plutarchi . . . moralia . . .* , trans. Xylander, p. 4.

87. *De regimine principum,* Molenaer ed., pp. 193–94.

88. Ibid., pp. 206–7.

89. See n. 44 above.

90. Jean Gerson, *Tractatus de parvulis trahendis ad Christum,* in *Opera omnia,* 3: 277–91. The reference is to pp. 283–84.

91. *De educatione liberorum,* Book I, Kopp trans., pp. 41–45.

92. Ibid., pp. 57–58.

93. *De pueris instituendis,* Margolin ed., p. 29.

94. Ibid., passim. The same arguments are made in Erasmus's *Education of a Christian Prince,* trans. Lester K. Born (New York, 1968), p. 140.

95. *De officio mariti liber,* in *Opera omnia,* 4: 322.

96. On this last point, see Quintilian I, 12, 8–9.

97. Ibid. I, 12, 11; also I, 1, 19.

98. *De pueris instituendis,* Margolin ed., p. 48.

99. Quintilian I, 11, 2.

100. Ibid. X, 7, 1.

101. Ibid. X, 2, 1.

102. See n. 85 above.

103. "Neque abs re morales virtutes dixeris virtutes consuetudinis eorum lingua." See n. 85 above.

104. *Politics* VII, 13, 21–23.

105. Ibid., VII, 12, 7; Vives, *De officio mariti liber,* in *Opera omnia,* 4: 322.

106. Aegidius Romanus, *De regimine principum,* Molenaer ed., p. 195.

107. "Mala enim consuetudo, diu inroborata, est inextinguibilis." This phrase is quoted by Nonius Marcellus, *De compendiosa doctrina ad filium* (ed. L. Quicherat [Paris, 1872], p. 137), who attributes it to Varro's *De liberis educandis.*

108. Seneca, *De clementia* I, 3.

109. Vives, *De disciplinis,* Heine trans., p. 44.

110. Vives, *De institutione feminae christianae* (1523), in *Opera omnia,* 4: 258.

111. Galen, *De sanitate tuenda libri sex* I, 12, 5f.

112. E.g., Otto Brunfels, *Weiber und Kinder Apoteck . . .* (Strassburg, 1535), xliii recto.

113. Dan die iugent fast die lehre nicht, so sie nicht zu ausdrücklichem nachsprechen gewehnet wird" (visitation articles for Electoral Saxony, printed in Karl Pallas, ed., *Die Registraturen der Kirchenvisitationen im ehemals sächsischen Kurkreise,* Geschichtsquellen der Provinz Sachsen [Halle, 1906–14], 41 [Allgemeiner Teil]: 91).

114. For all relevant citations see Lodge, *Plato's Theory of Education,* chap. 4.

115. Quintilian I, 2; for the Renaissance, see, e.g., Vergerio, *De ingenuis moribus,* 7 verso.

116. For a good discussion of this subject and references to authors, see Gregor Müller,

"Educazione morale-civile," *Bildung und Erziehung im Humanismus der italienischen Renaissance* (Wiesbaden, 1969), esp. pp. 204–10 on Francesco Filelfo.

117. E.g., Wimpheling, *Adolescentia,* Herding ed., pp. 188f., 208; idem, *Isidoneus,* Freundgen trans., pp. 82f.; Vives, *De disciplinis,* Heine trans., p. 26.

118. For a discussion of Augustine's theology with reference to education, and for relevant passages, see Rudolf Strauss, *Der neue Mensch innerhalb der Theologie Augustins* (Zurich, 1967), particularly pp. 52–55.

119. *De vera religione,* trans. J. H. S. Burleigh, Library of Christian Classics, vol. 6 (Philadelphia, 1953), pp. 48ff.

120. *De eruditione principum,* in *Sancti Thomae Aquinatis . . . opera omnia,* 16: 287–93; Vegio, *De educatione liberorum,* Kopp trans., pp. 137–59; Wimpheling, *Adolescentia,* Herding ed., pp. 209ff; Erasmus, *Pietas puerilis* (also called *Confabulatio pia*) in *Colloquia familiaria,* in *Opera omnia* (Leiden, 1703), vol. 1, cols. 648–53; Vives, *De disciplinis,* Heine trans., pp. 56–57.

121. Vives, *De disciplinis,* p. 33.

122. Quintilian II, 4, quoting Cicero, *De oratore* II, xxi, 88.

123. *De pueris instituendis,* Margolin ed., pp. 50–51.

124. E.g., Quintilian I, 8, 8.

125. Vergerio, *De ingenuis moribus,* 11 recto.

126. For references to the large number of Italian writers who saw this as the object of education, see Müller, *Bildung und Erziehung,* pp. 321–22.

127. Vegio, *De educatione liberorum,* Kopp trans., pp. 159–63.

128. This fact is too evident in all these writings to require proof. Even Erasmus, despite his talk about the ploughboy, concerned himself almost exclusively with the well-born, hoping that ordinary mortals would be beneficially influenced if they observed the children of prominent men working hard at their studies ("si conspexerint heroum liberos a primis statim annis dicari studiis"); see *De civilitate morum puerilium* (1529), in *Opera omnia* (Leiden, 1703), vol. 1, col. 1033.

129. See the discussion of the Erasmian ideal as put into action by Johann Sturm in Walter Sohm, *Die Schule Johann Sturms und die Kirche Strassburgs . . .* (Munich and Berlin, 1912), pp. 31ff.

130. *De pueris instituendis,* Margolin ed., p. 55. As usual, Erasmus can be quoted in self-contradiction. In his *De ratione studii,* Margolin ed., p. 125, he recommends domestic tutoring as superior to public education. But this is so only for the well-to-do. Erasmus insisted on public control over schools for ordinary boys.

131. Quintilian I, 1, 11.

CHAPTER 4

The Ownership of Books in England, 1560–1640: The Example of Some Kentish Townsfolk

BY PETER CLARK

It is perhaps paradoxical that despite the enthusiastic concern of much recent historical research with the expansion of educational facilities and the changing pattern of popular ideas in that crucial century or so before the English Revolution, the role of the book, arguably one of the most critical contact points causing those two movements to relate and react, has been comparatively neglected.[1] We have, for instance, no exhaustive survey of English printers, publishers, readers, and the books they sold or read comparable to H. J. Martin's splendid *Livre Pouvoirs et Société à Paris au XVIIe Siècle* (Geneva, 1969).[2] Rather, we have a series of mainly unrelated studies on particular aspects of the overall problem. Some scholars, like Wright or Bennet, have sought to depict the English reader and his tastes by concentrating almost exclusively on the content of extant printed works.[3] Needless to say, this approach is pitted with difficulties. It leads too often to an overconcern with literary quality and fails to distinguish the stylistically mediocre best seller from the multitudes of remaindered copies. It fails, perhaps, to differentiate enough between London and provincial taste. Most serious of all, it cannot take into sufficient account those apparently widely sold secular works such as ballads or almanacs of which only a few copies survive.[4] Work on the book trade itself has generally been confined to an analysis of the mechanics, personalities, scandals, and petty bickering of the London printing industry.[5] As far as the provincial trade is concerned, it is probably true to say that with a few exceptions—the work on the Oxford and Cambridge stationers being the most notable—we probably know less about the ordinary day-to-day distribution of books than we do about the underground trade in prohibited works of Puritan or Catholic extremists.[6]

Turning from book production to consumption we have a number of analyses of individual libraries—usually those of political grandees like the "wizard" earl of Northumberland, Sir Walter Raleigh, or the parliamentary earl of Essex.[7] How-

Earlier versions of this paper were read at the Davis Center, Princeton, in November 1972 and at the New England Conference for British Studies, Dartmouth, in May 1973. I am very grateful to those present for their comments and criticisms.

ever, one of the few historians to get anywhere near that large mass of English folk who actually bought books in this period has been S. R. Jayne. His *Library Catalogues of the English Renaissance* (Berkeley, 1956) provides a checklist of 848 libraries owned in England during the period 1500–1640, often using as a source inventories of personal wealth. Though an important pioneering work, it is limited in value by Jayne's decision to list only libraries containing fifteen or more separate titles and to rely for most of his primary material on lists from the scholastic communities of Oxford and Cambridge. The main purpose of this paper will be to repeat Jayne's question—Who owned books?—but to follow a broader approach, widening his criteria to include all references to books and applying them to a sample of inventories of personal wealth for three somewhat more typical provincial communities—the towns of Canterbury, Faversham, and Maidstone in the county of Kent—over the period c. 1560 to 1640.[8]

However, before we look at the private ownership of books we must consider briefly what other facilities for reading existed in the years up to 1640. By the 1570s the church hierarchy had in some measure succeeded in establishing in every parish church a small collection of books: the Bible, the common prayer book, the *Paraphrase* of Erasmus, and Foxe's *Acts and Monuments* (in greater churches) were all supposedly available for parochial consultation. In practice few English churches ever owned all at any one time, and most had great difficulty in keeping hold of what they did have: incumbents and wealthier parishioners purloined them, or else they fell victim—like parish registers—to that endemic disinterest in the welfare of church fabric and property which characterized the first phase of English Protestantism. Sometimes a parson, local landowner, or officer of the church court would donate a volume or more. About 1600 Thomas Ayhurst, a Maidstone merchant, declared in his will: "I do give so much money as will buy Mr Calvin's *Institutions* in English of the fairest and plainest letter, together with a chain to be fastened to a desk at the lower end of the parish church of Maidstone for the better instruction of the poor and simple there." But in general the parish library really flourished only from the last part of the seventeenth century.[9] A few of the greater urban communities like Bristol, Norwich, and Gloucester did found libraries under civic auspices; but they were never very successful, nor did the idea catch on. No Kentish town had a civic library before 1640, though it is possible that favored townsfolk had access to the fairly extensive school libraries which we find at Faversham, Sandwich, and Tonbridge. At Tonbridge by 1640 the visiting reader might have found copies of Camden's *Britannia*, Selden's *Titles of Honor*, Speed's *History*, Robert Ward's *Animadversions of Warre*, Foxe, and works by that prolific Puritan William Perkins.[10]

Nonetheless, in most cases the adult Kentishman needed to own a book before he could read it. Contrary to Jayne's suggestion that the nonacademic laity had only small collections before 1590, there is considerable evidence that a number of the wealthier members of the county community in Kent owned quite extensive libraries. The civil lawyer (and commissary for Canterbury diocese) Christopher

Nevinson, who lived at Adisham, had over 1,200 volumes by his death in 1551—among them, a massive section on canon law, many histories and maps (41 items), patristic and classical texts, as well as a large number of the more important reformist works of Bucer, Bullinger, Calvin, Luther, Martyr, and Melanchthon. Another lawyer, Thomas Rolfe of Canterbury, had a collection which merited its own librarian in 1562; while William Lambarde, the legal historian, was a noted Kentish bibliophile.[11] Kentish clergy and schoolmasters were also often interested in book acquisition on a large scale. John Greshop, master of the grammar school at Canterbury who died in 1580, left over 350 volumes, a veritable cornucopia of theological, controversial, moralistic, and pedagogic works. Nor was incipient bibliomania confined to professional men. The aristocratic Cobham and Sidney families both had large accumulations of books by the end of the sixteenth century. In the 1620s and 1630s Robert Sidney, second earl of Leicester, acquired countless volumes, ranging from works on martial discipline, St Augustine's *Confessions,* Montaigne's *Essayes,* and Leonard Digges's *Pantometria* to Raleigh's *History of the World,* Bacon's *De Dignitate et de Augmentis Scientarum,* royal manifestos, and the most recent coranto or latest newssheet; at his elbow were the current booksellers' catalogues. Lower down the social ladder, Sir Edward Dering's accounts for the early 1620s reveal an almost frenetic level of purchases. On 11 July 1623, for instance, he bought 41 books at a cost of almost £4; and during the whole of that year he purchased nearly 200 volumes, including pamphlets by the vitriolic Thomas Scott, plays by Shakespeare and Jonson, and Machiavelli's *Il Principe.* Not all Kentish gentlemen were quite so spendthrift, of course, but by 1640 our evidence would suggest that almost every county landowner of note had several shelves of books at home.[12]

For lesser folk, outside the landed and professional ranks of society, our evidence for book ownership is inevitably less complete. A little piercing light is shed by the evidence of witnesses in law suits. We hear of Elizabeth Baker, the wife of an Otham yeoman, who one night in 1607 was, according to her maid, "at her book reading as she uses many times to do before she goes to bed." In another case the witness tells how a Faversham man, Bartholomew Dann, assaulted his wife and "when she had been reading and leaving her book in some place . . . he would catch the book out of her hands and tear it in pieces or otherwise fling it away."[13] However, the only material presenting a tolerably rounded picture of book ownership among ordinary folk in this period is to be found in the inventories of personal goods which were taken after death by appraisers (usually friends or neighbors) and which had to be registered in the appropriate church court by the executor or administrator before probate was granted. In the period from the early 1560s until 1640 there are for Canterbury diocese approximately 130 volumes (or boxes), each containing from 200 to 250 inventories.[14] For the purpose of this survey we have taken as our sample all those complete inventories which survive for the inhabitants (male and female) of three towns: Canterbury, the leading urban center in East Kent with 5,000–6,000 inhabitants; Faversham, a prosperous port on the North Kent coast with strong metropolitan ties and a population nearing 2,000; and Maidstone, a growing social, industrial, and marketing center in the middle of the county with a population size similar to Faversham.

The total number of inventories in our sample is 2,771. Of these, 1,694 belong to Canterbury inhabitants (1,314 townsmen, the rest women), 643 to Faversham folk (529 male), and 434 to Maidstone folk (357 male). A few further points need to be made about this sample. In the first place, it obviously underrepresents women in these communities, mostly because a widower could claim his late spouse's property as his own from marriage. Secondly, the low number of Maidstone inventories is mainly due to the fact that for some unknown reason they do not survive for the 1570s and 1580s. Finally and most important, our sample is socially selective. It not only fails to include a hundred or so citizens whose wills were proven in the Prerogative Court at Lambeth Palace (and whose inventories may or may not survive in sacks at the Public Record Office) but also those many ordinary townsfolk (probably the majority) who did not make a will and for whom no inventory was taken unless their estate was contested. On the other hand, many of the latter—including servants, day laborers, and the like—often had no property to speak of anyway. In all we have perhaps a 30 percent sample of the adult citizens dying in these towns from about 1560 to 1640; but for those leaving any significant amount of property the coverage is probably nearer 75 percent.

Having established the limitations of our sample, we should also note that the inclusion of a book in the potpourri of personal possessions does not necessarily mean that it was read. A book might be inherited by someone unable to read, pushed to one side, and forgotten. Not infrequently, books are found listed among the bric-a-brac at the end of an inventory or referred to as old and tattered (though this might equally well be a comment on their overuse). But while our sample probably includes volumes which were never read or even remembered by their owners, there is a crude compensating factor: that is, our sample almost certainly underregisters the incidence of books whose owners read them regularly. There are three reasons for this underregistration: the negligence of the appraisers (although this was probably uncommon, since church courts and kinsfolk were usually quite vigilant about omissions); the practice by which the dying man or woman distributed a few close possessions to spouse or children from the deathbed; and, most serious, the tendency of the appraisers to lump books together in an omnibus category such as "all the goods in the study." Overall, then, we probably have a fairly accurate picture of book owners in our three urban communities.

What do the inventories tell us of the progress of book ownership before 1640? Our evidence for townsmen is the most detailed. Looking at Table 4.1 we find that in the 1560s fewer than one in ten of the Canterbury inventories referred to a book; the comparable figures were somewhat higher at both Faversham and Maidstone, but the samples in both cases were small. By the 1580s Canterbury book ownership had risen so steeply that well over one in four of the inventories referred to a book, and the next decade saw a further rise, with over a third listing a volume or more. Over the next two decades the rate of increase slackened off, but the direction

TABLE 4.1
Incidence of Book Ownership among Male Townsmen in Kent
(Percentage of Decennial Sample)

	1560s	1570s	1580s	1590s	1600s	1610s	1620s	1630s
Canterbury	8	21	29	34	33	39	45	46
	(36)	(58)	(87)	(151)	(165)	(275)	(251)	(291)
Faversham	15	21	17	32	41	33	40	49
	(20)	(48)	(54)	(60)	(64)	(77)	(95)	(111)
Maidstone	21			24	32	37	46	44
	(19)	—	—	(21)	(50)	(71)	(93)	(103)

Note: Numbers in parentheses indicate sample size.

remained upward. At Faversham the breakthrough in male book ownership is revealed in the inventories recorded for the 1590s: in that decade over 30 percent of those dying owned a book. Our Elizabethan figures for Maidstone are, as we said, incomplete, but by the first decade of the seventeenth century book ownership there was probably only slightly behind that in other centers. Finally, the last two decades of the prerevolutionary period saw book ownership rise above the 40 percent level in all three towns.

Because our female sample is so much smaller, a detailed analysis of book ownership on a similar decennial basis is impractical. However, by dividing the period we have chosen in half, we can see some degree of movement. Before 1600 a sample of 76 female inventories for Canterbury showed a 14 percent book ownership level; after 1600 the comparable rate was 29 percent, in a sample of 304. Maidstone's rate of increase was similar, rising from about 14 percent before 1600 to 27 percent afterwards. It would be unrealistic to put too much stress on these figures. It is disconcerting to find that at Faversham the level of book ownership as indicated by female inventories remained static at 21 percent throughout the whole of our period. Nonetheless, we would probably not be too far wrong if we said that whereas ownership of books among men in the early seventeenth century reached about 40 percent, among women the overall level was nearer 25 percent.

Though these overall figures are interesting they have one drawback: they conceal fluctuations (albeit fairly small ones) in the social composition of our sample over eighty years. To overcome this problem and, at the same time, shed further light on who owned books, we must look at the incidence of book ownership by relating it, first, to a breakdown of the structure of inventorial wealth and, second, to a set of occupational groupings (Tables 4.2–4.4).

When the incidence of books is correlated with inventorial wealth, certain points are fairly clear. Among townsmen with goods worth no more than £24, the chances of owning a book, while improving over the period as a whole, remained low, even just before 1640. At Canterbury and Faversham fewer than a quarter of the male inhabitants in that category owned a book; Maidstone had the highest figure, with 37 percent owning books, but this was still below the average of 44 percent for the

TABLE 4.2
Book Ownership among Kentish Townsmen according to Categories of Inventorial Wealth
(Percentage of Sample for Each Category)

Inventorial wealth in £	Canterbury			Faversham			Maidstone		
	1560 –89	1590 –1619	1620 –40	1560 –89	1590 –1619	1620 –40	1560 –89	1590 –1619	1620 –40
Up to 24	16	19	23	2	14	23	—	19	37
25–39	15	40	45	6	63	38	—	24	26
40–59	40	46	53	60	50	56	—	44	29
60–79	—	49	56	28	36	78*	—	33*	50
80–99	11*	50	50	43*	38*	50	—	50	50*
100–149	19	65	64	8	60	56*	—	30	62
150–249	31	54	57	38*	57	81	—	36	56
250–499	50*	57	69	38*	56*	59	—	53	61
500–999	86*	78	61	33*	36	86*	—	44*	92
1,000 and above	—	100*	83	—	40*	60*	—	100*	50*

*Sample smaller than 10.

whole town. Conversely, at the other economic extreme, among people worth £500 or more in personal property, book ownership was already at quite a high level in the first part of our period, and there was no striking advance over the rest of the era. On the whole, it seems likely that the most important growth of book ownership occurred among the middling economic categories. Having said this, however, we must admit that there was no precise or straightforward relationship between wealth and book ownership among townsmen. The same was also true for women.

As we can see from Table 4.3, once again there are considerable ambiguities in the correlation of wealth and the incidence of books. Yet, some broad outline is visible. Among poorer women it was still very much the exception to have a book

TABLE 4.3
Book Ownership among Kentish Townswomen
according to Categories of Inventorial Wealth
(Percentage of Sample for All Three Towns)

Inventorial wealth in £	c. 1560–1600	1601–1640
Up to 24	5	14
25–39	20	36
40–59	33*	28
60–79	43*	33
80–99	25*	46
100–149	40*	42
150–249	50*	47
250–499	100*	52
500–999	100*	30
1,000 and above	—	80*

*Sample smaller than 10.

in one's possession in the seventeenth century; among the wealthy it had become the norm; and for those in the middle economic range (the wives, widows, and daughters of respectable tradesmen and craft-workers) it was more and more usual—but it was still true only of a minority. At the same time, it is dangerous to talk of female book ownership in isolation: we must not forget that quite a few married women enjoyed access to their husbands' collections.

Earlier, we suggested that professional folk, lawyers, schoolmasters, and clergy possessed some of the most extensive libraries in prerevolutionary Kent. How far does our material shed light on the variations in book ownership among major occupational groupings?[15] The answer is to some extent provided by Table 4.4. As we might have expected, the professionals came out best with the highest level of book ownership throughout the period under discussion: at no time in any of the towns did it fall below 72 percent. Next came gentlemen: in the twenty-odd years before the summoning of the Long Parliament, two out of every three gentlemen dying in our towns were known to own a book of some kind; at Faversham and Canterbury the ratio was as high as three out of four. In the important textile centers of Canterbury and Maidstone those working in the silk and clothmaking crafts also tended to be above average in the ownership of books. Other groups with an above-average rate of ownership included those engaged in the lucrative distributive trades. In contrast, book ownership was below average among the food and drink trades (with their large contingent of poor, unlicensed victuallers), the small

TABLE 4.4

Book Ownership among Kentish Townsmen according to Occupational Groupings
(Percentage of Each Grouping Sample)

	Canterbury			Faversham			Maidstone		
	1560 –89	1590 –1619	1620 –40	1560 –89	1590 –1619	1620 –40	1560 –89	1590 –1619	1620 –40
Gentry	38*	77	73	50*	45	75	—	56	64
Professional	73	80	90	—	100*	100*	—	100*	83*
Clothing trades	31	41	45	13*	60	100*	—	31	67*
Leather trades	19	35	39	29*	17	75*	—	29*	9
Food and drink	11	40	31	21	42	56	—	50	43
Textile industry	30	40	54*	0*	57	0*	—	33	61
Household goods	33*	42	43	—	100*	0*	—	0*	57*
Distributive	33*	60	60	25*	67*	67*	—	55	50
Building trades	22*	21	36	9	17*	40*	—	36	29*
Rural: yeoman	38*	41	31	18*	29	37	—	33*	48*
Rural: husbandman	0*	0	0*	0*	0*	0*	—	0*	33*
Rural: laborer	0*	0*	0*	0*	—	0*	—	0*	—
Rural: misc.	—	33*	0*	0*	0*	33*	—	50*	0*
Service industries	14	23	24	14*	33	13*	—	25*	47
Servants	0*	0*	33*	0*	0*	0*	—	—	—
Misc.	0*	24	25	20	36	28	—	0	—
Unspecified	14	19	31	16	18	27	—	19	27

*Sample smaller than 10.

building crafts (except at Faversham), and occupations with a rural bent (yeomen, husbandmen, laborers, and the miscellany of other barely skilled workers).

Inventories can tell us who owned books, but they are less helpful in indicating what kind of books these were. In only about a quarter of our sample are books specified in any detail, and even then the listing is often only partial, with just one or two books mentioned by title and the remainder lumped together as "the other books" or "five more small books." There are, of course, a number of apparently complete lists. A servant to a Canterbury glover, John Brooke, who left goods worth just about £4 in 1607 had in his possession a small Bible, two catechisms, *The Governance of Virtue,* and *A Godlie Garden* (both religio-moralistic tracts): in all they were priced at three shillings and fourpence. When Alice Cornelius, a respectable Canterbury widow, died in 1579, she owned a Bible, Erasmus's *Paraphrase,* the New Testament, a service book, and a volume of Augustine's *Meditations.* In 1630, after retiring from gentle life to become a Canterbury almsman, Thomas Norton bequeathed a psalmbook, *The Principles of Religion,* a book on the nature of God, and *A Posie of Godlie Prayers.* [16]

On the other hand, to draw any meaningful conclusions from our library lists we must categorize them with some care. The first column in Table 4.5 includes those where ownership was limited to one specified volume; the second includes those which listed several books, all specified; the third, where several books were owned but only one itemized; and the fourth, where several books were owned and more than one, but not all, were itemized. For this survey we have brought together evidence from all three towns but excluded women because of the small female

TABLE 4.5
References to Book Titles in Inventories of Kentish Townsmen
(Percentage of Sample)

	Extent of ownership[a]			
	I	II	III	IV
Bible	82	38	92	42
Testament	4	9	1	12
Service Book	5	12	2	9
Psalter	2	11	0	7
Foxe's *Acts & Monuments*	0	6	1	10
Prayerbooks	1	5	0	2
Law Books	2	3	1	3
History books (including chronicles)	1	3	1	3
Other religious works	2	9	1	7
Other secular works	1	4	1	5
Sample of references	141	146	180	165

Note: This table excludes the book lists of professional men (lawyers, schoolteachers, etc.).

[a]The categories indicated by roman numerals are explained in the text.

sample. What does our picture show? In all four categories we can see that the most frequently owned book was the Bible. Among those townsmen who owned only one book, in eight cases out of ten that volume was the Holy Scripture; while for those citizens who possessed several specified books, the Bible comprised nearly 40 percent of their total specified holdings. The next most popular items were the service book, the psalmbook, and the Testament, with chronicles, law books, and other secular works many furlongs behind. Among those townsmen who specified only part of their library, theological works were again clearly predominant. The admittedly less complete information we have about female libraries would suggest a similar picture.

Two things are striking about these library lists. The first is the ubiquity of the Bible: even among those people (often poorer folk) who owned only one work, the volume they chose was the Bible, often a fairly expensive item. The second is the apparent absence of those secular works like occupation books, historics, ballads, and almanacs which historians working mainly from the production end of the book trade have seen as the most striking new phenomenon of the Elizabethan period. It may be that these secular works lie hidden among the unspecified items of our partial library lists—though their absence is equally striking from those lists which appear to be complete. It may be that they were omitted by the appraisers as items of little value. It may be that because the purchasers of these secular works never bothered to bind them, they just fell to pieces very quickly. It may be that their owners regarded them as ephemera, to be flipped through and then discarded. Whatever the reason, their absence is puzzling and should make us a little more cautious of accepting orthodox assertions that these secular works were important, widely influential items in the cultural mainstream of prerevolutionary England.

If we turn now from readers' preferences to location—where books were usually kept—our picture is again far from complete, mainly because appraisers frequently listed a person's books at the end of the inventory without reference to room. To some extent, this doubtless reflected a book's mobility about the home. On the other hand, there is considerable evidence that important books such as the Bible were a permanent fixture of one room, resting on a special lectern or purpose-built shelves. As Table 4.6 indicates, throughout our period the hall, the main reception room in the house, was the most preferred resting place for a family's book or books. At the same time, the post-1600 evidence would suggest that an increasing number of owners were less concerned with this kind of public display and kept their books by them in their bedchamber. Though it is true that some books may have migrated to the bedchamber as a consequence of their owner's last illness, it seems likely that a growing number of people, like the Otham woman whom we mentioned earlier, had a volume or so by their bed to read long before their final hour. Again, the growing number of books lodged in closets (often by the bedchamber) would suggest the same increasing sense that a book was the private concern of the reader alone. It is more difficult to know whether the increased number of books which we find in the kitchen is an expression of the housewife's desire to have a book by her as she worked or a result of the growing

TABLE 4.6
Distribution of Books About the House, Kent
(Percentage of Period Sample)

	c.1560–1600	1601–1640
Hall	48	39
Study	20	14
Parlor	16	12
Bedchamber	9	18
Kitchen	5	9
Shop	2	1
Closet	0	5
Elsewhere	0	2
Sample	62	296

Note: The overall sample includes male and female inventories for all three towns.

tendency for the master of the house to read prayers for the servants outside the hall.

Having sought to establish the dimensions and nature of the rise in book ownership in this period, we shall now try to answer that crucial question, What caused the increase? One factor, no doubt, was economic. As we saw, those citizens who belonged to higher economic groupings or to prosperous trades were more likely to own a book than those at the other end of the economic ladder. The fact that books cost money (as new, roughly a halfpenny a folio)[17] was only one fairly small element in the equation which we shall discuss in more detail shortly. It is tempting to see book ownership as an aspect of the rising level of conspicuous consumption among respectable folk in our towns. It may have become just as fashionable to own a book and put it on a hall lectern as it was to extend one's parlor, buy maps for its walls, or fill it with expensive furniture. There was of course an important difference, one which probably helps to explain the incomplete correlation between higher economic groups and book ownership. Unlike the acquisition of a new parlor or the purchase of maps, the possession of a book required a facility to read if the owner was to maximize its social value.

Book ownership, then, has to be seen as part of the general advance in literacy. Other evidence for literacy levels is often difficult to evaluate, but an analysis of the signatures and marks made by witnesses in ecclesiastical court litigation does provide some rough and ready index of the most basic writing skill. For this survey we have used a sample of 533 people from our three towns who gave evidence in the Canterbury diocesan courts in the years 1628–40;[18] after making their statement the deponents were required to subscribe it with a mark or signature. Obviously, with such a small sample our conclusions must be tentative, but Table 4.7 would suggest that the level of subscriptional literacy among males in the three towns was fairly constant, running at about four-fifths of all the witnesses. For women, the only reliable source is the Canterbury figure, but from this we can see

TABLE 4.7
Ability to Make a Signature, Kent, 1628–40
(Percentage of Group Sample)

	Place of residency		
	Canterbury	Faversham	Maidstone
Male	79 (280)	89 (67)	86 (42)
Female	18 (116)	11 (18)	50 (10)

Note: Numbers in parentheses indicate sample size.

that one in five of the female witnesses could sign their names. As we should expect, however, the value of these global literacy figures is limited by the biased social distribution of the sample. In order to remedy this we have categorized the male literacy sample according to the occupational groupings used earlier (Table 4.8). Any direct comparison between subscriptional literacy and book ownership by occupational groupings is, of course, out of the question. It seems likely that more people could read than sign their names, but the ratio is uncertain, although R. Schofield has suggested one of 3:2.[19] Nonetheless, there is some correlation, comparing Table 4.4 (the columns for 1620–40) and Table 4.8, between high or low levels of literacy and book ownership. Thus, the frequent incidence of book ownership among gentlemen and the professional classes was matched by 100

TABLE 4.8
Analysis of Male Subscriptional Literacy in Kent
by Occupational Groupings

	Deponents from all three towns		Deponents from Canterbury only	
	No.	% making signature	No.	% making signature
Gentry	90	100	59	100
Professional (excluding clergy)	19	100	17	100
Clothing trades	45	89	34	91
Leather trades	11	64	8	63
Food and drink	47	83	34	82
Textile industry	25	44	17	47
Household goods	10	40	7	36
Distributive	22	100	14	100
Building trades	23	70	15	67
Rural: yeoman	32	84	26	85
Rural: husbandman	12	25	8	0
Rural: laborer	8	0	8	0
Rural: misc.	5	60	4	50
Service industries	8	50	3	33
Servants	19	84	19	84
Misc.	6	67	1	100
Unspecified	7	71	6	67

percent subscriptional literacy rates. Conversely, husbandmen and rural laborers not only had a minimal taste for book ownership but were in almost all cases illiterate. Even more interesting, however, are the discrepancies. Why were yeomen apparently quite literate (84 percent) but yet inactive book buyers (about 34 percent). Was it perhaps because while the growth of internal trade and a cash crop economy made simple literacy (the ability to check a pro forma bond or sign a receipt) a farming necessity, the yeoman was still concerned to preserve his nationwide reputation as a plain, honest country man without all the educational or social pretensions which owning a book implied? Again, why the converse discrepancy between literacy and book ownership levels among textile workers? Here, the answer may be more straightforward and relate to the sharp economic polarization of the industry: whereas both prosperous master and poor artisan probably appear in our literacy figures (and balance each other off), only the masters were wealthy enough to leave an estate and thus dominate our inventorial sample. Subscriptional literacy figures are clearly interesting but taken in isolation may fail to reveal all the bumps in the educational boardwalk.

What cannot be denied is that the spread of literary skills, of which the growth of subscriptional literacy and book ownership were manifestations, owed a great deal to the expansion of educational facilities. All three of our towns had grammar schools in this period: Canterbury from 1541, Maidstone from 1549, and Faversham from 1576. But these were much less important in promoting educational change than the ubiquitous petty or dames' schools about which, at least in the urban context, we know only too little. A major problem is caused by the fact that while licenses for these schools survive in considerable numbers, perhaps half the petty schools functioning in prerevolutionary Kent were unlicensed.[20] Taking the licensed schools and as many of the unlicensed ones as we can find from church court presentments, it is possible to say that Canterbury (population c. 6,000) had at least twenty-five such schools in operation at one time or another from the mid-1570s until 1600: in the next four decades thirty-eight teachers were known to have kept school in the city—all outside the grammar school. Faversham, with a population probably less than a third of Canterbury's, had at least six petty school teachers before 1600 and twice that number in the next forty years. Maidstone, with a rising population of about 2,000, had six teachers before 1600; after 1600 this jumped dramatically to twenty-eight. Such schools might often have been short-lived as teachers moved on to better jobs or were ousted by the authorities, but it seems likely, for instance, that there were about ten petty schools functioning at any one time in early Stuart Canterbury. Their first priority was to teach children reading skills.

How was this growing educational level and potential demand for books converted into the rising graph of book ownership? First, there was the limited response of public reading facilities. Second, and more important, there was the massive expansion in book production and sales. The rise of the English printing industry is well documented and need not concern us here. What does require more discussion is how people purchased their copies, since with the general suppression of the provincial presses in 1557, virtually all legitimate printing was executed in London. Considerable evidence exists that some wealthier folk, gentry, lawyers, merchants, went up to St. Paul's churchyard for their books, while others had friends send copies down. In 1638, for instance, Sir Thomas Peyton wrote from Chelsea to Henry Oxenden, a modest landowner who lived outside Canterbury: "I have sent you such new books as are of the rarest perusal."[21] But ordinary townsfolk had to make do with local supplies. In the first part of our period the most important source was the London bookseller (or his factor), who brought wares down to town fairs. If the most famous fairs for booksellers were Stourbridge Fair just outside Cambridge and the Oxford Fair, London booksellers also certainly toured small provincial fairs. In 1583 the Stationers' Company accused John Wolfe and his associates of pirating copyright works and then running "up or down to all the fairs and markets through a great part of the realm" to sell them. Canterbury Fair, we know, was visited by metropolitan booksellers in Elizabeth's reign. But by the 1570s anyway, a growing number of provincial towns also had their own resident booksellers.[22] Unfortunately, we know little about the first two Canterbury stationers, John Gye and Clement Bassock;[23] but there is much more evidence about Joseph Bulkley, who received his freedom in 1590. Bulkley quickly built up a thriving trade selling books to Christchurch Cathedral, citizens, and country folk. His stock probably came down by boat from London to the port of Faversham and was then carted overland to the city. Within a decade Bulkley was successful enough to lease a city rectory and build himself a new town house: he even became a common councillor. In the 1620s he commissioned the London publication of at least one book, a recent sermon, which was to be sold at his shop in Canterbury. At least two of his sons joined the London printing industry, one of them, Stephen Bulkley, becoming a royalist printer at York in the early 1640s.[24]

Demand for books in Canterbury was so brisk by 1600 that there was plenty of room for competition. Esdras Johnson combined schoolteaching and bookselling in St. Andrew's parish in the 1590s; George White, who died in 1612, had a large stock of theological works, a number of books on heraldry and history, three medical volumes, and sixty small pamphlets (probably a mixture of sermons, almanacs, and ballads). Nearer 1640 Nicholas Johnson sold "small books as psalters, testaments, primers, ABCs" not only in the city but in neighboring towns and markets as well.[25] Selling basic texts for children (and also probably for adults) had become profitable enough for ordinary town retailers to keep a stock of them. Stephen Wissenden, a Canterbury mercer, had one and a half dozen primers (at 1s. 8d. a dozen) and a dozen hornbooks among his shop wares in 1597.[26] Forty years later Star Chamber decreed that "no haberdasher of small wares, ironmonger, chandler, shop-keeper" could sell books unless previously apprenticed to a London stationer—almost certainly to no avail. Book ownership was clearly a major beneficiary of the enormous growth of English internal trade in this period.[27]

Many books, needless to say, were not purchased new. There was an active market in secondhand books in which gentry, clergy, and ordinary folk participated. The comparative frequency of references to book thefts by 1600 would suggest that demand was to some extent met by stolen volumes. It seems likely that the existence of this secondhand market adds a new dimension to the problem of book prices. From the references we have in account books, prices of new books appear to have remained fairly high throughout our period. On the other hand, our inventories show that the price of a used book might vary widely according to condition. A tattered Bible coming onto the market after the owner's death (as many probably did) could well be picked up for a shilling or less by a poorer reader.[28]

So far we have suggested that the expansion of book ownership in the period 1560–1640 was fueled by a combination of rising living standards among respectable citizens and an associated dissemination of basic literary skills through the development of primary education, together with an improved sales network for books. But these points do not, it seems to me, add up to the complete answer. The dominant theological flavor of the reading matter for which evidence has survived would suggest a priori grounds for thinking that a man's religious attitude was another possible determinant. It is no coincidence, perhaps, that all three of our towns experienced something of a Puritan awakening in Elizabeth's reign which especially affected the merchantry and other well-established groups. Preachers and lecturers constantly enjoined the careful reading of the Bible and urged that the master of the house should declare extracts to his assembled household, family, and servants. In the early seventeenth century strict ethical Puritanism of this kind was increasingly outpaced in respectable urban life. Instead, from the 1610s there was a major growth of quasi-separatism, especially among inhabitants at the lower end of the social ladder in Canterbury and also at Maidstone. Conventicles which we know about invariably stressed the exhaustive examination of the Scriptures, not only at the weekly meeting but every day at home. From our Canterbury evidence it would seem that quite a few members of that narrow book-owning minority among poorer folk had dissenting contacts. It may be that in some cases the acquisition and avid perusal of the Scriptures predated and actually prompted their entry into a conventicling group, but we have no direct evidence of this. What does seem certain is that a personal copy of the Bible had become an essential spiritual asset not only for the prosperous godly but for poorer zealous folk as well: usually, it was the only book they owned.[29]

This chapter has concentrated for the most part on book ownership in towns. Evidence for the non-upper-class sectors of rural society is much less easy to uncover. Samples are usually too small for any successful repetition of our inventorial analysis for a single community, while grouping parishes together causes more problems than it solves. The few signs that we do have, however, would suggest that the Kentish countryside saw a somewhat disparate distribution of book ownership. In clothing areas such as the Weald, in the great cereal lands east of Canterbury, or in parishes with close market ties to larger urban centers, the level of ownership was probably quite high, with the same complex of generating factors more or less applicable, though at a lower pitch. On the other hand, in

Romney Marsh, the forested down lands west of Canterbury, and the marshland zone of North Kent none of these factors was operative—poverty was rife, schooling poor, conservatism overwhelming.[30]

What about other areas of England? Our information is once again sparse, but we can make a few interesting comparisons. In a group of Worcester wills and inventories A. Dyer found that references to books rose, overall, from about 4 percent in the 1550–89 period to 16 percent in the 1590s. If we make some allowance for the low level of ownership among the female section of his sample, we can guess that book-ownership among Worcester townsmen in the 1590s was running at about 23 percent, roughly two thirds of the level in our Kentish towns. Turning to 259 inventories, mostly for countryfolk, surviving for Oxfordshire in the period 1550–90, we find only three references to books—all belonging to townspeople. The failure of the high concentration of book ownership and book-sellers in the university to influence and infiltrate the adjoining countryside is striking. Two factors may have been important: first, the growth of internal trade affected the Midlands more slowly than the South East; second, Oxfordshire as a whole was far behind Kent in casting off religious conservatism. A somewhat later set of Bedfordshire inventories, again mainly rural, provide more data. In a sample of 166 for the years c. 1617–19, 22 (or just over 13 percent) had books, mostly Bibles. If the picture is obviously an improvement over the previous one, book ownership was clearly way behind its level in the Kentish towns. Here the rural bias of the Bedfordshire sample seems decisive; book ownership among the small group of town dwellers included was markedly higher than the average for the whole sample. Our final evidence relates to rural parishes in mid-Essex, mostly for the period after the Restoration, and tends to confirm the Bedfordshire story. Of 163 inventories for the period 1633–90 only 23 (14 percent) included a reference to a book; almost all belonged to prosperous people.[31]

To sum up, we can say that the three towns examined here saw a major growth in book ownership in the period 1560–1640, affecting not only prosperous *potentiores* but also in some measure the lower ranks of respectable society as well. While this expansion was part of the general rise of living standards and educational proficiency, it also had a dominant religious content and theological motif. Thus, if the level of book ownership was much higher in provincial towns than in the countryside, there is little positive evidence that the citizenry were sharing in that boisterous, secular, middle-class culture which some historians would have us believe existed in and after the reign of Elizabeth.

NOTES

1. The two standard texts on educational change in this period, J. Simon, *Education and Society in Tudor England* (Cambridge: Cambridge University Press, 1966), and K. Charlton, *Education in Renaissance England* (Toronto: University of Toronto Press, 1965), have only brief references to the role and impact of the book.

2. For more continental work on books and book ownership see A. Labarre, *Le Livre dans la Vie Amiénoise du Seizième* (Louvain: Nauwelaerts, 1971), a work with an excellent bibliog-

raphy; and also C. Lannette-Claverie, "La Libraire francaise en 1700," *Revue Francaise d'Histoire du Livre* 2 (1972): 3–43.

3. L. B. Wright, *Middle Class Culture in Elizabethan England* (Chapel Hill: University of North Carolina Press, 1935); H. S. Bennet, *English Books and Readers*, vol. 1, *1475–1557*, vol. 2, *1558–1603*, vol. 3, *1603–1640* (Cambridge: Cambridge University Press, 1952–70).

4. E. F. Bosanquet, *English Printed Almanacks and Prognostications* (London: The Bibliographical Society, 1917). For an interesting paper on the vagaries of book survival, see O. M. Willard, "The Survival of English Books Printed before 1640: A Theory and Some Illustrations," *The Library*, 4th ser. 23 (1943): 171–90.

5. For example, E. G. Duff, *A Century of the English Book Trade . . . 1457 to 1557* (London: The Bibliographical Society, 1905); W. W. Greg and E. Boswell, eds., *Records of the Court of the Stationers' Company* (London: The Bibliographical Society, 1930); L. Rostenberg, *Literary, Political, Scientific, Religious and Legal Publishing and Bookselling in England, 1551–1700* (New York: Franklin, 1965), vol. 1; C. Blagden, "The English Stock of the Stationers' Company in the Time of the Stuarts," *The Library*, 5th ser. 12 (1957): 167–86.

6. R. Jahn, "Letters and Booklists of Thomas Chard (or Chare) of London, 1583–84," *The Library*, 4th ser. 4 (1924): 219ff.; D. Paige, "An Additional Letter and Booklist of Thomas Chard, Stationer of London," ibid. 21 (1941): 32ff.; G. J. Gray, *The Earlier Cambridge Stationers and Bookbinders and the First Cambridge Printer* (Oxford: Oxford Bibliographical Society, 1904), pp. 25ff.; S. Gibson, ed., *Abstracts from the Wills and Testamentary Documents of Binders, Printers, and Stationers of Oxford from 1493 to 1638* (London: The Bibliographical Society, 1907). For other provincial booksellers see H. R. Plomer, "More Petitions to Archbishop Laud," *The Library*, 3rd ser. 10 (1919): 135ff.; idem, "Some Elizabethan Book Sales," ibid. 7 (1916): 318ff. The most recent account of the Puritan and Catholic presses is by L. Rostenberg, *The Minority Press and the English Crown* (Nieuwkoop: De Graaf, 1971).

7. G. R. Batho, "The Library of the 'Wizard' Earl: Henry Percy, 9th Earl of Northumberland (1564–1632)," *The Library*, 5th ser. 15 (1960): 246–61; W. Oakeshott, "Sir Walter Ralegh's Library," ibid. 23 (1968): 285–327; V. F. Snow, "The Lord General's Library, 1646," ibid. 21 (1966): 115–23. F. Wormald and C. E. Wright, *The English Library before 1700* (London: Athlone Press, 1958), are mainly concerned with institutional libraries.

8. For a more general discussion of educational change in Kent during this period, see P. Clark, *The Rise of a Provincial Community: Religion, Politics, and Society in Kent, 1500–1640* (Hassocks: Harvester, 1976), chap. 6.

9. Canterbury Cathedral Library (CCL), X.9.11, fol. 12v; X.9.14, fol. 24; Kent Archives Office (KAO), PRC 39/33, fol. 297, 328-v; CCL, Z.3.15, fol. 99v. For an exceptionally good parochial library see that of St. Mary Bredman, Canterbury, listed in CCL, U3/2/5. *The Parochial Libraries of the Church of England* (London: The Faith Press, 1959), pp. 64ff.

10. P. Clark and P. Slack, eds., *Crisis and Order in English Towns, 1500–1700* (Toronto: University of Toronto Press, 1972), p. 29. KAO, Fa/FAc 44, 52, 63; Sa/QEm 1, fols. 53v–54; Tonbridge School, School Inventories. I am most grateful to the Librarian of Tonbridge School for helping me to see these documents.

11. S. R. Jayne, *Library Catalogues of the English Renaissance* (Berkeley: University of California Press, 1956), p. 14; Lambeth Palace Library, Muniment Book Fl, fols. 65v–81v et passim; CCL, X.2.24, fol. 78; *Hodgson's Sale Catalogue of Lambarde MSS and Books, July 19, 1924*.

12. As early as the 1540s, 47 out of 113 wills found for clergy in Canterbury diocese referred to books, in some cases large collections (M. J. Peter, "A Study of the Administration of the Henrician Acts of Supremacy in Canterbury Diocese" [Ph.D. diss., Loyola University, Chicago, 1959], p. 66). KAO, PRC 21/4, fols. 169–75; D. McKeen, "A Memory of Honour" (Ph.D. diss., Birmingham University, England, 1964), p. 714; KAO, Sydney MSS, Accounts, 310, 313A, 322, 325(1), 327, 332; U350 E4.

13. CCL, X.11.10, fol. 141v; Z.3.5, fols. 63v–64v.

14. KAO, PRC 10, 11, 27, 28.

15. Occupational categorization is necessarily something of an arbitrary business, but provided the resulting evidence and correlations are handled with reasonable caution, the approach does provide some valuable insights: in any case, at the moment there is no obvious alternative. For a discussion of the problems of such an approach in a slightly different context, see P. Clark, "The Migrant in Kentish Towns, 1580–1640," in Clark and Slack, *Crisis and Order*, pp. 128, 156–57.

16. KAO, PRC 10/37, fol. 348; 10/9, fols. 333v–34v; 28/15, fol. 121.

17. F. R. Johnson, "Notes on English Retail Book-prices, 1550–1640," *The Library,* 5th ser. 5 (1950–51): 84ff.

18. KAO, PRC 39/39–52.

19. R. S. Schofield, "The Measurement of Literacy in Pre-Industrial England," in *Literacy in Traditional Societies,* ed. J. Goody (Cambridge: Cambridge University Press, 1968), p. 324.

20. The licenses are in CCL, License Registers (General), 1–16; the visitation returns are mostly in CCL, X, Y, and Z series; for a fuller discussion of this material see Clark, *The Rise of a Provincial Community,* chap. 6.

A similar point about the limited coverage of school licenses is made by R. O'Day, "Church Records and the History of Education in Early Modern England, 1558–1642: A Problem in Methodology," *History of Education,* 2 (1973): 120ff.

21. M. E. Bohannon, "A London Bookseller's Bill: 1635–39," *The Library,* 4th ser. 18 (1938): 418ff.; D. Gardiner, ed., *Oxinden Letters, 1607–1642* (London: Constable, 1933), p. 142.

22. A. Growoll, *Three Centuries of English Book Trade Bibliography* (New York: Dibdin Club, 1903); M. Plant, *The English Book Trade* (London: Allen and Unwin, 1939), p. 262; CCL, City Archives, AC 3, fol. 85v.

23. J. M. Cowper, *The Roll of the Freemen of the City of Canterbury* (Canterbury: privately printed, 1903), p. 272; R. B. McKerrow, *A Dictionary of Printers and Booksellers, 1557–1640* (London: The Bibliographical Society, 1968), p. 26.

24. Cowper, *The Roll of the Freemen,* p. 255; for shipments of books recorded in the Faversham Port Books: Public Record Office (PRO), E 190, 646/8, fol. 10v; 641/13, fol. 2; 646/10, fol. 4. CCL, AC 3, fol. 269; F/A 24, fol. 140; JQ 1614; New Foundation, Treasurers' Accounts, 12–13; Y.3.2, fol. 11v; KAO, PRC 10/52, fol. 180; McKerrow, *Printers and Booksellers,* p. 54. For Joseph's estate at his death see PRO, C3/436/17. H. R. Plomer and R. H. Peddie, "Stephen Bulkley, Printer," *The Library,* 2d ser. 8 (1907): 42ff.

25. KAO, PRC 10/24, fols. 3–5; 10/35, fol. 160; PRO, SP 16/434, fol. 169v; SP 16/434A, fol. 20.

26. KAO, PRC 10/25, fol. 379; see also PRC 10/70, fol. 54.

27. F. A. Mumby, *Publishing and Bookselling* (London: Cape, 1956), p. 104; A. Everitt, "The Marketing of Agricultural Produce," in *The Agrarian History of England and Wales: IV, 1500–1640,* ed. J. Thirsk (Cambridge: Cambridge University Press, 1967), pp. 502ff.

28. KAO, U350 E4; Sa/AC 5, fol. 85; Sa/AC 6, fol. 330v; QM/SB 145; Johnson, "English Retail Book-prices," pp. 84ff.

29. See Clark, *The Rise of a Provincial Community,* chaps. 5, 10, 11. For instance, John Drought, a small Canterbury turner who owned a Bible at his death in 1630, was a nonconformist and radical activist in the previous decade (KAO, PRC 28/15, fol. 219; U951 Z17/2, no. 58; CCL, X.5.10, fol. 120v).

30. For more on this, see Clark, *The Rise of a Provincial Community,* chap. 6.

31. A. D. Dyer, *The City of Worcester in the Sixteenth Century* (Leicester: Leicester University Press, 1973), p. 250; M. A. Havinden, ed., *House and Farm Inventories in Oxfordshire, 1550–1590* (Oxfordshire Record Society, 1965); *Victoria County History: Oxfordshire,* 2 (London: Constable, 1907): 42ff.; F. G. Emmison, ed., "Jacobean Household Inventories," *The Bedfordshire Historical Record Society* 20 (1938): 50–143; F. W. Steer, ed., *Farm and Cottage Inventories of Mid Essex, 1635–1749* (Colchester: Essex County Council, 1950).

PART III

The University and Society in the Eighteenth Century

CHAPTER 5

Evangelical Religion and Colonial Princeton

BY HOWARD MILLER

In recent investigations Lawrence Stone and Richard Kagan have suggested that the eighteenth century was for the universities of England, Spain, France, and Italy a period of numerical decline and intellectual stultification, that as their clientele contracted, the institutions of England and of Catholic Europe also remained for the greater part of the century relatively impervious to the intellectual advances being made in the universities of Scotland and Protestant Europe.[1] The present essay will argue, in contrast, that during much of the eighteenth century colonial Princeton in British North America was a vigorous institution both numerically and intellectually and that its vigor resulted at least partially from the evangelical origins of the small college and specifically from Princeton's Presbyterian character.[2] The first section of the essay will deal in a general way with the colleges of colonial America and suggest reasons for their successes and troubles in the late colonial period. The second section will deal with the Presbyterian clerics and laymen who established Princeton and with the evangelical revival that provided the immediate impetus for the college's foundation. The third will analyze some of the ways in which that revival, the Great Awakening, affected educational theory and practice at Princeton. And, finally, the essay will conclude by investigating in three sections the impact of the revival on the students of colonial Princeton, many of whom, like the biblical Samuel, were dedicated before birth to the service of God and more specifically to the furtherance of the evangelical revival. In promoting that revival, it will be argued, the Presbyterians made of colonial Princeton a vigorous institution that contrasted markedly to the stultifying universities of England and much of the continent.

The writer wishes to acknowledge and express his appreciation for the kindness of Professor James McLachlan of Princeton University in making available the biographical information he and his able assistant, Ms. Constance Escher, have collected for the forthcoming dictionary of Princeton's colonial student body. The paper simply could not have been researched without their cooperation. And the thoughts of David F. Allmendinger on the experience of nineteenth-century college students have been at all times most helpful and a constant reminder of how different the eighteenth-century experience was.

I

Of course, all of the colleges of eighteenth-century British North America were, relatively speaking, vigorous institutions that survived to become the premier colleges and universities of nineteenth-century America. Unlike many of the remarkably short-lived institutions established in the latter century, the colleges created in the colonial period—Harvard, William and Mary, Yale, Dartmouth, King's, Queen's, and the Colleges of New Jersey, Philadelphia, and Rhode Island—proved to be permanent foundations. The reasons for their success are varied. Harvard, especially, and Yale to a lesser degree, were seen by their founders as institutions vital to the success of Puritanism's "errand into the wilderness"; and thus support for those colleges, paltry and grudging though it sometimes proved, was deemed a responsibility of more than casual significance.[3] In addition, William and Mary, Harvard, and Yale were legally supported by established churches, a mixed blessing insofar as each of those schools incurred the opposition of dissenters from the favored denominations, but finally, an obvious advantage. Moreover, by the time the revival broke out in 1740, Harvard had celebrated its first centenary, and both Yale and William and Mary were approaching their fiftieth anniversaries; each could therefore call upon a growing body of alumni for what support colonial assemblies might withhold. And several of the colleges established at the mid-eighteenth century benefited from an early form of boosterism. In Philadelphia city fathers joined with Benjamin Franklin to create in the College of Philadelphia an institution to serve the needs of the British empire's second metropolis. And in New York City many Protestants joined in supporting King's College, although the Presbyterians' opposition to Anglican control of the college prevented it from flourishing as it might otherwise have.[4]

As the acrimonious debate over control of King's indicates, each of the colonial colleges was clearly identified with a particular religious denomination. That denominational identity might render a school vulnerable to occasional charges of sectarian ambition, but its denominational connection was also the colonial college's chief means of support and hope for success. Already in the eighteenth century had begun the process that by 1800 would make the American college characteristically the center of a denominational community, charged with educating that community's young and training its clergy.[5] And particularly strong were the denominational identities of three colleges established in the aftermath of the evangelical revival: The Dutch Calvinists' Queen's (now Rutgers), the Baptists' College of Rhode Island (now Brown), and of course, the Presbyterians' College of New Jersey at Princeton. Thus from colonial assemblies, loyal alumni, municipal leaders, and purposive religious groups, the colonial college was assured of financial support; and though trustees and presidents might fret over parsimony in any of those sources, their colleges nonetheless survived.

Other reasons abound for the success of the colonial colleges. In no colony was there more than one permanent institution of higher learning before 1776; each school, then, enjoyed the advantages of an educational monopoly. They also benefited from the strong leadership of determined founders and early presidents:

Dartmouth's Eleazar Wheelock and King's Samuel Johnson are the first to come to mind. Moreover, the colonial colleges, by and large, appear to have been receptive to innovations in curriculum and pedagogy and seem to have picked carefully through the imported New Learning of the eighteenth century, accepting new ideas here, discarding them there, and everywhere adapting the intellectual currents of the Enlightenment to colonial needs and tastes.[6] Those same institutions appear also to have served well a deferential society feeling the first rumblings of a democratic revolution that eventually would transform the American social landscape. For the most part, the colonial colleges trained those sons of the rich who desired a higher education, but they also became increasingly accessible to the sons of the middle and lower classes, or at least to the more extraordinary of those sons. The colleges therefore helped maintain traditional social arrangements while at the same time unwittingly laying foundations for quite different ones.[7]

But by emphasizing the basic similarities of the colonial colleges' experiences, one may miss significant differences in those experiences. For instance, although all survived the colonial period, the fortunes of American colleges in the later part of that period varied widely. Some prospered, while others almost closed their doors. For at least some of those colleges, a key to that variety of experiences may lie in their attitudes toward the Great Awakening, the revival of evangelical religion that divided colonial society as never before and forced upon America's educators choices of the most fundamental nature.[8]

Harvard and Yale at first cautiously endorsed and then emphatically opposed the revival. Heads of the two colleges almost instinctively recoiled from the enthusiastic demonstrations that attended the sensational preaching of the English itinerant, George Whitefield, in the first years of the 1740s. They closed the doors of Harvard and Yale to the Great Itinerant, who thereupon informed the world that the light of New England's colleges "was become darkness." Harvard, though, appears not to have been harmed by her opposition to the revival. By 1740 the college at Cambridge was the center of a genial, liberal Christianity that was Arminian in its theological tendencies, optimistic in its estimation of human nature, and in general, a comfort to the aspiring, materialistic descendants of the early Puritans, who had strayed far from the rigors of their fathers.[9] Harvard's constituency simply was in no hurry to follow George Whitefield—or Jonathan Edwards either—in returning to the stringencies of seventeenth-century Puritanism, let alone to the dark determinism of sixteenth-century Calvinism. Harvard, in short, risked little in opposing the revival; and the college prospered in the late colonial period because its alumni—now its constituency—prospered and because Harvard, by its reaction to the revival, did not alienate that constituency.

The experience of Yale is more complicated. The Connecticut college had been established in 1701 as a reaction to the perceived liberal tendencies at Harvard. In 1740 it was firmly controlled by the Old Light opponents of the Awakening and superintended by the Reverend Thomas Clap, who, as rector, was committed to maintaining at any cost Congregational orthodoxy at Yale. That orthodoxy had been sullied dramatically in the Great Apostasy of 1722, when Rector Timothy

Cutler signaled his conversion to the Church of England by concluding Yale's commencement exercise with a benediction straight from the Anglican Book of Prayer. In the aftermath of that astonishing event, Yale and its leaders grew increasingly defensive, seeing in the slightest deviation in belief or practice a direct assault upon the Truth as received by the college's pious founders. Consequently, they were in no mood to tolerate any manifestation of enthusiastic religion at Yale. But within a year of Clap's inauguration in April of 1740, George Whitefield preached on New Haven's green, the Presbyterian evangelist Gilbert Tennent delivered no fewer than seventeen blistering sermons in the village, and Yale's best known alumnus, Jonathan Edwards, defended the Awakening in his 1741 commencement address, "Distinguishing Marks of a Work of the Spirit of God." Shortly thereafter, Clap expelled a senior, David Brainerd, for allegedly insulting the authority of the college; and in the following April the college had to be closed down completely in the face of student protests against Clap's high-handed tactics, all of which were seen by revivalists as manifestations of the rector's hostility to the Awakening. In 1744 that view was vindicated when Clap expelled two students for attending their parents' separatist church while on vacation. That expulsion solidified the revivalists' opposition to Clap's control of the college.[10] Although for political reasons Clap belatedly switched to the New Lights, he expended the better part of his tenure opposing the revival, asserting extreme claims for Congregational privilege at Yale, and protecting and extending his own authority in both the college and colony.

Clap—and Yale—paid a price for opposing the revival. Alienated supporters of the Awakening sent their sons elsewhere to be educated, either to Princeton or simply to the study of an evangelical clergyman. Moreover, a wide array of citizens—Separates, Anglicans, Baptists, and Quakers—made common cause against the legal establishment of the Congregational Church in Connecticut and the privileges of its college at New Haven. Again, Yale forfeited the goodwill and support of that coalition. By 1763 the rector's methods had provoked petitions to the colonial assembly calling for his removal from office; by 1766 most of the tutors had left the college, as had all but about fifty students, and those who remained once more called upon the assembly to dismiss Clap. Having brought the college to the point of ruin, the controversial rector in that year bowed to the inevitable and resigned. For twelve years then Yale survived under the leadership of the Reverend Naphtali Daggett, and in 1778 a new era in the school's history began with the inauguration of the Reverend Ezra Stiles as president of Yale. The tolerant Stiles was a marked contrast to the dogmatic and authoritarian Clap, and he saw his move to New Haven as a turning point in the fortunes of Yale. In the year of his inauguration Stiles wrote a sermon on the prophet Ezra, his namesake, and in it sounded his call for a change at New Haven: "There was a Restoration of the School of the prophets, and Ezra became the first President or Head of the College at Jerusalem, after the return from Babylon."[11]

It is possible to argue that Yale's troubles in the late colonial period were simply a result of Thomas Clap's unfortunate personality and that only a conciliatory president like Ezra Stiles was required to revive the wounded school. But that interpretation would not measure the intensity of the Connecticut evangelicals' antipathy to the Old Light leanings of the school at New Haven. Nor would it adequately explain the Shepherd's Tent, a school established briefly by the Reverend Timothy Allen in New London in 1742 to provide an evangelical alternative to Yale. Nor would an emphasis on Clap's personality explain the decision of many of Connecticut revivalists to cooperate with middle-colony Presbyterians to create at Princeton an institution facing none of the problems that plagued Yale during Clap's tenure.

II

Early in the tour that later took him to Harvard and Yale, George Whitefield found himself in the tiny village of Neshaminy, on the main post road between Trenton, New Jersey, and Philadelphia. He had been invited there by "old Mr. Tennent," William Tennent, the pastor of Neshaminy's Presbyterian Church, to address a crowd that quickly swelled to more than three thousand. Whitefield "melted down" the multitude as he had done elsewhere, moved many to tears, and then retired for lunch to Tennent's home. There the Englishman discovered a new institution of higher learning, this one altogether different from his alma mater— ancient, dissolute Oxford. Whitefield was struck by the simplicity of the school next to Tennent's home and quickly noted the implications of that simplicity. The academy was "a log-house, about twenty feet long, and nearly as many broad," and to the evangelist it seemed "to resemble the school of the old prophets." Indeed, the school was intended to educate latter-day prophets. There Tennent was training for the evangelical ministry "gracious youth" who would be sent out "into the Lord's vineyard." Seven or eight had already graduated, and a foundation was "being laid for the instruction of many others." Whitefield was told, though, that there was opposition to the school, which was derided by its enemies as the "log college." The devil, in the form of lifeless, formal clergymen, raged against it; and its graduates were excoriated by the "carnal" ministers whom they fervently exposed. But, Whitefield concluded, Tennent's work was of God and would therefore prosper.[12]

And prosper it did. The derisive epithet became a badge of honor, and the "Log College" between 1727 and 1746 educated a generation of evangelical Presbyterian ministers and educators, including three of Tennent's four sons.[13] His eldest, Gilbert, had been educated by his father and been dedicated to the ministry before the family emigrated from the north of Ireland, and in America served as his father's assistant in the Log College. In that capacity he doubtless superintended the education of his younger brothers—William, Jr., John, and Charles—all of whom became Presbyterian ministers. In effect, William Tennent's academy separated from the rising flood of emigrants from Ulster to the middle colonies promising young men to serve the Presbyterian Church in America.[14] For example, the young Ulsterman Samuel Blair found his way to Neshaminy after immigrating to New Jersey in 1722, and his countryman Samuel Finley probably entered the Log College after arriving in America in 1734.[15]

Perhaps the early career of Charles Beatty best illustrates the social and religious function of Tennent's school. Beatty was born, probably in 1715, in Ireland's County Antrim, the son of a Scotch-Irish officer in the British army who died in Charles's youth. In 1729 the young man, his mother, and an uncle sailed to America. Beatty had received a Latin education in Ulster, but his family's poverty forced him to forego plans for further education while he peddled utensils in the middle colonies. Tradition relates that while on his rounds, young Beatty called on the Reverend Tennent, who was astonished when addressed in perfect Latin by a peddler. After assuring himself that Beatty was as pious as he was intelligent, Tennent urged the young man to abandon his wares and to embark upon ministerial studies at the Log College, which Beatty agreed to do. Tradition or no, the fact is that for twenty years the school on the post road attracted dozens of pious young men, many of them poor immigrants, who were trained there for the Presbyterian ministry by William and Gilbert Tennent.[16]

These men, according to Whitefield in 1739, were "looked upon as persons who turn the world upside-down."[17] In truth, the Tennents and other revivalists had, by their impassioned defense of evangelical religion, severely strained the unity of American Presbyterianism. They insisted on the primacy of vital piety over learning in the ministry; they urged Christians to judge the spiritual state of their ministers and to flee those deemed unregenerate; and they resisted every effort to impede the progress of revival in the colonies. In 1740 Gilbert Tennent delivered his blistering warning of "the dangers of an unconverted ministry," and Whitefield's itinerations spread the revival up the seacoast and down again. One year later, in a tumultuous synodical session, the Presbyterian Church split officially into Old and New Sides—the opponents and supporters of evangelical religion, respectively.[18]

The schism in the Presbyterian Church was simply the most dramatic and visible result of the great burst of energy that the Great Awakening released in American society. In effect, the revival shook to their foundations all of the institutions of colonial society—church, family, school, and the state itself. The energy of the revival flowed from the dynamics of evangelical religion, and usually in ways that are quite complex and as yet little understood. For the most part, they need not detain us here. But one of the critical distinctions between the New and Old Side Presbyterians was that the supporters of the revival both possessed and harnessed that energy while their opponents did not.[19]

The source of that crucial difference is not immediately obvious. There was, to be sure, a geographical division between Old and New Sides. Many of the revivalists were either New Englanders or of New England ancestry, while their Old Side opponents tended—though not always—to be recent emigrants from Ulster.[20] Inherent in that difference was another, an educational distinction. Most of the New Englanders had been educated either at Harvard or, more likely, at Yale, while most of the Ulstermen were graduates of the Scottish universities.

Moreover, there was an ecclesiological rift between the New Englanders and Ulstermen. The former, predictably, were strongly influenced by the congregational polity of New England; on the other hand, the Scotch-Irish usually insisted upon strictly following presbyterian ecclesiology and opposed any compromises with congregationalism. But there is an important exception to these generalizations: the Presbyterian schism was largely the result of a generational division that bridged all these other divisions. Younger New Englanders and younger Ulstermen (such as Tennent's students) tended to ally against the older Scotch-Irishmen. (The elder Tennent is the important exception that fixes the rule.) Then, as now, youth was no guarantee of vitality, but the relative ages of the antagonists in the Great Schism cannot be ignored when one seeks the source of the New Sides' vigor.

The crucial difference between the two sides, however, was in their expectations for America's future. For whatever reason, the New Sides responded to an exhilarating vision of a revived America's future; their opponents could, or would, not. The Presbyterian revivalists shared Jonathan Edwards's conviction that with the Awakening dawned the glorious final chapter not only in the history of the English colonies but in the history of man.[21] There were, of course, other sources of the revivalists' vigor and of the energy they released in society. Their psychological and epistemological precepts produced confident evangelists who aroused congregations to unprecedented levels of response. Edwards and his Presbyterian disciples did achieve dramatic results by addressing their hearers' "affections" and by dangling sinners over the bottomless pit of hell. But celebrated sermons like Edwards's "Sinners in the Hands of an Angry God" were effective finally because the men who preached them at the same time persuaded Americans that they lived in the last days, that the beginning of the millennium awaited only the reformation of colonial society, and that reformation could begin only in the hearts of regenerate men.[22] It should be noted that the revivalists did *not* expect the momentary return of Christ and the attending apocalypse. Their vision was certainly an ecstatic one, but it was also tempered and temperate. They were, of course, determined to transform individual lives, and the records of the Awakening teem with the accounts of those conversions. But the revivalists were no less persuaded that social institutions too must be transformed prior to the millennium.[23] Those dual convictions, interrelated and mutually dependent, produced the central distinguishing mark of New Side Presbyterians—their insistence that transformed men reform the institutions of colonial society as a precondition of the millennium.[24]

That insistence fueled a flurry of New Side activity in the middle colonies and the upper South at the mid-century. The revivalists launched ambitious missionary projects, sending their brethren to follow the Scotch-Irish down the backbone of the Appalachians as they pushed from central and western Pennsylvania, first through the Shenandoah Valley of Virginia, and then to the Carolina back country. On the frontier the Presbyterian minister was nearly always the most educated and respected man in any new community and as such exerted formidable influence on the embryonic institutions of each western settlement. At the same time, the revivalists ministered to older communities, treating them in effect as urban frontiers. They established charitable societies to aid the poor, evangelized black Americans both free and slave, and set in motion trans-Atlantic fund drives to pay for their wide-ranging godly activities.[25]

And the revivalists endeavored mightily to reform the family, that institution they deemed—outside the church itself—most crucial to the shaping of any society. To that end, they engaged in admittedly traditional exhortations: pious parents were to lead the young by example; youth was to heed and follow that example; and the clergy were to lead all in their duties. But to those traditional exhortations evangelical religion added a new awareness of the importance of youth. Ministers on the eve of revival worried constantly about the condition of their young charges—frivolous, heedless youths who seemed to embody the corruptions that threatened to undermine, if not destroy, the entire society with themselves. Ministers and parents were surprised, then, to discover that those same youths were also particularly susceptible to evangelical religion. Boys and girls astonished their elders by abandoning their accustomed frolics and, instead, demanding of their ministers the way to salvation. The earnestness of the young prompted the clergy to deliver—often for the first time—sermons directly addressed to youth, and the aroused young people responded in gratifying ways.[26] They organized themselves into holy bands to encourage each other in godliness and to reprove any falling therefrom. And the clergy fervently hoped that, in this instance, roles would be reversed, and the example of youth not be wasted on age.

III

These evangelical convictions and concerns were immediately translated into educational practice. Institutions of learning, in one sense, were no more—or less—important to the revivalists than other institutions. All had to be transformed. But even in the eighteenth century, Americans placed upon their schools a heavy burden—the task, in essence, of shaping society by molding the young. Of course, all societies have in some way invested education with the same task. But that simple observation, universal though it may be, masks a multitude of varied experiences. For the American Presbyterian revivalists, the social function of education was as complicated as it was crucial and was at all levels intimately related to the dynamics of evangelical religion.[27] The Presbyterians were the heirs of a tradition dating back to John Knox in which the Presbyterian Church usually stood beside a school for the godly instruction of the young. In addition, virtually all of the Presbyterian revivalists had themselves received a college education, either in New England, in Scotland, or in the Log College.

But disagreements over the relation of learning to piety made education a matter of bitter controversy among American Presbyterians on the eve of revival. Old Sides blasted the revivalists as enemies of learning and denounced the Log College as the seedbed, not of wisdom, but of wickedness and contention. Retaliating, the

New Sides insisted that learning be balanced with piety and charged their opponents with undoing that crucial balance.[28] But when that balance was righted by pious educators, the revivalists believed, educational institutions would be most potent instruments of social reformation.[29] The New Sides were all the more confident in that belief because theirs was a new society with little or no institutional past to confine them in their endeavors. Admittedly, each carried with him recollections of his own education, but in the middle colonies the New Sides determined to establish educational institutions peculiarly suited to the demands of a new, revived, reformed society. That determination, in turn, made their educational theories remarkably purposive and effective forces.

The first New Side schools—like the Log College—were institutional manifestations of these educational theories. In Newark and Elizabethtown, New Jersey, the Reverends Aaron Burr and Jonathan Dickinson, respectively, opened their homes to boys and young men for instruction in the classics and for direction of their moral development. Both Burr and Dickinson were New Englanders, and both were early supporters of the revival that began in the same year they opened their schools.[30] In 1744, amid the wreckage of the revival, Samuel Finley, a graduate of the Log College, established a similar institution in his home in Nottingham, on the Pennsylvania-Maryland border. One year later, the elder Tennent died; and Burr, Dickinson, and Finley joined with Tennent's sons and other Presbyterian ministers and laymen to establish a college that would continue and enlarge upon the educational efforts of the Log College. In 1746 they were incorporated as the Board of Trustees of the College of New Jersey.[31] The school was located first at Elizabethtown and then at Newark, where it absorbed the academies of its first two presidents, Jonathan Dickinson and Aaron Burr. In 1756 Burr moved it to Princeton, the village between New York and Philadelphia that gave its name to the college informally long before it did so officially.

To even the casual observer it should be obvious that the college at Princeton was a vigorous institution, vitally affecting American Presbyterianism and the trans-Atlantic reformed community of which that denomination was an important part. Without lapsing into the filiopietism of some of the school's earlier historians, it is possible to observe that, with some fluctuations in the rate of growth, Princeton's student body continued to increase during the colonial period as the school's constituency also increased and dispersed throughout the colonies. Moreover, Princeton provided increasingly diverse services for that constituency, preparing young men to enter business and to study medicine and the law as well as theology. For that reason, and more, it had a significant impact on a considerable and influential segment of colonial society. Finally, colonial Princeton made noteworthy contributions to the development of the larger culture of which its constituency was a part, most notably in the importation and dissemination of the Scottish Enlightenment.

But it is not always easy to determine the extent to which colonial Princeton flourished, simply because it was a new institution in a relatively young and underdeveloped society, nor is it easy to determine the extent to which its success

flowed from its relationship to evangelical religion in general and to Presbyterianism in particular. All other considerations aside, Princeton's location and
the conditions under which it was chartered greatly enhanced the school's chances
of success. In 1746 the New Jersey school was the only institution of higher
learning between New Haven and Williamsburg. Others—King's, the College of
Philadelphia, Queen's—would soon follow, but Princeton's location and its brief
headstart probably contributed substantially to the ease with which the school
attracted and maintained its colonial enrollment. Moreover, Princeton's charter
was consciously designed to attract students from the religiously heterogeneous
middle colonies, guaranteeing that, as there was no established religion in New
Jersey, none would be favored at Princeton. And none was. Princeton was
obviously a Presbyterian institution, but it attracted Anglican students from both
South and North, Dutch students from the middle colonies, and a surprisingly large
number of New England Congregationalists. Both by necessity and principle,
then, the Presbyterians welcomed to their new college all orthodox Protestants,
and that fact surely contributed to its colonial success.[32]

But these factors are probably not so crucial in explaining the school's success as
are several other factors more directly related to the evangelical and, specifically,
the Presbyterian nature of the college. One of these was totally fortuitous—the
mortality rate of the school's colonial presidents was astonishingly high. In a
thirty-year period Princeton had six presidents, four of whom died within the
single decade between 1757 and 1766. The deaths of Aaron Burr, Jonathan
Edwards, Samuel Davies, and Samuel Finley alarmed the Presbyterians, and
rightly so. But the rapid succession of vacancies allowed the college's board of
trustees to bring to Princeton—if briefly—an unusually large number of men of
great repute and, in Edwards's case, of international renown. Each, as president,
strengthened Princeton's relations with that part of the colonies from which he
came; and significantly, the presidents did not come from the same part. When
Burr moved the college from Newark to Princeton, he brought several young men
from Connecticut with him; the brief tenure of Edwards certainly increased
awareness of Princeton not only in Massachusetts but also in the trans-Atlantic
reformed community in which the great man loomed so large. When Samuel
Davies came from Hanover County, Virginia, to succeed Edwards, he became the
first link in a bond with the South that would become one of the most pronounced
characteristics of eighteenth- and nineteenth-century Princeton. Davies's successor, Samuel Finley, in turn helped to solidify Princeton's connections with the
middle colonies during his five-year tenure. And when Finley died, the board
appointed as his successor the Reverend John Witherspoon, a celebrated Scottish
clergyman, who in coming to Princeton strengthened further the school's relations
with the trans-Atlantic reformed community. Their contemporaries could find
little meaning and no good in the successive deaths of the Princeton presidents, but
it is clear in retrospect that the rapid succession of renowned men from different
sections of the Atlantic community greatly increased the reputation and hence the
fortunes of the Presbyterian school.[33] Harvard and Yale, in contrast, regularly

recruited their presidents from the Congregational establishments of Massachusetts and Connecticut, respectively.

Of course, the presidential succession only highlights the obvious: Presbyterians at the mid-century were a numerous and far-flung people. From their first settlements on Long Island, in and around Philadelphia, and on the eastern shore of Maryland, the Presbyterians had pushed to the western borders of virtually all the colonies south of New York and were vigorous majorities in many frontier communities. At the same time, the Presbyterian hierarchy of session, presbytery, and synod unified the scattered denomination into a community that was increasingly purposive after the reunion of Old and New Sides in 1758. That hierarchy could and did launch intercolonial campaigns to increase interest in and support for a wide range of evangelical projects that grew out of the Awakening, the most important of which was Princeton itself. Neither New England Congregationalism nor the bishopless hierarchy of American Anglicanism could lay claim to such an effective tool with which to shape institutions of learning. Moreover, the Presbyterian hierarchy was directly connected, through the Synod of Philadelphia, to the vital Presbyterian community of Great Britain, particularly that of Scotland. At strategic junctures in Princeton's colonial history that connection was used to provide psychological and financial support for the American college.[34]

Finally, colonial Princeton flourished because it spawned an evangelical educational empire that, in turn, sustained the college well into the nineteenth century. Scores of academies were established by Presbyterian ministers in the middle colonies and upper South in the latter half of the eighteenth century, and almost without exception, their founders were the sons of Princeton. Ignored until recently by historians, the Presbyterian academies are absolutely crucial to an understanding of colonial Princeton.[35] The first of them—Tennent's Log College and Burr's and Dickinson's New Jersey schools—were in fact the cultural conduits whereby much of the Scottish Enlightenment was transported to British North America. The first academies transferred to the colonies the curricular and pedagogical theories of the British dissenting academies and the Scottish universities, the only truly robust academic institutions in eighteenth-century Great Britain. Gradually, that cultural function was absorbed by the school at Princeton, which in effect grew out of these first academies.

A second wave of academies was established in the wake of the revival. The most important of these was the one in Pequa, Pennsylvania, superintended by the Reverend Robert Smith, a Presbyterian cleric whose life is particularly revelatory of the forces shaping the Presbyterian educational experience in colonial America. Born in Ulster of pious Scotch parents, Smith immigrated with them to Pennsylvania at seven. At fifteen his life was touched by George Whitefield, and at his parents' urging, Robert determined to enter the ministry. To that end he entered Samuel Blair's academy, where he was educated during the height of the great revival. In 1750 he simultaneously accepted the call of the Pequa Church and married Blair's daughter. At Pequa he established an academy in which he instructed boys and young men in the classics, thus preparing them to attend the college at Princeton. The product of one academy that predated the revival, Smith then established after the Awakening another school that supplied Princeton with students for over forty years.[36]

The third wave of academies followed the second almost immediately. In Basking Ridge, Elizabethtown, Lower Freehold, and Hackensack, New Jersey; Carlisle, Chestnut Level, and Providence, Pennsylvania; in August, Fauquier, and Prince Edward counties in Virginia; in Crowfield and Sugar Creek, North Carolina; in Charleston, South Carolina—in short, down the length of the colonial frontier—young ministers, Princetonians, established academies that provided the college with a considerable portion of its colonial student body.[37] By 1775 Princeton was graduating young men, like North Carolina's Spruce Macay, who had received their classical education in the academies of that third wave. In North Carolina, Macay almost certainly studied at the Reverend David Caldwell's school in Guilford County. Caldwell, in turn, graduated from Princeton in 1761 after attending Robert Smith's Pequa Academy.[38] And Smith, as noted, was trained at the academy of Samuel Blair, a graduate of the original Log College.

The Presbyterian academies not only supplied Princeton with a significant portion of its student body, but also insured that that body would be socially and chronologically heterogeneous. To that extent the academies clearly contributed to the college's vitality. On the frontier especially, but also in the more settled regions, the Presbyterian educators urged pious (and impious) parents to enroll in the local Presbyterian academy those sons who otherwise would have no opportunity for an education. Consequently, in those schools, the sons of the poor often rubbed shoulders with the sons of the educators themselves and of the middle class. Likewise, there was a great variety of ages among the academies' students. The sketchy information available suggests that in the academies young adults, urged into the schools by their ministers, mingled with the sons of the clergy, some of whom entered the academy as very young boys. As a result, young men who entered Princeton from one of the academies were accustomed to a student body that was heterogeneous both in age and social origin, which is to say that the student body of colonial Princeton should not have surprised them.[39]

IV

The impact of evangelical religion on colonial Princeton is nowhere more evident than in its effect on the college's student body. Likewise, in no better way can one relate evangelical religion to the vitality of the school than to investigate the ways in which the progress of evangelical religion at the mid-century brought to Princeton young men from an ever wider spectrum of colonial society.

Princeton's colonial student body was not large. Between 1746 and 1776, 490 graduates and at least 80 nongraduates entered the college.[40] Most of those young men, though certainly not all, fell into one of three more or less distinct groups according to their social origins. One rather large group consisted of the sons of the colonial commercial and landed elite, who were usually at Princeton preparatory to entering one of the secular professions or simply to acquire the liberal education deemed essential for a gentleman at the mid-century. A second group consisted of the sons and nephews of a different kind of elite, that is, of the colonial clergy. After their years at Princeton, many of these followed in their relatives' footsteps, although others did not. Those in the third group were in no way related to the secular or clerical elite. These young men, often from the frontier, had been converted by Presbyterian ministers and had then made their way to Princeton, often to prepare there for the Presbyterian clergy themselves. Frequently, these men were from the lower levels of colonial society and clearly used Princeton as an instrument of social advancement. Obviously, these three groupings do not exhaust the possible ways of dissecting and analyzing the makeup of colonial Princeton. Moreover, the statistical evidence upon which much of the present hypothesis rests is still fragmentary; hence the thesis must be a tentative one. But the three groups do provide a framework in which to test part of the thesis of the present essay, i.e., that each of the three groups was affected directly and sometimes dramatically by the imperatives of evangelical religion.

The first group of students were the sons of Protestants who were also colonial officials, wealthy merchants and shippers, landowners, and planters; the Lees of Virginia; the Bayards, Jaunceys, and Livingstons of New York; the Stocktons and Ogdens of New Jersey; and the Bradfords and Shippens of Pennsylvania are only the most obvious examples. Well on their way to becoming dynasties, these great families at the mid-century were part of an increasingly powerful and unified gentry that owned huge estates, often in several colonies; dominated the learned professions of law and medicine; and through their newspapers greatly influenced public opinion in colonial America.[41] The social standing of other well-to-do students was scarcely less secure, if not quite as high. Philip Freneau ('71) was the son of a wealthy New York wine merchant who left estates in three New York counties as well as in New Jersey and Connecticut, while the 1761 graduate Lawrence Van Derveer inherited parts of estates in New Jersey, Maryland, and Virginia.[42] Other Princetonians were the sons of colonial officials: the father of Joseph and Benjamin Woodruff, both 1753 graduates, was a member of the New Jersey Council as well as a merchant in the West Indies trade and left an estate inventoried at over £3,500.[43] Other Princetonians were also descended from well-to-do merchants: Andrew Hodge ('72), Morgan Lewis ('73), Cornelius Low ('52), and James Jauncey ('63), whose father was reported to have left an estate of £100,000.[44]

One fact about these sons of the commercial and landed elite is immediately obvious. As a group, their educational experiences prior to entering Princeton were much more varied than those of other groups at the college. Many had been educated privately by tutors. Southern planters, in particular, contracted with young college graduates to come south for a year to instruct their sons, who sometimes then enrolled at their tutors' alma maters. Just such a process brought James Madison to Nassau Hall in 1769. Other sons of the elite, like Morgan Lewis, the son of a New York merchant who signed the Declaration of Independence, were educated first at classical and then at grammar schools. Still others came to Princeton as boys and attended the grammar school that Burr established in conjunction with the college. Or, like Philadelphia's Joseph Reed ('57), they attended similar institutions in other cities, such as the Academy of the College of Philadelphia.[45] But these young men's educational experiences, varied as they were, very rarely included attendance at the Presbyterian academies. Philip Freneau did attend the school of the Reverend Alexander Martin ('65), and William Churchill Houston ('68), the son of a wealthy North Carolina landowner, studied at the academy of Joseph Alexander ('60).[46] But virtually no young man of wealth who later enrolled at Princeton first attended the principal Presbyterian academies at Pequa, Nottingham, and Londonderry.[47] The academies' rural locations may have made them inconvenient to an elite that, in the middle colonies at least, was characteristically urban. But for whatever reason, the sons of the elite were not regularly sent from their homes to obtain their elementary education at the Presbyterian academies. Consequently, they did not as frequently as some other Princetonians come under the influence of the young, charismatic educators at the various New Side "log colleges."

Possibly for that reason, the sons of the commercial and landed elite seldom entered the ministry. Instead, they regularly entered the professions or businesses of their fathers. Thomas Melville ('69), the son of a Boston merchant, entered the mercantile business in the Bay Colony, just as Andrew Hodge ('72) continued his father's business in Philadelphia. New Jersey's Robert Ogden ('65) followed his father into the law; and Isaac Handy, upon graduating in 1761, returned to Maryland to preside over a large estate, as had his father.[48] Other wealthy young men followed secular professions or vocations different from their, fathers'—in one common pattern, the sons of merchants became doctors and lawyers. William Channing ('69) and William Stevens Smith ('74) were but two sons of the mercantile elite who became lawyers after attending Princeton, while Hugh Hodge ('73) and James Smith ('57) turned to medicine. Some, like Hugh Hodge, were younger sons (his older brother Andrew would inherit their father's Philadelphia business) and doubtless turned to the law or to medicine simply because they could not follow in their fathers' steps.[49] For these sons of the commercial and landed elite, colonial Princeton clearly afforded an opportunity to enter the professional elite of doctors and lawyers that was everywhere slowly emerging in the British colonies at the mid-century.

But for all their secular background and subsequent secular careers, the influence of evangelical religion on this group of young men was significant and often crucial. Many of them came from families that had been affected in one way or another by the Great Awakening, whether they were New England Congregationalists, middle-colony Presbyterians, or southern Anglicans. But, beyond that, some of the wealthier students were directly related to the colonial clergy, usually through their mothers. David ('63) and Ebenezer Cowell ('66) were the nephews of the Reverend David Cowell, the pastor of Trenton's First Presbyterian Church and a charter trustee of Princeton.[50] Likewise, John McPherson ('66), the son of a wealthy planter, was the nephew of the Reverend John Rodgers, one of the leading Presbyterian clergymen in the colonies. The Livingstons of New York also were related to the clergy: Henry Philip ('76) was the maternal grandson of the Reverend Dirick Ten Broeck, an influential minister of the Dutch Reformed Church.[51] And Jonathan Dickinson Sergeant ('62), later a distinguished Philadelphia lawyer, was the maternal grandson and namesake of Princeton's first president. Others, like future congressman Nathaniel Niles, were descended from the New England clergy; and at least one, Maryland's John Bay ('65), was both the grandson and the nephew of Presbyterian clerics.[52]

At Princeton these and other well-to-do young men were exposed to an exhilarating concept of public service that proceeded directly from the New Sides' dedication to social reformation. All of the colonial presidents, but especially Samuel Davies and John Witherspoon, insisted that society would be reformed—and redeemed—only when led and served by regenerate men.[53] Witherspoon encouraged his students to enter the ministry, of course—a year spent studying theology with the president after graduation appears to have become a rite of passage that even James Madison undertook before succumbing to the temptations of the law. But clearly more important to the Scotsman than making a minister of every Princetonian was the creation of a godly laity. To that end, he encouraged his students to view all professions and businesses as opportunities for serving God.[54] Surely that change in emphasis helped encourage his students' entry into a wide range of secular professions. Indeed, Witherspoon's Princeton seems to have produced a peculiar evangelical variant of the renaissance man, a man who upon graduation might practice law *and* medicine while also running for public office and joining projects to reform colonial society.[55]

For some of Princeton's wealthier students, though, the impact of evangelical religion was more direct than the influence of Witherspoon's general exhortations or of ministerial kinsmen. William Bradford ('72), for instance, grew up in a home dominated by the conflicts of the Great Awakening and the polemics they produced. His father, the wealthy Philadelphia publisher of the *Weekly Advertiser,* between 1748 and 1753 printed most of what Gilbert Tennent had to say publicly, and the younger Bradford was much impressed by the great evangelist. Possibly for that reason, Bradford read theology with Witherspoon upon graduation before deciding, like Madison, to read law instead.[56] In much the same way, Thomas Henderson ('61) was greatly affected by Gilbert Tennent's younger brother, William, who was his pastor at Freehold, near Princeton. After graduating and studying medicine, Henderson returned to Monmouth County, where, like his wealthy father, he served for forty years as a ruling elder in the Freehold Church.[57]

When the influence of evangelical religion became strong enough, the sons of the well-to-do entered the ministry. Many of Witherspoon's wealthier students obviously considered entering the ministry; and they must have had difficulty withstanding the pressures of the evangelists who frequently stopped at the college on the way to and from New York or Philadelphia. Some did resist. In 1754, for example, Whitefield himself attended commencement and afterwards urged the

class's valedictorian, William Shippen, to commit his obvious oratorical skills to
the service of God. Only very reluctantly did young Shippen decide instead to
follow in his family's long-established medical practice in Philadelphia. On
others, though, the impact of Whitefield and other evangelists was transforming.
Peter Fish ('74), the son of a wealthy Long Island farmer, was converted by
Whitefield at thirteen and apparently was determined thereafter to follow the Great
Itinerant's example and become a minister.[58] And Benjamin Woodruff ('53) grew
up surrounded by a wide circle of evangelicals that included upon occasion
Whitefield and the same David Brainerd who had been expelled from Yale by
Thomas Clap. Woodruff's father, a wealthy merchant in Elizabethtown, New
Jersey, was also an elder in the local Presbyterian church and in the early 1750s
entertained a steady stream of evangelicals. Perhaps because of the godly visitors
in his father's home, Benjamin, whose mother was an Ogden, became a Presbyterian minister and remained for forty-four years the pastor of the church in
Westfield, New Jersey.[59]

Other well-to-do young men, like New Hampshire's Samuel Livermore ('52),
planned to enter the clergy but appear to have changed their minds while at college
or shortly thereafter. Some were persuaded by disapproving fathers to abandon
plans for a career in the ministry. One wealthy young man, Morgan Lewis, had
been encouraged by his mother to enter the Anglican clergy, but his father, a New
York merchant, was unalterably opposed and finally persuaded his second son to
enter the practice of law instead. And sometimes the situation was reversed.
Young men had to persuade pious fathers that they were better suited for the law
than for the ministry. Oliver Ellsworth ('66) had to placate his pious father by
studying theology for a year after leaving Princeton, but he finally convinced both
his father and his teacher that he was best suited for the law by spending the first ten
pages of his first sermon in defining precisely all the terms he would use in the
exercise. Samuel Spring ('71), on the other hand, persisted in his determination to
become a minister and with his mother's help finally overcame the objections of
his father, a wealthy farmer from Massachusetts.[60]

The career of Lewis F. Wilson perhaps best demonstrates the impact of evangelical religion on the wealthier Princetonians. Admittedly atypical, Wilson's career
is instructive precisely for that reason; its eccentricity throws into relief the effect
of evangelical religion as it worked with full force on the wealthy at Princeton.
Wilson was born in 1753, one of two sons of a West Indies planter. As a boy he
moved with his father to London, where he received his elementary education. At
seventeen he traveled with an uncle to America, where he enrolled at Princeton,
possibly to escape the depravities of the English universities. Under Witherspoon's care, he was converted in the remarkable revival of 1772, a convulsive
experience that saw the majority of that year's class enter the Presbyterian ministry. Deeply affected by the revival, Wilson, an Anglican, sailed to England to take
holy orders. Once there, though, he decided instead to enter the Presbyterian
ministry, thereby causing his father to disinherit him. Undaunted, Wilson returned
to Princeton and studied theology with Witherspoon while serving as a tutor at the

college. But at the beginning of the Revolution he was persuaded by one of his fellow tutors to study medicine. He practiced for a brief time and then accepted the invitation of his classmate and brother-in-law, the Reverend James Hall, to practice in Iredell County, North Carolina. For five years he served the frontier community that Alexander ministered to, but in 1791 Wilson himself was ordained to the Presbyterian ministry, apparently having lived for almost twenty years with a guilty conscience for deserting the study of divinity. Wilson's father, in the meantime, had forgiven his son's apostasy and provided for his economic needs, and that financial independence appears to have enabled Wilson to experiment with the career opportunities for a Princeton graduate in the new republic. Finally Wilson settled upon the Presbyterian ministry as a career, surely because of the evangelical college at Princeton and the abiding influence of the men he had met there.[61]

V

There were at colonial Princeton the sons of another colonial elite, an elite based not at all on wealth but on profession. Fully one of every ten of Princeton's colonial graduates was the son or nephew of a clergyman; some in fact were members of what amounted to clerical dynasties. The three sons of Jonathan Edwards— Timothy ('57), Jonathan, Jr. ('65), and Pierpont ('68); Israel Evans ('72); and James Frelinghuysen ('50) were the grandsons as well as the sons of well-known clerics. Thomas Craighead ('75) could trace his ancestry back through at least four generations of English and Scottish Presbyterian ministers.[62] This group included some of Princeton's most renowned colonial sons: the minister-educator sons of Robert Smith, Samuel Stanhope ('69) and John Blair ('73); Benjamin Rush ('60), nephew of Samuel Finley, signer of the Declaration of Independence, and self-appointed conscience of the young American republic; and, of course, the younger Aaron Burr ('72), the third vice president of the United States.[63] Moreover, the sons of the clergy represented virtually all the major denominations of colonial America. Though most were Presbyterians, others were Anglican (Thomas Claggett, '64), Dutch Reformed (James Frelinghuysen, '50), Baptist (Benjamin Stelle, '66), and Congregationalist (Ralph Pomeroy, '58).[64]

By virtue of their parentage, these young men were at all times directly influenced by the progress of evangelical religion in colonial America. Some, indeed, grew up in the midst of the most controversial repercussions of the Great Awakening. The three grandsons of William Tennent who graduated from colonial Princeton—John Van Brugh Tennent ('58), William Tennent III ('58), and William Macky Tennent ('63)—were surely affected by the role played by their grandfather, their fathers, and their uncles in the celebrated battles of the 1740s.[65] And Ralph Pomeroy ('58) could hardly forget that when the revival was at its hottest in 1742, his father, the Reverend Benjamin Pomeroy of Hebron, Connecticut, had been arrested with the notorious revivalist James Davenport and had been brought to trial before the Connecticut General Assembly in 1744 for threatening with his itinerations the ecclesiastical order of the colony.[66] These young men were under the constant influence of their fathers, among whom were some of the most dynamic and impressive men in colonial America: Jonathan Edwards, Aaron Burr, Samuel Finley, and John Witherspoon. But their fathers also knew each other, were frequently related to each other, and were cooperating in effecting a religious revolution in colonial America. Consequently, the young Princetonians were influenced not only by their remarkable fathers but by what must have been at times an impressive group of single-minded men. That group included Whitefield himself, by whom, significantly, several of the clergy's relatives were strongly influenced if not actually converted. That influence was sometimes indirect, as in the case of Richard Hutson ('65). Whitefield converted his father, a South Carolina law student and actor, who then entered the ministry himself. Likewise, Alexander Craighead, the father of Thomas Craighead ('75), had itinerated with both Whitefield and Gilbert Tennent during the Awakening. For others the impact of Whitefield was immediate and direct, as when the evangelist passed through Princeton in 1763 and settled the young Thomas Claggett's tentative decision to follow his father into the ministry.[67]

Unlike the sons of the commercial and landed elite, the relatives of the clergy usually attended the Presbyterian academies, which, of course, often were superintended by their fathers and uncles. Some, like Connecticut's Samuel Kirkland ('65), probably studied with their minister fathers at home, while others were sent by their fathers to the home of an uncle to be educated. In the case of Ebenezer Pemberton ('65), his father, a judge, sent him at age seven to Boston to be educated by his uncle Ebenezer Pemberton, a Presbyterian cleric who had been quite active in establishing Princeton. Likewise, John Woodhull ('66), William R. Davie ('76), and Benjamin Rush were sent to study at the academies of their respective uncles, the Reverends Caleb Smith, William Richardson, and Samuel Finley— Presbyterians all.[68] More regularly, though, the sons of the clergy attended academies superintended by their fathers, obviously so in the case of the sons of Finley, John and Samuel Blair, and Robert Smith, but less obviously so in the instance of a young man like Charles McKnight ('71), who received his classical education in his minister-father's Mattison Grammar School in Lower Freehold, New Jersey. And the sons of the Princeton presidents—Jonathan Edwards, Jr., John Witherspoon, Jr. ('73), and his brother David ('74) among them—attended the grammar school established at the college by Burr, which functioned in the colonial period as another Presbyterian academy.[69]

But for all of the impact of their fathers and other evangelicals, the majority of these young men did not enter the ministry upon leaving the school at Princeton. Instead, they became merchants or, more frequently, doctors and lawyers, which is to say that they regularly entered those professions also chosen by the sons of the commercial and landed elite. One of the sons of Jonathan Edwards, Pierpont, became a lawyer, judge, and U.S. congressman; while his brother Timothy developed a successful mercantile business first in New Jersey and then in Massachusetts. The three sons of Samuel Finley followed their cousin Benjamin

Rush into the practice of medicine rather than following their father into the ministry. And, reversing a clerical tradition that went back at least to his great-great-grandfather Solomon Stoddard, the younger Aaron Burr abandoned his intentions to study theology after only a year of study with the Reverend Joseph Bellamy. Instead, young Burr began to read law with his brother-in-law, Tapping Reeve, himself a 1763 Princeton graduate who had likewise chosen the law over the profession of his father, the Reverend Abner Reeve of Long Island, and who in Litchfield, Connecticut, established the first private legal school in the colonies.[70] It should be noted that the younger Burr had been orphaned as a child when his mother, his father, and his grandfather Edwards died at close intervals. Consequently, he was raised in the home of his uncle Timothy Edwards, who, as noted, had already become an established merchant rather than following his father into the ministry.

Even though they chose secular careers, the sons of the clergy were often moved by dramatic and transforming conversion experiences. Benjamin Young Prime ('51), the son of the Reverend James Prime of Connecticut, has left a moving description of the spiritual turmoil that finally ended with his conversion, throughout which he was led and comforted by his father. Prime decided to practice medicine rather than preach the Word, possibly because he himself was rather sickly, but surely *not* because he had failed of conversion.[71]

Nor was the decision not to enter the ministry lightly taken. On the contrary, it was often quite a traumatic experience. Ebenezer Pemberton, for instance, after studying with the uncle whose name he shared, graduated from Princeton, and read theology for a year before deciding against the ministry, according to family tradition, "from his physical sensibility and religious scruples." His uncle was bitterly disappointed and gave to Princeton the library he had promised his nephew, who appears to have spent the rest of his life searching unsuccessfully in the law and in teaching for a rewarding alternative to the clerical career he had reluctantly rejected as a young man.[72]

Benjamin Rush has left the most poignant expression of the trauma occasioned by rejecting "divinity." His uncle and teacher, Samuel Finley, and Rush himself, had expected that he would enter the ministry upon leaving Princeton. But Rush could never be satisfied that he had been "called" to the "sacred desk." President Samuel Davies, himself one of the colonies' most effective orators, then encouraged the young man to study law instead. Finley objected, though, that the legal profession was full of temptation and instead urged his nephew to "set a day for fasting and prayer and ask of God to direct you in the choice of a profession." The young man did so and followed Finley's further advice to study medicine if he could not in good faith give himself to the ministry.[73] But the choice was a very difficult one for Rush, who greatly admired those of his classmates who had decided upon a clerical career. In 1761, one year after his graduation, he congratulated his classmate Enoch Green for having "obeyed nature's dictates in the sublime study of Divinity" and declared that "to have officiated in the Sacred Desk would be my most delightful employment." Disappointed as he was by his "incapacity" for the study of divinity, Rush could nevertheless be reassured by the New Side doctrine that every profession was a calling of God whereby the righteous could serve: "To spend and be spent for the Good of Mankind is what I chiefly aim at."[74] And spend himself Rush did. He was at the forefront of virtually every reform movement in the new republic, earning from his contemporaries a reputation as an officious busybody and from his latest biographer the apt label of "revolutionary gadfly." Possibly Rush's frantic efforts to do good to and for others in the new republic reflect as much his guilt at rejecting the ministry as his New Side dedication to godly effort in any and all callings.

Many sons of the clergy, of course, did follow their fathers into the ministry, and several of these are very significant exceptions to the rule that most did not. Chief among them were the sons of Robert Smith—Samuel Stanhope and John Blair. The former became the president first of Virginia's Hampden-Sydney College and then of Princeton (1794–1812); the latter served in the same capacity at New York's Union College. Likewise, Samuel Kirkland ('65), the son of the Reverend Daniel Kirkland of Connecticut, was the founder of Hamilton College, while Israel Evans ('72), another fourth-generation Presbyterian minister, served as one of the most effective chaplains in the Revolution and later as an influential New Hampshire cleric. And few churchmen were as busy in the new republic as Jonathan Edwards, Jr., the only one of the great man's sons to follow his father into the ministry. There were others—John Davenport ('69); John Evans Finley ('76), President Finley's nephew; Benoni Bradner ('55)—more than twenty in all.[75]

The careers of the clergymen's sons reveal a truth that Christians, and particularly evangelical Christians, learn anew each generation: the fervor of one generation cannot often be transferred intact to another. For the truth is that the conversion experiences of the clergy's sons appear often to have been perfunctory or the undramatic, predictable culmination of years of parental nurture. And when one of the clergy's sons did decide to enter the ministry, his decision was seldom a traumatic one. For the most part, he determined early to follow his father and did not deviate from that decision: such was certainly the case with both the sons of Robert Smith. Indeed, the career decision appears to have been traumatic only when the minister's son determined, for whatever reason, not to follow his father's example.

Whether they entered the commercial and landed gentry or followed their fathers into the ministry, the sons and nephews of the clergy among Princeton's colonial sons had a direct influence on the vitality and success of the college in the latter half of the eighteenth century. Clearly, they were among the college's staunchest supporters and performed for Princeton a wide range of services. While studying medicine in Edinburgh, Benjamin Rush almost single-handedly charmed a troubled Mrs. John Witherspoon into allowing her husband to immigrate to America. At the same time, back at the college the trustees had chosen Samuel Blair, Jr., Rush's classmate, to superintend Princeton in the event Rush's campaign was not successful.[76] But it fell to another son of the clergy, Samuel Stanhope Smith, to become the first alumni of the college to fill Princeton's highest

office. Others of the clergy's relatives served as trustees of the college, Andrew
Hunter ('72), Frederick Frelinghuysen ('70), and John Woodhull ('66) being but a
few.[77]

The career of one trustee, William Macky Tennent ('63), illustrates the services
performed by the sons of the clergy for the college. Tennent was, in fact, doubly
descended from Presbyterian clerics: he was the paternal grandson of the elder
William Tennent and the maternal grandson of an Irish clergyman. In Tennent's
case, if not in others, his clerical heritage impelled him into the Presbyterian
ministry. He served churches in Connecticut and Pennsylvania and was a life-long
supporter of Princeton, serving on the college's board from 1785 until 1805.
Perhaps more important, Tennent rose to high positions of authority in the
Presbyterian hierarchy—he was moderator of the General Assembly in 1797—and
from those offices he advanced the interests of his alma mater. That support clearly
contributed to the college's success. Equally obvious, it measures the impact of
evangelical religion on the lives of Princetonians who, like Tennent, were the sons
of the colonial clergy.[78]

VI

That the sons of wealthy merchants, landholders, and public officials patronized
colonial Princeton is not surprising; nor was it particularly unusual for the sons of
the clergy to be given a higher education. The wealth of one and the occupational
status of the other determined that usually, if not invariably, the sons of the two
elites would attend some institution of higher learning. That assumption was not
justified in the case of a third group of students at colonial Princeton. They were the
sons of small farmers and businessmen, laborers, and artisans, whose presence at
the Presbyterian college measures the extent to which Princeton was, for a large
part of its colonial student body, a significant instrument of social mobility. That
social function was largely a result of the evangelical revival and measures another
important way in which the revival produced the vitality of colonial Princeton.

It is not possible to be precise in designating young men for inclusion in this
group, but some generalizations can be made. Where they survive, the wills of
their fathers indicate estates usually inventoried at less than £500. That of John
Warford, "yeoman" of New Jersey and father of Princeton's '74 graduate of the
same name, was inventoried at £82, while the estate of Philip Fithian's father, also
of New Jersey, was valued at £444. And although Joseph Rue's father left two
small farms in New Jersey to his six children, his estate was valued at only £366.[79]
(At the same time, the colonial gentry regularly left estates inventoried at two to
five thousand pounds.)[80] In the absence of readily available wills, the economic and
social status of other graduates may be deduced from their fathers' occupations.
Many Princetonians—like John Wilkes Kittera ('76), Luther Martin ('66), and
Elihu Thayer ('69)—were the sons of small, often poor farmers.[81] The fathers of
others combined farming with supplementary trades: the father of William Ramsey
('54) was a cattle drover, while Josiah Sherman's father was a shoemaker and

cordwainer as well as a Connecticut farmer.[82] Still others were the sons of artisans and small businessmen. William Whitwell ('58) was the son of a Boston whalebone cutter, Andrew King's father was a clothier, and Alexander McWhorter ('57) was the son of a linen merchant.[83] Finally, the circumstances under which they came to and remained at Princeton also indicate the poorer Princetonians' economic status. Before coming to Princeton many of these young men had to raise money themselves to pay for their education, principally by keeping school, as in the cases of Samuel Doak, William Graham, and Thaddeus Dod.[84] And some could attend Princeton only if supported by scholarships. For instance, when David Rice accompanied Samuel Davies to Princeton in 1758, the young Virginian was supported by a fund earlier solicited by Davies and Gilbert Tennent on their "begging tour" of Great Britain. When that money stopped, Rice contemplated leaving Nassau Hall because of his shabby wardrobe but was persuaded to stay by the wealthy Richard Stockton ('48), who apparently advanced Rice the money for clothing suitable to colonial Princeton.[85]

For the most part, these young men were the first in their families to attend college. Generally, they came to Princeton either at the encouragement of their mothers—and sometimes of their fathers—or they were recruited by their Presbyterian ministers. Frequently, parents and pastors cooperated. In any case, the dynamics of evangelical religion were the primary motivating force in the individual decisions that, taken together, made of colonial Princeton an effective means of social mobility for a significant part of its colonial student body.

Ironically, pious lay parents were sometimes more successful in directing their sons into the ministry than their pastors were in persuading their own sons to follow in that calling. Children of the laity were sometimes dedicated to the ministry even before birth, much as the Old Testament's Hannah had promised to Jehovah any son that was conceived in her barren womb. In at least two instances—those of John McMillan and Alexander McWhorter—parents promised to God a child that would replace a son who had just died. These dedicated sons became, respectively, the leaders of Presbyterianism in western Pennsylvania and in North Carolina.[86] Another became a president of colonial Princeton. Samuel Davies took seriously the dedication implied in his name. "I am a son of prayer, like my name-sake *Samuel* the prophet; and my mother called me *Samuel* because, she said, I have asked him of the Lord. . . . This early dedication to God has always been a strong inducement to me to devote myself to Him by my own personal act; and the most important blessings of my life I have looked upon as immediate answers to the prayers of a pious mother."[87] Others—Daniel McCalla ('66), James F. Armstrong ('73), Elihu Thayer ('69)—were the sons of pious lay parents who did not explicitly dedicate their sons to the ministry but early and vigorously impressed upon their offspring the importance of religion.[88]

In these instances, pious fathers and mothers agreed that it was desirable, indeed that it was essential, to send their sons to college, even if for the first time in their family's history. In other cases, that unity was lacking, fathers staunchly resisting the innovative career suggested by a son and his mother. Frequently, then, a young man and his mother sought the support of their pastor in overcoming a father's reluctance. On the frontier, the resulting familial-ministerial conflict was a familiar one. In Virginia's Shenandoah Valley, for instance, the farmer fathers of Caleb Wallace and William Graham both opposed their sons' wish to obtain an education preparatory to entering the clergy, and only a determined phalanx of Presbyterian ministers and Princetonians was able to overcome those paternal objections. William Graham enlisted the aid of both his mother and his pastor, the Reverend John Roan, in persuading his father to allow him to enter the ministry. Graham's neighbor, Caleb Wallace, had been converted by Samuel Davies, whose aid he then secured in overcoming his father's objections to his leaving the farm. Moreover, Wallace added to the pressure of President Davies that of James and David Caldwell, other neighbors who had themselves attended Princeton. Finally the elder Wallace relented; but not until his son was twenty-five years old was he allowed to leave his father's farm to enroll at Princeton.[89]

It is clear, then, that on the frontier, especially, Princeton-educated clergymen intruded into Presbyterian families, frequently became figures of authority in opposition to obstinate fathers, and with great effect altered the lives of a significant group of colonial Princetonians. The point cannot be emphasized too firmly. Virtually from its inception, Princeton produced graduates who then established academies which in turn prepared young men to come to Princeton. Those graduates—William Graham, John McMillan, Thaddeus Dod—then themselves established their own academies and thus extended the Presbyterian educational empire, which by 1800 included many such academies as well as colleges in every state west and south of the Hudson. In the colonial period that system of academies functioned to locate, prepare, and then send to Princeton young men from those parts of American society that heretofore had not regularly sent their sons to any college.[90]

Samuel Doak was one such young man. He was the son of a Scotch-Irish farmer who immigrated first to Chester County, Pennsylvania, and then to Augusta County in the Shenandoah Valley of Virginia, where Samuel was born. The young man worked on his father's farm until he was sixteen, when he was converted by one of the several Presbyterian ministers in the valley. After overcoming his father's objections by renouncing his small share of the small farm, Samuel and another boy built a hut next to the nearby Presbyterian academy, where Samuel studied first with the Reverend Robert Alexander and then with the Reverend John Brown, a member of Princeton's second graduating class. Between 1773 and 1775 Doak attended Brown's alma mater, where Witherspoon apparently confirmed him in his decision to enter the Presbyterian ministry. Upon graduation he studied theology with both Robert Smith at Pequa and with William Graham in the Shenandoah Valley. For two years he also tutored at Hampden-Sydney, the college across the Blue Ridge in Prince Edward County established by Robert Smith's sons, Samuel Stanhope and John Blair, with whom Doak also studied theology. Finally, he went to eastern Tennessee and established his own academy, which later became Washington College. Doak's experience—his humble birth, his problems with his father, the formative impact of several Presbyterian minister-educators, and his own career as an educator—is characteristic for the generation of Princetonians that established the educational empire which grew out of and then sustained Princeton in the last half of the eighteenth century.[91]

Like Doak, many of the poorer students at colonial Princeton were the products of that system of academies, and like him, many of them entered the Presbyterian clergy after graduating from Princeton. And like some of their wealthier classmates, some of the Princetonians of moderate circumstances were converted by George Whitefield. But more frequently than the conversions of their peers, the experiences of the poorer students were permanently transforming steps to a ministerial career.

The experience of John McMillan illustrates that fact. The son of a poor Scotch-Irish farmer who had dedicated him to the ministry before his birth, John attended both John Blair's Fagg's Manor academy and Robert Smith's school at Pequa, where he was converted at age fifteen by Whitefield. Before he received these "first religious impressions," he had "at times some checks of conscience, and was frequently terrified by dreams and visions in the night, which made me cry to God for mercy." But, "these seasons were of short duration," and like "the morning cloud and the early dew they quickly passed away." Whitefield led the boy to understand that he "was a lost undone sinner, exposed to the wrath of a justly offended God" and that he could do nothing to save himself. Shortly thereafter he went to Princeton, arriving just as a revival broke out. In that event his conversion was sealed: he "got some discoveries of Divine things which I had never had before," and now realized that divine law was not only holy, just and spiritual, but also that it was good, and that conformity to it would make me happy."[92] At each step of his conversion McMillan was guided by dynamic, impressive men who instructed him as to what conversion should and should not be. And the revivalists who led him superintended institutions that were designed to allow the young man to work out the implications of his conversion and finally to prepare for the Presbyterian ministry, the logical conclusion of his conversion experience. McMillan's experience—education at a Presbyterian academy, at least two years at Princeton, ordination to the Presbyterian ministry—was replicated in the lives of many colonial Princetonians of moderate means.

Not all of these young men, though, were impelled into the ministry by a transforming conversion experience; for some, the reasons for seeking ordination were quite practical. Joseph Rue ('76), the son of a New Jersey farmer, had already begun to work as a shoemaker when he lost an arm in an accident. Rue had been raised in the congregation of the younger William Tennent, and now he decided to follow the profession of his minister, for whom he apparently had great affection. Rue graduated from Princeton in 1776, studied theology with Tennent, and was ordained over the Presbyterian Church at Pennington, New Jersey, where he remained for forty-one years.[93]

Other poorer young men came to Princeton with every intention of entering the ministry but did not do so. Some, like Joseph Lyon ('63), possibly were deterred by problems of health.[94] Others, like their wealthier colleagues, were distracted by the practice of law. The experience of Hugh Henry Brackenridge is instructive because his early life is illustrative of that of many poorer young men who followed through on their decision to enter the ministry. Brackenridge was the son of a very poor Scotch-Irish farmer in York County, Pennsylvania. A precocious child, Brackenridge was encouraged by his pious mother and by his pastor to prepare for the ministry, which he did, first in neighborhood schools and then at Wither-spoon's Princeton, graduating in 1771. Indeed, he was even licensed in 1777. But Brackenridge never presented himself for ordination and instead studied law, edited a political periodical, and finally served in the United States Congress and on the Supreme Court of Pennsylvania. In short, he discovered politics.[95]

Although it was not the case with Brackenridge, some young men of moderate means risked the wrath of pious fathers when they succumbed to the temptations of politics, medicine, or the law. Andrew Kirkpatrick ('75), the son of a modest farmer, dutifully studied theology with the Reverend Samuel Kennedy to satisfy his father's desire that his son become a minister. But after six months the Princeton graduate left Kennedy and began to read law with another son of Nassau Hall, William Paterson ('63). His father carried out his threat to drive Andrew from his home if he abandoned theology, and Mrs. Kirkpatrick apparently supported her son's legal education to the extent that she could with her own savings. Significantly, Kirkpatrick, having rejected the ministry for himself, was among the staunchest advocates of a seminary to train young men for the clergy and was the chairman of the Board of Trustees of the Princeton Theological Seminary from its creation in 1807 until his death in 1831.[96]

While some of Princeton's poorer students abandoned an intention to study theology, many never aspired to enter the clergy. John Wilkes Kittera ('76) was the son of a modest farmer who also was an elder in Robert Smith's Pequa Church. Almost certainly, then, young Kittera received his classical education at Smith's academy, thus coming under the influence of the minister-educator both at school and in services. Upon graduating from Princeton, however, Kittera began to study the law, apparently never having considered the clergy as a possible career. Luther Martin ('66) was also the son of a poor farmer and, like Kittera, turned to the law after departing Nassau Hall. And the Ramsey brothers, David ('65) and Nathaniel ('67), chose medicine and law as the professions through which they would overcome their humble origins.[97] Their careers and those of other poorer Princetonians who did not enter the clergy serve finally, though, to emphasize the rule to which they are apparently the exceptions: in the colonial period most Princetonians of moderate means appear to have entered the ministry and to thereby have strengthened the clerical community upon which the college in the eighteenth century ultimately depended for its support.

VII

A brief discussion of the impact of evangelical religion on Princeton's colonial student body does not, of course, thoroughly explain the vigor of the college at the mid-century. No mention has been made, for instance, of the colonial

curriculum—of the effect of the Scottish moral philosophy on colonial Princetonians; of their response to the embryonic social sciences presented by their
professors in classes on natural philosophy, chronology and history, composition
and criticism. Princeton's curriculum was fundamentally influenced by the course
of study at the Scottish universities and, for that reason, directly exposed colonial
students to the creativity and vitality of the Scottish Enlightenment.[98] That exposure, greatly strengthened by Witherspoon's coming to the colonies, clearly was a
significant factor in the intellectual vigor of Princeton. Moreover, the present
essay's emphasis on the dynamics of evangelical religion does not completely
explain the fact that in the colonial period Princeton's clientele was expanded both
socially and geographically. Much more must be known about the social origins of
every colonial graduate and nongraduate before that expansion can be adequately
understood.

Nor is the essay intended to argue a necessary or universal relation between
evangelical religion and institutional or intellectual vigor. As noted, colonial
Harvard flourished while opposing the Great Awakening, and indeed, in the
American experience evangelical religion has probably more often been the foe
than the ally of intellectual advance. This was certainly true at Princeton after
1800, as the expansive evangelical fervor of the eighteenth century solidified into a
rigid orthodoxy—ironically, just as the European universities began to rouse from
their stultification. But that the specter of French infidelity and doubts about the
virtue of American republicans led nineteenth-century Presbyterians to make of
Princeton a bastion of orthodoxy should not obscure the fact that the college in the
eighteenth century had been a very different institution, that the evangelical
religion that held the nineteenth-century school in its numbing grip had helped
make eighteenth-century Princeton a dynamic institution, one of the most vital
products of the American Enlightenment.[99]

NOTES

1. See especially Marius B. Jansen and Lawrence Stone, "Education and Modernization in Japan
and England," *Comparative Studies in Society and History* 9 (1967): 208–32; Lawrence Stone, "The
Size and Composition of the Oxford Student Body, 1580–1909," in *The University in Society,* ed.
Lawrence Stone, 2 vols. (Princeton, 1974), 1:3–110; Richard L. Kagan, "Universities in Castile," in
ibid., 2: 355–405; and Kagan, *Students and Society in Early Modern Spain* (Baltimore, 1974).
2. Guy Howard Miller, "A Contracting Community: American Presbyterians, Social Conflict, and
Higher Education, 1730–1820" (Ph.D. diss., University of Michigan, 1970), pt. 1; and Douglas
Sloan, *The Scottish Enlightenment and the American College Ideal* (New York, 1971), chap. 1.
3. Samuel Eliot Morison, *Three Centuries of Harvard, 1636–1936* (Cambridge, Mass., 1946), pp.
3–163; Margery Somers Foster, *"Out of Smalle Beginnings...": An Economic History of Harvard
College in the Puritan Period* (Cambridge, Mass., 1962); Richard Warch, *School of the Prophets: Yale
College, 1701–1740* (New Haven, 1973).
4. Carl and Jessica Bridenbaugh, *Rebels and Gentlemen: Philadelphia in the Age of Franklin* (New
York, 1965), chap. 2; William L. Turner, "The College, Academy, and Charitable School of
Philadelphia: The Development of a Colonial Institution of Learning, 1740–1779" (Ph.D. diss.,
University of Pennsylvania, 1952); Patricia U. Bonomi, *A Factious People: Politics and Society in
Colonial New York* (New York, 1971), pp. 176–77; David C. Humphrey, "King's College in the City
of New York, 1754–1776" (Ph.D. diss., Northwestern University, 1968).
5. Miller, "A Contracting Community," chap. 9. But see David B. Potts, "American Colleges in

the Nineteenth Century: From Localism to Denominationalism," *History of Education Quarterly* 11 (Winter 1971): 363–80, for a contrasting view.

6. For an overview see Lawrence A. Cremin, *American Education: The Colonial Experience, 1607–1783* (New York, 1970), esp. pts. 1 and 4. Also useful are Norman S. Fiering, "President Samuel Johnson and the Circle of Knowledge," *William and Mary Quarterly*, 3rd ser. 28 (April 1971): 199–236; and Warch, *School of the Prophets*, chaps. 8–9.

7. Warch, *School of the Prophets*, chap. 10, is a particularly effective discussion of this process at early Yale. See also James Axtell, *The School upon a Hill: Education and Society in Colonial New England* (New Haven, 1974), chap. 6.

8. The best account of the American phase of the Great Awakening is the introduction to Alan Heimert and Perry Miller, eds., *The Great Awakening* (Indianapolis, 1967). A more extensive and sometimes perverse analysis may be found in Heimert's controversial *Religion and the American Mind* . . . (Cambridge, Mass., 1966).

9. The best discussion of that liberal religion is Conrad Wright, *The Beginnings of Unitarianism in America* (Boston, 1955); but see too Heimert, *Religion and the American Mind*, pt. 4.

10. Warch, *School of the Prophets*, chap. 4; Louis L. Tucker, *Puritan Protagonist: President Thomas Clap of Yale College* (Chapel Hill, 1962); and Stephen Nissenbaum, ed., *The Great Awakening at Yale College* (Belmont, Calif., 1972).

11. Edmund S. Morgan, *The Gentle Puritan: A Life of Ezra Stiles, 1727–1795* (New Haven, 1962), pp. 302, 316–18.

12. William V. Davis, ed., *George Whitefield's Journals, 1737–1741* (Gainesville, Fla., 1969), p. 351.

13. Archibald Alexander, *Biographical Sketches of the Founder and Principal Alumni of the Log College, Together with an Account of the Revivals of Religion, under Their Ministry* (Princeton, 1845); Thomas C. Pears and Guy S. Klett, comps., "A Documentary History of William Tennent and the Log College," *Journal of the Presbyterian Historical Society* 28 (September 1950): 173–74.

14. The best discussion of the reasons for the emigration from Ulster is in R. J. Dickson, *Ulster Emigration to Colonial America, 1718–1775* (London, 1966); and the most thorough analysis of the American experience of those emigrants is James G. Leyburn, *The Scotch-Irish* (Chapel Hill, 1962).

15. Alexander, *Biographical Sketches*, pp. 265, 303–4.

16. Ibid., p. 358; William B. Sprague, "Charles Beatty," *Annals of the American Pulpit: or Commemorative Notices of Distinguished American Clergymen of Various Denominations*, 9 vols. (New York, 1860), 3: 119.

17. Davis, *Whitefield's Journals*, p. 351.

18. *Records of the Presbyterian Church in the United States of America, 1706–1788* (New York, 1969), pp. 155–61; Leonard J. Trinterud, *The Forming of an American Tradition: A Re-examination of Colonial Presbyterianism* (Philadelphia, 1949), pt. 1.

19. The best effort to explain the social impact of the revival remains Richard L. Bushman's suggestive *From Puritan to Yankee: Character and the Social Order in Connecticut, 1690–1765* (Cambridge, Mass., 1967), esp. pt. 4.

20. For a competent discussion of the geographical division and its implications see Boyd S. Schlenther, "The Presbytery as Organ of Church Life and Government in American Presbyterianism, 1706–1788" (Ph.D. diss., University of Edinburgh, 1965), pp. 24–47.

21. Stephen J. Stein, "A Notebook on the Apocalypse by Jonathan Edwards," *William and Mary Quarterly*, 3rd ser. 29 (October 1972): 623–34; C. C. Goen, ed., *The Works of Jonathan Edwards: The Great Awakening* (New Haven, 1972), "Editor's Introduction."

22. Jonathan Edwards, "Sinners in the Hands of an Angry God," in *Jonathan Edwards*, ed. Clarence H. Faust and Thomas H. Johnson, rev. ed. (New York, 1962), pp. 155–72.

23. For example, see Aaron Burr, *The Watchman's Answer to the Question, What of the Night* . . . (New York, 1757).

24. See especially Miller, "A Contracting Community," pp. 98–106. But for a quite different view of the distinctions between the Old and the New Side, see Elizabeth A. Ingersoll, "Francis Alison, American Philosophe, 1705–1779" (Ph.D. diss., University of Delaware, 1974).

25. For the journals of two New Side ministers involved in missionary and fund-raising activities, respectively, see Guy S. Klett, ed., *Journals of Charles Beatty, 1762–1769* (University Park, Pa., 1962); and George W. Pilcher, ed., *The Reverend Samuel Davies Abroad: The Diary of a Journey to England and Scotland, 1753–55* (Urbana, 1967).

26. For a refined example of such sermons see Samuel Davies, *Little Children Invited to Jesus Christ* . . . (Boston, 1762).

27. The best articulation of the Presbyterian view of education's social function was made by New York's William Livingston in the bitter debate over the chartering of King's College in 1752–53. See Milton M. Klein, ed., *The Independent Reflector; or, Weekly Essays on Sundry Important Subjects More particularly adapted to the Province of New York by William Livingston and Others* (Cambridge, Mass., 1963), pp. 171–214.

28. *Presbyterian Records,* pp. 141, 145, 146.

29. Gilbert Tennent, *Remarks upon a Protestation Presented to the Synod of Philadelphia, June 1, 1741* (Philadelphia, 1741), p. 41; Samuel Finley, *Christ Triumphing and Satan Raging* . . . (Philadelphia, 1741), p. 20; [Samuel Blair, Jr.], *An Account of the College of New-Jersey* . . . (Woodbridge, N.J., 1764), pp. 5–6.

30. Sprague, "Aaron Burr," *Annals,* 3: 68–72; Keith J. Hardman, "Jonathan Dickinson and the Course of American Presbyterianism, 1717–1747" (Ph.D. diss., University of Pennsylvania, 1971).

31. Alison B. Olson, "The Founding of Princeton University: Religion and Politics in Eighteenth-Century New Jersey," *New Jersey History* 87 (Autumn 1969): 133–50; Margaret W. Masson, "The Premises and Purposes of Higher Education in American Society, 1745–1770" (Ph.D. diss., University of Washington, 1971), pp. 53–63.

32. *A General Account of the Rise and State of the College, Lately Established in the Province of New-Jersey, in America; And of the End and Design of Its Institution* (New York, 1752), p. 4. Phyllis Erenberg has recently estimated that 70 percent of Princeton's students between 1746 and 1799 were Presbyterians and that 18 percent were Anglicans. More striking, she finds that 75 percent of the school's students during that period came from outside New Jersey and that an astonishing 50 percent of them were born outside New Jersey, Pennsylvania, and New York. Erenberg's work is among the most provocative in a recent rash of doctoral dissertations on colonial higher education (Phyllis V. Erenberg, "Change and Continuity: Values in American Higher Education, 1750–1800" [Ph.D. diss., University of Michigan, 1974], pp. 220–23). David Humphrey, on the other hand, has found that 80 percent of King's colonial students were raised within 30 miles of the New York City campus and that more than one-half of them were from Manhattan itself. In addition, while he found that 40 percent of students who matriculated between 1754 and 1764 were members of the Dutch Reformed Church, between 1766 and 1776 the college's attraction for the city's Anglican population became pronounced: 75 percent of the young men who enrolled in that decade were communicants of the Church of England. See Humphrey, "King's College," pp. 329–30, 342.

33. For an extended discussion of the Presbyterians' reactions to the deaths of the Princeton presidents, see my "The 'Frown of Heaven' and 'Degenerate America': A Note on the Princeton Presidency," *Princeton University Library Chronicle* 31 (Autumn 1969): 38–46.

34. Synod of New York to the Presbyterian General Assembly of Scotland, 3 October 1753, *Presbyterian Records,* p. 257; *To the Worthy and Generous Friends of Religion and Learning: The Petition of Gilbert Tennent and Samuel Davies, in the Name of the Trustees of the Infant College of New Jersey* . . . (London, 1754), p. 2 (typescript in Firestone Library, Princeton University).

35. But see Douglas Sloan's helpful chapter on the Presbyterian academies in his *American College Ideal,* pp. 36–72.

36. Jacob N. Beam, "Dr. Robert Smith's Academy at Pequa, Pennsylvania," *Journal of the Presbyterian Historical Society* 8 (December 1915): 145–61.

37. For an exhaustive list of the Presbyterian academies, see the appendix to Sloan's *American College Ideal,* pp. 281–84.

38. Samuel Davies Alexander, "Spruce Macay," *Princeton College during the Eighteenth Century* (New York, 1872), p. 188; E. W. Caruthers, *A Sketch of the Life and Character of the Rev. David Caldwell* . . . (Greensborough, N.C., 1842), pp. 18–20.

39. Sloan, *American College Ideal,* pp. 60–61n.

40. I am particularly indebted to Professor McLachlan of Princeton for these figures.

41. The significance of this elite is only now beginning to be appreciated by historians, and much more work needs to be done on crucial aspects of its emergence at the mid-century, especially on the role that shared collegiate experiences and intermarriage played in the development of the elite. But see Carl Bridenbaugh's helpful discussion in *Cities in Revolt: Urban Life in America, 1743–1776* (New York, 1955), chap. 9; and P. M. G. Harris's provocative "The Social Origins of American Leaders: The Demographic Foundations," *Perspectives in American History* 3 (1969): 159–344. Especially interesting is Appendix A, in which Harris distinguishes between the sons of a "secular" and a "professional" upper class in early America. For colonial Princeton, at least, it seemed more helpful to distinguish between the sons of a "secular" and a "sacred" elite. Indeed, Professor Harris's profes-

sional upper class—which includes the clergy, doctors, and college presidents—becomes essentially a sacred upper class (excepting only the doctors who were not also clerics) when one remembers that colonial college presidents were always clergymen. Both Bridenbaugh's and Harris's work should now be read in light of the recent novel and frequently convincing thesis of Professors John Murrin and Rowland Berthoff. After investigating land-holding patterns on the eve of the Revolution, among other things, Berthoff and Murrin consider the American Revolution as a "social accident" and suggest that the events of 1776 may have prevented what they aptly call a "feudal revival" in America. See "Feudalism, Communalism, and the Yeoman Freeholder: The American Revolution Considered as a Social Accident," in *Essays on the American Revolution*, ed. Stephen G. Kurtz and James H. Hutson (Chapel Hill, 1973), pp. 256–88. Then see [Joseph O. Brown], *The Jaunceys of New York* (New York, 1876); Betsy C. Corner, *William Shippen, Jr.: Pioneer in American Medical Education* (Philadelphia, 1951); William Ogden Wheeler, *The Ogden Family in America* (Philadelphia, 1907).

42. New Jersey Historical Society, *Documents Relating to the Colonial History of the State of New Jersey . . .* (Newark, N.J., 1880–), *Abstracts of Wills*, 4: 153–54; 5: 539.

43. Ibid., 4: 487.

44. Lorenzo Sabine, *Biographical Sketches of Loyalists*, 2 vols. (Boston, 1864), 1: 572.

45. Douglass Adair, "James Madison," in *The Lives of Eighteen from Princeton*, ed. Willard Thorp (Princeton, 1946), pp. 137–40; John F. Roche, *Joseph Reed: A Moderate in the American Revolution* (New York, 1957), p. 6.

46. Glenn A. Glenn, *William Churchill Houston, 1746–1788* (Norristown, Pa., 1903), pp. 6–8.

47. One exception was John Henry ('69), who did attend Finley's Nottingham Academy near his father's Maryland estate. It should be noted, though, that Henry was the grandson of another John Henry, one of the earliest Presbyterian ministers to Maryland, who in America married the daughter of an Irish baronet (Sprague, "John Henry," *Annals*, 3: 5n; *Dictionary of American Biography*, s.v. "John Henry").

48. Alexander, "Thomas Melville," *Princeton*, pp. 129–30; "Andrew Hodge," ibid., pp. 152–53; "Robert Ogden," ibid., p. 99; "Isaac Handy," ibid., p. 71.

49. *DAB*, s.v. "William Stevens Smith"; Alexander, "William Channing," *Princeton*, p. 128; "Hugh Hodge," ibid., pp. 164–65; "James Smith," ibid., p. 50. For James Smith's merchant father, who was also a Princeton charter trustee, see Franklin B. Dexter, *Biographical Sketches of the Graduates of Yale College with Annals of the College History*, series I–III, 1701–78 (New York, 1896–), 1:207–11.

50. Alexander, "David Cowell," *Princeton*, p. 83; "Ebenezer Cowell," ibid., p. 105. For the will of their father, an extensive landholder and deputy-surveyor of West Jersey, see New Jersey, *Abstracts of Wills*, 4: 94.

51. Alexander, "John McPherson," *Princeton*, pp. 110–11. For the will of Philip Livingston, Henry's father and signer of the Declaration of Independence, see New Jersey, *Abstracts of Wills*, 5: 314.

52. Alexander, "Jonathan Dickinson Sergeant," *Princeton*, pp. 79–80; Clifford K. Shipton, "Nathaniel Niles," *Sibley's Harvard Graduates: Biographical Sketches of Those Who Attended Harvard College*, 16 vols. to date (Boston, 1873–), 16: 391–92; *DAB*, s.v. "Nathaniel Niles."

53. See especially Samuel Davies, *Religion and Publick Spirit: A Valedictory Address to the Senior Class Delivered in Nassau-Hall, September 21, 1760* (Portsmouth, N.H., 1762), pp. 4–7.

54. Sloan, *American College Ideal*, pp. 103–45; Miller, "A Contracting Community," chap. 7.

55. Cremin, *American Education*, pt. 4.

56. *DAB*, s.v. "William Bradford"; Alexander, *Princeton*, pp. 148–49.

57. *DAB*, s.v. "Thomas Henderson"; James Burtis, "Henderson Family in Monmouth County" (bound MS, Firestone Library, Princeton University).

58. Corner, *William Shippen*, pp. 6–7. For the will of Peter Fish's father see New-York Historical Society, *Collections of the New-York Historical Society . . .* (New York, 1868–), *Abstracts of Wills*, 7: 242.

59. Aaron Burr to David Cowell, 7 November 1753, in William L. Ledwith, "Six Letters of President Burr," *Journal of the Presbyterian Historical Society* 1 (September 1902): 320; Charles A. Philhower, "Benjamin Woodruff," in William R. McKinney et al., *Commemorative History of the Presbyterian Church in Westfield, New Jersey, 1728–1928* (n.p., 1929), p. 164.

60. *DAB*, s.v. "Samuel Livermore," "Morgan Lewis"; William G. Brown, "The Early Life of Oliver Ellsworth," *American Historical Review* 10 (April 1905): 546–48; Sprague, "Samuel Spring," *Annals*, 2: 85–86.

61. John M. Wilson, *The Blessedness of Such as Die in the Lord: A Sermon, Preached at Bethany, Iredell County, North Carolina, February, 1805* . . . (Salisbury, N.C., 1805), pp. 24–28; Sprague, "Lewis F. Wilson," *Annals,* 3: 570–72.

62. Sprague, "Israel Evans," *Annals,* 2: 138; Frederick L. Weis, *The Colonial Clergy of the Middle Colonies: New York, New Jersey, and Pennsylvania, 1628–1776* (Worcester, Mass., 1957), p. 221.

63. Samuel Holt Monk, "Samuel Stanhope Smith: Friend of Rational Liberty," in Thorp, *Eighteen from Princeton,* p. 86; "John Blair Smith," *The Assembly's Magazine; or, Evangelical Intelligencer* 1 (June 1805): 267; David F. Hawke, *Benjamin Rush: Revolutionary Gadfly* (Indianapolis, 1971), chap. 1; *DAB,* s.v. "Aaron Burr, Jr."

64. George B. Utley, *The Life and Times of Thomas John Claggett* (Chicago, 1913); Alexander, "Benjamin Stelle," *Princeton,* pp. 115–16; "Ralph Pomeroy," ibid., p. 53; Dexter, "Benjamin Pomeroy," *Biographical Sketches,* 1: 485–88.

65. Stephen Wickes, "John Van Brugh Tennent," *History of Medicine in New Jersey and of Its Medical Men from the Settlement of the Province to A.D. 1800* (Newark, N.J., 1879), p. 421; D. K. Ludwig, "Memorabilia of the Tennents," *Journal of the Presbyterian Historical Society* 1 (September 1902): 352–53; Shipton, "William Tennent III," *Sibley's Harvard Graduates,* 14: 338.

66. Sprague, "Benjamin Pomeroy," *Annals,* 1: 394–95.

67. *DAB,* s.v. "Richard Hutson"; Alice M. Baldwin, "Sowers of Sedition: The Political Theories of Some of the New Light Presbyterian Clergy of Virginia and North Carolina," *William and Mary Quarterly,* 3rd ser. 5 (January 1948): 64. The case of Claggett is particularly interesting because his father, William, took holy orders as a middle-aged man, having already established a prosperous plantation in Maryland (John N. Norton, *The Life of Bishop Claggett, of Maryland* [New York, 1859], pp. 21–22; Utley, *Claggett,* p. 7).

68. Thorp, "Samuel Kirkland," *Eighteen from Princeton,* p. 26; Shipton, "Ebenezer Pemberton," *Sibley's Harvard Graduates,* 16: 197; Sprague, "John Woodhull," *Annals,* 3: 304; Blackwell P. Robinson, *William R. Davie* (Chapel Hill, 1957), pp. 18–26.

69. Sprague, "Jonathan Edwards, Jr.," *Annals,* 1: 653–54. The evidence for the Witherspoon boys' attending the grammar school is circumstantial but persuasive, given the boys' ages (eleven and eight) at the time of their father's immigration.

70. *DAB,* s.v. "Pierpont Edwards"; Samuel H. Fisher, *The Litchfield Law School, 1775–1833* (New Haven, 1933), pp. 1–2, 12–13.

71. The account is reprinted in full in Charles W. Wheelock, "Dr. Benjamin Young Prime (1733–1791), American Poet" (Ph.D. diss., Princeton University, 1961), pp. ix–xvii.

72. Shipton, "Ebenezer Pemberton," *Sibley's Harvard Graduates,* 16: 197–98.

73. Quoted in J. Kendall Wallis, "Benjamin Rush: Universal Doctor," in Thorp, *Eighteen from Princeton,* p. 52.

74. Benjamin Rush to Enoch Green, Philadelphia, 1761, in *Letters of Benjamin Rush,* ed. Lyman H. Butterfield, 2 vols. (Princeton, 1951), 1: 3.

75. Sprague, "John Davenport," *Annals,* 3:92; Mrs. J. Harry Gorley, "The Clan Finley" (typed MS, c. 1892, Presbyterian Historical Society, Philadelphia), pp. 13–14; Alexander, "Benoni Bradner," *Princeton,* p. 34. In her study of the student bodies of Princeton, Dickinson, Union, King's, and the College of Philadelphia, Erenberg found that between 1746 and 1799, 63.3 percent of the sons of ministers themselves became clergymen ("Change and Continuity," p. 248). In marked contrast, David Humphrey finds that only two of King's colonial students followed their fathers into the ministry. The same number from the mercantile and professional elite chose a clerical career, while the majority of those other students who entered the ministry did so only after pursuing and then leaving another vocation ("King's College," pp. 362–63).

76. For an account of Rush's campaign see Lyman H. Butterfield, ed., *John Witherspoon Comes to America* (Princeton, 1953); Sprague, "Samuel Blair, Jr.," *Annals,* 3: 268–69.

77. *DAB,* s.v. "Andrew Hunter," "Frederick Frelinghuysen"; Sprague, "John Woodhull," *Annals,* 3: 304–6.

78. Sprague, "William Macky Tennent," *Annals,* 3: 26; Alexander, "William Macky Tennent," *Princeton,* p. 89.

79. New Jersey, *Abstracts of Wills,* 4: 367, 465; 5: 177.

80. See, for example, the wills of Richard Stockton (New Jersey, *Abstracts of Wills,* 6: 375); Philip Livingston, father of Henry Philip Livingston, '76 (ibid., 5: 314); Nicholas Bayard, father of Nicholas Bayard, '75 (New York, *Abstracts of Wills,* 6: 428–30).

81. "Thomas Kittera and His Descendants," *Journal of the Presbyterian Historical Society* 2 (December 1903): 172; Henry P. Goddard, "Luther Martin, The 'Federal Bull-dog,'" Maryland

Historical Society, *Fund Publications* 24 (1887): 12; Shipton, "Elihu Thayer," *Sibley's Harvard Graduates,* 16: 539. Erenberg finds, unsurprisingly, that only 26 percent of the sons of farmers at her five colleges between 1746 and 1799 returned to the farm after graduation ("Change and Continuity," p. 248).

82. Caldwell Woodruff, "The Ramsey Family," *Vineland Historical Magazine* 26 (July 1941): 233–42; Shipton, "Josiah Sherman," *Sibley's Harvard Graduates,* 13: 488.

83. Shipton, "William Whitwell," *Sibley's Harvard Graduates,* 14: 367; Sprague, "Andrew King," *Annals,* 4: 397n; "Alexander McWhorter," ibid., 3: 208.

84. Janie P. C. French, *The Doak Family* (Chattanooga, 1933), pp. 63–64; Hugh B. Grigsby, "The Founders of Washington College," Washington and Lee University, *Historical Papers* 2 (1890): 15–16; [Cephas Dod], "Autobiography and Memoir of Rev. Thaddeus Dod" (MS in Presbyterian Historical Society), p. 6.

85. Robert Davidson, *History of the Presbyterian Church in the State of Kentucky with a Preliminary Sketch of the Churches in the Valley of Virginia* (New York, 1837), pp. 65–66.

86. Joseph Smith, *History of Jefferson College: Including an Account of the Early Log-Cabin Schools, and the Canonsburg Academy* (Pittsburgh, 1857), p. 414; "Alexander McWhorter," *Presbyterian Magazine* 3 (July 1853): 330.

87. Quoted in George W. Pilcher, *Samuel Davies: Apostle of Dissent in Colonial Virginia* (Knoxville, Tenn., 1971), p. 5.

88. Sprague, "Daniel McCalla," *Annals,* 3: 320; "James F. Armstrong," ibid., 3: 389; "Elihu Thayer," ibid., 2: 104–5.

89. Henry Ruffner, "Early History of Washington College, Now Washington and Lee University," Washington and Lee University, *Historical Papers* 1 (1890): 61; William H. Whitsitt, *Life and Times of Judge Caleb Wallace* (Louisville, 1888), pp. 9–13. For a thoughtful discussion of the impact of mature students on New England student populations in the nineteenth century, see David F. Allmendinger, Jr., *Paupers and Scholars: The Transformation of Student Life in Nineteenth-Century New England* (New York, 1975), esp. pp. 130–38.

90. Miller, "A Contracting Community," pp. 189–95; Donald R. Come, "The Influence of Princeton on Higher Education in the South before 1825," *William and Mary Quarterly,* 3rd ser. 2 (October 1945): 359–96.

91. French, *Doak Family,* pp. 63–64; Sprague, "Samuel Doak," *Annals,* 3: 392–94.

92. Dwight Guthrie, *John McMillan: The Apostle of Presbyterianism in the West, 1752–1833* (Pittsburgh, 1952), pp. 8–12; quotations from John McMillan, "Biography" (MS in Presbyterian Historical Society), pp. 1–3. For a description of a more traumatic conversion experience of a young man who, like McMillan, was dedicated to the ministry at birth, see "Alexander McWhorter," *Presbyterian Magazine* 3 (July 1853): 330n.

93. George Hale, *A History of the Old Presbyterian Congregation of the "People of Maidenhead and Hopewell," More Especially the First Presbyterian Church of Hopewell at Pennington, New Jersey . . .* (Philadelphia, 1876), p. 66.

94. Samuel R. Winans, "Biographical Sketches of the Elders Who Served in the First Presbyterian Church of Elizabethtown, New Jersey, Fifty Years Ago" (1869 MS in the Presbyterian Historical Society), p. 2.

95. Daniel Marder, *Hugh Henry Brackenridge* (New York, 1967), pp. 24–31.

96. James Grant Wilson, *Memorials of Andrew Kirkpatrick, and His Wife Jane Bayard* (New York, 1870), pp. 15–17.

97. "Thomas Kittera and His Descendants," *Journal of the Presbyterian Historical Society* 2 (December 1903): 172; Goddard, "Luther Martin," p. 12; W. F. Brand, "A Sketch of the Life and Character of Nathaniel Ramsey," Maryland Historical Society, *Fund Publications* 24 (1887): 45; *DAB,* s.v. "David Ramsey."

98. Sloan, *American College Ideal,* pp. 103–17; Francis L. Broderick, "Pulpit, Physics, and Politics: The Curriculum of the College of New Jersey, 1746–1796," *William and Mary Quarterly,* 3rd ser. 6 (January 1949): 42–68.

99. Miller, "A Contracting Community," chap. 10.

CHAPTER 6

The Aristocracy and University Reform in Eighteenth-Century Germany

BY CHARLES E. MC CLELLAND

In 1700, the Holy Roman Empire contained thirty-two universities. Some were large, old, and famous—like Leipzig, Vienna, and Heidelberg. Most were small, relatively new (founded since the Reformation), and obscure. But even the famous universities had fallen on evil days by the end of the seventeenth century. So moribund were the German universities, so low was their reputation, that many reformers—such as Leibniz—called for their abolition and replacement by specialized academies. Such sentiments existed in France, too, and the traditional university system there was finally dismantled during the revolution. In Germany, however, such radical solutions did not come about. Many universities survived into the nineteenth century, and the German university became a model for foreign emulation.

One traditional explanation for the survival of these medieval educational institutions in an age of reform and revolution lies in the power of inertia and the stubborn resistance of the guildlike corporations of professors. But not all survived. The ones which closed their doors during the period of the Napoleonic wars—fourteen in all—had largely been the least able to reform themselves. The newly founded universities of the eighteenth century—Halle, Göttingen, and Erlangen—had managed to survive by adapting to the new pedagogical and scientific needs of the time; and many of the other survivors had followed their reforming lead. Berlin (founded 1810) and Bonn (1818) cannot, of course, be considered as "survivors," although their structure and purpose clearly reflect the reform traditions already successfully employed by the eighteenth-century reform-oriented university.

The question is, Why was it especially the *reformed* universities that survived? For despite their adaptation to new pedagogical realities, there were still many voices calling for the abolition of universities during the Napoleonic period. One possible explanation is that the reformed universities met the needs of the German states and of those social groups which used the university. The social and political background of German university history has not, however, been a prominent feature in the works of university historians. The reason for this sociopolitical blind spot has more to do with the unwillingness of German historians to place universities in any sociopolitical context than with the lack of any objective connection.

The aim of this study is to demonstrate a close connection between the reform and survival of the German university system in the eighteenth century and the needs of certain elites in German society, combined with the desire of some German governments to raise the degree of integration between social, political, and cultural elites. The study will concentrate on one social elite (the nobility), one state (Hanover), and one university (Göttingen) in particular; but its findings are not atypical of other regions, governments, and reforming universities of the eighteenth century. Its implications for the general relationship of society, state, and university are extensive.[1]

For the moment, however, let us see how parts of the traditional German system of higher education were "modernized" by the workings of social and political forces beyond the control of the universities themselves.

I

At the beginning of the eighteenth century, most universities in central Europe stood in poor repute. Scholasticism was the method, orthodoxy the content of most instruction. Medicine was openly ridiculed, natural science was almost exclusively the province of the new royal academies, and the movements in philosophy and law which later came to be labeled "enlightened" faced great hostility. Lectures, textbooks, and teaching staff changed little, since they were expected to transmit static truths, not develop new ideas. Latin, the universal language of Christendom's intellectuals, was still the medium of instruction and publication. Practically speaking, and in terms of the numbers of students listening, theology and law were the important branches of university learning. In the Catholic universities of Germany, which constituted over a third of all institutions, philosophy and theology were often the only faculties. Until the late eighteenth century, they were dominated by such teaching orders as the Jesuits. In those German states where central bureaucratic administrations of a more or less despotic type had emerged, the universities had begun serving the state by training doctors of law for the expansion of princely power, just as they had previously trained priests and pastors for the interests of their respective churches.

With few exceptions, universities were small and provincial, often so much so that they hardly deserved the name *university* at all. Kiel and Rostock, for example, often had only twenty-five or thirty new students each year. Even as training grounds for functionaries of the law courts and churches, the German universities were out of step with the age. Theology still moved largely in the wake of Luther and the Counter-Reformation, and except for the renaissance of natural law, legal studies aimed at producing narrow Roman-law jurists who would be docile, dependent instruments in the hands of absolute princes. At their worst,

German universities around 1700 served only the limited interests of church and princely bureaucracy and served neither very well. Under the circumstances it is not surprising that influential groups of the population shunned university training altogether.

By the end of the eighteenth century, in contrast, Germany could boast several excellent universities, led by Halle and Göttingen. Their pioneering efforts had been envied and copied, in turn, by other institutions, and dissatisfaction with the remaining "unreformed" universities reached intense levels by the 1790s and 1800s. The new university of Berlin, opened in 1810, was as much the crowning of the eighteenth-century reform movement as the beginning of a new epoch in the history of German higher education. By the dawn of the nineteenth century, scholasticism and hidebound religious orthodoxy were on the defensive if not driven out of the universities; medicine and natural sciences were academically resurgent; Latin had given way to the vernacular; the thought of the Enlightenment and neohumanism had conquered a place for themselves, particularly in the increasingly prestigious philosophical faculties; and even law faculties had become intellectually exciting. The entire purpose of the university had been redefined. Instead of passing on static truth in a dead language, the best German universities pursued knowledge in a dynamic way, adding the dimension of research (for both teachers and students) to the traditional tasks of teaching and learning. How does one account for this change in curriculum and ethos among the best universities? Traditional university histories have largely answered this question instrumentally, by merely describing what happened. The broader social and political context of university reform, which they ignore, might offer a more satisfying explanation—that of social causation.

Let us consider briefly the relationship of university and society at the beginning of the eighteenth century.

The evidence indicates that German universities around 1700 were largely self-sustaining corporations existing under princely protection and ecclesiastical supervision, but lacking any deeper social support. The most numerous estate, the peasantry, traditionally had the least to do with universities, although there may well have been more peasants attending them than in the nineteenth century. Nor could one say that the bourgeois estate as a whole constituted the natural clientele of universities around 1700, since one very important element of the bourgeoisie—the oligarchs and citizens of Germany's many towns—had little use for universities and certainly did not bestir themselves to maintain such institutions (although a very few, like Cologne and Strasbourg, were "city" universities). Universities were, to be sure, predominantly bourgeois in their clientele and staffs, but they drew heavily on a small segment of the bourgeoisie, one Mack Walker has recently called the subclass of "movers and doers,"[2] those who left the fixed place in life guaranteed and decreed by the German towns to join the comparatively rootless class of professionals, civil or ecclesiastical, who belonged to another world wherever they lived. In training, language, clothing, life expectations, life style, and function, the academic bourgeoisie was far removed from the traditional world of the German *Bürger*, as the frequent clashes between urban philistines and university students or professors might indicate.

The German noble estate was as little a class in the modern sense as the bourgeoisie. The difficulty of including all those with noble patents and family background in one term is enormous, so much so that even today the historian has the greatest difficulty in saying anything precise about the German nobility. The geographic, political, religious, and economic differences among all those families entitled to use the *von* before their names was probably greater in central Europe in the eighteenth century than anywhere else at any time. No scholar can be sure even of the size of this social group, except that it was larger than that of England and smaller than that of Poland or Hungary. Some nobles were working farmers, others mere *seigneurs* collecting rents, still others members of princely bureaucracies, yet others court nobles. Some were poor sovereigns over tiny, but autonomous, domains, while others were rich but servile to a territorial prince. The German language richly reflects the complexity of the German nobility, with such prefixes to the term *nobility* as *old, new, imperial, territorial, court, country, high, low, patent,* etc.

Attitudes toward education naturally varied as much among the noble families as among the bourgeois. Although the nobility had attended German universities in large numbers during the sixteenth and early seventeenth centuries, they had deserted these institutions by the beginning of the eighteenth century, an indication that universities had become increasingly irrelevant to their needs. Young noblemen had learned to prefer the knightly "academies" (*Ritterakademien*), which taught social graces and military arts. These academies stressed the building of character over knowledge for its own sake, in keeping with the German version of the Renaissance idea of the gentleman. The academies offered worldly breadth rather than scholastic depth; and a grand tour or, occasionally, a short visit to a foreign university completed the ideal cosmopolitan gentlemanly education begun in the academies, especially for those noblemen bent on a diplomatic or civil service career.

Given the structure, tastes, and needs of German society as a whole around 1700, many observers regarded the existing universities as hopelessly irrelevant, too numerous for their existing clientele, and unlikely to change in such as way as to attract more and better students. Yet the very end of the seventeenth century and the first half of the eighteenth witnessed the opening of four new universities: Halle, in Prussia (1694); Breslau, in Silesia (1702); Göttingen, in Hanover (1737); and Erlangen, in the Frankish principality of Bayreuth (1743). Although Breslau was little more than a Catholic seminary, the other three universities shared a modern, pioneering spirit. Two—Halle and Göttingen—became large and prosperous despite the superabundance of universities already in existence. Both had large state governments standing behind them, to be sure; but more importantly, they succeeded in attracting a disproportionate number of the "movers and doers." They succeeded, in other words, not only because of strong government support (and control), but because they apparently appealed to certain important groups in German society.

II

Halle, founded in 1694, is conventionally called the first modern German university, with Göttingen playing the role of conscious imitator. Halle's beginnings, in contrast to Göttingen's, were somewhat haphazard. Halle originally had a Ritterakademie which, thanks to the fortuitous presence of Christian Thomasius, a jurist and outspoken leader of pedagogical modernism, attracted so many students that it was raised to university status. The other side of the university was the theological faculty, which was Lutheran-Pietist. The Pietists originally combated Lutheran orthodoxy, too, but as they grew entrenched at Halle, they became increasingly dogmatic in their own way. Throughout most of the eighteenth century, Halle never overcame the philosophical and practical contradictions which sprang from its origins as a merger between a cavaliers' school and a seminary of the strictest moral earnestness.

Göttingen, Halle's great and successful rival, was much more carefully planned. As early as the beginning of the eighteenth century, Hanoverian officials were clearly dissatisfied with the arrangement whereby Hanoverians were supposed to attend the university of neighboring Brunswick-Lüneburg, in Helmstedt. Furthermore, their words made clear their concern for the education of the upper classes in a more "practical" and fashionable manner. As Chancellor Benjamin Beischärff complained in 1710, "noble youth and agile geniuses," especially those destined for military careers, were damaging themselves and the state with their poor training. Law, he groaned, was "negligent, casual, and without any special application" to the realities of contemporary administrative needs. Theology was also taught in an "impractical" way. Beischärff was so repelled by the universities' performance that he eschewed the term entirely and, like Leibniz and other thinkers of the period, recommended setting up academies instead. Such academies would offer broader curricula than the Ritterakademien but would be teaching, rather than research, institutions.[3]

Beischärff's call for a new higher education system went unheeded until a quarter of a century later. When the Hanoverian government did create a state university, it was modeled on Halle, retaining the forms and privileges of universities, as well as the name *university*. It is characteristic of the thinking of the leading Hanoverian privy counselor of the time, Gerlach Adolf von Münchhausen, that Göttingen clung to many conservative practices in form while joining in the movement toward curriculum modernization initiated on a large scale by Halle. Many historians have seen in Göttingen's moderation, in its cautious avoidance of extremes, and in its attempt to combine traditional and progressive elements the secret of its success. What were the specific elements of this approach to university reform at Göttingen? In particular, what were the innovative elements, the ones which have caused many previous scholars to argue that Göttingen has an even better claim than Halle to the title of Europe's first modern university? And what did the modernity of Halle, Göttingen, Erlangen, and subsequently reformed universities have to do with social movements and the needs of state?

Göttingen offers the historian the clearest and fullest evidence for answering these questions. From its inception, the new university was less a royal then an estate institution, since the noble-dominated estates put up the lion's share of the operating expenses.[4] The electoral dynasty lent its moral and political weight to the enterprise, which, tradition claims, interested the culturally undistinguished Elector George II less for itself than for the prestige it would lend him in his bitter rivalry with the King of Prussia.[5] The elector's diplomatic weight was doubtless useful in obtaining imperial and papal recognition of Göttingen; but the main impetus came from the bureaucracy, with strong support from the noble-dominated *Stände*.

Münchhausen, who in effect governed the affairs of the university from his office in Hanover, faced formidable hurdles. He was opening a new university at a time when many believed universities ought to be abolished, either because there were too many of them or because they had outlived their usefulness in an enlightened age. Halle had proven that a new university could survive and even thrive, but it had to be large to be effective, and to be large it had either to lure students away from the other universities or attract the sort of student who had previously avoided higher education. Since nobles and wealthy students in general paid higher fees than the many ordinary "in-state" students (*Landeskinder*), Münchhausen deemed it necessary to attract a maximum of *Vornehme und Ausländer* (notables and foreigners) in order to bring money into the country and help defray the cost of the university. Yet "academic mercantilism," as this system has been called,[6] was not the only motive for attracting nobles and foreigners. Their presence would heighten the visibility of the new university and lend it some of their own social prestige. That, in turn, would attract other students.

In seeking to attract young noblemen and ambitious but wealthy commoners, the planners of Göttingen did not deviate from the dreams of all university administrators. Who did not prefer rich, elegant, and well-prepared students to impoverished, provincial, underprivileged students (simply called *paupers* in the less euphemistic language of the eighteenth century) who begged for free meals and for dispensation from lecture fees? What is remarkable about Göttingen's history (even in comparison with Halle's) are the decisive innovations made to please and attract the upper-class students. Historians have often written that Göttingen, like Halle and Erlangen, was fashionable with nobles.[7] Just how fashionable, we shall see later in this paper. But what has not been made clear is the degree to which the founders of Göttingen set out to lure this class of students by a series of curricular and other reforms. Münchhausen and his aides set out to avoid a long list of university characteristics distasteful to young noblemen, while placing new emphasis on forms of education fashionable among them. Insofar as much of the "modern" movement in ideas was fashionable with the nobility, it appears that Göttingen was consciously constructed as a modern university in order to make it a relatively aristocratic university. Such a linkage of educational modernity and a class which—especially in Hanover—has traditionally been associated with reaction will need further discussion later. First let us turn to what Göttingen's planners sought to avoid in the German university heritage and what they sought to introduce or augment.

A typical avoidance tactic was Münchhausen's insistence that theology play a quiet role at Göttingen. Münchhausen did not wish to diminish the authority of the church but, rather, to avoid the acrimonious disputes among Protestant sects (e.g., Pietists, orthodox Lutherans) which had been raging in Germany since the end of the seventeenth century. The university statutes consequently forbade denunciations of teachers for "heretical" opinions.[8] Münchhausen hoped thereby to avoid the fate of Halle, which had come under the influence of an increasingly rigid Pietism. The position of the theologians was thus considerably weakened from the start, and Münchhausen sought to further guarantee peace by appointing doctrinally neutral professors of theology. The energies of students and professors could be turned to concerns more productive (and more secular) than squabbles over orthodoxy. In this sanction against heresy charges and other forms of exaggerated scholastic feuding, one can see the germs of academic freedom, which later in the century made Göttingen a favored residence even of nonuniversity intellectuals. The freedom in Göttingen to think, write, and publish was unsurpassed elsewhere in Germany. Even though Göttingen's theologians had to be good Lutherans,[9] the spirit of intellectual liberty left to them allowed Göttingen to develop into a major center of "enlightened" Biblical criticism and church history.

Not only did Münchhausen cool the religious zeal of the theological faculty, but he also went out of his way to accommodate Catholics (especially noblemen) who might wish to study in Göttingen. He thus made arrangements whereby Catholic students could exercise their faith. The deference Münchhausen showed to Catholic Vienna in obtaining an expensive imperial charter for the university undoubtedly sprang more from political expedience and concern for attracting wealthy Catholic students than from any particular sense of ecumenicalism.

In his selection of professors, Münchhausen also took pains to avoid quarrelsome or overly controversial scholars who might drive away students by their extremism. He made sure that the most important prerogatives of appointment lay in the hands of the government and its agents. Such an approach, which contrasted with the usual guildlike prerogatives of German faculties to make their own appointments, might at first appear an unwarranted presumption and a threat to academic freedom. In the context of the eighteenth century, however, it was the only guarantee against the nepotism, favoritism, and seniorism which prevailed at most universities. By giving the faculty only a right to suggest candidates upon invitation, Münchhausen sought to avoid divisive quarrels and factionalism in the faculties, especially the sort which derived from conflicts of personal interest. Münchhausen was not unwilling to seek the advice of scholars themselves in making appointments; but he considered it wiser to rely on the advice of those he knew to be relatively impartial, whether outside the university or within it. One of the by-products of this policy was the recruitment of a faculty which had a supraregional and even international reputation.

More important than avoiding the mistakes of others, Münchhausen and his advisers sought to offer something new and positive as an inducement to students and professors. The professors, in addition to enjoying a climate of liberal scholarly discussion and publication, received the added inducement of high salaries and the promise of high fees.[10] Münchhausen did not hesitate to use the elector's political influence to obtain the release of professors from the service of other rulers (professorial mobility was still not an established principle). He paid moving expenses, arranged for quarters in Göttingen, and otherwise made an offer from Göttingen almost irresistible. Münchhausen personally supervised the recruitment of the professoriate. In general, his chief criterion was the fame of the scholar, which he knew would quickly draw attention to Göttingen. For this fame, which almost universally derived from nationally recognized publications, Münchhausen was willing to pay the best prices in Germany.

Göttingen soon acquired the reputation it subsequently held, as one of the chief seats of scholarship and science in central Europe. The Society of Sciences, established there in 1751, made it a leading intellectual center, one of the few cities in Europe to have both a university and a scientific academy. The library, which was generously endowed from the first, attracted many serious scholars, so that by the end of the eighteenth century Göttingen probably had more learned men per capita than did any other city in Germany.[11] The *Göttinger gelehrten Anzeigen* attained a leading place in the literary and scientific life of Germany, drawing upon professors for most of its contributions. Although it is difficult to prove that Münchhausen's preference for publishing scholars induced the beginning of the research and publication ethic so apparent in nineteenth-century German universities, the effect was to place a premium on teachers who could also publish, and whose publications were sufficiently significant to draw attention to their institutional base.[12]

The relative weight given to the four faculties (theology, medicine, law, and philosophy), the curriculum allocations within each one, and training institutions set up outside the faculties also shed much light on the social and political motivations in the thinking of Münchhausen and his advisers. We have already noted the relatively severe limitations placed on the traditional censorship powers of the "first" faculty, that of theology. The medical faculty, as at Halle, was relatively weak. J. G. von Meiern, one of the planners of the new university, expressed the typically low contemporary regard for medical men: he urged "the creation of ten or fifteen young exterminating angels [per year], so that people can be delivered methodically to the cemetery."[13]

More significant than the curriculum in these two faculties were the emphases set in the other two, philosophy and law. Of these two, philosophy still held a distinctly inferior place, as it always had in traditional German academic organization. The philosophical faculty remained largely an antechamber to the higher faculties, for teachers as well as for students. And it did not lose its preparatory function until later in the eighteenth century, even at Göttingen. Yet the struggle for equality with the other three faculties had already begun, and Münchhausen added to the weight and importance of the "philosophical" subjects—e.g., history, languages, and mathematics—by his insistence that these fields were more than remedial areas for poorly prepared freshmen.

Münchhausen took special pains in the composition of the philosophical faculty. True, he was personally suspicious of radical innovations in speculative philosophy.[14] It is also true that Göttingen did not shine as brilliantly as Halle before the expulsion of Christian Wolff, the greatest contemporary German Enlightenment philosopher. But even here, Münchhausen waived his baroque distaste for Wolffianism on the pragmatic grounds that it was fashionable and would therefore draw students.[15] And while the philosophical faculty as a whole started out somewhat disadvantaged in comparison to the rights and status of the others, certain disciplines—notably history, mathematics, and eloquence—were lavishly promoted when compared to other universities. The proposed salary for one history professor, Treuer, was quite close to that of the top legal professor (Gebauer) and top theologian (Rambach).[16] Münchhausen himself emphasized the importance of history, and specifically of modern history, in choosing candidates for professorships. This attitude pervaded Göttingen, so that even a contemporary theology professor there called history not only the "favorite science of our time" but also the proper substitute for legal studies among those notables and foreigners (in this context, nobles, Englishmen, and Russians) whose wealth, life on country estates, and luxurious unemployment might make law superfluous.[17] Indeed, some 10 percent of Göttingen students in the eighteenth century were enrolled in the philosophical faculty—a figure far higher than the average at other institutions.[18] In this movement one can legitimately see the beginnings, or rather the refounding, of liberal education on the university level.

Among the offerings in the philosophical faculty—in addition to the traditional introductory course of logic, metaphysics, and ethics—Göttingen offered lectures in "empirical psychology," the law of nature, politics, physics, natural history, pure and applied mathematics (including surveying, military and civilian architecture, etc.), history and its "auxiliary sciences" (such as geography, diplomatics, science, and art), and ancient and modern languages.[19]

Such a program, as it existed by the 1760s, indicates a step away from purely propaedeutic intentions and shows that the attempt to give a broad, if dilettantish, survey of useful knowledge to "notables and foreigners" was not an empty promise. Private lectures, agreed on by teacher and student, and constituting a major source of income for the professors, presumably covered an even wider span of fashionable and useful subjects.

The backbone of the Göttingen curriculum from the start was the legal faculty. Münchhausen left no doubt about the reason for care about this branch of learning. "That the legal faculty be filled with famous and excellent men is necessary above all, because that faculty must induce many rich and distinguished people to study in Göttingen," he wrote.[20] To some extent, no doubt, Münchhausen's comment reflected sober mercantilistic calculation: law was the field which attracted the best-paying students, whether noble or not. The result would be a degree of fiscal self-sufficiency for the university and an augmentation of what we would now call Hanover's balance of payments. Yet a certain degree of class-consciousness, beyond deference to the merely rich, can also be seen in Münchhausen's thoughts. The kind of law taught at Göttingen deferred to the resentments of many German nobles against the high-handed innovations of increasingly absolute rulers and was designed to reinforce their position and rights under the laws of the moribund empire, common law, and private law.

A typical exchange between Münchhausen and a Mecklenburg *Landrat* shows the pains taken by the former to stress the aristocratic interest which underlay legal studies at Göttingen. The Landrat asked Münchhausen about a rumor that Göttingen would teach "regalistic" law, which was, after all, the official creation of the king of England. Münchhausen groaned about the pernicious effects of such rumors, "especially as I hope to attract the rather numerous Mecklenburg nobles and to fix their predilection for Göttingen." Accordingly, Münchhausen replied that George II had personally warned the law professors that they would gain no favor with him by teaching regalistic law—on the contrary. Aside from royal indifference, the fierceness of Hanoverian noble families in defense of their liberties and prerogatives would certainly militate against regalism at Göttingen. "I do not know how people come by such allegations," Münchhausen sighed, "since they could figure out for themselves that the law professors would not act so unreasonably against themselves as to adopt regalistic principles of law, whereby they would load themselves down with odium, especially in the eyes of the *noblesse,* and would gain thanks from nobody."[21]

Thus, even Roman law, which could be and was used to legitimate princely incursions, was taught at Göttingen in a manner favorable to the defense of *older* rights against the absolute princes. Georg Strube, whose *Jurisprudence* was used as a supplement to the introduction to Justinian's *Institutes* and *Digest (Pandekten)* at Göttingen, made this plain in a letter to Münchhausen. At the same time, he also indicated part of the motivation for the toleration of Catholics at Göttingen. "Catholics are themselves persuaded," he wrote, "that their publicists [i.e., teachers of civil law] are worthless. The principles of Thomasius and Ludewig, being much too princely, have scared them away from attending Halle; if we teach them a more convenient civil law, and one more in line with the laws of the Empire, then it can be hoped that their best people will come to us."[22] Significantly, the Göttingen legal faculty paid more attention to feudal law, German common law, German and European constitutional law, legal history, and trial law (especially that of the two imperial courts at Wetzlar and Vienna) than to the traditional Roman fare of the seventeenth century.[23] Indeed, it was not until Pütter was hired in 1746, primarily to teach the practical subject of *Reichsprozess,* or imperial trial law, that Göttingen's legal reputation began to soar. Reichsprozess was a key to litigation against arbitrary administrative acts and therefore especially interesting to the nobility as a class. Pütter gave an entirely fresh, practical bent—unparallelled in Germany at the time—to legal education.[24] He and the Göttingen school made major contributions to the codification of German law, thereby diminishing the power of pure Roman law as a weapon in the hands of centralizing rulers.

In addition to philosophical subjects for the dilettante and law for the place-seeking nobles, Göttingen offered perhaps the best training in courtly arts available at any European educational institution. Dancing, drawing, fencing, riding, music, and conversation in modern languages were all offered in addition to the regular curriculum. Riding alone was taken so seriously that one of the university's largest eighteenth-century buildings (torn down only recently) was an indoor riding hall. The stallmaster was held in such high regard that his place in academic processions came before that of the associate professors (*Extraordinarien*).[25] No doubt, many noblemen decided to spend a few semesters at Göttingen principally because of its potential as a courtly finishing school. Indeed, with the strengthened philosophical faculty for the training of the mind and the various excellent facilities for the exercise of the body, Göttingen may be said to have transformed the relationship of the three ''higher'' faculties (theology, medicine, and law) to the philosophical faculty and the worldly arts: in effect, the new university combined the traditional strengths of Ritterakademien and traditional universities. Even if courtly training at the university later fell into disrepute or degenerated into mere dueling and horseracing, the new function placed on the philosophical faculty remained a breakthrough and laid the groundwork for neohumanism in the university, with its emphasis on the subjective, rather than objective, benefits of study.[26]

III

Earlier I stated that Göttingen, even more than Halle, was laid out consciously along ''modern'' lines. The term *modern,* however, requires some qualification, and it will be necessary to return to this point later on. Let us assume for the moment that it means the opposite of ''traditional,'' that it had not only an etymological but a real connection with ''mode'' or fashion, and that the setters of fashion in eighteenth-century Germany still tended to be the nobility. Another, more Whiggish test of modernity is the degree to which, for example, the Göttingen curriculum and ethos approached that of later times. Or we can recall the Weberian association of modernity and rationalization. By any of these standards, a good case can be made for Göttingen's relative modernity.

As we have seen, the Göttingen planners evinced great solicitude toward the notables in general and toward noble youth in particular in bringing about these departures from traditional curriculum and purpose. Even if Göttingen attracted more aristocrats, could these not be dismissed as a handful of dilettantes unrepresentative of the noble class at large? Or did university study increase among the nobility?

A survey of the social origins of the Göttingen student body is one way to ascertain its component of nobles. Table 6.1 shows the results of a 5 percent sample taken from the matriculation lists of the university at ten-year intervals. For the total sample, the average proportion of nobles is nearly 13 percent. Since contemporaries reported that impoverished nobles often matriculated under non-noble names to escape the higher fees imposed on their class,[27] the real figures are perhaps somewhat higher. Although the noble population of the Holy Roman Empire is unknown, one might not go too far wrong in guessing that it was comparable to that of France—a maximum of 2 percent of the whole population.

Not only were nobles represented at Göttingen disproportionately to the population; they were also there in much higher numbers than at other universities. Other large universities had to content themselves with half as many. The noble enrollments at Strasbourg, for example, averaged 5 percent in the eighteenth century; Jena had about the same proportion. Leipzig had an average of a little over 7 percent, as did Heidelberg. A few small, limping universities such as Kiel and Rostock did, to be sure, have large percentages of nobles in their student body (up to 12 percent sometimes at Kiel); but these percentages are relatively meaningless because of the mere handful of total students usually enrolled (as few as eight one year at Kiel). Only Halle among the larger universities showed a similar pattern, with as much as 11 percent of its student body being noble in the 1690s. Nevertheless, Halle slipped to only 7 percent in the decades from 1710 to 1740, and finally to 4 percent in the 1740s—partly, no doubt, because its aristocratic clientele abandoned it for Göttingen.[28] Many universities had very few noble students: at Würzburg and Tübingen, for example, less than 5 percent of the students were noble. Furthermore, and perhaps more important in the eyes of contemporaries, Göttingen outclassed all other universities in its number of higher nobles—princes, dukes, imperial counts, and others who owed obeisance only to the emperor himself. The wealthier nobles frequently brought along a retinue of servants and a private tutor, customarily resided in relatively opulent quarters, and

TABLE 6.1
Noble Students at Göttingen, 1737–97

Year	Total no. of students	% of nobles	% of nobles studying law
1737	297	10	55
1747	279	13	73
1757	183	15	50
1767	257	8	45
1777	334	12	79
1787	372	14	68
1797	366	15	62

Source: Goetz von Selle, ed., *Die Matrikel der Georg-August-Universität zu Göttingen, 1734–1837,* 2 vols. (Hildesheim and Leipzig, 1937), vol. 1. The table is based on a 5 percent sample.

were given pride of place in classrooms and official exercises of the university. Thus, their economic and psychological impact on the town and university was well out of proportion to their numbers, high as these were.

As Table 6.1 indicates, the vast majority of the noble students enrolled in the legal faculty. Few enrolled in the medical and theological faculties, so that the remaining nobles can be assumed to have come with the intent of studying in the philosophical faculty or with nothing specific in mind (sometimes they did not list a faculty of preference). Although the philosophical faculty was small in comparison to the law faculty, the Göttingen planners lavished considerable attention on it, as we have seen. Noblemen who wanted to round out their general education probably made up a large percentage of the students, who in any case could later enter a "higher" faculty.

Parallel to the return of large numbers of noblemen to the universities, or rather to the most modern of them, one can discern a certain influx of noblemen into other spheres, notably into government. Hanover and Prussia, the homes of the new university reform idea, both experienced some version of this phenomenon. But the situations were different in important respects. Both states had seen conflict between strong rulers and indigenous nobilities during the seventeenth century, and both dynasties had availed themselves of the assistance of commoners trained in the law—known simply as *doctores*—in attempts to overcome feudal privilege. In Prussia, the long struggle ended with the compromise between Frederick the Great and the nobility, the terms of which granted the nobles a safe place in army, state, and society at the price of surrendering political privileges. In Hanover, the fortuitous departure of the elector and his family to assume the British throne led to the long-term triumph of the indigenous nobility. It began to assert itself more vigorously and successfully against the bourgeois doctores. Not only did Hanover's estates, dominated clearly by the nobility, thrive in the eighteenth century; but even the electoral civil service was increasingly usurped in spirit and personnel by the nobles.[29]

Yet the conquest of power was not uncomplicated. For one thing, many sixteenth- and seventeenth-century doctores had been ennobled (even though, or perhaps because, a doctorate was then considered a sort of patent of nobility), and some had attempted to legitimate their nobility by acquiring land and marrying into the older families. Another complicating factor was that a few noble families tended to predominate in the diets. Furthermore, though the dynasty was absent, it had not given up all claim to sanction policy decisions. A court nobility which had thrown in its lot with the electoral house continued to exist around the palace in Hanover, and it did not suffer as often from the absence of its royal master under the first two Georges as it did under the third. Despite intermarriage and resulting family connections, there was plenty of room for competition both among the noble families and between them and the well-established families of former doctores, whether formally bourgeois or noble.

Besides the struggle for power, the nobles faced economic problems. Hanoverian noble estates were not large enough or rich enough to provide a luxurious style of life. As Hanover's major constitutional historian has said, "The existence of the upper classes rested wholly or in part on the civil service; perhaps in no other part of Germany was the civil service so often a source of wealth.''[30]

As property holdings declined in importance among Hanoverian, Prussian, and probably all other German nobles in the eighteenth century, surrogate sources of "honor," the essential quality of a nobleman after lineage, had to be sought elsewhere.[31] Some writers began to stress the honorific value of a university education. For example, a major eighteenth-century chronicler of the nobility, C. F. Pauli wrote approvingly that "noblemen frequently took academic degrees and honors and showed thereby that they were the most qualified for political posts of honor, and they therefore demanded preference before their [social] equals.''[32] Significantly, it was the brilliant new universities, with their emphasis on excellence and a famous faculty, that succeeded in convincing part of the nobility that some extra margin of honor was to be gained by university attendance. It is tempting to reflect on the reciprocal influence of the two concepts of fame and honor. Fame, one might suggest, was the equivalent of honor for a bourgeois scholar. The more famous the scholar, the more honor the aristocratic student derived from hearing his lectures. And while a student, noble or not, might actually learn more from a conscientious young teacher without a wide reputation, the nobleman would later wish to boast that he had studied under "the famous Professor So-and-so." Thus, in terms of money, power, and social psychology, the nobles responded to the reformed universities in a warm way.

Given the attractiveness of the civil service to the aristocracy, the traditional learnedness of the nonnoble or new noble civil servants, and the lead provided by some of Hanover's most prominent old nobles, it is not surprising that university attendance—or at least a state examination based on university legal curriculum—became increasingly the norm in the course of the eighteenth century, at least for holders of certain offices.[33]

The highest echelons of the Hanoverian administration became generally more exclusive in two ways between the departure of the dynasty in 1714 and the accession of George III in 1760. First, the proportion of noble officeholders generally rose. Second, the level of education for both noble and nonnoble officials increased markedly. Both phenomena are indicated in Table 6.2. If one divides this period into two equal parts, 1714–36 and 1737–60, one can see the following patterns. In the first period, the members of the *Geheimes Ratskollegium* (Privy Council)—the chief ministerial and legislative body of Hanover—were all noblemen, but 17 percent of them were of the new noble families (fewer than four generations in the nobility); the educational accomplishments of the new nobles were much greater than those of the old nobles (100 percent vs. 53 percent university attendance). In the second period, however, all the members of the Privy Council were old nobles, and 89 percent of them had attended a university. In the Chancellery, or *Geheime Kanzlei,* the proportion of nobles to nonnobles (2:1) was reversed between the two periods, but university attendance rose to 100 percent in both cases. The Privy Chancellery was, incidentally, losing power during this period.

The *Ober-Appelations-Gericht,* or High Court of Appeals, in Celle was divided

TABLE 6.2

Social Origins and University Attendance of Hanoverian Central Government Officials (in Percentages)

Office	Appointees, 1714–36 (N = 193)				Appointees, 1737–60 (N = 124)			
	Old nobility[a]	New nobility	Commoners	All appointees	Old nobility[a]	New nobility	Commoners	All appointees
1. All offices								
Social origin	64	24	12		68	20	12	
University attendance	45	76	71	56	76	100	89	82
2. Privy Council								
Social origin	83	17	0		100	0	0	
University attendance	53	100	0	59	89	0	0	89
3. Privy Chancellery								
Social origin	50	17	33		0	33	67	
University attendance	0	67	50	28	0	100	100	100
4. High Court of Appeals								
A. Noble bench								
Social origin	100	0	0		100	0	0	
University attendance	67	0	0	67	58	0	0	58
B. Learned bench								
Social origin	0	79	21		0	83	17	
University attendance	0	82	100	86	0	100	100	100

5. Exchequer								
Social origin	100	0	0		75	25	0	
University attendance	64	0	0	64	83	100	0	88
6. War Chancellery								
Social origin	78	22	0		100	0	0	
University attendance	29	50	0	33	73	0	0	73
7. Justice Chancellery								
Social origins	42	37	21		48	28	24	
University attendance	40	78	80	63	83	100	83	88
8. Court Marshal's Office								
Social origin	73	27	0		100	0	0	
University attendance	13	0	0	9	33	0	0	33
9. Household								
Social origins	86	14	0		90	10	0	
University attendance	38	20	0	32	53	25	0	50

Source: Compiled from Joachim Lampe, *Aristokratie, Hofadel und Staatspatriziat in Kurhannover, 1714–1760*, 2 vols. (Göttingen, 1963).

Note: This table does not include the "secretaries" at the lower end of the bureaucratic hierarchy, an additional 135 persons. They were overwhelmingly commoners by origin and were not as well-educated as the higher officials. Nevertheless, more secretaries attended universities in the second period than in the first, an increase from 41 to 56 percent.

[a]At least four generations old.

into a hereditarily aristocratic bench and a "learned bench," so that competition on the basis of education was probably not as keen here as elsewhere. This may explain why the percentage of old nobles attending universities dropped slightly, from 67 percent in the first period to 58 percent in the second, despite an official rescript aimed at raising it. But there were nobles sitting on the *Gelehrte Bank* as well, as Table 6.2 indicates, and the percentage of university attendance among these nobles rose between the two periods.

The *Justizkanzlei* (Justice Chancellery) shows a similar configuration: more nobles in the upper, important offices and considerable increases in the number attending universities. The Justice Chancellery was 79 percent noble in the first period but 76 percent noble in the second. Of all the noblemen, 58 percent had university training in the first period, as opposed to 89 percent in the second period.

In the War Chancellery (*Kriegskanzlei*), where educational qualifications were understandably somewhat lower, the pattern was nevertheless similar. Counselors were always noble; but whereas 22 percent of them in the first period had at least been nobles of recent origin, the old families completely dominated the chancellery in the second. At the same time that old blood won out over new, the proportion of old nobles attending universities rose from a mere 29 percent to 73 percent.

Finally, by way of control, it might be useful to cast a glance at the court, where the supreme test was high birth and education was quite secondary. Is there any parallel to developments in the political administration? The answer is yes. The percentage of officers of the Household from the ancient nobility increased between the first and second periods; both the old and the new court nobility were more likely to have attended a university in the latter time period, even though the increase was from a rather low 32 percent to 50 percent.

Both the nobles of the court and those of the bureaucracy often attended the Ritterakademien and traveled to attain worldly polish. The high nobility of the bureaucracy, however, was twice as likely to take the further step of attending the university. The newer nobility was the group that had most often attended a university; being somewhat insecure in their birth status, newer nobles were most likely to back it up with the status of education. As in the seventeenth century, when the bourgeois doctores had held many high posts in the Hanoverian government, it was the commoners, rather than the aristocrats of either type, who held the highest degrees (usually doctor of laws): noblemen were not expected to bother with certification.

One can draw some tentative conclusions from this prima facie evidence. Clearly the Hanoverian administration became both more exclusive in terms of birth and better educated in terms of university attendance in the nearly half-century for which we have evidence. The amount and intensity of university study varied with social status, so that old nobles almost never bothered with a doctorate and commoners almost always had one. This is an important point for the social and political history of Hanover, but not such a vital one for the fortunes of the university at Göttingen, which rested more on the *presence* of students than on their taking degrees. Since the bachelor's degree had fallen into disuse everywhere in Germany and the master's was more a byword for professorial venality and student abuse than a true sign of magisterial accomplishment, the doctorate had already become the only worthwhile degree. Functionally, inscription at a university and a year or more of attendance represented the German equivalent of the baccalaureate.

One could conclude from Table 6.2 that in all branches of the higher civil service attitudes toward higher education changed markedly from the first to the second half of the total period, even if we had no other evidence of the attitudes in government circles which produced the new university itself. Academic observers of the time, however, commented on the desire of young nobles to acquire university training, in contrast to their indifference prior to the eighteenth century. Professor Treuer, one of the original history professors at Göttingen, commented on the preference of young nobles—more than previously—for "study and scholarship," which could pave the way for "important posts" in Hanover.[34] Late in the century, almost all persons who reached high office in Hanover had been students of the jurist Pütter in Göttingen.[35]

To be sure, the nobles in the higher administration of Hanover constituted only a small fraction of Göttingen's noble alumni. For one thing, the size of the central administration was minuscule when compared to the pool of noble alumni. For another, the holders of high posts were generally men already in the autumn of life when appointed, so that only the last few appointees before 1760 would have been able to attend Göttingen—and, indeed, did so heavily, forsaking such former favorites as Leipzig and Helmstedt. Only one-third of the members of the Household from 1714 to 1736 had attended universities; half the appointees for 1737–60 had done so, and over 75 percent of them had spent at least one semester at Göttingen. Göttingen was also the heavy favorite among those in the other administrative posts. What is most interesting about the figures for members of the Household is that they show such an increase, particularly in favor of Göttingen. Household duties did not require special legal or other training, beyond what a decent Ritterakademie would have provided. This form of support for the university must be kept in mind when explaining Göttingen's success. In addition to a curriculum and professoriate tailored to the tastes of the nobility, Göttingen strove from the outset for a style and a set of extracurricular arrangements which would attract even those students who were uninterested in a civil service career.

IV

The testimonial and statistical evidence points in the same direction. Göttingen was planned in such a way as to attract noblemen and other notables. It clearly succeeded in attracting a disproportionate share of the nobles, whom one can easily recognize in the university statistics. We have also seen the concomitant rise of higher education qualifications among the ranks of higher civil servants, both noble and nonnoble, during the half-century in the middle of which Göttingen was founded. It is now time to consider a few questions more carefully. To what extent was Göttingen typical? If one can call the revised curriculum and general ethos of Göttingen, Halle, and their imitators a reform, to what extent was it a *modernizing* reform? To the extent that the aristocracy participated heavily in the reform movement, is it justifiable to associate university reform with the nobility as a social group? What role did the bourgeoisie play? Aside from being the instrument of the wealthier classes in their attempts to justify their leading positions in life, did the university have any important effects on them?

Göttingen hardly typified the German university system of the eighteenth century. Halle (but only partly by plan) shared with Göttingen the desire to have a modern curriculum and to attract the upper classes. Erlangen, to be sure, was a conscious copy of Göttingen. It did have a comparatively fashionable curriculum and did attract a large number of noblemen. But Erlangen remained more of a Ritterakademie and a local university than Göttingen or Halle.[36] But other German universities did not rush to follow the lead of the new-model institutions. It is significant that educational reform succeeded best in new universities; the old ones lacked the will to reform, or saw their interests threatened by innovation. Corporate rule by the professors meant, in general, lethargy and corrupt practices (characteristics of many corporations in eighteenth-century German life). Halle, Göttingen, Erlangen, and a few others were able to overcome such lethargy because the state virtually ran them and intended to align university life with the perceived needs of state and society. In other universities, however, habit and privilege often successfully beat back attacks by enlightened (and sometimes benighted) princely bureaucracies and ministers bent on reform. Only late in the eighteenth century, when enlightened despotism reached its zenith and the unreformed universities (especially in Catholic states) had few defenders left, were the principles of the new universities put into practice on a large scale. And even then, the Napoleonic wars, the further development of pedagogical and scientific principles, and other changes in thought and conditions revised much of the detail of the Göttingen reform model. Indeed, given the limited student market of the eighteenth century, Göttingen's planners could not have even wished other universities successfully to copy their ideas; Göttingen's success, they assured themselves, lay in its differentness. Nevertheless, Halle and Göttingen did serve as reform models. Even though they were atypical, the ideas for which they stood eventually entered the German reform tradition and worked on well into the nineteenth century.

In contrast to the universities within the earlier German university tradition, Göttingen and, to a slightly lesser extent, Halle were clearly moving in the direction of our own time—modernizing by the Whig definition. They taught in the vernacular and deemphasized the grammatical study of ancient languages. They placed new emphasis on common and recent law while diminishing the canonical value of Roman law—a movement which has left traces on German law, even though it is a "code" law, up to the present time. They deemphasized religious orthodoxy, and Göttingen at least demoted theology to a much lower rank than it had held in centuries; it virtually lost its tutelage over the other faculties. This attention to the here and now went beyond religious questions. It encouraged a developmental, scientific approach to reality and, above all, "practical" studies, in place of the static scholasticism, eternal verities, and speculation of the preceding century. History, especially modern history, augmented the study of the speeches of antiquity. Instruction in mathematics took on a more applied tone. Philosophy turned its attention toward problems of life and away from casuistry. Students were encouraged to read books on their own, to exercise their bodies as well as their minds, to think practically, and to develop themselves in an all-around manner which the later idealists would sneeringly describe as "shallow," but which lived on in an idealized form in the conceptions of Humboldt and other nineteenth-century university reformers.

Indeed, much of the criticism of the Göttingen model in the late eighteenth century came from men who accepted many of its reform premises but criticized it as being too utilitarian. Coming from philosophers who were becoming more and more idealistic, philologists who were insisting on more scientific rigor and specialization, or theologians who wished to arrest the march of materialism, such criticisms (many of which emanated from late eighteenth-century Göttingen and Halle themselves) are understandable. Yet it is debatable whether neohumanism and idealism should necessarily be associated with modernity, or Berlin considered more modern than Göttingen, simply because they came at a later date. In some respects, the revival of classical studies—even though on an incomparably more scientific basis—can be regarded as a rejection of some aspects of modernity incorporated in the German Enlightenment and in the Göttingen reform model. The fact that Göttingen, in the late eighteenth century, was a leader in the philological renaissance should not surprise us. The famous philological seminar there not only rejuvenated theology by liberating it from dogmatics; it also gave a rejuvenated theology and, later, philosophy a certain leverage against the preponderance of the legal faculty. Nor should one overlook a certain social dynamic in this process: theology students, who were mostly poor young men, could achieve through philological studies a certain prestige as scientists and thinkers; the richer and more aristocratic legal students could be despised, not openly for their better social position and career prospects, but for their mundanity, secularism, and "unscientific," broadly based training. In the end, many noblemen shared this view themselves, as the case of the Humboldt brothers shows.

In any case, the earmarks of nineteenth-century "classical" education in Germany, visible most concretely in the *Gymnasium,* were not merely a monopoly of the middle class. The mastery of symbols of classical culture, which Pierre Bourdieu has called the monopolization of cultural capital, served the function, among other things, of drawing a line between the upper levels of society—the upper middle class and the aristocracy—and the lower. It also drew a line against certain members of the aristocracy who preferred to maintain their rural and untutored life style—for example, the Prussian *Krautjunker.* And by the end of the nineteenth century, even the proud, self-made entrepreneurial class, the *Besitz-bürgertum,* proved in the long run unable to resist sending its sons to the "useless" German universities. The process of legitimization through university attendance, once begun by the nobility in Halle and later Göttingen, eventually spread to virtually all classes of society except workers and farmers.

The Halle-Göttingen reforms may be seen as modern in two other respects. In the simple etymological sense, *modern* meant "à la mode," or "fashionable." The success of Halle, and then of Göttingen and Erlangen, in attracting the most fashionable sector of German society back to the universities implied both a change in curriculum to suit the tastes of this sector and, by the success of this change, the opening of a new dynamic toward university reform to suit the needs of society. In contrast to their earlier habits, university administrators and, eventually, professors and diets were persuaded that change is a good thing—particularly if it means growth.

In Weber's terms, rationalization is the key to modernity. In this sense, too, the Halle-Göttingen reform model was clearly modern, since the purpose was to make education *zweckrational* by introducing the subjects and educational purpose—preparation for life as well as for a wider range of careers than provided for by the medieval university—of the knightly academies. The paramount importance of law studies at Halle and Göttingen, the concomitant specialization and growth of bureaucracy in many German states, and the rise of "liberal education" in arts and sciences (a self-consciously gentlemanly form of education) indicate a meshing of the needs and purposes of the leading political and social circles with the offerings and purposes of higher educational institutions.

At the same time, educational modernization in this case did not mean political or economic progress. It may have contributed to it in the long run. But in the short run it undoubtedly reinforced the grip of the aristocracy and the upper bourgeois service class on privilege and power. Both Hanover and Prussia, although in different modes, survived the Napoleonic period with their bureaucratic forms of government stronger than ever. It would be too audacious to suggest that bureaucracy and aristocracy survived the revolutionary era solely because, by 1789, the bureaucracies and aristocracies of most large German states had behind them the prestige and legitimacy of rational modern education. But this form of prestige and legitimacy certainly played some role in retarding political and even social modernization in Germany even during the industrial revolution.

In the case of eighteenth-century university reform we see an irony of history: modernization of certain sectors of society (education, administration) was carried out by men who were less bent on modernizing the world than on dominating it. Furthermore, the effects of reforms were not necessarily the ones hoped for. Let us consider, for example, the effect of reform on the creation of a modern attitude toward the pursuit of knowledge and a modern notion of the role of the professor. The attitude toward science and scholarship at Göttingen came close enough to our own to be recognized as at least a precursor. Yet this modern look was more the result of an aggregate of conditions than of conscious policy. Publication of "research results" was regarded more as an advertising technique for the university than an end in itself. Nevertheless, like the Protestant merchant in his attitude toward money, the Protestant professors began to look upon published works as signs of grace. And while publication was still motivated largely by hopes of financial gain, *Ruhmsucht,* or the addiction to fame, was a growing motive.[37] Professor Michaelis, writing in the 1760s, gave vent to the ambivalencies surrounding the role of "science" (i.e., any systematic research or scholarship leading to published results, no matter what the field) in universities. While he sought to defend the role of the university purely as a teaching institution, he also acknowledged that institutions that hire famous, publishing scholars have the best chance of success. Mere good teachers, or even mere *young* scholars whose reputations were not yet fully established, did the university less good than mature, publishing scholars, he reasoned.[38] Even in the realm of textbook writing (a significant part of scholarly production in the eighteenth century), a certain dynamism consistent with modern ideas of changing "truth" began to emerge. At Göttingen, it was considered rather shameful to teach courses on the basis of textbooks written by the older generation or by non-Göttingen professors.Thus, even though some commentators believed *discovery* of new truths—or, more precisely, new natural phenomena and laws—was difficult to institutionalize and remained tied to genius and accident, systematic *codification* of knowledge was now expected of each fresh generation of scholars. The minimum requirement of professors was that they keep abreast of developments in their "field" (a much wider terrain than it would become later). By the mid-eighteenth century, professors at Göttingen and at some other universities were involved in five separate kinds of scholarly production that had only a tangential bearing on their teaching duties. The closest to teaching was the writing of textbooks. The second form of production was the writing of reference and "scientific" books, purchased by libraries, government bureaus, and some laymen, not to mention other scholars and students. The third type of scholarly labor entailed writing occasional pieces for the multiplying "learned" journals, such as the *Göttinger gelehrten Anzeigen.* Fourth, many professors wrote for the general public and not infrequently involved themselves in issues of momentary interest quite outside their specialties. And finally, professors frequently performed what we would now call consultation services. Jurists wrote legal opinions that were often regarded as having the force of law; medical men had outside practices; theologians held church offices; and at Göttingen, some members of the university were members of the Society of Sciences and contributed to scientific research. The Göttingen professor thus resembled his counterpart of today more than his predecessor in the twilight decades of scholasticism. He had the incentive (fame, promotion, requests for consultations), the facilities (in Göttingen's fine library, perhaps the greatest of its kind in Europe), the liberty (freedom from heavy censorship and from theological tutelage), and the leisure (due to high salaries and fees) to carry out scholarship and writing in a way comprehensible to us today. The ethos behind research and scholarly publication certainly became clothed in more idealistic garb in the nineteenth century; but as the vast number of forgotten and unoriginal publications from that century (and from our own) indicates, publication was often merely a means of gaining temporary secular advantages for the author or his institution rather than of advancing *Wissenschaft*.

As this discussion of the origins of the modern research ethos indicates, one can seek the inspiration for a new attitude toward knowledge as much in the tastes and prejudices of certain social classes as in the linear development of a noble human thirst for enlightenment. To what extent did the aristocracy really lead university reform? Should one not also mention the bourgeoisie, since the vast majority of professors and students were of that class? What new relationships, if any, developed between the nobility and the educated commonality, or among various strata of these two broad classes, as a result of university reform? Aristocratic patronage and interest had definite limits, and many of the pioneering traits of Göttingen cannot be traced from such involvement. The institution of the seminar, which eventually came to be a hallmark of German university education in the nineteenth century, owed more to the needs of bourgeois theology students than to those of the nobles. And the majority of law students and cameralists were commoners. It is also difficult to make an argument for any special class origins for neohumanism, an area in which late-eighteenth-century Göttingen was a leader. Neohumanism may well have had a *social* character, especially with the generalization of Gymnasium education among the bourgeoisie in the nineteenth century, but it cannot be proved that it had a *class* character, adhering to only one class.

What one can argue is that Göttingen was founded with the role of nobles and other "notables" as a *sine qua non* of its existence. One may also argue that Göttingen succeeded beyond the wildest dreams of its founders and ultimately served as the model for more "bourgeois" institutions, such as the University of Berlin. Yet the formula which won the admiration of Humboldt and other later reformers (many of whom had attended Göttingen) had been created especially to attract nobles, and the style of academic culture it stood for was on a much different level from the traditional university. If Göttingen became a model for general university reform, it was not because the university gave up its noble-tailored curriculum, but because the commoners attended it with this style in mind. Michaelis could argue in the 1760s that poor students should be discouraged from studying at the university, since, in effect, the employment market was too narrow to accommodate them afterwards. But he was careful to rule out excluding them, and he gave as his reason the unhealthy effect exclusion would have on social cohesion—on the "useful emulation of the wealthy."[39] In throwing out this casual explanation, which must have seemed obvious enough to eighteenth-century pragmatists, Michaelis delivered a clue to the success of reformed universities in drawing new support. The new middle class of eighteenth-century Germany— Walker's "movers and doers"—was, in its way, departing from the standard pattern of middle-class higher education almost as much as the nobles who attended Göttingen. Although it is hard to imagine that Münchhausen and other members of the exclusive old nobility of Hanover would have desired it, Göttingen forged a new kind of education which was able to bend the edges of *Stand* limits and prepare the way for a new stratum in German society. This stratum, too small to be a class, nevertheless achieved a commanding position in Germany through its manipulation of the administrative system, specifically the state, the church, and the professions. Wilhelm Roessler has pointed out the rise of this new stratum (which he calls, too vaguely, the "educated class") and argues that the aristocracy was the first source of its members in the early eighteenth century. He sees in the fusion of the scholarly and traditional ruling classes the beginnings of a "rationalization" of noble authority in the form of systematic administrative training.[40] Roessler further argues that the self-image of the new middle class (which was primarily responsible for the revival of German culture in the late eighteenth century) set it apart from the traditional middle class, and that, more than any other class, the new middle class emulated the nobility, not only in terms of domestic architecture, servant employment, and so on, but also in a cosmopolitan life style and knowledge of the world.[41] Much evidence from the late eighteenth century itself argues that the perception of social distance between the nobility and at least the new middle class, and therefore the barriers to a degree of emulation, were diminishing. Göttingen professors themselves remarked on this phenomenon.[42]

Contemporary literature, such as Goethe's *Wilhem Meister,* indicates that the new *Bildungsbürgertum* regarded education as the most promising path toward a narrowing of social distance between itself and the nobility it admired. Although we cannot argue that social distance diminished in fact—we simply do not know about intermarriage rates and other such indicators—the *perception* of narrowed distance has interesting connotations for the history of higher education. A generation or so after the opening of Göttingen and a generation or so before the opening of Berlin, university training had become fashionable again. Its ideology was that of professional training coupled with modern social and literary graces, of practical utility combined with social exclusiveness. The broad middle class did not yet give its allegiance to the new reformed university, judging by the conjunction of stagnant enrollments and rising population. Indeed, purely utilitarian voices clamored for the dissolution of the traditional university form into more professionally channeled schools (as actually happened in France after the revolution). The main rationale for retaining the university format centered on the humanistic function of the philosophical faculty, which had already begun its meteoric rise at Göttingen.

The philosophical faculty at Göttingen was preeminently responsible for the shift of emphasis in "gentlemanly" education from external to internal values, from *galant,* modern dilettantism to a serious philosophical commitment to *Bildung.* This process cannot be discussed here. One should keep in mind, however, that the urgent preoccupation of the Berlin reformers with "philosophical" training both at the Gymnasium and university level ran in somewhat the same direction of the Göttingen reforms decades before. The differences must not be forgotten. But the notion that there *was* a *Bildungsgut,* or fund of knowledge and thinking techniques, which every truly educated man must have, ran counter to the purely professionalizing tendencies of many Enlightenment institutions (and those set up by Napoleon in France). The Berlin reformers, to be sure, suppressed crass references to the class they wished to attract and seemed generally less aware of social divisions than their predecessors at Göttingen. But the type of study they proposed to make obligatory for the future *Bildungsschicht* tacitly implied leisure, solid (and expensive) schooling, and early exposure to a refined life style. These were the characteristics of noblemen and children from wealthy and educated families. Even a casual glance at matriculation lists of the eighteenth and nineteenth centuries shows how drastically the poorest class of students, *pauperes,* dwindled over time. Seventy-three years after the founding of Göttingen, the founders of Berlin University spoke and wrote of an educational ideal which was far from a copy of Göttingen. Yet the purposes and aims they set were almost unthinkable outside the context of earlier university reform. Above all, the lofty tone of the Berlin reformers contrasted with the practical one of Münchhausen. The former had so internalized and idealized the benefits of university education that they now called it "noble" in the moral sense. Nor was the titled aristocracy so conspicuous in Berlin, overwhelmed as it was by the crushing size of Germany's largest student body. Yet Berlin was far from being the foundation of a resurgent middle class. If its founders thought less in class terms than had the men of the early eighteenth century, it was because they had learned the thought habits of the "educated class," one composed of both nobles and bourgeois, dedicated to the administration of the state and organized culture, and hostile to the "philistine" and ordinary style of both the commercial bourgeoisie and the crude, titled bumpkins of East Elbia. The tremendous aura of prestige that surrounded German universities from the founding of Berlin on was not merely a reflection of their scientific achievements. Equally, it derived from their association with the small elite class which directed, supervised, and initiated so much through the bureaucratic structures of the German states.

It is likely that these states would have developed some other higher educational system equally serviceable to the reigning bureaucracy had the Göttingen reform model with its stress on gentlemanly, philosophical education not been available. They could have set up specialized schools, as in France, to train their elites and create a shared ethos among them. The end results for scientific and scholarly achievement might have been far less, but German elites might have been somewhat more open. The salvation of the German universities, even though it cost the price of reform, was possible partly because a few German universities had been able to ally themselves with powerful social forces and meet their needs. Few universities elsewhere before 1789 had been able to do this. The long-lasting impact of German universities on educational systems abroad is well known. It should thus give cause for thought that the origins of the modern university system in Germany appear to have been bound up with an attempt to stabilize and legitimate the rule of the more flexible part of the aristocracy with the aid of a small elite recruited from the middle class.

NOTES

1. I hope to explore these implications in another, longer work.

2. Mack Walker, *German Home Towns: Community, State, and General Estate, 1648–1871* (Ithaca, N.Y., 1972), p. 119.

3. Benjamin Beischärff, memorandum entitled "Wie eine Academie Electorale . . . anzurichten," Stolberg, 16 October 1710, Hist. lit. 83, Niedersächsische Staats- und Universitätsbibliothek, Göttingen.

4. The university was one of the two important new creations of the Hanoverian state in the eighteenth century. The other was the High Court of Appeals in Celle. Both, significantly, were financed by the estates (*Stände*), in which the nobles predominated. The estates paid three-quarters of the university's annual operating expenses, with the remnant coming from the *Klosterfonds*, a special fund deriving from secularized ecclesiastical properties. The elector's exchequer thus made no contribution, at least at the outset, to the current budget of the university.

5. Götz von Selle, *Die Georg-August-Universität zu Göttingen, 1737–1937* (Göttingen, 1937), p. 14.

6. R. Steven Turner, "The Prussian Universities and the Research Imperative, 1806–1848" (Ph.D. diss., Princeton University, 1973), p. 70.

7. Selle, *Göttingen,* p. 27.

8. Selle somewhat dramatically, but not incorrectly, saw in this provision "the pivot for the great turning in German life, which moved its center of gravity from religion to the state" (Selle, *Göttingen,* p. 41).

9. Reinhold Wittram, *Die Universität und die Fakultäten,* Göttinger Universitätsreden, no. 39 (Göttingen, 1962), p. 7.

10. See undated estimate, probably from 1734, in Hist. lit. 83, leaves 131–33, Niedersächsische Staats- und Universitätsbibliothek, Göttingen. Salaries for full professors ranged up to 900 thaler plus pensions, and the professors could expect very high incomes from fees from the many noble students' *privatissime* tutoring sessions. Professor Pütter, the famous cameralist, demanded a fee of 100 thaler per course from noble students. See Wilhelm Ebel, *Zur Geschichte der juristischen Fakultät und des Rechtsstudiums an der Georgia Augusta,* Göttinger Universitätsreden, no. 29 (Göttingen, 1960), p. 22.

11. The Göttingen library is still one of the best university libraries in the world, with impressive eighteenth-century holdings. Professors were encouraged to treat it as their own, even students were given borrowing privileges. Professor Pütter identified such privileges as "an advantage which hardly any other library in Germany, and perhaps in other areas, can challenge" (Johann Stephan Pütter, *Versuch einer academischen Gelehrtengeschichte von der Georg-Augustus-Universität zu Göttingen,* 2 vols. [Göttingen, 1765–88], 1: 219).

12. See the excellent discussion of the "research imperative," with an emphasis on the difference between eighteenth-century "fame" and "publication" on the one hand and nineteenth-century "prestige" and "research" on the other, in Turner, "Prussian Universities." Turner argues forcefully that there was a fundamental difference between the public-oriented writings of eighteenth-century *scholars* and the discipline-oriented writings of nineteenth-century *scientists.* Emphasis on a primary orientation toward research in professorial recruitment, he correctly points out, was lacking in most of the eighteenth-century definitions of professorial roles, even in those given by Göttingen professors. In many other universities, research orientation was lacking completely. Doubtless, scientific reference groups, with their internal prestige structures, were much stronger and more influential in the nineteenth century. Yet the shift in values from teaching to research excellence was perhaps not so sudden as Turner argues. Fame and prestige undoubtedly rested on different bases, in the first case, more on the educated public and in the latter, the specialized scientific community. Yet both drew attention to the scholar and his teaching institution, enabling professor and university to compete more readily with others. Göttingen appears to have been the first university to use this potential in a systematic way. Given the absence of specialized scientific communities and the comparative breadth of education in the eighteenth century, fame and publication, it may be argued, served the same social (recruiting) function as prestige and scientific research in the nineteenth, even though the results for the furtherance of *science* were quite different.

13. Quoted in Selle, *Göttingen,* p. 27.

14. See Wittram, "Universität," p. 8. In his attempts to reduce its many claims to being first and best to the modest scale of the eighteenth century, Wittram perhaps goes too far in denigrating the

"appearances" which Göttingen attempted to keep up. Academic freedom, for example, may have been far from perfect when compared to a later time, but it was still considerable to Münchhausen's contemporaries.

15. Gerlach Adolf von Münchhausen, "Nachträgliches Votum" for the *Geheimer Ratskollegium*, 16 April 1733, printed in Emil F. Roessler, *Die Gründung der Universität Göttingen* (Göttingen, 1855), p. 36.

16. See the university cost estimates in Hist. lit. 83, leaves 131–33, Niedersächsische Staats- und Universitätsbibliothek, Göttingen.

17. Johann David Michaelis, *Raisonnement über die protestantischen Universitäten in Deutschland*, 4 vols. (Frankfurt am Main, 1768–76), 1: 193–234. It is rather remarkable that Michaelis, a theologian, considered the well-being of the philosophical faculty to be more vital than that of his own to the health of the university.

18. Turner, "Prussian Universities," p. 30.

19. As cited in Pütter, *Versuch*, 1: 296–308.

20. Münchhausen, "Nachträgliches Votum," in Roessler, *Gründung*, p. 34.

21. Münchhausen to Professor Gebauer, Hanover, 8 April 1737, in Roessler, *Gründung*, p. 140.

22. Georg D. Strube to Münchhausen, Hildesheim, 1 November 1734, in Roessler, *Gründung*, p. 248. Strube was a Hanoverian official and a friend of Münchhausen.

23. See the course listings for public lectures as of 1765 in Pütter, *Versuch*, 1: 281–89.

24. Ernst Landsberg, *Geschichte der deutschen Rechtswissenschaft*, 4 vols. (Munich and Leipzig, 1880–1910), 3: 322.

25. Christoph Meiners, *Über die Verfassung und Verwaltung deutscher Universitäten*, 2 vols. (Göttingen, 1801), 2: 147.

26. Münchhausen and Michaelis's opinions on this point contrast strongly with those of Meiners, writing three decades later. Meiners ridiculed the effort of Göttingen to train "courtiers" and pleaded for a shift away from purely utilitarian subjects (*Verfassung und Verwaltung*, 2: 36). At the same time, his conception of the purpose of education was more idealistic, moralistic, and limited than Münchhausen or Michaelis's.

27. Götz von Selle, ed., *Die Matrikel der Georg-August-Universität zu Göttingen, 1734–1837*, 2 vols. (Hildesheim and Leipzig, 1937), 2:1.

28. Johannes E. Conrad, "Die Statistik der Universität Halle während der 200 Jahre ihres Bestehens," *Festschrift der vier Fakultäten zum zweihundertjährigen Jubiläum der vereinigten Friedrichs-Universität Halle-Wittenberg* (Halle, 1894), pp. 18–20.

29. The curial constitution of Hanover degenerated as the townsmen and prelates either gave up sitting separately, did not attend sessions at all, or were outmaneuvered when they did sit separately, depending on which province one observes. See Ernst von Meier, *Hannoverische Verfassungsgeschichte*, 2 vols. (Leipzig, 1898–99), 1: 225ff. Meier observes: "The same estate [nobles] which dominated in the diets also became the ruling element in the civil service" (ibid., 1: 462).

30. Ibid., 1: 517.

31. For the financial crisis of the Prussian nobles, see Fritz Martiny, *Die Adelsfrage in Prussen vor 1806 als politisches und soziales Problem* (Stuttgart and Berlin, 1938).

32. C. F. Pauli, *Einleitung in die Kenntnis des deutschen hohen und niederen Adels* (Halle, 1753), pp. 30f. Pauli implied, furthermore, that much of the jockeying among the nobles for positions of honor derived from the massive confusion about their rank owing to the convoluted development of titles since the late Middle Ages. For an elaborate description of the contemporary hierarchy, as Pauli saw it, see ibid., pp. 36–38.

33. The High Court of Appeals in Celle, founded in 1711, was an "aristocratic" creation in the sense that the noble Stände provided the funds for it. It provided a dualistic legal review system, with a "learned bench" to represent the Roman-law tradition of the doctores and a "noble bench" to represent the German (common) law interests of the nobility. The first pushed, the second braked the centralizing, despotic tendencies of the electoral house. Significantly, the High Court of Appeals was the first Hanoverian governmental body to require an examination in law. An electoral rescript of 1711 laid down the rule that "noble persons [on the bench] should not be less well provided with sufficient erudition for the administration of their office than the learned [i.e., nonnoble] persons" (Meier, *Hannoverische Verfassungsgeschichte*, 1: 480). Yet nobles were not expected necessarily to have doctorates. Furthermore, in the course of the eighteenth century, educational qualifications requisite for more stringent examinations were strengthened, but primarily for the lower, local offices. A typical

lower office, that of second officer in an *Amt* or local agency of the government, was held by a bourgeois or new noble who had to pass university-based legal examinations. The place of first officer was often held by a young noble of old family, who was exempted from the examination, even though he may have attended a university (ibid., 1: 549ff.). In fact, many higher offices required university training by custom as time went on, so that the exemption of the old nobility from examinations for the lowest offices appears to have guaranteed a minimum of sinecure without express qualification, but not a maximum of power and income.

34. Ibid., 1: 462.

35. Ibid.

36. For a brief description of the creation of Erlangen University in 1743 (on the foundations of a Ritterakademie), see Theodor Kolde, *Die Universität Erlangen unter dem Hause Wittelsbach, 1810–1910* (Erlangen and Leipzig, 1910), pp. 5–12.

37. Meiners, *Verfassung und Verwaltung,* 2: 14.

38. Michaelis, *Raisonnement,* 1: 272ff.

39. Ibid., 2: 168.

40. Wilhelm Roessler, *Die Entstehung des modernen Erziehungswesens in Deutschland* (Stuttgart, 1961), pp. 95, 129.

41. Ibid., p. 153.

42. Meiners, *Verfassung und Verwaltung,* 2: 20. Pütter, in his writings of the 1790s, emphasized the relatively small social distance between the lower nobility and the Bürger, encouraging marriage between these two estates. See his *Über den Unterschied der Sände* (Göttingen, 1795) and *Über Missheiraten deutscher Fürsten und Grafen* (Göttingen, 1796).

PART IV

Elementary and Secondary Education in the Nineteenth Century

"Between the Scylla of Brutal Ignorance and the Charybdis of a Literary Education": Elite Attitudes toward Mass Schooling in Early Industrial England and America

BY CARL F. KAESTLE

In the 1930s Merle Curti wrote a finely balanced account of the social ideas of American educators in which he noted, among other things, the social conservatism of American common school advocates and their firm attachment to capitalism and the existing social structure.[1] Curti's insights were lost upon the generally laudatory tradition that then prevailed in educational historiography. Recently, however, a new group of historians have reasserted the conservatism of early schoolmen and have made it the major thrust of an attempted revision of American educational history. Public schooling is seen, not as the product of democracy, humanitarianism, and rationalism, but of class interest and the fear of disruption.[2] According to the revisionists, the system which developed is and has always been conservative, racist, and bureaucratic.[3] School reformers from Horace Mann to the present have promoted middle-class goals while manipulating the poor and the non-WASP.[4]

This rediscovery of the reformers' social conservatism appears to contradict previous comparisons of English and American developments in education. While acknowledging a substantial transatlantic reform community, earlier comparative scholars emphasized contrast. Americans conceived of education as a natural right, while the British saw it as a privilege. The Americans' commitment was thus principled and complete; the Englishmen's, pragmatic and limited. The system which thrived in democratic America floundered in England, not only on the

This paper was delivered in briefer form at the annual convention of the American Historical Association in New Orleans, 30 December 1972. I wish to acknowledge gratefully the support for this research provided by the Shelby Cullom Davis Center for Historical Studies at Princeton University and by the Research Committee of the Graduate School, University of Wisconsin, Madison. I am indebted to Lawrence Stone, Bernard Bailyn, David Tyack, Kenneth Lockridge, and Maris Vinovskis for sympathetic criticism of this essay.

religious problem but on what Cobden called the Englishman's "insatiable love of caste."[5] Although there is some merit to the characterization of British society as deferential and hierarchical and American society as more democratic and fluid, such generalizations overlook the spectrum of views on education within England and miss the essential similarity of the dominant American educational ideology before 1825 to the ideas of the particular alliance of English reformers who advocated mass schooling in the early industrial period.

The advocacy of mass schooling for social stability, which was a minority view in England at the beginning of the nineteenth century but finally prevailed against vigorous aristocratic opposition, was the mainstream reform view in America during these years and was virtually unopposed among American elites. With no truly conservative opposition to placate, American urban reformers nonetheless repeated the social justifications for mass education offered by their English counterparts. Thus, the recent trend to see our early schoolmen as having been centrally concerned with social order and middle-class consolidation has simply confirmed the fact that, for the first quarter of the nineteenth century at least, there were strong similarities in the views of English and American school advocates and much borrowing from England by Americans. Thus, we may think of this as a transatlantic reform movement in both the comparative and generative senses, a movement which provided the initial impetus for mass education institutions in England and in America combined with indigenous ideas to make its influence strongly felt on this side of the Atlantic as well. In their arguments for education, both English and American advocates emphasized collective goals—such as the reduction of crime and disruption and, to some extent, increased economic productivity—rather than individualistic goals—such as intellectual growth or personal advancement.[6] This feature has led to the controversial and somewhat sinister characterization of "education for social control" rather than for individual opportunity and, similarly, of religion for social control rather than for individual redemption.[7] I prefer simply to associate the arguments of leading school advocates from 1800 to 1825 with collective rather than individualistic goals; to talk of education for social stability, a feature of virtually all schooling systems; and to point out that the ideology cannot very usefully be labeled "conservative" or "liberal." The schooling of the masses was consonant with English liberalism of the day, even though it was an interventionist tactic; however, English liberalism of the early nineteenth century is in many respects conservative according to present-day usage. On the other hand, there were conservatives of the early industrial period, those I shall call educational Tories, who were firmly opposed to the education of the masses, for social stability or any other reason. Thus, I prefer to call the school advocates simply reformers, which is equally imprecise but has fewer normative connotations.

In the early nineteenth century, then, there were two contrary attitudes toward mass schooling among English elites, and both had roots in the eighteenth century. Opponents of mass schooling hearkened back to the writings of Bernard Mandeville and Soame Jenyns, who had attacked charity schools and argued for the necessity of an ignorant labor force.[8] The reformers' arguments, in turn, had been anticipated, though in more cautious terms, in the annual sermons of Anglican clergymen promoting charity schools.[9] After 1790, however, the argument intensified, and the education of the poor became a leading public controversy. The debate lasted some thirty years, preceding and then overlapping the English debate on state vs. voluntary support for education. Education for social stability gained advocates as the effects of the industrial revolution on the lower classes became increasingly apparent: cities filled up, crime increased, and poverty became more visible. Malthus, Smith, and Bentham justified mass education in the new industrial society in order to rescue a brutalized working class from vice, overpopulation, and antagonism toward the upper classes. After the turn of the century, increased charity schooling was advocated by several different groups, including the Utilitarians and the religious humanitarians. On this subject men as different as James Mill, William Allen, Francis Place, and Patrick Colquhoun shared similar arguments and institutional programs.

At the same time, however, opponents of mass schooling gained strength because of the educational activities of Dissenters, the fear of political radicalism fueled by the French Revolution, and the widespread opposition to any alteration of the English class structure. This Tory–High Church opposition to mass education rested on two basic arguments: that it would make the lower classes unfit for their necessary occupational role and that it would subvert proper authority by disseminating seditious and atheistic ideas. The first argument was based on a static concept of the occupational structure: because "every step in the scale of society is already full, the temporal condition of the lower orders cannot be exalted, but at the expense of the higher."[10] This fear was trumpeted from the pulpit, in the press, and before Parliament in a hundred variations. What shall we do for food when our ploughboys all become poets, they demanded.[11] There was no shortage of bankers, only of dutiful servants.[12] The teaching of writing had led to a flood of discontented, unemployed youths entering London from the countryside.[13] Even within the menial class, education would create a surplus of presumptuous upper servants and a shortage of "under servants." Give a boy some education and his parents would think him worth more money.[14] Farmers, leaving the plough in the furrow, would demand places in counting houses.[15]

In their second general argument, that mass education would lead to disorder, the conservatives predicted a multitude of dire effects, centering on political sedition, vice, and religious dissent. Mechanics who read politics would become disrespectful and insubordinate, dissolving the bonds between the classes.[16] Servant girls who read novels would be corrupted.[17] Dissenting Sunday schools were nurseries of sedition.[18] Lancasterian schools promoted atheism.[19] If good and bad principles were circulated freely among the common people, bad principles would undoubtedly win out.[20]

These aristocratic views were not confined to the upper class. The ideology of a static, deferential society was widely diffused. Hannah More's efforts were frustrated, according to her sister, by a coalition of "hard-hearted farmers, little cold country clergy, [and] a supercilious and ignorant corporation."[21] A farmer told Miss More that "of all the foolish inventions and new-fangled devices to ruin the country, that of teaching the poor to read is the very worst."[22] Both Hannah More and William Allen complained of parents' suspicions and superstitions regarding their fledgling institutions.[23] Andrew Irvine explained in 1815 that opposition to mass education stemmed from "a deep-rooted prejudice" that had "long prevailed among all classes of the community."[24] Indeed, after the Anglican bishops finally endorsed Sunday schools, they encountered resistance from their parish clergy.[25] The Elizabethan world picture died hard, and degree was not to be shak'd without great trepidation.

The vigor of this conservative position put advocates of mass schooling on the defensive in the early nineteenth century. Educational reformers of varying persuasions proclaimed that writing and arithmetic were more dangerous than reading and thus should be carefully limited.[26] Again and again the school advocates insisted that moral training, including rudimentary reading, would make men content with their lot, not ambitious, and that education would increase social stability, not disruption.[27] Although each side in the debate relied primarily upon traditional beliefs and common-sense assertions, both also attempted to prove their case by reference to observed facts. Then, as now, the actual effects of education were elusive, and both reformers and their opponents adduced evidence to fit their arguments. Schooling coincided with low crime rates, argued the education advocates, citing comparisons of Ireland and Scotland.[28] To rebut this "vulgar truism," an opponent presented figures from France to show that crime rose in the areas where instruction was increased.[29] Monitorial school reports, however, boasted of towns whose poor children had been visibly transformed into sober, industrious, polite youth.[30] *Blackwood's Magazine* retorted, "All those dogmas respecting national education have been, to a great extent, tested by experiment, and lamentable indeed are the results. . . . As education has increased amidst the people, vice, and crime, have increased."[31] Conservatives argued that the mutiny at the Nore had been instigated by unemployed clerks who should have been raised to the plough. Another argued in Parliament that this mutiny resulted from the crew's reading newspapers at nightly meetings.[32] Education was also blamed for riots in agricultural areas. On the contrary, replied schooling advocates, it is a "fact" that disturbances are greatest in Kent and Sussex, where the poor are the most ignorant.[33] The press opposed such agrarian violence as rick-burning, but few of the perpetrators could read.[34] Parliamentary testimony was produced to assert that the connection between disturbances and education was "in direct opposition to facts."[35]

Despite the apparent impossibility of resolving the issue by amassing evidence, the reformers gradually prevailed. They argued that mass schooling would serve the very goals the conservatives prized: stability, deference, and discipline. Education would prevent rebellion by humanizing the workers, whom industrialization had turned into "savages."[36] Education would teach resignation to one's lot and attach the poor to the given social structure.[37] Most important, education would reduce crime. Prevention was better than punishment, and cheaper.[38] Wherever schools were opened, prisons would be closed. In addition to the moral training they provided, the schools' custodial function was important: they would reduce crime and vagrancy simply by getting children off the streets.[39] Persuaded or not, and many were not, the conservatives were forced into acquiescence. Unable to halt the successful educational efforts of Dissenters, and openly fearful of losing working-class members to Dissent, the English Church had no choice but to establish its own educational program; and thus the Tory–High Church faction was dragged kicking and screaming into the nineteenth-century industrial world, in which mass education was unavoidable.

By 1825 the opponents of mass schooling, not the advocates, were on the defensive. It became a rhetorical ritual for those who opposed expansion of general education to deny that they were "advocates of ignorance" or descendents of Mandeville.[40] Lord Brougham rejoiced that educational bigotry was finished, and the *Edinburgh Review* declared in 1818 that "the disgraceful opposition is extinct."[41] In 1826, however, the journal was still referring, somewhat less confidently, to the "almost expiring controversy"; and Andrew Irvine argued that the opposition, though silent, was still effective.[42] Whenever a further, worrisome extension of the curriculum was suggested, the High Church bishops fell back to their old line.[43] Mass education was fought out in a stage-by-stage process. The Tories, having been brought around to the reformers' initial position, nevertheless remained vigilant to preserve the status quo.[44] They had compromised, but only on the basis of the course set out by Hannah More, to steer "between the Scylla of brutal ignorance and the Charybdis of a literary education."[45]

It is difficult, however, to keep such a ship on course. Mass education, no matter how strictly controlled, carries with it the potential for opportunity and mobility. If you teach a man to read in order that he may know his place, he may learn that he deserves yours. The conservatives perceived this potential. Indeed, many school advocates were also unsympathetic to social mobility. Others, however, while they generally denied that mobility was their intent and denied that it would happen, occasionally let the cat out of the bag. Sometimes they admitted that although most would not rise, some would. They hastened to add, however, that these few would be especially loyal because ambition attaches one to the system. Some mobility, then, would be a good thing.[46] Lord Brougham went even further, saying he longed to see some talented working-class men treading on the heels of the complacent upper class.[47]

When meritocracy raised its alien head in England, it typically brought down a storm of renewed protest and dire predictions from conservatives. Thus the dialogue continued, keeping English mass education to its characteristic collective aims: social stability and a productive citizenry.[48] In America this dialogue between advocates and opponents of mass schooling did not take place. This contrast was noted at the time. Benjamin Shaw, a member of the British and Foreign School Society, wrote in 1817, after a tour of America, "I am ashamed to reflect that in my native country, Great Britain, there are so many in opposition to the education of the poor, and to that system which is here an undisputed good."[49] Although some historians have attributed this contrast to national differences in social philosophy—namely, to a positive egalitarian thrust in America—it is important to see the difference as a more subtle one of the political and social context. The relative absence of a Tory opposition in America allowed school advocates to express in less guarded terms their approval of a modicum of social mobility through schooling, a feeling shared by many English reformers. Yet individual opportunity, although accepted by school advocates in both countries, was not a central educational goal in either.

Long before the so-called common school revival, reformers in American cities were adopting English arguments and English institutions for educating the poor. American reformers eagerly established Sunday schools, monitorial schools, and, later, infant schools, all based explicitly on English models. From New York, Thomas Eddy corresponded eagerly with Patrick Colquhoun about the education of the poor, while his son-in-law visited Lancaster's famous Borough Road school in London. Divie and Joanna Bethune's enthusiasm for Sunday schools and infant schools can be traced across the Atlantic. Quaker Roberts Vaux, while keeping in touch with English coreligionists, helped found Philadelphia's charity school system on the monitorial system. Similar institutions mirrored a similar social philosophy. The institutions were the tools of moral education, aimed especially at the increasingly volatile urban working class. Appropriate habits had to be instilled and the bonds between social classes reinforced.[50] While American orators, particularly legislators, often paid homage to the republican ideal of informed citizenship, there was actually scant attention to this function in the schools of America's major cities.[51] In the first quarter of the nineteenth century, the main thrust in mass education in America was charity schooling, and the urban reformers' collective values were very similar to those of their English counterparts. The important difference between America and England in the period 1800–1825, then, is not in the social uses of popular education, but in the widespread consensus among American elites about its desirability. Unlike the English Tories, conservative Americans generally advocated schooling for social stability. They feared ignorance, not instruction. The more skeptical they were about the survival of the republic, the more they favored mass education.[52]

The most thorough discussion of educational thought in the early national period is still Rush Welter's *Popular Education and Democratic Thought in America*. His main effort is to trace an evolution from republican educational values, which he calls conservative, to democratic educational values, which he calls liberal. Compared to the English Tory view of education, of course, republican educational theory in America was not conservative. Thus, his terminology is problematic, especially in the case of "liberal conservatism."[53] Furthermore, by focusing on the writings of political elites, Welter overestimates the effect of political theory, and thus of the American polity, upon the actual functions of schools. This is especially true of urban education. In Boston, New York, or Philadelphia, the differences between Federalists and Republicans had less effect on popular education than did the overriding concern with moral education for the poor and the immigrant. This is not to deny a role for political theory, but simply to place it in a more complex explanatory framework which recognizes that different arguments for mass schooling had a different impact, or a different relative emphasis, in different types of American communities. My research suggests that the central thrust of early English educational reform—moral education for social stability— also provided the main theme and central purpose of educational development in American cities of the early national period. Although it is true, as Welter emphasizes, that educational thought among American elites became more democratic (meaning more economically and politically egalitarian) as the nineteenth century progressed, it remains for further research to delineate more carefully between educational theory and actual practice, to document more fully changes in educational theory over time, and to determine more accurately the role of education in demographically different communities.[54] My purpose here is to point out the essential similarity of the ideas expressed by English and American advocates in urban settings during the initial stages of the institutionalization of mass schooling. Although they were similar, however, they were not identical.

Despite social values and institutional forms shared with the English, the Americans displayed a greater tolerance for individual mobility. Yet this cannot be explained by the assertion of an American egalitarian consensus, which implies that mass schooling was designed to implement equality of opportunity. On the contrary, mobility was actually quite incidental. Nor is the difference explained by the notion that Americans conceived of education as a natural right, which was a minor theme at best. The American tolerance for mobility is explained, rather, by the virtual absence in America of a Tory opposition to mass education. Reformers in America had no tactical reasons for reserve on this issue. The argument that mass education would make workers unfit for their station and spread sedition and dissent among the lower orders was almost totally lacking.

Almost, but not quite. Some waning Federalists used Tory or pseudo-Tory arguments against mass education in America. Harrison Gray Otis, for example, fretted about the incompetent schoolmaster, who "travels, like a pedlar, with bundles of trashy pamphlets and orations on his back, scattering his miserable wares through all the cottages and workshops and kitchens in the country." Defending an elite class of learners, Otis warned a Harvard centennial crowd not to "trust to the promises of the conductors on the modern intellectual railroad, to grade and level the hills of science, and to take us along at rates that will turn our heads and break our bones."[55] Another Federalist, Joseph Cogswell, said that in New England it was "rare that a child destined to live by the labour of his hands, cannot find the means of acquiring quite as much book learning, as will be useful to him in his business, and often a great deal too much to allow him to remain contented with his lot and place in life."[56] An Indiana man complained of schooling for those "who were better suited to their station without it," and the *Philadelphia National Gazette* editorialized as late as 1830 for a "comparatively uneducated" labor supply.[57] Otis, however, was more worried about cultural leveling than economic leveling, and the other comments, though thoroughly Tory, are more notable for their rarity than for their frequency. These scattered American conservatives could not mount anything like the vigorous public campaign of their English elitist cohorts.

It remains only to trace two limited strains of Tory educational thought that extended beyond the early national period. Some American conservatives perceived, correctly, that free secondary education posed a greater threat of occupational mobility than the rudimentary education of the earlier charity schools. A debate over the founding of the New York Free Academy in 1847 provides an example of opposition couched in such terms. Touted by the public school establishment and by Democratic politicians as the "keystone of the arch" of the educational system, the Free Academy was opposed by the Whig press. A letter printed in the *Journal of Commerce* argued that "to send the children of persons possessing small means to college, is doing them an injury rather than a favor. It is of this description of college educated individuals that the ranks of pettifoggers and quacks are filled. They are too proud of their superior education to work either as clerks or mechanics, or to follow any active business except what is termed 'professional.' "[58] As in England, the conservative attack elicited a cautious response from the advocates, who claimed that the practical orientation of the academy's curriculum would dignify manual work and "remove the foolish prejudice which now induces thousands to abandon the honest and healthy pursuits of their fathers, in order to establish themselves in professions, and mercantile pursuits which are already crowded to excess."[59] As in the case of English Sunday school and monitorial school advocates fifty years before, the defense was not that social mobility was good, but rather that education did not cause it. In America, however, the Tory-like opposition was weak, and thus the outright advocacy of occupational mobility was more frequent. In this case, the Democratic press, unlike the Board of Education, was unrestrained in its assertion that the academy would "improve and illustrate one of the peculiar characteristics of our people," which was, "irrespective of their circumstances and business in life, to be looking up. Every man expects to be wiser and wealthier, and to rise in the estimation of his countrymen."[60]

The New York City Whigs, then, were American neo-Tories on the education issue, but their public denunciation of commoners' rising into professional ranks marks them as unusual among school critics. The fear that schooling would change people's occupational qualifications in dysfunctional ways becomes a minor, plaintive theme in American educational debate. Later in the nineteenth century, disillusionment with the public schools and their grandiose claims prompted Richard Grant White to this Tory tirade:

Crime and vice have increased year after year almost *pari passu* with the development of the public-school system, which, instead of lifting the masses, has given us in their place a nondescript and hybrid class, unfit for professional or mercantile life, unwilling and also unable to be farmers or artisans, so that gradually our skilled labor is done more by immigrant foreigners, while our native citizens, who would otherwise naturally fill this respectable and comfortable position in society, seek to make their living by their wits—honestly if they can; if not, more or less dishonestly; or, failing thus, by petty office-seeking.[61]

The argument is echoed again in the twentieth century by Kansas poet Walt Mason, who complained: "Still the schools go on cramming the young with knowledge few of them will ever need; spoiling excellent farmers to make third-rate lawyers; running promising plumbers to furnish some more spellbinders." But Mason, characteristically American, concluded, not that there should be less education, but that there should be a more practical high school curriculum.[62] Thus was Tory rhetoric domesticated in America, until finally more education for more people came almost always to seem a good thing. In fact, the most widespread opposition to secondary education in the nineteenth century came from an antielitist working class, rather than from the heirs of Mandeville; and it was based on the negative liberal principle that since only a few would benefit from high schools, all should not be made to pay.[63]

Tory opposition to education was substantial in America on only one issue: the schooling of slaves. Whether we see American slaveholders as agrarian capitalists or as antibourgeois seigneurs, whether we see their aristocratic arguments as the essence of slave society or as superficial rationalizations, the fact remains that a majority of slaveholders who wrote about education, especially after 1830, rejected the characteristic reform argument about schooling for social stability. Some writers on slave education began to argue on general, rather than racial grounds, and in doing so sounded remarkably like the English Tory–High Church opposition of the 1790s. On the issue of mass education, these Southern slaveholders became more aristocratic while the English aristocrats became more bourgeois.

The charity school rationale—training for obedience and subordination—had been promoted with reference to slaves in eighteenth-century America, most notably by the Society for the Propagation of the Gospel in Foreign Parts.[64] After the Revolution, the S.P.G.'s missionary activities ceased in the United States; and the efforts at black schooling by groups like the Quakers, who associated education more with manumission than with submission, were increasingly discouraged in the South. After 1820, in response to slave revolts and abolitionist literature, laws prohibiting education became standard features of the slave codes.[65] These were the immediate reasons for the stringent laws against teaching the slaves, and they were frankly admitted. But challenges to this prohibition, both from Northern critics and a minority of Southern reformers, prompted a broader justification, for which, consciously or unconsciously, one group of slavery apologists borrowed a Tory view of education.

Southern critics of the ban on slave education, echoing both the S.P.G. missionaries and the early urban reformers like Patrick Colquhoun of London and Thomas Eddy of New York, argued that the education of slaves, if thoroughly religious and otherwise limited, far from causing rebellions, created a bond between master and slave, and indeed, that the best-behaved slaves were those who could read.[66] In response, the more aristocratic slaveholders developed a defense of slave ignorance similar to George Fitzhugh's defense of slavery as a desirable form of labor, an argument that did not depend upon race, and thus they began to sound like Tories. In England in the 1790s, for example, a High Churchman had argued that the laboring poor had a "serious advantage" in that all they required was "industry and innocence," qualities that could be learned from their parents. They are free of all the "distressing perplexities" and cares of wealth.[67] A widely read anonymous tract applied the same argument to the American slave in the 1830s. Learning brings "more anxiety than enjoyment." The slave escapes the "harassing cares" of knowledge and position and is left, as he naturally prefers, to his "rustic pleasures." In addition, the two central Tory arguments are asserted: "The situation of the slave is, in every particular, incompatible with the cultivation of his mind. It would not only unfit him for his station in life, and prepare him for insurrection, but would be found wholly impracticable in the performance of the duties of a labourer."[68] But if these objections applied to slave labor, did they not apply to free white labor as well, as the English aristocrats had argued? Only a few Southern writers made this striking extension explicit. William Harper, a true heir of Bernard Mandeville, was one who did:

The slave receives such instruction as qualifies him to discharge the duties of his particular station. The Creator did not intend that every individual human being should be highly cultivated. . . . It is better that a part should be fully and highly cultivated, and the rest utterly ignorant. To constitute a society, a variety of offices must be discharged, from those requiring but the lowest degree of intellectual power to those requiring the very highest, and it should seem that the endowments ought to be apportioned according to the exigencies of the situation.[69]

Thus, the Tory–High Church view was alive and well in South Carolina in the 1850s. But as George Frederickson has argued in response to Eugene Genovese's formulation of an antibourgeois Southern culture, such aristocratic arguments were not politically viable in the *herrenvolk* democracy of the antebellum South.[70] Despite the appeal of the hierarchical argument to some Southern elites, slave ignorance was predominantly and ultimately justified on racial grounds. Nowhere in America did the Tory view of education prevail.

    This comparison of England and America presents us with a case study of the selective transatlantic crossing of institutional ideas. The notion that social stability demanded mass education, a hotly contested view in England, was readily accepted in America. The reasons for the absence of a Tory opposition to mass education in America, except as a minor theme, are various. The most obvious reason is that there was no formal nobility and no established church in America. To the extent, then, that the Tory opposition to mass education was a trait of the nobility proper and of the High Church establishment, it simply had no constituency in America. As we have seen, however, the static, hierarchical view of society enjoyed broad support in England; and many American elites, though lacking coats of arms, held paternalistic and disdainful attitudes toward workers and the poor. Furthermore, many Americans, particularly Federalists, underwent a revulsion against the French Revolution similar in kind if not in degree to that of their conservative English contemporaries. Shays's Rebellion, and the immigration of Frenchmen and United Irishmen, intensified the fear of sedition at home. These factors suggest that the uncontroversial nature of charity schooling in the early national period requires some further explanation.

Three additional factors distinguish the American situation from the English. First, America started from a higher literacy base. At the turn of the century, when American urban reformers were corresponding with their English counterparts about mass education, America was decades behind England in industrial and urban development, but ahead in literacy. Thus, the Americans did not fear a literate public; indeed, as their English liberal correspondents warned them, they had great reason to try to maintain the literacy level in the face of increasing industrialization.[71] The objects of charity education in America, then, seemed neither so numerous nor so dangerous as in England. Second, the relationship between general literacy and rebellion was perceived differently in America, simply by virtue of the nation's beginnings. Despite reactions against the French Revolution and anxieties about sedition at home, virtually all Americans had, of necessity, a more ambivalent attitude toward revolution; after all, they had rebelled against England, and the very success of that rebellion, some pointed out, was due to the widespread and right-minded judgment of the country's yeomen.[72] Third, and perhaps most important, American mass schooling efforts became increasingly acculturative as immigration increased. Even before the 1830s, despite the fact that a majority of the working class was still native, the rhetoric and mission of schoolmen in the coastal cities were heavily influenced by the threat of immigrant vice, infidelity, and crime. In England, despite increasing class alienation, there was a native laboring class, and conservatives could hope more reasonably to rely upon institutions other than schools to transmit values like deference and subordination. This hope proved illusory. English conservatives finally accepted the educational program of the reformers, and Parliament's particular interest in the schooling of the London Irish illustrates the special connection between charity education and the acculturation of aliens.[73] In America the use of schools for ethnic conversion became a central theme.

It was the congruence of all these conditions—social, political, and cultural—which accounts for the absence of a Tory opposition in America and thus the consensus among American elites, in contrast to the controversy among English elites, on the issue of mass education. Consensus among elites, however, does not imply a conflict-free society. Indeed, American urban reformers saw mass education as necessary to alleviate growing class conflict, and the schoolmen's rhetoric is laden with battle metaphors. Their justification of mass education, based on collective values they perceived as necessary, has been an enduring legacy, but it presents a problem of historical interpretation. Earlier defenders of the liberal tradition, such as J. S. Schapiro, believed that bourgeois liberalism was a good thing because it contained within its program the seeds of democratic liberalism, as the aristocrats had feared.[74] Whether the study of education confirms that faith or whether, on the contrary, a system developed which basically served collective goals while professing individualistic goals, is one of the crucial research problems that face historians of education today.

In its charity school origins, however, mass education in both countries was frankly justified on grounds of stability, with little pretense to providing equality of opportunity or intellectual enlightenment. If we keep this distinction in mind, we may avoid the anachronism of characterizing early school reformers as hypocrites who said one thing and intended another. These were the sons of James Mill and William Allen, not of Condorcet and Tom Paine. Although they strove to protect the position of the great middling ranks of society, these advocates of mass education were a progressive force in the nonnormative sense that they defeated the previously dominant elite attitude: outright opposition to the education of the working class. The demise of the Tory view of education is interesting in itself, as a chapter in the history of conservatism. But the demise of Tory opposition is also important, as I have suggested, in underlining the central importance of schooling for social stability in early industrial England and America.

NOTES

1. Merle Curti, *The Social Ideas of American Educators* (New York, 1935; rev. ed., 1959), chaps. 3 and 4.

2. Michael B. Katz, *The Irony of Early School Reform: Educational Innovation in Mid-Nineteenth Century Massachusetts* (Cambridge, 1968); idem, *Class, Bureaucracy, and Schools: The Illusion of Educational Change in America* (New York, 1971), p. xviii and passim.

3. Michael B. Katz, ed., *School Reform: Past and Present* (Boston, 1971), pp. 2–3.

4. On the Progressive period, see Clarence J. Karier, Paul Violas, and Joel Spring, eds., *Roots of Crisis: American Education in the Twentieth Century* (New York, 1973); Colin Greer, *The Great School Legend: A Revisionist Interpretation of American Public Education* (New York, 1971); and Joel Spring, *Education and the Rise of the Corporate State* (Boston, 1972).

5. Frank Thistlethwaite, *America and the Atlantic Community: Anglo-American Aspects, 1790–1850* (Philadelphia, 1959), chaps. 5 and 6; Rush Welter, "Democratic Theory and Education in English and American Thought" (Paper delivered at the Symposium on the Role of Education in Nineteenth-Century America, Chatham, Massachusetts, June 1964), published in revised form in *American Writings on Popular Education: The Nineteenth Century,* ed. Rush Welter (Indianapolis, 1971), introduction.

6. The argument that education would increase productivity was not as characteristic of the early industrial period as it was later. See E. G. West, *Education and the State* (London, 1965), pp. 118–19; John Vaizey, *The Economics of Education* (London, 1962), chap. 1; and Maris A. Vinovskis, "Horace Mann on the Economic Productivity of Education," *New England Quarterly* 43 (December 1970): 550–71.

7. On religion as social control see Charles I. Foster, *Errand of Mercy: The Evangelical United Front, 1790–1837* (Chapel Hill, 1960); and Clifford E. Griffin, *Their Brothers' Keepers: Moral Stewardship in the United States, 1800–1965* (New Brunswick, N.J., 1960). This interpretation is challenged in Lois W. Banner, "Religious Benevolence as Social Control: A Critique of an Interpretation," *Journal of American History* 60 (June 1973): 23–41.

8. Bernard Mandeville, *The Fable of the Bees; or, Private Vices, Public Benefits,* 2 vols. (Edinburgh, 1772), 1: 216–18; Soame Jenyns, *A Free Enquiry into the Nature and Origins of Evil* (London, 1757).

9. See, for example, Isaac Watts, "An Essay towards the Encouragement of Charity Schools," *Works . . .* (London, 1753), 2: 755f.; Thomas Ashton, *A sermon preached . . . at the yearly meeting of the children educated in charity schools . . .* (London, 1787), p. 21; Joseph Pott, *A sermon preached . . . at the yearly meeting of the children educated in the charity schools . . .* (London, 1794),

pp. 18–19. See also R. A. Soloway, *Prelates and People: Ecclesiastical Social Thought in England, 1783–1852* (London, 1969), pp. 353–56.

10. John Weyland, *A letter to a country gentleman on the education of the lower orders . . .* (London, 1808), p. 5.

11. Ibid.

12. John Simeon, 24 April 1807, in Great Britain, *Hansard's Parliamentary Debates*, IX, col. 544.

13. Weyland, *Letter*, p. 53.

14. William Davis, *Hints to Philanthropists; or, a Collective View of Practical Means of Improving the Condition of the Poor and Labouring Classes of Society* (Bath, 1821), p. 11; Catherine Cappe, *An Account of Two Charity Schools*, quoted in Harold Silver, *The Concept of Popular Education: A Study of Ideas and Social Movements in the Early Nineteenth Century* (London, 1965), p. 29.

15. George Rose, 13 July 1807, in Great Britain, *Hansard's Parliamentary Debates*, IX, col. 800.

16. *Blackwood's Magazine* 17 (1825): 549.

17. Davis, *Hints*, p. 11.

18. Bishop of Rochester, second general visitation, 1800, in J. Henry Harris, *Robert Raikes: The Man and his Work* (London, 1899), p. 93; Ford K. Brown, *Fathers of the Victorians: The Age of Wilberforce* (Cambridge, 1961), pp. 168–69, 178, 211.

19. John Bowles, *A Letter Addressed to Samuel Whitbread . . .*, 2d ed. (London, 1808), pp. 11–12.

20. William Windham, 24 April 1807, in Great Britain, *Hansard's Parliamentary Debates*, IX, col. 547.

21. Martha More, *Mendip Annals*, quoted in Mary Sturt, *The Education of the People: A History of Primary Education in England and Wales in the Nineteenth Century* (London, 1967), p. 12.

22. Richard D. Altick, *The English Common Reader: A Social History of the Mass Reading Public, 1800–1900* (Chicago, 1957), pp. 68–69.

23. On More, see Harris, *Raikes*, p. 89; on Allen, see Frederic Hill, *National Education: Its Present State and Prospects*, 2 vols. (London, 1836), 1: 46–47.

24. Andrew Irvine, *Reflections on the Education of the Poor* (London, 1815), p. 45.

25. Soloway, *Prelates and People*, p. 362.

26. Sarah Trimmer, *The Oeconomy of Charity*, 2 vols. (London, 1801), 1: 99; Patrick Colquhoun, *A New and Appropriate System of Education for the Labouring People* (London, 1806), p. 13.

27. See, for example, the many articles on monitorial education in the *Edinburgh Review* between 1806 and 1813 and in the *Philanthropist* between 1811 and 1819.

28. For example, Irvine, *Reflections*, pp. 24–26.

29. Baldwin F. Duppa, *The Education of the Peasantry in England . . .* (n.p., n.d.), pp. 4–5, 106.

30. See, for example, Second Annual Report of the Lancasterian School in the Town of Douglas, Isle of Man, 1812, in Carl F. Kaestle, ed., *Joseph Lancaster and the Monitorial School Movement: A Documentary History* (New York, 1973), p. 127.

31. *Blackwood's Magazine* 22 (1827): 427.

32. Weyland, *Letter to a Country Gentleman*, p. 55; Sir T. Thurton, 4 August 1807, in Great Britain, *Hansard's Parliamentary Debates*, IX, col. 1053.

33. Richard Whately, *The Duty of those who disapprove the education of the Poor . . .* (London, 1830), p. 4.

34. Thomas Wyse, *Education Reform; or, The necessity of a national system of education* (London, 1836), p. 386.

35. Hill, *National Education*, p. 110.

36. For examples, see *Gloucester Journal*, October 1785, in Harris, *Raikes*, p. 73; Thomas Beddoes, *Extract of a Letter on Early Instruction, particularly that of the Poor* (London, 1792); Colquhoun, *System of Education*, pp. 67–69; Francis Place, *Improvement of the Working People* (London, 1834), pp. 5–6.

37. Irvine, *Reflections*, p. 18; Samuel Wilderspin, *A System for the Education of the Young . . .* (London, 1840), pp. 5–7.

38. Irvine, *Reflections*, pp. 23–27; *First Report . . . select committee appointed to inquire into the education of the lower orders of the metropolis* (London, 1816), pp. 77–80.

39. Irvine, *Reflections*, pp. 32–33.

40. Richard Lloyd, *A Letter to a Member of Parliament . . .* (London, 1821), p. 31.

41. Henry Brougham, *Practical Observations upon the Education of the People . . .* (London, 1825), p. 31; *Edinburgh Review* 30 (1818): 486.

42. *Edinburgh Review* 45 (1826): 194; Irvine, *Reflections*, p. 6.

43. Soloway, *Prelates and People,* p. 385.

44. See, for example, Edward Grinfield, *A Reply to Mr. Brougham's "Practical Observations upon the Education of the People . . . "* (London, 1825), pp. ii–iv, 9–11.

45. *Letters of Hannah More,* quoted in Silver, *Concept of Popular Education,* p. 48.

46. Irvine, *Reflections,* pp. 20–22; Ralph Wardlaw, *Essay on Joseph Lancaster's "Improvements in Education"* (Glasgow, 1810), pp. 36–37; Alexander Christison, *The General Diffusion of Knowledge One Great Cause of the Prosperity of North Britain* (Edinburgh, 1802), pp. 8–10.

47. Chester W. New, *The Life of Lord Brougham to 1830* (Oxford, 1961), p. 340.

48. On the "conservative aims of English reform in this period, see Bernard N. Schilling, *Conservative England and the Case against Voltaire* (New York, 1950), chaps. 7 and 8; Altick, *English Common Reader,* pp. 141–44; and Brown, *Fathers of the Victorians,* p. 4.

49. Benjamin Shaw to the British and Foreign School Society, in British and Foreign School Society, *Report* (London, 1817), p. 58.

50. See Carl F. Kaestle, *The Evolution of an Urban School System: New York City, 1750–1850* (Cambridge, 1973); and Stanley K. Schultz, *The Culture Factory: Boston Public Schools, 1789–1860* (New York, 1973). On Vaux, see Joseph J. McCadden, *Education in Pennsylvania, 1801–1835, and Its Debt to Roberts Vaux* (Philadelphia, 1937), esp. pp. 150, 209–10.

51. A sampling of such republican arguments for the 1790s is found in Frederick Rudolph, ed., *Essays on Education in the Early Republic* (Cambridge, 1965); and for the period after 1825, in Welter, *American Writings on Popular Education.*

52. See David B. Tyack, *George Ticknor and the Boston Brahmins* (Cambridge, 1967), pp. 204–8.

53. Rush Welter, *Popular Education and Democratic Thought in America* (New York, 1962), p. 79.

54. On the general shift in reform sentiment in Jacksonian America, see W. David Lewis, "The Reformer as Conservative: Protestant Counter-Subversion in the Early Republic," in *The Development of an American Culture,* ed. Stanley Cohen and Lorman Ratner (Englewood Cliffs, N.J., 1970), pp. 64–91; and David B. Davis, ed., *Ante-Bellum Reform* (New York, 1967), introduction.

55. James S. Loring, *The Hundred Boston Orators . . .* (Boston, 1853), pp. 196–97.

56. Joseph Cogswell, quoted in James McLachlan, *American Boarding Schools: A Historical Study* (New York, 1970), p. 317n.

57. Curti, *Social Ideas of American Educators,* p. 88. For similar examples see Edgar W. Knight and Clifton L. Hall, eds., *Readings in American Educational History* (New York, 1951), pp. 149, 341. For related arguments against women's education, see Mary S. Benson, *Women in Eighteenth-Century America* (New York, 1935), p. 145; and Thomas Woody, *A History of Women's Education in the United States* (New York, 1929), vol. 1, chap. 3.

58. *Journal of Commerce,* 22 May 1847, in Mario E. Cosenza, *The Establishment of the College of the City of New York as the Free Academy in 1847 . . .* (New York, 1955), pp. 146–47.

59. Townshend Harris et al., *Memorial . . . to Establish a Free Academy . . .* (New York, 1847), p. 7.

60. *Daily Globe,* 25 May 1847, in Cosenza, *Free Academy,* pp. 149–50. For an analysis of the early graduates of the academy which demonstrates that the conservatives' fears of occupational mobility were justified, see Kaestle, *Evolution of an Urban School System,* pp. 104–9.

61. Richard Grant White, "The Public-School Failure," *North American Review* 131 (1880): 546. For similar arguments during the 1870s and 1880s, see David B. Tyack, "Education and Social Unrest, 1873–1878," *Harvard Educational Review* 31 (Spring 1961): 194–212; and, by the same author, "Bureaucracy and the Common School: The Example of Portland, Oregon, 1851–1913," *American Quarterly* 19 (1967): 489.

62. Walt Mason, "Who's to Weed the Onions When Everybody is Highly Educated?" *Literary Digest,* 68 (1921): 50–52. Late-nineteenth-century antecedents for this argument—Tory anxieties about mobility coupled with pleas for practical education—are found in Gail Hamilton, *Our Common School System* (Boston, 1880); and in J. R. Kendrick in *The Forum,* September 1889, p. 74.

63. Elmer E. Brown, *The Making of Our Middle Schools* (New York, 1902), pp. 317–18; Katz, *Irony of Early School Reform,* pp. 80–93; Frank T. Carleton, *Economic Influences upon Educational Progress in the United States, 1820–1850* (Madison, Wis., 1908; paperback ed., Teachers College Press, 1965), pp. 65–70.

64. See Samuel Auchmuty to the Society for the Propagation of the Gospel in Foreign Parts, 19 September 1761, S.P.G. Letter Book B., no. 2 (microfilm); and Auchmuty to Daniel Burton, 10 September 1764, quoted in Frank Klingberg, *Anglican Humanitarianism in Colonial New York* (Philadelphia, 1940), p. 151.

65. Carter Woodson, *The Education of the Negro Prior to 1861* (New York, 1915).

66. Charles C. Jones, *The Religious Instruction of the Negroes in the United States* (Savannah, 1842), pp. 210–15; J. B. O'Neall, "Slave Laws of the South," in *Industrial Resources of the Southern and Western States,* ed. J. D. B. DeBow (Boston, 1852), p. 279.

67. William Paley, *Reasons for Contentment: Addressed to the Labouring Part of the British Public* (London, 1793), p. 11. On Fitzhugh and the antibourgeois character of the slave South, see Eugene D. Genovese, *The World the Slaveholders Made: Two Essays in Interpretation* (New York, 1969), pp. 95–102, and pt. 2 passim.

68. *The South Vindicated from the Treason and Fanaticism of the Northern Abolitionists* (Philadelphia, 1836), pp. 68–69. The same arguments were presented to Frederick Douglass; see his *Narrative of the Life of Frederick Douglass, An American Slave, Written by Himself* (1845; Cambridge: John Harvard Library paperback edition, 1969), pp. 58–59. That the arguments were widespread and the prohibition effective is apparent from the slave narratives collected in Norman R. Yetman, ed., *Life under the "Peculiar Institution": Selections from the Slave Narrative Collection* (New York, 1970); see pp. 16, 26, 39, 56, 106, 149, 152, 161, 177, 189, 225, 227, 273, 274, 276, 296, 299, 313, 332.

69. William Harper, "Memoir on Negro Slavery," in DeBow, *Industrial Resources,* p. 217.

70. George M. Frederickson, *The Black Image in the White Mind: The Debate on Afro-American Character and Destiny, 1817–1914* (New York, 1971), pp. 64–70.

71. See Patrick Colquhoun to Thomas Eddy, London, 16 February 1803, in Samuel L. Knapp, *The Life of Thomas Eddy* (London, 1836), p. 149. On literacy, see Lawrence Stone, "Literacy and Education in England, 1640–1900," *Past and Present* 42 (February 1969): 68–139; and Kenneth Lockridge, *Literacy in Colonial New England* (New York, 1974). The contrast with English literacy levels is most striking for New England. See Lockridge, *Literacy,* pp. 88–89. That Southern literacy rates were only slightly greater than English is consistent with the lingering Tory attitude toward the education of blacks in the South.

72. For example, see Jonathan Fisk, "On Education" (1798), quoted in Kaestle, *Evolution of an Urban School System,* p. 63.

73. House of Commons, *First Report; Minutes of Evidence Taken Before the Select Committee appointed to inquire into the Education of the Lower Orders of the Metropolis* (London, 1816), pp. 4, 6, 8, 11.

74. J. Salwyn Schapiro, *Liberalism and the Challenge of Fascism: Social Forces in England and France, 1815–1870* (New York, 1949), pp. 397–403.

CHAPTER 8

Working-Class Demand and the Growth of English Elementary Education, 1750–1850

BY THOMAS W. LAQUEUR

English elementary education underwent remarkable and far-reaching changes in the century spanning the industrial revolution. From an enrollment in 1818 of some 630,000 children—about 6.5 percent of the population—the number of students on school registers grew by 1851 to over 2 million—or 13 percent of the population. There were 450,000 Sunday school scholars in 1818 and five times that number by mid-century.[1]

More often forgotten, there was also a radical change in the arrangements for the control and financing of education. In the mid-eighteenth century no more than 20–30 percent of enrollment was found in schools paid for and consequently controlled by a public body, religious or secular.[2] The great majority of students were not in the grammar and charity schools which have captured the historians' imagination. Rather, their parents purchased elementary education in the open marketplace from thousands of private teachers who operated small schools for a profit. Public control of schooling came slowly. In 1833 still only 40 percent of all students were in schools under outside control; by 1851, 68 percent of students had at least part of their education financed by some public body, be it church or chapel, the government, or a local authority.[3] Lowe's Revised Code, the Forster Act of 1870, and the Mundella Act of 1880 making school attendance compulsory finally and perhaps irrevocably removed the education of children from the control of their parents.

The century being considered also saw the transformation of the school as a social institution. Private schools in 1750 could have contained no more than the handful of students that might fit into a teacher's front room or workshop. Even the publicly financed charity schools of the mid-eighteenth century had enrollments of only twenty to twenty-five children.[4] Schools in preindustrial England seldom kept records of admissions or attendance; they did not publish rules about discipline, dress, or deportment; they were not divided into classes with set curricula nor were they taught in accordance with an accepted system of pedagogy. In short, the rationalized, disciplined, highly structured, professionally staffed, and essentially public organization which is the modern school came into being during the nineteenth century.[5]

II

How and why did these changes take place? What insight might an answer offer toward an understanding of working-class response to the social and economic pressures of industrialization?

Historians have offered a wide range of different and occasionally contradictory explanations. There is agreement, however, that the answer lies somewhere on the supply side of the equation, that it rests upon an understanding of how or why some outside agency sought to increase the number, nature, or quality of school places. The role of working-class demand in the transformation of elementary education has been largely ignored and, if noted at all, relegated to an obscure and ill-lighted corner.

A standard textbook on the history of education, for example, begins with a somber description of social conditions in the late eighteenth century. These conditions, it argues, "made it obvious that something would have to be *done for* the poor."[6] Subsequent chapters chronicle exactly what was done to supply the working classes with school places: "Bell, Lancaster, Robert Owen, Wilderspin, David Stow—all have contributed to make English elementary education."[7] The "religious difficulty" in English education is interwoven throughout the narrative: vigorous opposition to Graham's Factory Bill in 1843, for example, meant that "a State system of education was postponed for nearly thirty years."[8] Continued controversy between church, dissenters, and voluntarists; the Newcastle Commission; the Revised Code; and Forster's Act are presented as if they indeed formed the exclusive stuff of educational history.

But such explanations are not limited to old textbooks. Professor Lawrence Stone, for example, asserts that "the rise of popular elementary education was very largely an incidental by-product of the struggle between Anglicans and Dissenters for the allegiance of the lower classes."[9] Professor Asa Briggs, in focusing on the rise of "national," or state, education, argues that, on the contrary, this rivalry was "the main obstacle to the further development of an educational system."[10] Professor Harold Perkin in his more recent work follows Stone by claiming that the founding of the British and Foreign School "provoked into existence the rival National Society, and by their competition and constant agitation for State education [they] stimulated the expansion of elementary education." Even the school curriculum, he argues, was determined by this rivalry between the suppliers of public education: "The traditionalists could no longer confine the teaching to religious and moral education, reading the Bible and learning the catechism and the Ten Commandments. Useful knowledge became the watchword."[11] Professor J. F. C. Harrison goes so far as to deny explicitly the role of demand in effecting educational change: "The working class had no distinctive educational ideology of their own . . . and had no alternative but to accept the instruction offered in the middle class Sunday and day schools.''[12]

Even when the working-class consumer of education is given a part to play, it is as an advocate of state intervention, a not altogether congenial role. True, as Professor Simon notes, many Chartists supported the educational provisions of Graham's Factory Bill.[13] But this support must be seen, in part at least, as opposition to the dissenting clergy who led the anti-Factory Bill forces and to what they represented. Cries of ''The New Poor Law,'' and not slogans in favor of the bill, characterize Chartist participation at public meetings.[14] Clearly, suffrage was the main thrust of the Chartist leadership, and if they felt that education would follow it ''as day succeeds night'' they were not anxious to encourage that succession actively.[15] The kind of government which would be elected were the charter to become law might well be trusted with providing schooling for working-class children, but state intervention under the old constitution was viewed by Chartists with suspicion born of the New Poor Law and the 1839 Police Act. Citing an occasional petition to Parliament for a measure furthering education, like that of the Miner's Association in 1847, only emphasizes the decades of working-class indifference or even hostility toward a national system of schools.[16] And it obscures the fact that demand for education was expressed through very different channels.

Even those historians who stress the counterrevolutionary thrust of educational provision in the nineteenth century relegate the working-class consumer to a relatively minimal, passive place in their narratives. Elementary schooling grew, they argue, out of the need perceived by middle-class patrons to reimpose on the lower orders a certain discipline that had been lost through the social dislocations of industrialization. Day schools by the thousands were founded to act as agencies of social control. The child and his parents, meanwhile, figure only as victims of these new repressive institutions, except on those rare occasions between 1817 and 1820 and again between 1839 and the mid-40s when Radicals and Chartists provided some alternative schooling.[17]

There is, of course, considerable truth in each of the accounts outlined above. But they begin to appear suspect as being too one-sided when considered alongside histories of secondary and higher education in which the consumer, not the supplier, of education plays the leading role. Grammar schools changed their curriculum to cater to middle-class demand for a more practical education; hundreds of lower secondary schools grew up to meet the requirements of the burgeoning commercial orders. The revivification of the great public schools, when not attributed to the efforts of Dr. Arnold, is generally interpreted as a response to the demands of the socially ambitious professional and manufacturing classes. Birkbeck College and a succession of redbricks were founded to circumvent the religious and curricular restrictions of Oxbridge. Strangely, only in the history of elementary education is attention focused exclusively on the supply of school places.

There are, moreover, at least four specific difficulties with this account which suggest that it needs to be broadened. First, it cannot explain why anyone, especially a working-class parent,bothered to send his children to school. School attendance was not compulsory in England until 1880, and so there quite clearly would have been no growth of enrollment if parents had not *chosen* to send their children to some school, be it public or private. Secondly, explanations in terms of supply alone cannot account for expansion of education before the time when the agencies responsible for the great increase in school places—the Anglican and dissenting school societies—were created in 1810. Even after that date they explain growth only in the public sector, and yet privately provided schooling grew apace for at least a generation more. From the demise of the charity school movement in the 1730s to the resurgence of educational philanthropy in the early nineteenth century, the private school, created by and wholly dependent on local demand, was at the cutting edge of slow but steady educational advances.

The persistence of private-venture schools raises a third objection. Why did parents continue to patronize these small, ill-organized, and allegedly inefficient seminaries which charged on the average four times as much as their publicly subsidized competitors? Until mid-century the majority of students remained enrolled in these comparatively expensive anachronisms. Even in 1851, when only one-third of all students were outside the public sector, there were still twice as many private as public day schools.[18] All of this suggests that the contest for the provision of primary education was not just between the British and Foreign and the National School societies but between private and public schools generally. The existence of this latter contest and its importance in working-class life are not explicable in terms merely of supply.

Finally, by concentrating almost exclusively on the triumphant institutions—the publicly financed, highly structured, and rationally organized schools—historians have obscured and forgotten the fundamental features of what these schools supplanted. As so often happens to losers, the ramshackle, improvised network of private schools patronized by the working classes has been denied its place in the sun. By their very nature, these schools were an integral part of the community and one of the most important reflections of its educational aspirations. An analysis of education and the working classes which excludes a careful evaluation of the kind of schooling parents freely decided to purchase for their children is, therefore, deficient.

III

Changes on the supply side of education, although very important, do not in themselves provide a sufficient explanation of what actually happened. There existed a considerable and highly discriminating working-class demand for education, both before and after the founding of the two great school societies, which directly affected the scale and structure of educational provision. The struggle between the older private schools which lived by satisfying this demand and the new, publicly financed schools was in a larger sense a contest between a preindustrial institution thoroughly integrated into the local community and a modern organization imposed on the community from the outside. Old patterns of behavior had to give way to new before public education could supplant its more primitive predecessor.

Indirect evidence from many angles can be provided to show that there was a high demand for education even before 1750. Basic literacy, the immediate product of elementary instruction, was already high by that date. The male literacy rate, about 60 percent, held up for the next half century despite the pressures and dislocations of rapid demographic growth, migration to the cities, and factory employment; after 1800 it actually began to increase. Female literacy, about 35 percent at mid-century, grew slowly and uninterruptedly from 1750 to 1850.[19] The 200,000 copies of Tom Paine and the "short and popular antithetical tracts" that were "circulated through every part of the kingdom, but especially the north, with a degree of system and zeal, which have scarcely ever been exceeded" all found an audience created largely by the much maligned private-venture schools.[20]

It is difficult to estimate either the total number of children enrolled in all schools during the middle of the eighteenth century or the proportion of this number whose education was financed by some public body. What appears to be a charity school turns out to be a private school in disguise when examined more closely.[21] The small parish school, six of whose scholars were supported by an endowment and the remaining fifteen out of their parents' pockets, defies classification. It would not be far wrong, however, to suppose that at most 60,000 students—one-quarter to one-third of the total enrollment—were attending publicly financed schools.[22] The remaining two-thirds or three-quarters purchased their education on the relatively open educational marketplace of the day. Of course, there was no compulsion to attend any school, public or private; the relatively high literacy rate in England was achieved by parents' voluntarily sending their children to school.

Moreover, demand for education among the working classes was highly discriminating. Even when publicly financed schools began to appear in large numbers after 1810, parents did not flock to have their children admitted. When both options were available, they often chose to send their children to the private, fee-paying schools rather than to the free, publicly supported ones. James Kay's testimony to the 1837 Parliamentary Inquiry into the Education of the Poorer Classes illustrates this peculiar predilection.

Kay, later Kay-Shuttleworth, sought to convince the committee that the national system of publicly supported schools which he advocated for a host of reasons, many having little or nothing to do with the welfare of the poor, would in fact attract working-class children.[23] Certain committee members, however, brought up on the classical economic doctrine that a superior product at a lower price ought to outsell an inferior one at a higher price, found it difficult to understand why nearly free public schools were not as popular as theory might predict. It puzzled Mr. Pusey:

Why there should be so large a number as 4,000 boys in Manchester in attendance upon those private day schools, where you state the instruction afforded to be of a very ordinary and inferior description, whilst it appears that at the Lancastrian day school, where it is of a superior kind and where the instruction is gratuitous, there are but 721 boys; and at the National School, where it is also gratuitous, there are 280 boys at attendance. Can you state the reason why parents give preference to the worst kind of education, for which they are obliged to pay.[24]

Kay fumbled for an answer and ended up arguing that parents did not in fact give preference to "the worse kind of education" but rather that Manchester was so large a town that the public schools in question could adequately serve only their neighborhoods. This, he said, they did. But in response to a question from the young Gladstone, he admitted that public schools met with little success, even though they sometimes paid a bounty to attract children; to Pusey he confessed that the National School on Granby Row, which was built to accomodate 500, actually had registered only a little over half that number.[25]

Kay did not, however, enlighten the committee as to the real educational ecology of the area around Granby Row. While the National School stood half empty, at least seven private-venture schools flourished within a 500-yard radius of its doors. There may, indeed, have been more such schools, too small or too transitory to be listed in a commercial directory.[26] In fact, therefore, with free schooling on their back door, parents nevertheless preferred to pay 4–8d. per week to send their children to the allegedly inferior private schools.

This preference is reported again and again during the 1830s, '40s, and '50s. J. P. Norris, in one of his reports to the Committee of Council, noted that in Burslem there were two dame schools in every street. Out of a population of 225,000, 9,400 children of the same class that patronized National schools attended private-venture schools instead. He was shocked to discover that 4 percent of the population attended schools costing on the average 6d. per week; while 2.4 percent attended the supposedly superior church schools, which only cost them on the average a third as much. The most expensive schools, he concluded, were the most popular.[27]

An 1837 investigation into the causes of the Warrington National School's unpopularity came to a similar determination. "Facts elicited," it reads, "have necessarily led to the conclusion that whilst a sense of duty and interest induces a large proportion of the working class to make considerable pecuniary sacrifices for the mental cultivation of their off-spring, the means by which they pursue their end are in general inadequate."[28] That is, parents were reluctant to send their children to the church school.

But while working-class demand discriminated against the public school, it was apparently also attuned to the quality of education. The Manchester Statistical Society noted with disapproval the existence of a couple of schoolmasters of great ability, though "much given to drink," whose pupils went to other schools or onto the streets while their masters were on the binge but filled their schools again when they returned to sobriety.[29] Henry Mosely reported to the Committee of Council in 1844 that the quality of instruction determined the success of a school. St. Mary's Sheffield was appreciated by the working classes "as evidenced by the fact that

698 children resort to it.'' Excellent schools in fifteen other towns are cited as ''examples scarcely less instructive than those which I have before enumerated of the value the labouring classes attach to a good education and the just estimate they are accustomed to form in respect to it.''[30] The converse was also true; parents shunned schools which provided inferior instruction. Mosely cites, for example, a school ''started with great pretensions and a high fee [where] the poor, impressed with the idea that the education was good, sent their children in great numbers. . . . they found out its real merits and the numbers have gradually fallen off.''[31] In the town of Barrow parents quickly dispensed with the young parish schoolmaster who refused to teach anything but Latin.[32] William Lovett recalls that his mother removed him from a school where he ''made but little progress'' to one where he ''learned to write tolerably well, and to know a little arithmetic and the catechism.''[33]

It is also clear that discriminating working-class demand stimulated the supply and broadened the curriculum of public schools. ''The poor will have education,'' one National School committee stated, ''and if our system fails the schoolmaster of sedition and infidelity is not sleeping at his post.''[34] Publicly provided schooling thus grew up in large part to meet the demand for education which might otherwise have been satisfied in politically less reputable private schools. The argument of an anonymous clergyman who reported to the *Anti-Jacobin Review* in 1800 that he always paid for the education of his parishioners' children because otherwise they might fall into the hands of seditious and irreligious teachers was echoed by the High Church Tories who founded the National Society in 1811.

This Anglican organization, which controlled the great majority of public schools during the first three-quarters of the nineteenth century, soon found itself pushed by working-class parents to provide far more education than it had originally envisaged. By 1837 the society's secretary admitted that his schools ''carried writing instruction to a greater extent than the station of the children would necessitate, for the sake of keeping scholars under our discipline for a greater length of time.''[35] In fact, pressure from private and British and Foreign schools had caused the Anglicans to abandon their no-writing policy two decades earlier. The same pressures acted on Sunday schools. ''Dissenters,'' one vicar noted, ''entice children by larger supplies of intellectual food . . . and the schools of the establishment are compelled, however reluctantly, to make some advances in order to prevent absolute desertion.''[36]

In short, a good schoolmaster was appreciated and patronized; a bad one was ignored and allowed to starve. Moreover, working-class demand impelled public schools to provide more instruction than they would otherwise have been willing to supply. But while the quality and scope of education was clearly of concern to parents, the preference for private schools was far stronger in determining their choice; the working-class consumer of education during this period was above all hostile to public education. Why?

First, private schools may well have provided elementary instruction at least as successfully as their public competitors. Their value has been minimized by educational historians largely because they were so roundly condemned by the educational reformers of the nineteenth century whose pronouncements serve as the basis of modern accounts. To Kay-Shuttleworth private-venture schools were little more than day-care facilities taught by untrained incompetents; they were devoid of method and discipline; they were beyond the control of government and served no useful social role. But of course the secretary to the Committee of Council was not without his axe to grind, and working-class parents saw the situation differently.[37]

"They were odd affairs, those schools," remarked a late-nineteenth-century observer, "but the population supported them."[38] The dame and other private-venture schools of the late eighteenth and early nineteenth centuries were not what educational reformers looked for in a school, but many did apparently teach the skills of basic literacy. Wordsworth's characterization of his dame as "no bad teacher, but indifferent to method" must have applied to many such women throughout England. "The old dame did not affect to make theologians or logicians but she taught to read, and she practiced the memory."[39] F. W. Soutter, the labor leader, performed admirably during his half year in a British School; "hitherto," he noted, "my schooling has been limited to attendances at private schools run by ladies who apparently did their work well."[40] Of course, many private schools undoubtedly deserved the opprobrium heaped on them by nineteenth-century observers; but it is not clear that they were as a whole markedly inferior to the Gradgrind instruction of the National or British systems.

Secondly, and far more importantly, schools provided by religious bodies—particularly those provided by the overwhelming dominant Anglican National School Society—were suspect as foreign, as strange to the community. The discipline they sought to impose was either noxious in itself, made compliance expensive, or was thought to be irrelevant to elementary education. Teachers were self-consciously above and outside the community they purportedly served and were often viewed, like charity workers, as agents of oppressive authority.[41]

"The parents," according to the secretary of the National Society, "will, in their ignorance, not value the schools according to the kind of instruction they give, but they will take into account whether they are allowed to break the rules or not. *They resist the discipline of our schools to a surprising extent; they do not like the obligation of attending at fixed hours, and conforming to rules, having clean dress and short or tidy hair.*"[42] British and Foreign Society schools, according to the investigator of the Royal Statistical Society, enjoyed a social standing well below that of dame schools among the London working classes and even farther below common day schools. National schools, however, stood lowest of all. The costumes required were viewed as a mark of charity, the embarrassment of which parents would avoid if at all possible by sending their children to more expensive private schools; rules requiring girls as well as boys to wear short hair were viewed with hostility, and rules regarding cleanliness caused trouble and expense to parents which would be spared elsewhere.[43] The rector of Warrington in 1836 explained the unpopularity of his schools as the result of two women teachers who "had enforced church attendance, short hair, and other noxious forms of discipline" and a male teacher who had offended the community by becoming the secretary to a Tory politician.[44] The Reverend E. Wyatt Edgell, rector of N. Cray, Kent, abolished the rule requiring girls to cut their hair and wear uniforms as counterproductive to the success of his school. The standards of cleanliness and appearance required at most publicly provided schools, while perhaps desirable in themselves, were extremely difficult to maintain on a day-to-day basis by people without running water, adequate heat, or a cheap supply of soap and clothing. Private schools took these considerations into account and neglected to legislate on matters of personal appearance.

Teachers in most publicly supported schools were viewed by the patrons and parents alike as social upstarts, men and women who had transcended their class origins but were not yet comfortable in their new roles. As such, they were regarded with a mixture of admiration and resentment, and were even occasionally the objects of violence. One teacher at a London ragged school reported that his coat was taken by students as a sign of the class with which they were at war; assaults by pupils on teachers were common.[45]

Moreover, public education, like public charity, was examined closely for its ulterior motives. David Winstanley, the schoolmaster in Benjamin Heywood's factory village of Miles Platting, reported that "the uneducated poor speculate upon the motives of those who take upon themselves any office which is professedly for their good, much more than they are generally supposed to do, and . . . the result of our exertions depends in a great measure upon the motives they ascribe to us."[46] As for state provision of education, it, too, was suspect. State interference would only lead to a large staff of officers who would lay new taxes, "which, like all taxes, would be wrung from the working man."[47] East Londoners resisted school board officers as if they were the advance legions of an invading army.[48] Indeed, as Henry Pelling has noted, the working class advanced into the twentieth century with a profound distrust of government and authority and with little expectation of social amelioration from this quarter. In education, as in public housing or the poor laws, reform from the outside was viewed with deep suspicion.[49]

Conversely, private schools and their masters were part of the community and accepted as such. In some cases, politics may have been the decisive factor. Adam Rushton heard an elderly schoolmaster talk from a Chartist platform about "the prophecies and dreams of sages, patriots and martyrs which were now to be fulfilled. . . . So charmed were several youths at the meeting, including myself," he continues, "that we decided to attend his evening classes two nights a week. . . . For many years he managed somehow to make a living from the income of his poor school. Then the worthy man passed into the eternal silence, noted only by a few who had known and loved him. But beyond the bourne we are sure he could hear the welcome words, 'Good and faithful servant, enter thou into the joy of thy Lord.' "[50] Indeed, teachers at private-venture schools were often friends and neighbors—men and women whose health had been ruined in other forms of employment, who had been victimized for political or trade union activity, or who for some other reason needed the support of the community.

Moreover, the private school was more attuned to the rhythms of working-class life than was its public competitor. The miners' leader, John Wilson, may have been an exception in attending a different school every few months as he followed his father, a navvy, around the country.[51] But attendance at school was sporadic for a working-class child—a total of eighteen months to two years of education between ages five and eleven accumulated from a few days here, a couple of weeks there, when the family could afford school pence or clothes and when help was not required about the house.[52] "We senden them to school a bit, when we can afford it," one parent told an investigator; another said that children in her family of eight attended "by bits and snatches" owing to the father's having been frequently out of work.[53] A London street seller, age thirteen, reported that he had been to an "academy" kept by an old man but that he didn't know the charge because when his father was living "the schoolmaster used to take it out in vegetables."[54] The private school—with its lack of rules governing dress, appearance, and cleanliness; its easy admission and withdrawal procedures; and its unstructured curriculum—was the institutional analogue of this poverty-induced pattern of education.

There were other reasons why public schools were received so reluctantly by the working class. They never shed the stigma of charity. Many, especially National Schools, were so closely identified with a religious community that parents of a different persuasion were reluctant to send their children even if there was no other public school in the vicinity.

There may also have been supply constraints on the growth of public schooling, but these should not be exaggerated. In Manchester, Salford, and the associated townships, for example, there were not enough places for all potential students in 1851; but even so, publicly financed schools were underutilized. At the British, National, or denominational schools there were 19,516 students, although at 8 square feet per pupil, which was the rather limited space then thought necessary for one person, there was room for 21,731 more. Even doubling the area per pupil, there would still have been unused capacity.[55]

It might be objected that if working-class resistance to public weekday schools was really a powerful force, it should have limited Sunday school attendance as well. But Sunday schools were strange halfway houses between the private school, which was integrated into the community, and the externally imposed public school. While they promoted what might be called the bourgeois virtues of cleanliness, punctuality, and regular attendance, their teachers and their whole ethos were largely working class. Furthermore, the practical problems of washing, mending clothes, and doing chores ahead of time were minimized for once-a-week attendance; indeed, they might even become a special treat. Sunday schools were more akin to self-improvement organizations than to public weekday schools; they became part of the recreational and religious life of the community to an extent never achieved by schools financed from the outside.[56]

If the existence of a considerable and selective working-class demand for education is now admitted, some rather interesting answers can be given to the questions raised at the beginning. While the *public* provision of education stagnated in the second half of the eighteenth century and right up to the founding of the two school societies, private schooling, which grew up entirely in response to local demand, was to a large extent responsible for the creation of a remarkably literate working class. Because of this fact and because private schools maintained their share of the market until the late 1830s, the expansion of education even between 1818 and 1851 cannot be attributed solely to the supply of publicly financed schools. In fact, the continued existence of private schools, in so many ways different from publicly financed schools, was a spur to those who, for a variety of reasons, sought to supplant the older with the newer kind of schooling. Private schools maintained their hold on the working-class community even past mid-century because they, in contrast to publicly provided ones, were a part of and not an imposition upon the culture of those they served. The large, highly structured, disciplined, and well-ordered institution which is today recognized as a school was a novelty well into the nineteenth century. It was a child of the industrial revolution, and it was resisted as part of the new order. Its ultimate triumph must be seen as a part of the triumph of industrial society.

This essay has not argued that the unrestrained free market is or was the best way to allocate educational resources, or that working-class children received an equitable share of England's educational resources during the nineteenth century. Kay-Shuttleworth and others were no doubt right to criticize the quality of many private-venture schools, even if their publicly financed competitors were only marginally, if at all, better. But what has been suggested is that the base for the educational expansion of the late nineteenth century is to be found in the bewildering but widely supported network of small schools which grew up, like butchers' or bakers' shops, in response to community demand. Increased state intervention in education, public financing of schools, the introduction and extension of compulsory attendance for a prescribed number of years, were all progressive measures in their time. Taken together, however, they curtailed or even precluded a parent's ability to determine the content or structure of his children's education. Schooling became a question, not of private choice, but of public policy. Perhaps the crisis in American and even English education is to some extent the legacy of this development; perhaps a new place must be found for the voices of the consumers of education and of their parents.

NOTES

1. *General Table Showing the State of Education in England,* 1820 [151], xii; *Education [1851] Census,* 1852–53 [1692], xc, pp. 4–5.

2. It is impossible to derive accurate statistics either for total school enrollment or for the percentage of students in publicly financed schools for the mid-eighteenth century. Indeed, M. G. Jones despairs of determining their enrollment even in this more limited class of school. See *The Charity School Movement* (Cambridge, 1934; Frank Cass Reprint, 1964), pp. 24–26. I propose here to estimate a maximum enrollment figure for the number of students in publicly supported schools and a minimum

figure for total school enrollment; from these estimates, an upper limit for the percentage of total enrollment in publicly provided schools may be calculated. The 1,329 charity schools reported by the Society for the Propagation of Christian Knowledge (SPCK) in 1723 probably represent the high-water mark of the movement and may, therefore, be taken as a reasonable estimate of the number of such schools, supported by subscriptions, in existence in 1750. This may indeed be a high estimate. As Joan Simon has pointed out, in the case of Leicestershire, many of the schools which found their way into the official reports were not established subscription schools at all but small, ephemeral private institutions. If her conclusions hold true for the rest of England, the number given on the SPCK's 1723 list would have to be adjusted downward. See Joan Simon, "Was There a Charity School Movement?" in *Education in Leicestershire: A Regional Study,* ed. Brian Simon, (Leicester, 1968). In addition to the 1,329 charity schools, there were by 1750, according to the Commission of Inquiry into Charities, 1818–43, 1,260 endowed nonclassical schools and 933 educational endowments not attached to specific schools. See Jones, *The Charity School Movement,* app. 1, pts. *a* and *b.* Since there is probably considerable overlap between the schools reported by the SPCK and the endowed nonclassical schools, and since it is stretching the point to count as a school an endowment which might have paid for only one student, the total number of publicly supported schools in 1750 arrived at by adding the numbers in each of these categories (i.e., 3,522) is an extremely generous one.

The mean size of each school in 1750 (20.8 pupils) was derived by linear interpolation between the mean size of the schools on the 1723 list (17.6 students) and the mean size of nonmonitorial schools reported in 1818 (28.2 students). See *General Table,* 1820 [151] xiii.

Total enrollment in publicly supported schools—73,298 students—was calculated by multiplying the mean school size by the estimated total number of schools.

It is extremely difficult to estimate with any degree of confidence the percentage of the population enrolled in all schools in 1750. For the purposes of this calculation, I assume that all of the children who were in "new," or monitorial, schools in 1818 would not have been in school before 1811 at all. Of the total population 5.54 percent were in school in 1818—1.24 percent in the so-called new schools and 4.28 percent in all other schools. This procedure, in effect, yields a low estimate for the proportion of the population in school in 1811. I further assumed that there had been no significant changes in per capita school enrollment during the latter half of the eighteenth century. A more or less constant male literacy rate and a very slowly rising rate of literacy for females during this period, a rapidly growing population, and a decrease in the rate of growth of educational endowments after 1750 suggest that the assumption is warranted.

The population of England and Wales in 1750 was 6,140,000. See the estimates in P. Deane and W. A. Cole, *British Economic Growth, 1688–1959* (Cambridge, 1969), p. 6. Using the estimates derived above, it may be calculated that 27.8 percent of all students—i.e., 73,298 out of 262,922—were in publicly financed institutions. Since 73,298 represents a maximum estimate and 262,922 a minimum one, this percentage is the highest plausible estimate. A total enrollment in publicly financed schools of somewhat less than 60,000 seems more plausible.

3. It was reported that in 1833, out of 1,222,137 scholars, 700,672 (57.3 percent) attended infant and daily schools supported exclusively by payments from scholars. Since the overseer of the poor, who provided the raw data for this compilation, would have been more likely to overlook the small, ephemeral private school than the more well-established, endowed school or those supported wholly or in part by subscription, this is probably a low estimate of the percentage of students in schools supported by parents alone. See *Abstract of answers and returns relative to the State of Education in England and Wales,* 1835 [62] xliii, p. 1326; in 1851 see *Education Census,* pp. 4–5.

4. See n. 2 above.

5. My model for the "modern school" is derived in large measure from Robert Dreeben's *On What Is Learned in School* (Reading, Mass., 1968) and from Talcott Parson's pioneering article, "The School Class as a Social System: Some of Its Functions in American Society," reprinted in *Education, Economy and Society,* ed. A. H. Halsey, Jean Floud, and C. Arnold Anderson (Glencoe, Ill., 1961), pp. 434–55.

6. H. C. Barnard, *A Short History of English Education from 1760 to 1944* (London, 1947), p. 4; my emphasis.

7. Ibid., pp. 73–74.

8. Ibid., p. 121.

9. "Literacy and Education in England, 1500–1900," *Past and Present,* 42 (1969): 81.

10. Asa Briggs, *The Age of Improvement, 1783–1867* (London, 1959), p. 337.

11. Harold Perkin, *The Origins of Modern English Society, 1780–1880* (London, 1969), p. 295.

12. J. F. C. Harrison, *Learning and Living, 1790–1860* (London, 1961), p. 40.

13. Brian Simon, *Studies in the History of Education, 1780–1870* (London, 1960), pp. 269–74.

14. *Northern Star,* 1 April 1843; see also *Northern Star* for 11 March, 15 April, 22 April, 29 April, 6 May, 13 May, 20 May, 31 May, 3 June, and 17 June regarding Chartist response to Graham's Factory Bill.

15. *Northern Star,* 12 September 1846.

16. A. E. Dobbs, *Education and Social Movements, 1700–1850* (London, 1919), p. 230; see also p. 247.

17. See, for example, E. P. Thompson, *The Making of the English Working Class* (London, 1963), p. 377, and generally, his description of Sunday school education; M. W. Flinn, "Social Theory and the Industrial Revolution," in *Social Change and Economic Change,* ed. Tom Burns and S. B. Saul (London, 1967), pp. 14–17; Raymond Williams, *The Long Revolution* (London, 1961), pp. 35–36.

18. Calculated from table in 1851 *Education Census,* p. 4.

19. R. S. Schofield, "Dimensions of Illiteracy, 1750–1850," *Explorations in Economic History* 10, no. 4 (Summer 1973): 442–45.

20. For Paine see Richard D. Altick, *The English Common Reader* (Chicago, 1957), p. 70; for the tracts see *British Critic,* March 1798, p. 266.

21. See Simon, "Was There a Charity School Movement?"

22. See n. 2 above.

23. The underlying social assumptions of Kay's educational activities are lucidly analyzed by Richard Johnson in "Educational Policy and Social Control in Early Victorian England," *Past and Present* 49 (1970): 96–119.

24. *Report from the Select Committee on the Education of the Poorer Classes in England and Wales, together with the Minutes of Evidence,* 1837–38 (589), vii, Q 114.

25. Ibid., Q 114, Q 78.

26. This was determined by drawing a circle representing a 500-yard radius on a map of Manchester and noting how many of the 190 private schoolteachers listed in Pigot and Sons' 1833 *Directory of Manchester* taught within its circumference.

27. *Minutes of the Committee of Council on Education,* vol. II, 1852 [1480], xl, pp. 381–83.

28. Ms. File, Warrington School, National School Archives, Great Peter Street, London.

29. Manchester Statistical Society, *Report on the State of Education in the Borough of Manchester in 1834* (Manchester, 1835), p. 10.

30. *Minutes of the Committee of Council on Education for 1843–4,* 1845 [622], xxxv, 337, pp. 586–87.

31. Ibid., p. 587.

32. Simon, "Was There a Charity School Movement?," p. 587.

33. William Lovett, *The Life and Struggles of William Lovett* (London, 1876), p. 5.

34. On the National Society see H. J. Burgess, *Enterprise in Education* (London, 1958).

35. *Select Committee on Education of the Poorer Classes,* 1837–38 (589), vii, Q 749.

36. *Church Remembrancer* 3, no. 1 (1821): 13.

37. See Johnson, "Educational Policy."

38. *When I Was a Child,* by "An Old Potter" (London, 1903).

39. Quoted in Morris Marples, *Romantics at School* (London, 1967), p. 18.

40. F. W. Soutter, *Recollections of a Labour Pioneer* (London, 1923), pp. 16–17.

41. On the social position of teachers and parents' responses thereto, see Asher Tropp, *The School Teachers: The Growth of the Teaching Profession in England and Wales* (London, 1957), esp. chap. 3, pp. 33–35.

42. *Select Committee on Education of the Poorer Classes,* 1837–38 (589), vii, Q 747.

43. "Third Report of a Committee of the Statistical Society of London into the State of Education in Westminster," *Journal of the Statistical Society of London* 1 (1838): 454–56.

44. Rev. Horace Powys to J. C. Wigram, 4 June 1836, in Warrington National School File.

45. Tropp, *School Teachers,* p. 10.

46. Thomas Kelly and Edith Kelly, eds., *A Schoolmaster's Notebooks,* in Remains Historical and Literary Connected with the Relative Counties of Lancaster and Chester, vol. 8, 3rd ser. (Chetham Society, Manchester, 1957), p. 24.

47. "Report of a Meeting at Hulme," *Manchester Guardian,* 24 March 1849. The speaker was not an entirely disinterested party; he spoke as a private schoolmaster in opposition to a motion of support for the Lancashire Public School Association's proposals.

48. See David Rubinstein, *School Attendance in London, 1870–1904: A Social History* (Hull, 1959).

49. See Pelling's "The Working Class and the Origins of the Welfare State," in *Popular Politics and Society in Late Victorian Britain* (London, 1968).

50. Adam Rushton, *My Life as a Farmer's Boy, Factory Lad, Teacher, and Preacher, 1821–1909* (London, 1909), pp. 65–66.

51. John Wilson, *Memories of a Labour Leader* (London, 1910), esp. pp. 47–56.

52. Dobbs, *Education*, pp. 158–59.

53. Manchester Statistical Society, *Report on the State of Education in Pendleton in 1838* (Manchester, 1839), pp. 4–5.

54. Henry Mayhew for Charles Booth, *London Labour and the London Poor*, 1 (London, 1851): 473.

55. *Report of the Select Committee on Manchester and Salford Education . . . together with minutes of evidence*, 1852 (499), xi, p. 36.

56. These themes are discussed in detail in Thomas W. Laqueur, *Religion and Respectability: Sunday Schools and Working-Class Culture, 1780–1850* (London and New Haven, 1976).

CHAPTER 9

The Social Origins, Ambitions, and Occupations of Secondary Students in France during the Second Empire

BY PATRICK J. HARRIGAN

INTRODUCTION

Recent studies of nineteenth-century French education have stressed its relationship to such general historical themes as modernization, institutional adjustment to social change, loyalties to the emerging national state, and the acceptance by social and political elites of the values of intellectual elites. They have also argued that secondary education was a vital factor in social mobility, either by providing access to the top or by preserving hereditary elites. Sociologists and historians have similarly examined the impact of educational systems in other countries. As yet, however, we have few detailed studies of the relation between education and social structure for the nineteenth century and none for France. This chapter analyzes relations between secondary education, social structure, and immediate mobility in France in the 1860s.

What follows is based on a wide-ranging survey of secondary schools taken by the Ministry of Education during the 1864–65 school year. The survey—in the form of a questionnaire to academic rectors, departmental inspectors, and principals of public schools—posed over one hundred questions on such matters as the curriculum, texts, qualifications of teachers, relations between public and private schools, and public responses to those schools. Just why the survey was undertaken is unclear. It occurred at a time when Victor Duruy, then minister of education, hoped to reform the public school system and was worried about competition from Catholic secondary schools.

Financial aid for this project was given by the Canada Council and the Shelby Cullom Davis Center for Historical Studies at Princeton University. The University of Waterloo and the Institute for Social Research at the University of Michigan provided technical assistance. Victor Neglia of the University of Waterloo programmed the data. Donald Baker, Raymond Grew, Donald Lammers, and Jacques Ozouf offered invaluable suggestions at various stages of this project. To these and many more who are unmentioned but remembered I extend my thanks.

For our purposes, the key part of the questionnaire was a directive for each principal to list the occupations of the fathers of students likely to graduate in the next two years, the intended occupation of each of those students, and the occupations of all graduates of the particular institution during the last five years. Answers to that question provide information on the occupations of more than 27,000 students and the occupations of more than 13,000 of their fathers.[1] The survey also provides information on the location, tuition, size, type, and reputed quality of each school.

Unfortunately, the scope, at least, of Duruy's inquiry about students' and parents' occupations is apparently unique for France. Yet, few historians would wish for a more significant time or type of education for a single study. The 1860s were the years immediately following France's industrial mini-revolution. In their monumental study, *Social Mobility in Industrial Societies,* Seymour Lipset and Reinhard Bendix saw widespread social mobility as a concomitant of industrialization.[2] To be sustained historically, such a generalization needs further comparative studies of industrial and preindustrial societies, but France offers one case study of a transitional society. The decade of the 1860s was for France a period of political stability but also one of increasing tension between church and state, of increasing opposition to the government, and of mounting concern about France's place in Europe. Intellectuals and governmental ministers alike had begun to question the traditional structure and curricula of French education, and their concern would increase in the next decade after France's defeat in the Franco-Prussian War. France was a society in change and a self-conscious one that was reconsidering its political, social, and intellectual direction.

The demand for education was growing, and the ministry of education reflected and stimulated such demands by establishing new schools and inaugurating new programs during the Second Empire. It introduced a bifurcated program of science and classics in 1854, abandoned that, but soon devised a limited and special program within the secondary system. Catholic secondary schools, permitted by the Falloux Law of 1850, were rivaling public schools; but Catholic schools were more like public schools in clientele in the mid-1860s than at any other time.[3] Enrollment was rising more rapidly in secondary schools than in any other sector of education.

Of the three sectors of French education, secondary education offers the best opportunity to examine social differences and mobility in mid-nineteenth-century France. Higher education was then almost exclusively professional and limited to a small elite who had graduated from secondary schools. Elementary education was nearly universal for men, but taught only literacy and arithmetic. It offered no immediate nor intrinsic preparation for a particular occupation. Secondary education, on the other hand, had become a prerequisite for higher education and professional careers after the establishment of the *baccalauréat* examination in 1820 and its gradual strengthening over the next twenty-five years.[4] It was intended to develop elites while promising some access to a variety of social groups.[5] At the same time, a familiarity with classical learning was becoming a mark of status.[6] Thus, secondary education is an illuminating test of social opportunity, values, and movement.

PATTERNS OF RECRUITMENT

Duruy's survey allows us to examine the occupations of fathers and students in France as a whole, with distinctions made between *lycées* and *collèges communaux, enseignement secondaire spécial* and *enseignement secondaire classique,* and graduates and students. Among students it is possible to distinguish between actual careers of recent graduates and expected careers of those still in the last two years of studies. Moreover, one can compare students' occupations generally with those of their fathers, although, unfortunately, one cannot compare the expected and actual occupation of a particular student.

Although studies of particular occupations are revealing, such analysis is best left to another paper. The general data demands analysis first. Here, the discussion will focus first on the social background of students generally and then on differences between types of schools and programs. Next, the mobility patterns within secondary education will be considered. Education has implied mobility, but expectations of students are not necessarily the same as the first occupations of graduates. Distinctions among hopes and expectations suggest the degree to which the educational institution responded to the aspirations of contemporary society. A comparison of the occupations of fathers and graduates shows one effect of education on society, and presents a test of whether the educational system served to create new elites or to renew old ones.

The basic organization of French public education had been established during the revolutionary and Napoleonic years and reflected the assumptions of those years. Public education attempted to provide open access to careers, but open access to careers implied more a rejection of aristocratic notions that birth should determine social position than a desire to promote wide social mobility. The retention of tuition assured that secondary education would be available only to those Frenchmen who could afford it. It also was designed to produce a loyal, talented group of social and political leaders. It was liberal and utilitarian rather than conservative or democratic in theory. The penetration of secondary education in French society of the Second Empire permits us to examine the effect of a half century of social change on this educational system and its relation to mid-century society.

Schools and programs are important too. Although French public secondary education is often identified with the lycée, three times as many collèges communaux as lycées existed during the Second Empire. Collèges communaux, as their name implies, depended more on local financing than did the lycées, but they were theoretically equal with the lycées and offered exactly the same two programs of study. One program was the traditional classical curriculum; the other, a special four-year program within secondary schools. We need to know whether the lycées attracted social groups different from those in the collèges communaux and whether students in the classical program had different expectations, careers, and social origins from those in the special program.

French education promised that any student, regardless of birthright, who passed certain prescribed examinations could eventually enter the most prestigious *grande école*. But first, a student had to enroll in a secondary school. Tuition in them was high—at least 50–150 fr. annually, even for day students, and 300–1,500 fr. for boarding students—at a time when few unskilled workers had an annual wage of 1,500 fr. Scholarships were few, and they generally went to children of army officers or of civil servants. Moreover, secondary schools included an elementary division within them. Primary schools existed, but they offered only a four-year terminal program of studies and taught a different curriculum, notably omitting classical studies. Transfers from primary to secondary schools were rare. Thus, primary and secondary education were separate. Parents had to make a choice between these two tracks when their son was seven years old or, at the latest, by the time he was ten, at which time he would enter the *division grammaire* in a secondary school.

As a result of high tuition and the division between primary and secondary education, French secondary education was not available to the lower classes. Less than 2 percent of the students in French secondary schools during the 1860s were sons of unskilled rural or urban workers (see Table 9.1).[7] Tuition and the organization of secondary education were objective restrictions placed on the working classes. The position and values of the working classes themselves also limited their desire for secondary education. William Sewell, among others, has argued convincingly that the workers in mid-nineteenth-century France retained a corporate mentality, felt that their status in society was derived from membership in working-class organizations, and were not attracted to occupations that lacked a corporative sense,[8] occupations that secondary education promised. Moreover, the lower classes were often too concerned with mere survival and too sharply distinguished from the rest of society in everyday life to aspire to high social positions for their children.

If few unskilled workers sent their children to secondary schools, the lower middle classes did. One-third of the students in secondary schools were sons of peasants, skilled workers, and shopkeepers.[9] Even if we do not yet know the precise social background of French ruling elites in the 1860s, we may safely conclude that it was not 30 to 40 percent petit bourgeois.[10] French secondary education, however, was far more democratic than the contemporary political or social system. The high percentage of these petit bourgeois groups within secondary schools indicates the deep strength they retained in French society during the 1860s and the strength of their desire to join the upper classes. For the upper levels of these groups (the tuition demanded by secondary schools suggests that we are dealing with upper levels), secondary education promised that their sons could improve or at least retain status within a changing society and economy. To peasants, skilled workers, and shopkeepers, industrialization presented as much a

TABLE 9.1

French Secondary Education: Students' Social Origins, Ambitions, and Occupations, by Percentage in Occupational Categories

Occupational category	Fathers' occupations			Career preferences and reality			Adjusted % of graduates among graduates/students
	All schools[a]	Lycées	Collèges communaux	Student preference	Graduate occupation	Combined preferences and occupations[a]	
Government employee[b]	11.8	12.5	10.6	8.5	9.7	9.6	53
Professional	18.2	21.6	16.2	56.7	37.3	43.9	40
Law	6.3	8.0	4.8	15.0	10.7	12.1	42
Upper	8.5	10.1	7.1	31.5	18.8	23.2	37
Semi	3.4	3.5	4.3	10.2	7.8	8.6	43
Propriétaire/rentier	17.0	19.0	15.4	1.2	3.5	2.8	75
Agriculture	12.5	8.0	16.6	5.6	8.3	7.4	60
Peasant	12.3	7.9	16.4	5.6	8.2	7.3	59
Worker	0.2	0.1	0.2	0	0.1	0.1	100
Bourgeois (business)	12.9	16.1	9.8	3.3	4.0	3.6	55
Commercial	9.5	12.3	6.7	2.5	2.9	2.8	54
Industrial	3.4	3.8	3.1	0.8	1.1	0.8	59
Petit bourgeois	16.5	15.0	17.2	15.9	21.8	19.7	58
White collar	1.6	1.2	1.5	1.4	4.4	3.3	76
Commerce	14.9	13.8	15.7	14.5	17.4	16.4	55
Worker	7.8	4.4	11.1	1.4	2.6	2.3	66
Skilled	6.1	3.0	9.0	1.1	2.3	2.0	68
Unskilled	1.7	1.4	2.1	0.3	0.3	0.3	52
Miscellaneous	3.3	3.5	3.0	7.1	12.7	10.8	63
Industrie	1.3	1.6	1.0	2.6	3.6	3.2	58
Military (non-officer)[c]	1.3	1.4	1.2		5.4	4.5	65
Other	0.7	0.5	0.8	1.9	3.7	3.1	66
Total cases	12.605	6.030	6.077	9,191	17,124	26,376	

[a] In some instances it was impossible to determine whether a person was a student or a graduate, or whether he attended a lycée or a collège communal; therefore, the total cases for these general categories are somewhat more than the cases in the subcategories.

[b] "Government employee" includes only those clearly in the civilian administration.

threat to their social position and way of life as it promised progress, rationality, and opportunity. To groups that had long considered themselves part of the middle class but had increasingly been regarded as a lower class by ambitious and wealthy bourgeois, secondary schools were both a means to assert their own bourgeois status and to seek new bourgeois occupations for their children.

Lipset and Bendix have argued that those threatened by downward mobility in industrial societies since World War II have attempted to compensate by encouraging their children to rise through education.[11] The French experience of a hundred years earlier supports this model. Those whose occupations were threatened by industrialization constituted a strikingly high percentage of parents who enrolled children in secondary schools, even if many of their children eventually followed the same occupations as their fathers.

On the other hand, the fact that a large number of students intended to remain in petit bourgeois occupations implies that status factors and values were also important. An acquaintance with classical studies increasingly became the mark of a bourgeois in the nineteenth century. A secondary education was likely to give a self-defined bourgeois increased status among peers and may well have been a sign of success.[12] Moreover, secondary schools permitted children of petits bourgeois to mix with the hauts bourgeois, theoretically at least, as social equals. Certainly, the lower middle classes saw in secondary education both status and mobility. Later analyses of particular occupations may reveal which was most important.

The participation of particular elements of the lower middle class suggests some further conclusions about them. Even the difference between the number of skilled workers (774) who sent sons to secondary schools and the number of unskilled ones (214) who did is an important one, not in terms of their total percentage within the system of secondary education, which was minimal for both, but in distinctions between them. Artisans may generally have been falling into the lower classes, but some of them were successful or ambitious enough to seek secondary schools for their children. The presence of three and one-half times as many sons of skilled workers as of unskilled workers in secondary schools indicates that there remained a clear difference in either income or values among these manual workers. Only one-tenth as many children of agricultural workers as children of urban workers attended secondary schools. The former were even more isolated than industrial laborers. Peasants, on the other hand, made up more than one-eighth of the fathers whose sons finished secondary schooling.[13] If French peasants often resisted industrialization and liberal values, many believed, nonetheless, that secondary education was worth sacrificing manpower and hard currency.[14]

The sons of governmental officials were a major source of recruitment for secondary schools. Their 12 percent representation was almost as much as that of the sons of the commercial and industrial bourgeoisie combined (10 percent and 3 percent, respectively). Their fathers had achieved their own appointments in part because of their education, and their experience gave them a special appreciation of its social and economic implications.[15] In contrast, the commercial and industrial bourgeois depended more on their talents than on education per se for their social position. The highest percentage source of students in secondary schools (18 percent) were the professions, the groups most dependent on educational achievements for their occupations and status. Thus, previous experience affected attitudes toward the value of education.

The acceptance of the existing educational system, with its inherent possibilities for mobility by governmental administrators, those who implemented official policies, was particularly important in a nation not noted for its political stability. A bureaucracy recruited from within existing institutions and therefore having a stake in the preservation of those institutions is likely to demonstrate loyalty, try to elicit it from others, and provide a source of stability. Secondary schools taught a prescribed curriculum and narrowly defined approaches to it. They inculcated the values of governing elites at the same time that they promised access to those elites.

As secondary education promised new access to elite positions to some, so it provided a means for existing elites to preserve their status. Professionals sent their sons to secondary schools; so did *propriétaires* and *rentiers*. An ill-defined group, propriétaires and rentiers made up 17 percent of fathers of students in secondary schools; far fewer of the sons expected to live solely as a propriétaires or rentiers (see Table 9.1).[16] For the propriétaire, secondary education was a way to provide sons (perhaps the second- or third-born) with an opportunity for a new career that would preserve status. Institutions like the church and army had absorbed sons of the upper classes during the *ancien régime*. But social and economic changes during the nineteenth century necessitated the discovery of new ways to reproduce and distinguish elites. The primary institutional support became secondary education, necessary even for the army, and the upper classes recognized the importance of this expanding institution. Elites adopted new means to defend their traditional social position.

One may conclude that secondary education reached a sufficient number of social groups and promised enough social improvement to help stabilize French society from the lower middle classes through the upper groups. On the other hand it accentuated differences between them and the lowest classes, including the least successful of the traditional petits bourgeois. Marked social differences existed between the well-born or rich and other Frenchmen. Secondary education offered hope for some rather lower down to join the upper classes, but it also reinforced differences between workers and the rest of society.

The next question is how, within the secondary system, differences in curriculum and types of schools affected social mobility. Enseignement spécial, established in 1865 according to the guidelines set in the circular of 2 October 1863, was a four-year program of instruction in French, modern languages, geography, and applied sciences within secondary schools: it was "a cultural education but . . . [one that] will insist on the practical."[17] It was intended for sons of "the *négociant, industriel,* or *agriculteur*";[18] and in fact, the sons of workers, peasants, and *commerçants* did compose over half of students in our sample in this program. It was not confined to these groups, for a third of the students were sons of propriétaires, bourgeois, and employees of the government (see Table 9.2 and the Appendix to this chapter). But sons of workers, peasants, and shopkeepers were far more likely to take the special program than were sons of professionals or civil servants.[19]

The limited program of enseignement spécial appealed to groups who were not prepared to pay for long years of classical studies but who wanted something more than primary education for their children, perhaps only the prestige of attending a secondary school. Its literary and mathematical content was not "technical" in the modern sense of the word, and thus it attracted groups besides the industrial classes: it appealed to those who desired status or movement within their own group. Its appeal to the industrial (less to the commercial) bourgeois and the propriétaires suggests a possible variety among propriétaires but also suggests that these groups had a limited need for or interest in extended, classical studies. The industrial bourgeois who enrolled sons in enseignement spécial generally intended them to pursue careers in industry, while those who enrolled sons in enseignement classique expected them to enter the professions.[20] Certainly enseignement spécial had a limited attraction for the higher professions and the upper levels of govern-

TABLE 9.2
Enseignement Spécial: Students' Social Origins, Ambitions, and Occupations,
by Percentage in Occupational Categories

| Occupational category | Fathers' occupations | Career preferences and reality | | | Adjusted % of graduates among graduates/students |
		Student preference	Graduate occupation	Combined preferences and occupations	
Government employee	8.6	11.3	12.3	11.9	52
Professional	6.3	26.7	21.4	22.8	44
Law	0.6	2.5	1.5	1.8	38
Upper	2.0	8.1	5.2	5.9	39
Semi	3.7	16.1	14.7	15.1	48
Propriétaire/rentier	13.4	1.7	3.3	3.2	65
Agriculture	21.9	10.4	11.3	11.3	52
Peasant	21.3	10.4	11.1	11.2	52
Worker	0.6	0.0	0.2	0.1	100
Bourgeois (business)	10.8	4.1	3.4	3.6	45
Commercial	7.3	2.7	2.4	2.4	47
Industrial	3.5	1.4	1.0	1.2	41
Petit bourgeois	21.7	32.1	29.5	30.4	48
White collar	1.4	1.2	4.4	3.4	79
Commerce	20.3	30.9	25.1	27.0	45
Worker	14.3	4.3	7.3	6.2	63
Skilled	12.5	3.3	6.7	5.6	67
Unskilled	1.8	1.0	0.6	0.6	36
Miscellaneous	3.0	9.3	11.2	10.6	55
Industrie	0.8	5.2	3.1	3.8	38
Military (non-officer)	1.2	3.7	5.5	4.9	68
Other	1.0	0.4	2.6	1.9	86
Total cases	1,554	974	1,892	2,906	

ment. Well-educated themselves, the professionals and upper-level government employees sought the full program of secondary studies, which alone gave access to the grandes écoles of the state. The commercial bourgeois were also more attracted to enseignement classique than were the industrial bourgeois. The older bourgeois, some of whom had become notables during the July Monarchy, viewed education more as higher professionals and governmental administrators did.

One final point needs mention. Both the category of unskilled workers and the group identified solely as *industrie* enrolled a below-average number of sons in the program of enseignement spécial. The actual numbers for these categories are small, but since the number of sons of skilled workers in enseignement spécial were twice the normal average, the difference may be significant. Few unskilled workers sent their sons to any secondary school for any program. Whether the student entered because his parents sought that schooling or because he was recommended by a local curé or *instituteur,* the very enrollment of such a child in a secondary school may have been unusual enough to result in his pursuit of the more prestigious classical program.

Students in the lycées generally were from a higher social background than were students in the collèges communaux. Nevertheless, the difference in students' background between types of schools in the provinces was not so great as historians traditionally have claimed.[21] Of those peasants who sent their sons to secondary schools, substantially more did send them to collèges communaux than to the lycées (16 percent vs. 8 percent), as did skilled workers (9 percent vs. 3 percent). More collèges communaux than lycées were located in rural areas, offered the program of enseignement spécial, and required a relatively low tuition.[22] Nevertheless, these two groups, representing almost one-ninth of the population of lycées, were hardly excluded from them. There was little difference in the presence of children of rentiers, propriétaires, and the industrial bourgeoisie in the two types of schools (23 percent in collèges communaux vs. 19 percent in lycées). Figures for unskilled workers show a preference for collèges, but if parents whose occupation is designated simply as "industrie" are added to that group, there is no real difference between types of schools, as there is none for them between the programs of enseignement spécial and enseignement classique.

The two groups that clearly preferred the lycées to the collèges for secondary education, by nearly a two-to-one ratio, were the higher professions (distinguished from other professions in Table 9.1) and the commerical bourgeoisie. Both objective and subjective factors account for this deviation from the norm. Professionals were largely an urban group, and matriculation of their sons reflected the urban location of lycées. Moreover, they were well educated themselves, and they believed, probably rightly, that the instruction in lycées or a degree from one of them gave their sons better access to professional and administrative positions. The commercial bourgeoisie, too, generally sought professional careers for their sons. The expectations and careers of students in each type of school will be compared later, but objective realities need not have determined parental selection of schools. Myths can influence choices too.

There was a social difference between the clientele of lycées and collèges communaux, but that difference was not so much a matter of social class as it was of education or expectation. Those who had achieved their own positions through education and desired the same opportunity for their children, and those who attached a well-defined sense of status to particular types of education, tended to choose lycées. Those who attended lycées expected better jobs than did those who attended collèges communaux. Before discussing differences among students' expectations and occupations of fathers and graduates, let us conclude this analysis of parental occupations with reference to a prestigious Parisian lycée, the Lycée Bonaparte.

Unfortunately, the principal of the Lycée Bonaparte grouped students into eleven general categories and reported round numbers that suggest estimates, a lack of precision which limits the usefulness of the data. Nevertheless, his report, reorganized in accord with the categories used here, shows that 33 percent of the students in this Parisian grand lycée were sons of propriétaires, 25 percent were sons of petit commerçants, 20 percent sons of professionals, 17 percent sons of commercial bourgeoisie, and 5 percent sons of employés (primarily employed by the government).[23]

The 50 percent combined percentage for propriétaires and the commercial bourgeoisie implies that the Parisian lycées primarily served the notables that André Tudesq has described; 40 percent of the students of the Lycée Bonaparte expected to attend a grande école. Peasants, unmentioned in this report, apparently sent children to schools in their own areas. On the other hand, 30 percent of the students of Lycée Bonaparte are designated as sons of petits commerçants or employés. Even if that description was meant to include all petit bourgeois, they composed a surprisingly large group for a famous Parisian lycée.

We lack information concerning the expected occupations of individual students of Lycée Bonaparte and information about graduates, although other sources indicate that graduates of Parisian lycées dominated admissions to St. Cyr and to the *École Polytechnique,* the most renowned grandes écoles.[24] Should one conclude that the grand lycées supported existing class divisions by giving sons of the wealthy access to the grandes écoles, or, rather, conclude that the relatively high percentage of the lower middle classes indicates the presence of social mobility in nineteenth-century France? Available evidence permits neither conclusion. We do not know which students attended the grandes écoles. The information suggests that a hierarchial ranking of social groups by wealth is more appropriate for the Parisian lycées than it is for provincial schools, and that the clientéle of Parisian lycées were as distinguishable by social class from the provincial lycées as provincial lycées were from the collèges communaux. Most of all, it shows the need for more social analysis of French higher education, the difficulty of analyzing some sources, and the caution with which historians should approach their sources.[25]

STUDENT PREFERENCES AND CAREERS

So far, parental occupations have been emphasized. As important as these are for an understanding of the French social structure in 1865, they cannot alone show the impact of secondary education on later social patterns. For this, we must first compare the careers which students expected to pursue with the first positions graduates gained, and then relate parental occupations to those of graduates.

CAREER EXPECTATIONS.   At least half of the students expected to enter a profession (see Table 9.1). The clear preference for professional careers among students indicates the high status that the professions had in mid-nineteenth-century France. Lenore O'Boyle has argued that there was an excess of educated men in France.[26] Although the expectations of students do not directly substantiate Professor O'Boyle's argument, they support it and suggest a source for the excess—students in an expanding educational system sought first a professional career and the status it gave. Moreover, a blockage occurred even before careers began. While 57 percent hoped to enter the professions, only 37 percent did so, a three-to-two difference.[27]

Although secondary students evidenced a preference for the professions, they showed little interest in pursuing a business vocation. Only 3 percent of the students planned to take bourgeois positions in commerce or industry.[28] The radical difference between hopes for professional careers and other bourgeois ones reflects both the curriculum of secondary schools and status in France. Future businessmen did not regard a classical curriculum as relevant to them, and many successful bourgeois sought places in the professions or in government for their sons.[29]

Two differences—between school types and programs—need to be noted. The first, a distinction between lycées and the collèges communaux, directly relates to the preceding generalizations about professional hopes. The second defines especially relations between secondary education and industry.

There was an enormous difference in the way in which students in the lycées and those in the collèges communaux regarded opportunities in the professions. Of students in the lycées, 18 percent planned to study law; only 12 percent of those in collèges communaux did. For the other higher professions, an even greater difference existed. Of the students in lycées, 43 percent preferred a professional career or entry to a grande école, preparatory to such a career; of those in the collèges communaux, only 19 percent expressed such a choice. It is impossible to tell from this evidence whether parents who planned a professional career for their children sent them to lycées or whether the atmosphere of the lycées produced professional hopes. Both were probably factors. Regardless of the cause, students in the lycées clearly had higher career hopes than did those in the collèges communaux, although the two types of schools offered the same curricula and were theoretically equal. Parental background had a profound effect on expectations and careers, but so did attendance in a lycée.

Differences in students' expectations distinguished these types of schools much more than did the social origins of students. Parents from the higher professional groups, by a three-to-two ratio, preferred the lycées over the collèges communaux; but other upper-class groups—propriétaires, rentiers, and the commercial and industrial bourgeois—showed only a slight preference for the lycées over the collèges. About one-half of the students in the lycées and one-quarter of those in the collèges communaux were from upper- or upper-middle-class families (see Table 9.5). But about two-thirds of those in the lycées expected to become members of elite groups, as against only one-third of those in the collèges communaux.[30] The road to those elites was usually additional education and a professional career.

Since twice as many students in the lycées as in the collèges communaux intended to enter the higher professions, many more students in the collèges than in the lycées planned lower-middle-class careers. Twenty-three percent of the students in the collèges communaux, but only 13 percent of those in the lycées, wanted to enter the lower professions. Twenty-five percent of students in the collèges communaux expected to become peasants, workers, or soldiers; only 10 percent of those in the lycées did. The lycées were regarded as a means to join or to continue among the elite of France. The collèges communaux were regarded as offering mainly access to middle- or lower-middle-class groups or to an increased prestige within these classes.

For one group, however—the petit commerçant—that generalization does not apply. Rather more students in the collèges communaux (16 percent) than students in the lycées (14 percent) indicated that they would become commerçants, but that ratio is much less than we might expect, since the differences for all other lower-middle-class groups are much greater. Although there was a hierarchy of wealth and position among those engaged in petit commerce not indicated by the available evidence, a secondary education was not formally necessary for any petit commerçant. The relative similarity in the percentage of students planning a career in commerce between the lycées and the collèges communaux suggests that the status of the petit commerçant was high and that many believed that his was a viable career.[31] That career satisfied even many students in the lycées, primarily sons of the petite bourgeoisie, for whom a professional career entailed competition with wealthier children.

The expectations of students in the lycées and collèges communaux differed for reasons independent of curricula. But there were two different programs within secondary schools, and these two curricula also affected students' choices of careers.

Students in the program of enseignement spécial displayed more interest in jobs in industry than did those in the classical program, and over 10 percent of the graduates who attended the three schools of Arts et Métiers came from enseignement spécial. Nevertheless, the percentage of those who hoped for an industrial career was only about one-fourth of the percentage of those who sought a professional or government career, one-third of those who planned a career in the distinctly traditional area of petit commerce, and only a few more than those who intended to be farmers (see Table 9.2).[32] Enseignement spécial was modern in the sense that it emphasized modern rather than classical learning, but it was not "technical" in the twentieth-century sense of the word. Although Victor Duruy introduced it in 1863 after a period of sharp industrial expansion, its inauguration was not the direct result of these economic changes, nor did it prepare students directly for occupations created by France's new industry. It was a response to social change but not a response to recent economic change.

Enseignement spécial attracted those who could not afford the longer classical program or who regarded classical learning as unnecessary for their station in life. For some graduates it provided access to the lower levels of the administration or to lower professions—primary school teaching, veterinary science, and pharmacy. For many others, however, it offered no special preparation for their careers. The very high preference for commerce (31 percent) by students in the special program argues that the shopkeeper retained a social prestige among the lower and lower middle classes and that a secondary education was a sign of status among these groups. He was a bourgeois even if he was only a petit bourgeois.

Within secondary education generally, more than one-third of the students completing studies expected to follow lower-middle-class occupations. Some students had probably enrolled in secondary schools because they (or their parents) had higher hopes, but secondary schools screened some students even as they prepared others for more schooling. Moreover, status was as important a by-product of secondary education as mobility was, even for the petite bourgeoisie.

CAREER REALITIES.   Student expectations were not identical with the actual occupations of recent graduates (see Table 9.3).[33] Expectations and occupations were more similar in all general categories for enseignement spécial, however, than they were for enseignement classique. Students recognized the social limitations implicit in the special program, and their hopes more nearly approximated reality.

For secondary education in general, the number of students expecting jobs in the civil administration were similar to the number of recent graduates who took positions in the administration. The bureaucracy offered modest but sure advancement. Preferences for positions in both grand and petit commerce were only slightly less than graduates' employment in these occupations. Commercial careers retained a status in France, and a secondary degree increased an individual's status among peers, be he banker or shopkeeper.[34]

There was also little difference between expectations and reality for jobs in unskilled labor. The acceptance of any unskilled job by a graduate of a secondary school was rare—less than 0.5 percent took such a job—and it is not surprising that nearly as many students as graduates designated this occupation. Some choice, even if it was ultimately limited by social structure, is implied in this occupation. Whether a corporative mentality, despair, or a desire to lead fellow workers affected this choice, it was as likely to be evidenced in a student's last year as among graduates.[35]

The greatest difference between hopes and careers occurred for the professions. One and one-half times as many students expected to enter the professions as recent graduates had. A main avenue of mobility was narrower than it was thought

TABLE 9.3
Occupations in 1865 of Graduates by Year of Graduation (Percentages)

Occupational category	All graduates, 1859–63	Graduates of 1863	Graduates of 1859
Government employee	9.7	9.3	9.0
Professional: Law	10.7	12.8	10.8
Upper	18.8	22.4	18.0
Semi	7.8	7.9	7.2
Propriétaire/rentier	3.5	3.6	3.3
Agriculture: Peasant	8.2	4.7	5.5
Worker	0.1	0.0	0.1
Commercial Bourgeois	2.9	2.9	3.1
Industrial Bourgeois	1.1	0.5	2.6
Petit Bourgeois: White Collar	4.4	4.4	4.8
Commerce	17.4	17.7	20.1
Worker: Skilled	2.3	1.9	1.9
Unskilled	0.3	0.4	0.1
Miscellaneous: Industrie	3.6	2.9	2.7
Military (nonofficer)	5.4	3.8	4.8
Other	3.7	5.0	5.8
Percentage of all graduates, 1859–63	100.0	10.7	8.3

Note: Only 51 percent of the graduates were identified by specific year of graduation; thus, absolute numbers for each of the five years represent approximately 10 percent rather than 20 percent of the total. Unknowns are excluded from the table.

to be. On the other hand, far more graduates became white-collar workers, nonofficers in the military, propriétaires, and skilled workers than students had intended to.[36] Both white-collar positions and careers in the military offered hope for eventual advancement, but neither dependence on familial income nor a career as a tradesman did.

Students who were not admitted to a grande école might join a law or business firm in the hope that they might eventually be promoted to a managerial position. The military offered another alternative for graduates. Student preferences for St. Cyr, the French equivalent of West Point, and for the École Polytechnique, which trained artillery officers as well as civilian engineers and bureaucrats, were strikingly high. Among certain groups, the army officer corps carried high status. The officer corps had been a career traditionally preferred by the upper classes during the ancien régime and the Restoration. Its prestige was probably increased by foreign adventures and increasing nationalism in the Second Empire. If the army increased its prestige generally in French society after 1870,[37] it appears that its prestige was already high among the upper classes in the 1860s. The officers' corps, like the professions generally, also offered a chance for social advancement or preservation of upper-class status.

The lower levels of the army offered other similar inducements. Among secondary schools as a whole, twice as many graduates entered the military as students had expected to, and the variations exist primarily for those whose ranks are given.[38] Many who had vague plans for a military career but could not attend St. Cyr first had to enlist in lower ranks. For many others, disappointed in their original career hopes, the army may have offered the best alternative chance for mobility or a temporary occupation until better opportunities became available.[39] Four times as many graduates of the lycées entered the ranks of the military as students in lycées expected to; the differences for the collèges communaux was only three to two. Only half as many graduates of lycées as graduates of collèges communaux joined the lower levels of the military, but the greater difference between expectations and careers in this area for those in the lycées suggests that the military was an expedient for them.

In both the lycées and collèges communaux, students were disappointed in their professional hopes. Students in the lycées more often achieved their hopes for law than did students in the collèges communaux, but a greater percentage of students from the lycées who hoped to enter other professions were disappointed than were students with the same hopes in the collèges communaux. Differences between students' expectations and graduates' positions within the administration, industrial bourgeoisie, lower military, and among agriculteurs and propriétaires were magnified for the lycées. Graduates of the lycées who were denied admission to a professional school were more likely to rely on familial income, enlist in the army, or find another respectable bourgeois occupation than were graduates of the collèges communaux (see Table 9.5). The latter were more inclined to seek lower-middle-class occupations that reflected their own social origins.

Nevertheless, there was no great difference between the lycées and the collèges communaux in the relationship between expectations and careers for the majority of students and graduates. Students exaggerated the importance of their degrees, but students in the lycées and collèges communaux exaggerated it in like manner. Students about to graduate knew that the social status of their parents and their enrollment in one or the other type of school had already affected their careers, since schools did not offer equal opportunity.

Denied admission to a grande école and faced with unsatisfactory career opportunities, the wealthy student could have recourse to familial wealth. Three times as many graduates as students were listed as propriétaires. In an increasingly democratic and industrial society, however, neither familial income nor a skilled trade promised the same status for graduates as it had given their fathers. Graduates sought new positions, but there were only so many administrative and professional opportunities for graduates of secondary schools. For skilled workers and the lower middle classes in general, who could not always fall back on familial income, this blockage could be severe. If secondary schools, despite the financial sacrifices they entailed, did not provide new social opportunities, children had to return to family farms or small businesses that were threatened by an increasingly industrial economy.

The failure of secondary education to fulfill expectations is more widely attributable to larger social and economic trends in France than it is to intrinsic weaknesses in educational institutions. Nevertheless, secondary education promised social opportunities that it could not create. The curriculum was traditional and did not reflect the social or economic changes that France had experienced in the first half of the nineteenth century. Troubled or ambitious members of the lower middle classes expected to change their occupation through secondary education, but they were often disappointed. Unrealized hopes may have eventually contributed to social dissatisfaction among educated members of the future petite bourgeoisie, as promised mobility for their sons might have satisfied parents in the 1860s.

If secondary education could not satisfy everyone's desires, it was for many a road to new careers. Although professionals constituted the largest single group sending children to secondary schools (18 percent), three times that proportion of students hoped to follow a professional career and twice that percentage of graduates succeeded in doing so. The professions served as an important means of mobility for graduates of secondary schools, especially for graduates of the lycées. Twice the percentage of graduates of the lycées entered law or the higher professions (42 percent) as did the graduates of the collèges communaux (21 percent).

Slightly more graduates of all secondary schools took a place in the civil administration than their fathers had. An administrative position in government might be considered professional and the shift into it explained on the same basis as the shift into the professions. But the closer relation (53 percent and 47 percent) between graduates and fathers in government (see Table 9.4) suggests that its appeal was less than that of the private professions. The government granted a limited number of scholarships to its employees. This opportunity, combined with a sense of the social importance of education, encouraged large numbers of bureaucrats to send their children to secondary schools. At the same time, however, paternal frustrations at slow advancement in the bureaucracy may have convinced sons to seek a profession in which there seemed to be more immediate opportunity for a rise into the upper bourgeoisie. A higher percentage of graduates of enseignement spécial, the content of which restricted students' choices, and of the collèges communaux entered the administration. Graduates of the special program tended to take jobs in the lower levels of the administration, while graduates of the classical program found more positions in the middle levels (see Table 9.1).

The greatest movement into the professions, both in absolute numbers and in percentage differences between fathers and graduates, in fact occurred not in the traditionally respected legal profession, but in medicine, secondary-school teaching, and the army-officer corps (see Table 9.4). These three areas were growing during the Second Empire, although not rapidly enough to absorb all who desired to enter them. Both education and national strength were receiving increased attention from society. Although we know little about the medical professional, we might assume that scientific discoveries in general and some specific medical applications discovered by Louis Pasteur and his contemporaries created greater prestige and opportunities for doctors in the third quarter of the nineteenth century.[40]

TABLE 9.4
Fathers' and Graduates' Occupations, in Adjusted Percentages

Occupational category	All secondary schools[a]		Enseignement spécial[b]	
	Fathers	Graduates	Fathers	Graduates
Government employee	47	53	41	59
Professional	34	66	23	77
Law	38	62	27	73
Upper	25	75	28	72
Semi	31	69	20	80
Propriétaire/rentier	83	17	80	20
Agriculture	61	39	66	34
Peasant	61	39	66	34
Worker	66	34	79	21
Bourgeois (business)	70	30	76	24
Commercial	77	23	76	24
Industrial	76	24	78	22
Petit bourgeois	44	56	42	58
White collar	28	72	24	76
Commerce	47	53	45	55
Worker	75	25	66	34
Skilled	73	27	65	35
Unskilled	85	15	76	24
Miscellaneous	21	79	21	79
Industrie	27	73	20	80
Military (non-officer)	19	81	18	82
Other	16	84	28	72
Total cases	12,605	17,124	1,554	1,892

[a]Adjustment for graduates = .705
[b]Adjustment for graduates = .821

Three other categories—the lower military, white-collar jobs, and industrie—also expanded. The first has been discussed earlier; suffice it here to say that it was probably a second choice. Clerical positions, some of which offered possibilities for promotion and an eventual move to the bourgeoisie, required some education and were relatively more attractive to students in enseignement spécial.[41]

As graduates of secondary schools moved primarily into the professions, they moved in significant numbers out of other bourgeois categories: propriétaires, rentiers, and the commercial and industrial bourgeois. Five times as many parents (adjusted numbers) had been propriétaires or rentiers and two and one-half as many parents had been members of the commercial and industrial bourgeois as graduates were (Table 9.4). Sons of wealthy investors and businessmen sought new means to preserve social status and to gain access to positions of social and political power. Industrialization and democratization of society were felt most acutely by the propriétaire, but these changes did not lead to a desire among graduates of secondary schools to take positions in business. Despite a wide difference in graduates' occupations generally between the lycées and collèges communaux, nearly the same percentage of graduates of each type of school became members of the commercial or industrial bourgeoisie. In France, old status attitudes to business, reinforced by the classical curriculum and the values taught in secondary schools, led graduates to search in the professions for new social opportunity.

A number of other patterns are suggested by Table 9.4. Among lower-middle-class occupations, the stability between the number of fathers and of graduates in petit commerce reflects the status and strength of shopkeepers in France during the 1860s. Major shifts occurred from agriculture and skilled work.[42] Graduates of secondary schools considered commerce a satisfactory career. They regarded a life on the farm or in a trade with considerably less relish. Neither agriculture nor the ancient trades were providing new jobs, their status was declining, and graduates preferred to avoid them. Many peasants' sons did return to the family farm, however. Nineteenth-century education and social changes modified eighteenth-century patterns of succession to parental occupations, but they did not obliterate those patterns.

Between enseignement spécial and enseignement classique, there is one striking difference that so far has been unmentioned. Three times as many graduates from enseignement spécial entered a profession as their fathers had—a greater disparity than for the rest of secondary education, in which there were twice as many graduates as fathers in the professions. But graduates of the special program joined primarily the lower (semi-) professions. They also found positions within the civil administration, in petit commerce, and as clerks in private business. Social movement for the graduates of enseignement spécial was from manual labor and the lower levels of the petite bourgeoisie into white-collar jobs and the upper levels of the petite bourgeoisie.

The type of school a child attended had a substantial effect on the social stratum he would enter. Half of the graduates of lycées took positions historians traditionally regard as upper or upper middle class. That was almost twice the percentage of the graduates of collèges communaux who did, and three and one-half times the percentage of graduates from enseignement spécial (Table 9.5).[43] The type of school attended and program pursued affected graduates' occupations more than parental social status affected the school or program chosen for students. One-fourth of the fathers of those in the special program were from the upper or upper middle classes, but only one-eighth of the graduates of that program entered occupations that gave such status; about the same number of graduates of lycées achieved upper-middle-class occupations as their fathers had. The lycées prepared the future elites of France; the collèges communaux taught the future petit bourgeois, though they gave access to the elites for their best or more privileged students; enrollment in enseignement spécial generally restricted graduates' careers to middle-class or lower-middle-class occupations.

EDUCATION AND SOCIAL MOBILITY.   Although secondary education promised mobility, Table 9.5 clearly indicates that on the whole graduates did not im-

TABLE 9.5
Graduates' and Fathers' Social Status (Percentages)

Status	All secondary schools		Lycées		Collèges communaux		Enseignement spécial	
	Graduates	Fathers	Graduates	Fathers	Graduates	Fathers	Graduates	Fathers
Upper- and upper-middle-class	37	45	50	53	28	37	14	27
Middle-class	48	44	37	39	54	48	68	55
Lower-middle- and lower-class	6	9	5	6	8	12	11	16
Other	9	2	8	2	10	2	8	2

Note: For the purposes of this table, classes have been divided as follows: *upper and upper middle classes*—the upper professions, commercial and industrial bourgeoisie, propriétaires, rentiers; *middle class*—the civil administration, lower professions, peasants, white-collar workers, and those in commerce; *lower middle and lower classes*—workers (skilled, unskilled, and agricultural) and industrie; *other*—the lower military, priests and ministers, deceased, those designated as *sans profession*, and a few vaguely described (e.g., visiting South American relative).

mediately improve on the social status of their parents. Fewer graduates than fathers held upper-middle-class positions despite high student preferences for the professions.[44] For all but the wealthiest, secondary education had become a necessity for joining French elites. Yet a diploma from a secondary school did not assure high social status: it promised only that most graduates would pursue a career broadly described as middle class. Only the lycées gave graduates a fifty-fifty change of becoming members of upper social groups and of equaling immediately the status of the fathers. Those who attended the collèges communaux or who took the program of enseignement spécial were still faced with downward mobility if they were of upper-middle-class background. The only clear pattern of upper mobility was for graduates from the lower or lower middle classes. If they were able to achieve a secondary degree, they could usually count on a slightly higher occupational status than their fathers had.

Thus, secondary education promised mobility, but it did not assure upward mobility. Necessary for future professionals, it was as much a way for elites to preserve their position in a changing society as it was for new groups to enter elite groups. The upper classes sought secondary education for their children, and students hoped that it would provide entry to the upper classes. But few graduates immediately achieved positions that gave the status that they or their parents had hoped for. The new road to high social status in the transitional society of France's Second Empire was clear, but it was too narrow to accommodate all who sought it.

Among traditional class groupings, mobility was more horizontal than vertical. The relatively small number of secondary schools and the tuition required limited access to them. This limited access, their traditional curriculum, and the continuation of old French social values restricted the impact of secondary education on French society as a whole.

Nevertheless, French education was important for individual mobility. Many used it to find new occupations that would permit them to hold the same status as their fathers, when the alternative could have been downward mobility. Ambitious students who achieved scholastic excellence could rise in society. Regardless of the opportunity for mobility provided individual students by the system, secondary education did significantly affect the social background of future French elites. By the mid-nineteenth century, the baccalauréat degree was a *sine qua non* for a promising career in the government or the professions, and we might search diligently within the organization and teaching of secondary schools and the social background of certain graduates for a fuller understanding of the future values of French elites. Elites in France were then still small enough and access to them well enough defined for the impact of secondary education on society in general to be magnified geometrically among elites.

CONCLUSION

From this analysis of the data, certain broad conclusions stand out. A major one is that although the lower classes were excluded from secondary education, the lower middle classes made up a high percentage of those sending their sons to secondary schools.[45] Peasants, petits commerçants, and even artisans often sought secondary education as a means of providing their sons with middle-class occupations or status at a time when economic changes were threatening the traditional middle-class status of these groups. The agricultural laborer, perhaps the real proletarian of the nineteenth century, was the most isolated from the educational system.

The upper classes found in secondary schools an institutional means to preserve social position, but secondary education also provided upward mobility for some of the petit bourgeois. Among sons of shopkeepers, peasants, and artisans whose fathers could not employ them or bestow on them a viable business, a few entered law and the upper professions; more joined the civil administration and lower professions. Some were also sent to secondary schools for the status education gave to both parents and graduates.

Within the secondary system of education, there were clear differences between types of schools and programs within them. Enseignement spécial served those who believed that the classical program was inappropriate to their social needs, but it did not especially serve the industrial classes. Between the graduates of lycées and the collèges communaux, there was a social difference as marked as between the graduates of the programs of enseignement classique and enseignment spécial. Curricula affected parental choices and graduate careers, but so did preexisting values.

Student expectations were considerably higher than were graduates' immediate achievement. The high preference among students for the professions indicates the desirability of professional occupations in French society, but opportunities in them were limited. Lenore O'Boyle has found an excess of educated men in nineteenth-century Europe. Social blockage occurred even before men achieved a professional position. Most preferred positions were not in law but especially in the newer professions. Law served primarily traditional elites, but medicine, teaching, even St. Cyr, and the École Polytechnique attracted wider groups and provided vertical mobility for lucky sons of the petite bourgeoisie.

Generally, the preference for officers' careers among students in public secondary schools during the Second Empire is suggestive of relationships that existed among education, government, and society. The category "government" used in the tables includes only those in the civil administration. A broader conception of government, including all those who received their salaries from the state, would result in a significant increase of students, graduates, and fathers in this category.[46] The proportion of students and graduates in government shown in Table 9.1 would then increase to 30 percent and that of fathers, to 23 percent. These greater percentages are more revealing of the close ties between public secondary education and the political system of France. Those employed by the government were likely to seek public education for their children, and students and graduates of public education were even more likely to seek a career within the government. This tie between government and public education helped to preserve social stability in France while regimes were changing and assured that those who would later give direction to schools, the army, and the civil administration were schooled in the political and social perspectives of existing elites.[47]

As important as the relationship between government and education is the question of social mobility. Those who attended secondary schools believed that the baccalauréat offered substantial social opportunity. On the eve of graduation, students as a whole expected much better jobs than their parents held and than recent graduates had actually achieved. The *perception* of mobility through education was significantly higher than its actuality in nineteenth-century France. In recent times, many have seen education as a panacea for social ills and as the way for poor or minority groups to achieve equality with the more fortunately born. One hundred years ago, however, not only social reformers but also other elements of French society believed that education promised mobility—more mobility than it delivered. Students had high expectations and parents made substantial financial sacrifices to send sons to secondary schools. One might conclude that a myth that education engenders mobility has long existed, but *myth* seems too strong a word, for mobility certainly did exist.

But mobility was as often horizontal as it was vertical. For individuals whose parents chose the right schools and who excelled in classes, secondary education provided a means to raise themselves through the most available means. On the whole, however, while secondary education offered individual mobility, it preserved existing social structure. The social status of one's parents affected job possibilities more than did the kind of school attended. Many graduates struggled to achieve immediate social status equal to that of their fathers, especially graduates who came from the upper classes. Even with a seondary diploma, the son of an upper-class Frenchman was likely to take a position inferior to that of his father. The one clear avenue of social mobility was from lower-middle-class to middle-class occupations.

Desires for respected occupations were greater than openings in them. Society changed less than did expectations, which were magnified by the expansion of secondary educaition dictated by governmental ministers in Paris but also reflective of societal demands for more educational opportunities. In this atmosphere of limited openings to upper-class occupations, the lycées alone gave access to the upper classes, while other secondary schools offered access primarily to middle positions and increased status among middle-class and lower-middle-class positions. A graduate of a lycée had twice the chance of embarking immediately on an upper-middle career as did a graduate of a collège communale and four times the chance that a graduate of the special program did. Secondary education could not insure continued upper-class status to its students; much less could it offer a means to democratize French elites.

The limited mobility produced by secondary education suggests that desire for occupational advancement was not the only reason parents and children sought secondary schools. The preferences of students for occupations that did not require secondary education and the financial sacrifices of lower-middle-class parents to send sons to secondary schools show that other factors were at work.

In nineteenth-century France, graduation from a secondary school gave status as well as a possibility for mobility. A shopkeeper who sent his son to a secondary school may have been asserting his success among his peers by paying tuition and defining himself as a bourgeois, the social equal of the wealthy.[48] The graduate of a secondary school had a facility in the classics, and his educational achievement remained with him regardless of the occupation he later followed.

Marx defined classes according to their relations to production. Weber argued that status groups manifest differences in part by their life styles, and Tawney noted that the fact of class is not necessarily the same as consciousness of class. For an understanding of social relations in a society, we must consider not only the models of historians and sociologists but also the way in which contemporary social groups saw themselves. In nineteenth-century France, those social groups traditionally described as the petit bourgeois clearly conceived advantages other than occupational movement to be gained by a secondary education. They saw secondary education as a means to preserve their bourgeois status during a period of economic and social change which threatened that status. Few workers attended secondary schools, but many petit bourgeois did. The social distinction in secondary schools existed between the lower-middle groups on to the highest and the working classes, not between *notables* and others. Through secondary education, petit bourgeois could attempt to describe themselves as bourgeois at a time when social and economic distinctions between the grand and the petit bourgeois seemed to be expanding and the differences between the lower middle classes and the lower classes appeared to be narrowing.

One threatened group was the peasantry, and large numbers of peasants' children attended secondary schools. One hundred years later, a smaller percentage of children of peasants than children of unskilled workers would attend secondary schools. In the nineteenth century, small farmers were a part of the petite bourgeoisie and sought increased status or mobility for their sons through education. In the twentieth century, some democratization of secondary education had drawn more sons of workers into the system, but it had little expanded the participation of peasants.[49]

Secondary education, then, in its promises and relations to other governmental institutions was a temporary source of social stability in nineteenth-century France. Its structure provided elites with a means to reproduce themselves and offered access for a few to the elites. For many more of the petit bourgeois, it provided openings to the lower professions or middle levels of the bureaucracy, positions that gave a petit bourgeois status at a time when opportunities in agriculture, artisanal skills, and petit commerce were decreasing. It gave prestige to those who could continue in the traditional petit bourgeois occupations. It also, however, helped to define the lower classes as a separate element in society. It was neither wide enough nor powerful enough to change French social structure nor to assimilate great numbers of the petit bourgeois into a broadly based, open, new governing class. It was an institution that was liberal in the early-nineteenth-century sense of *liberal,* but it was not a democratic institution. Liberal institutions did not provide the traditional petit bourgeois with a means to compensate for their declining economic and social position, and they eventually searched for answers in the new conservatism of the late nineteenth century. With the growth of political democracy in the Third Republic, secondary education became less responsive to social demands. Its failure to reform or to create new opportunities made it an anachronistic institution, subject to increasing social criticism by the end of the century.

NOTES

1. For a more detailed discussion of the data and categories, see the Appendix to this chapter. The information is for male students only because the French system of public secondary education of the time excluded females. The report is contained in the Archives Nationales, F17/6843–6849. Hereafter, all *F* citations refer to the Archives Nationales.

2. Seymour Lipset and Reinhard Bendix, *Social Mobility in Industrial Societies,* Berkeley, 1959, p. 11. Ralf Dahrendorf has also argued that social mobility is a necessary characteristic of an industrial society and that in industrial societies social position is dependent on educational achievement (*Class and Class Conflict in Industrial Society* [Stanford, 1959], pp. 57–59).

3. See Patrick J. Harrigan, "Social and Political Implications of Catholic Secondary Education after the Falloux Law," *Societas* 5 (Winter 1975).

4. Jean Piobetta, *Le Baccalauréat* (Paris, 1937). A. Delfaur described the baccalauréat after 1810 as a "social institution . . . necessary for most careers in social and political life" (*Napoleon 1er et l'instruction publique* [Paris, 1902], p. 62).

5. In a letter to the Prefect of Morbihan, Victor Duruy wrote that "the humanities [i.e., the classical program], which require much time and money will preserve the privileges of the upper classes" (quoted in Viviane Isambert-Jamati, *Crises de la Société: Crises de l'Enseignement* (Paris, 1970), p. 75. Previous ministers of education made similar remarks. See Hippolyte Fortoul, *Rapport à l'Empereur* (Paris, 1853), p. 80; Victor Cousin, *Oeuvres* (Paris, 1846–51), 1: 38. There was increasing discussion among both Catholic and public educators about the proper education of different classes in the late nineteenth century.

6. Regine Pernoud, *Histoire de la bourgeoisie en France: Les temps modernes* (Paris, 1962), pp. 485–92; Gerard Vincent, "Les professeurs du second degré au debut du XXe siècle," *Mouvement social,* 1966, p. 52.

7. The percentage might be 3 percent if we assume that the majority of those designated simply as in industrie were unskilled workers.

8. William Sewell, "Social Mobility in a Nineteenth-Century European City: Some Findings and Implications" (Paper presented at the Institute of Advanced Study, Princeton, N.J., June 1972).

9. This figure would be 40 percent if we added other lower-middle-class groups. Some of those designated simply as *commerçant* may have been grands commerçants, but it is unlikely that many were (see the Appendix); and that group represents only 3 percent of the occupations.

10. The best study of French ruling elites is André Tudesq, *Les grands Notables en France, 1840–1849: Etude historique d'une psychologie sociale,* 2 vols. (Paris, 1964). He finds that a fused aristocracy and wealthy bourgeoisie composed the ruling elite.

11. *Social Mobility,* p. 238.

12. The very existence of a local secondary school was a status symbol for many communities. Inspectors' reports in the Archives Nationales regularly refer to such attitudes. For example, see F17/6256, 9197. See also Antoine Prost, L'Enseignement en France, 1800–1967 (Paris, 1968), p. 58.

13. Some of the more than 2,000 propriétaires were probably little different from a well-off peasant.

14. Professor Sewell's work has demonstrated that sons of peasants were more mobile than sons of manual workers in Marseilles between 1846 and 1851. Lipset and Bendix have argued that differences in value systems are unimportant and that mobility is "determined by occupational structure" (*Social Mobility,* pp. 55, 73). For France, at least, values were a factor.

15. Appointment to administrative positions in the Second Empire often depended on personal contacts. Civil service examinations were not established until the Third Republic, but education was a prerequisite for administrative positions. See Henri Chardon, *L'Administration de la France: Les Fonctionnaires* (Paris, 1908), pp. 140–46; Christian Chavenon, "L'Administration dans la société

française," in *Aspects de la Société Française,* ed. André Siegfried (Paris, 1954), p. 159; and John Armstrong, *The European Administrative Elite* (Princeton, 1973), pp. 86–87.

16. Few students might be expected to describe themselves as rentiers, but *rentier* was a rare designation even for fathers. The difference between student and graduate designations as propriétaires, however, suggests that sons of the propriétaires sought a better-defined career.

17. Circular of 2 October 1863, quoted in Felix Ponteil, *Histoire de l'enseignement en France* (Paris, 1966), p. 262. A similar *cours de français* preceded the new program, and graduates discussed here were really graduates of the former program. For a recent examination of the fate of these programs, see C. R. Day, "Technical and Professional Education in France: The Rise and Fall of L'Enseignement Secondaire Spécial, 1885–1902," *Journal of Social History,* Winter 1972–73, pp. 177–202.

18. Circular of Victor Duruy to Prefects, 9 August 1865, quoted in Isambert-Jamati, *Crises,* p. 75. The French words are preserved here because the term *industriel* is used vaguely, as Isambert-Jamati points out. It came to be used to mean a bourgeois, but early in the century it only meant one involved in industry. See Jean Dubois, *Le Vocabulaire politique et social en France de 1869 à 1872* (Paris, 1962), p. 323.

19. Our sample identified 12 percent of all secondary students and graduates as pursuing the special program. But 25 percent of the sons of skilled workers pursued the special program, as did 23 percent of the sons of peasants, 16 percent of the sons of shopkeepers, and only 4 percent of sons of professionals. (These percentages are not represented in the tables.) Among the professions, primary school teachers (included among semiprofessionals) were the only group exceeding the 12 percent norm, with 23 percent. Within the government, 16 percent of the sons of employés and 11 percent of the sons of a group I have designated as "low government" enrolled in enseignement spécial; higher levels of the administration produced much lower percentages. Of the sons of propriétaires alone (rentiers excluded), 10 percent were enrolled. Within the category of law, the highest proportions of students in the special program were sons of the simple notaire. No son of a judge or prosecutor was identified in the special program, although seventy sons of these were in the classical program. It should be noted that percentages of sons of all groups in enseignement spécial would actually have been higher than these percentages, since only a sample of that program was taken, but relative distribution among occupational groups would be little changed.

20. Expectations and first jobs of sons of particular occupational groups will be discussed in a related article, but this one instance needs mention here because it affects this more general discussion.

21. Lycées have traditionally been regarded as more prestigious, with clientèle and alumni from higher social classes. For a recent statement of this attitude, see Robert Anderson's article "Secondary Education in Mid-Nineteenth-Century France: Some Social Aspects," *Past and Present* 47 (1971): 130–32.

22. Tuition and board in the collèges averaged 649fr.; the average for lycées was 739fr. (Ministre de l'instruction publique, *Statistique de* [l'enseignement secondaire] *1865* [Paris, 1868], p. 253).

23. The categories and figures listed by the lycée were the following: army, 50; *magistrature,* 50; law, 40; commerçants notables, 150; commerçants petits, 350; bankers, 55; propriétaires and rentiers, 395; medicine, 60; education, 50; employés, 50; art, painting, 50.

24. F17/6926.

25. The weaknesses of Robert Anderson's article "Secondary Education in Mid-Nineteenth-Century France" are the claim that a few selected schools are typical and the failure to distinguish between sources that themselves offer only vague categories and others that list precise occupations.

26. Lenore O'Boyle, "The Problem of an Excess of Educated Men in Western Europe, 1800–1850," *Journal of Modern History* 40 (1970): 474–95.

27. The percentage of students expecting professional careers indicated in Table 9.1 is 57 percent, but since I have included within this category those who expected to attend a grande école—some of whom might have planned to pursue a career in government or business—50 percent seems a more accurate, though perhaps conservative, estimate.

The 37 percent includes those who entered professional schools. Five years after graduation, fewer were pursuing a profession or professional studies. The decline occurred especially among the upper professions; see Table 9.3. For a more detailed discussion of the professions, see Patrick Harrigan, "Secondary Education and the Professions in France during the Second Empire," *Comparative Studies in Society and History,* Summer 1975, pp. 319–41.

28. A slightly higher percentage is indicated since some students who expressed a desire to attend a

grande école may have intended a career in industry. Less than 6 percent of the graduates of the class of 1859, however, were designated as in commercial or industrial bourgeois positions in 1865. By then, most graduates had left a grande école. See Table 9.3 and notes 27 and 33.

29. Even if Landes's arguments about the effect of value considerations on French economic development may now be suspect in the light of recent research into the French economy, his argument about the low esteem of businessmen in France and the status concerns of French entrepreneurs—many of whom sought government careers or aristocratic marriages for their children—are supported by this evidence. See David Landes, "French Entrepreneurs and Industrial Growth in the Nineteenth Century," *Journal of Economic History,* 1949, pp. 45–61. It might be further argued that businessmen lacked social prestige because few had the traditional education that other elites did.

30. It may well be that the propriétaire who sent his son to a lycée was wealthier than the propriétaire who sent his son to a collège communal, but we cannot determine this from the evidence at hand.

31. A similar ratio exists both for those listed as simply *commerce* and for those listed under more specific occupations within commerce. See also Theodore Zeldin's remarks on the status of commerçants in *France: Ambition, Love, and Politics* (Oxford, 1974), pp. 95–112.

32. Combining industrial occupations gives a percentage of 14 percent. While this percentage is a bit low, since some graduates of certain "professional" schools entered industry, adjustments would still indicate respective ratios of about 8:3, 2:1, and 2:3. The École Centrale, for example, trained engineers, but some of its graduates became teachers, governmental bureaucrats, and army officers. A few were even ordained to the priesthood. See Léon Guillet, *Cent Ans de la Vie de l'École Centrale des Arts et Manufactures, 1829–1929* (Paris, n.d.), pp. 267ff. Guillet gives a synopsis of the careers of some "renowned" graduates.

The three schools of Arts et Métiers at Aix, Angers, and Chalons are a special problem. I have included the secondary students who attended them among semiprofessionals. Although this is not entirely satisfactory, too many categories confuse more than help, and including such students within a category of industry seems even less satisfactory. Edouard Charton noted a century ago that there was no firm information for their graduates, and we still lack it today, though C. R. Day is presently completing a study of these schools. Until his findings are completed, we must rely on scattered evidence. Charton wrote that graduates "occupied positions in industry, strictly speaking, in *chemins de fer, ponts et chaussées,* the navy and the army." These occupations would imply government service as well as private industry (Charton, *Dictionnaire des professions* [Paris, 1880], 1:65). Mortimer d'Ocagne found that most graduates of Arts et Métiers initially become skilled workers (120 *ajusteurs-mécaniens,* 15 *menuisiers-modeleurs,* 15 *fondeurs,* 10 *forgerons*), but most advanced at least to draftsmen. *Les Grandes Ecoles* [Paris, 1873], pp. 149–50). The "Notice sur les Ecoles Imperiales d'Arts et Métiers" by M. Le Brun, Inspector (F17/4317), listed the following occupations for graduates of 1861 and of 1862: workers, *chefs, sous-chefs, ajusteurs,* etc., in private industry, 110; the same categories in the government-supported railroads, 77; *mécaniciens* in the navy or government communication system (*messageries Imperials*), 47; *Ponts et chaussés* or *agents voyers,* 22; military, 4; unknown or other, 36. For those living in Paris, he found 71 engineers; 9 *directeurs;* 106 *chefs;* 159 *chefs* of railroads; 78 draftsmen; 20 *conducteurs des ponts et chaussés;* 6 mastermechanics; 30 in teaching, the military, and assorted fields outside industry; 21 simply in industrie; and a number of employés. An 1856 report entitled "Position des élèves" for the Ecole d'Arts et Métiers for Aix (F17/4335) describes nearly half as draftsmen, a fourth as master-mechanics (many in the service of the government), and the remainder as generally government employees—teachers, soldiers, or lower-level administrators. This report also indicates some upward mobility of the graduates of 1846, who were most often described as being in skilled occupations (*ouvrier-adjusteur,* etc.). In general, then, graduates of Arts et Métiers seem to have been employed as often by the government as by private industry. Some attained minor administrative posts, a few middle-level positions. See also Antoine de Saporta, "Une école d'Arts et Métiers," *Revue des deux mondes* 133 (October 1892): 557–85.

33. For the following, please note the adjusted percentages (explained in the Appendix) for each category of Tables 9.1 and 9.2. These tables group graduates generally. For many we are able to determine the precise year in which they graduated. These are represented in Table 9.3. The only significant differences between the graduates of 1859 and those of 1863 are a decline for the upper professional group five years after graduation from secondary schools (partly attributable to graduation from the grandes écoles), an increase in the industrial bourgeoisie (attributable to an increase in engineers who would have graduated from grandes écoles), an increase in petits commerçants, and an increase in the lower military. Law remains a stable category with a natural decline in law students from

the class of 1859 matched by increased numbers of *avocats, magistrats,* and *notaires.* None of the graduates of the class of 1863 were described as *avocats;* they could not have been in 1865, but this serves as a check of the general accuracy of the report.

34. Among petits commerçants, the difference between anticipated and actual occupations is a result of differences for specifically designated occupations (butchers, bakers, etc.). It is 2:1 for these; it is equal for the vague designation *commerce.* This may reflect only a greater precision in descriptions for graduates, but it may indicate that even those students who decided to seek a traditional petit bourgeois job were still unsure of specific opportunities open to them. Such careers in local areas may have depended on openings at a particular time as much as they depended on familial connections. At least, the difference is to specifically lower-middle-class occupations rather than to a vague descriptive category.

35. In the same way, there is a commensurate relation between skilled workers' occupations among students and graduates in the lycées. Only 0.5 percent of students in the lycées planned to become skilled workers, and only 0.6 percent did. In the collèges communaux 18 percent expected to engage in skilled labor, but 38 percent of the graduates worked in those jobs. In a lycée the rare acceptance of such work, for whatever reasons, was also indicated by students. Against this argument it should be noted that there was a greater differential between students and graduates of lycées in industrie than there was for those in the collèges communaux. If principals or graduates from the lycées described socially unacceptable positions vaguely as *industrie,* there would be no difference in skilled labor between graduates of lycées and collèges communaux. It seems more probable that a position in industrie implied a possibility of advancement and described a variety of occupations in private business.

36. The category "others" in Table 9.1 is distorted because it includes deceased graduates.

37. See Paul de La Gorce, *The French Army* (New York, 1963), pp. 7–11.

38. "Military" here and elsewhere in this chapter excludes officers and those enrolled at St. Cyr. It includes those designated as sergeant or as of a lower rank and those described simply as *militaire;* it also includes lower ranks in the navy, but instances of sailors are minimal. The 2:1 ratio is an adjusted one. The number of nonofficers among graduates was 171 and among students, 12, an adjusted ratio of 8:1. The adjusted ratio for *militaire* is 3:2. Despite conscription, the differences are significant in an age when conscription was not universal and substitutes could be hired.

39. Other opportunities do not seem to have become available, since 6 percent of the graduates of the class of 1859 were in the lower military in 1865 and 5 percent of the class of 1863 were. The difference here is too slight and the cases too few, however, to be more than suggestive. Supporting the idea that the military was an alternative for students with other hopes is the trend upward for the lower military (2.4 percent vs. 5.2 percent) among schools that evidenced a higher percentage of graduates in bourgeois positions. (This sample is not indicated in the tables.) Those who expected a bourgeois position may have preferred a military career or enlistment to a lower-status civilian job.

40. A recent study of the French administration during the Restoration shows that promotion was slow and that increasing dissatisfaction was felt at the lower and middle levels: see Nicholas Richardson, *The French Prefectoral Corps, 1814–1830* (Cambridge, 1966). See also C. H. Chavenon, "Administration". For doctors' improving but unsure status, see Zeldin, *France,* pp. 23–43, and Charton, *Dictionnaire,* p. 348.

41. Lipset and Bendix found that large industry provided the usual avenue of mobility for white-collar workers in the twentieth century (*Social Mobility,* p. 179). All the occupations in this category cannot be listed here, but it should be noted that most of them are specific enough to allow one to conclude that they were generally lower-middle-class jobs rather than training positions for future executives. Almost 6 percent of the graduates of the collèges communaux became white-collar employees; less than 3 percent of graduates of the lycées did. The category of *industrie* is vague; it implies lower positions because higher ones were usually specified. See n. 42, and the Appendix to this chapter.

42. Figures shown in Table 9.4 indicate that there was a greater similarity in the percentage of fathers and sons in agriculture (61 and 39 percent, respectively) than there was for artisans, or skilled workers (73 percent vs. 27 percent). Nevertheless, some of those who eventually would succeed their fathers as propriétaires might have described themselves simply as *agriculteurs.* The higher percentage of graduates than fathers designated as in industrie implies a closer relation between fathers and graduates among skilled workers. Even if a closer relation does exist, however, the vaguer description of graduates suggests that occupations which a generation earlier deserved a specific appellation were regarded in the 1860s simply as a part of industry. Personal skills that once permitted a small but independent business may by that time have offered only higher pay in the employment of another. In

any event, skilled work and farming was the almost exclusive preserve of those whose parents had followed one of these occupations.

43. Because of the vagueness of certain occupational descriptions—notably *droit,* propriétaire, and industrie—the class groupings indicated in Table 9.5 have their limitations. A graduate of the program of enseignement spécial in law or industry may well have had restrictions placed on his future career that a graduate of a lycée did not. If so, that would exaggerate the differences among schools and programs already mentioned. The propriétaire who sent his son to a lycée may have been wealthier than the propriétaire who sent his son to a collège communal, but on the available evidence, we have no means to distinguish them.

44. It must be remembered, however, that we are comparing *first* jobs of graduates with those of their fathers and that therefore the difference shown here might be lessened or even reversed by a comparison of later graduate careers with those of fathers. Far fewer graduates than fathers were described as propriétaires or rentiers, but inherited wealth might have permitted some graduates to use those appellations later. Nevertheless, professional careers would have been indicated early, and they were the main avenue to assured higher status.

45. Certainly Antoine Prost's judgment that "only a very limited elite receives a complete secondary education" must be moderated (*L'Enseignement en France,* p. 34). Similarly, Jean Rohr's comment that secondary students during the Second Empire came essentially from the bourgeoisie (*Victory Duruy, ministre de Napoléon III: Essai sur la politique de l'instruction publique au temps de l'Empire Libéral* [Paris, 1967], p. 66) is sustained only if a broad definition of bourgeoisie is used.

46. The expanded category would include all teachers, military, and students in St. Cyr and the École Polytechnique. Although some graduates of the École Polytechnique took civilian jobs, some of the graduates of schools like Centrale, Mines, and Arts et Métiers—not included in the expanded category—would have been employed by the government. So would some law graduates. The vast majority of prefects in the Third Republic, for example, had a law degree (Jeanne Siwek-Pouydesseau, *Le Corps Prefectoral sous la Troisième et la Quatrième Republique* [Paris, 1969], pp. 31–34). Thus, percentages are minimal but accurate within a point or two.

47. When the independent system of Catholic secondary education increased its enrollment of graduates in the grandes écoles, the Third Republic restricted Catholic secondary schools. See Patrick Harrigan, "The Social Appeals of Catholic Secondary Education during the Third Republic," *Journal of Social History,* 8 (1974-1975): 122–41.

48. Saint-Marc Girardin believed that sending sons to a secondary school was the mark of bourgeois status (*De l'instruction interimédiaire et des ses rapports avec l'instruction secondaire* [Paris, 1847], p. 372).

49. After World War II, only 17 percent of the farmers' sons in elementary schools went on to secondary schools. The only smaller percentage was for agricultural laborers (13 percent). Yet 21 percent of the sons of unskilled workers continued their education. The highest participation in secondary education, then as in the nineteenth century, was by sons of senior officials and of professionals. See A. Girard, "Selection for Secondary Education in France," in *Education, Economy and Society,* eds. A. H. Halsey, Jean Floud, and C. A. Anderson (New York, 1961), pp. 183–94. See also Christian Peyre, "L'origine social des élèves d'origine ouvrière," in *Ecole et Société* (Paris, 1959). This neglected article considers secondary students of 1936–37 and after 1943–44. The percentage of students in secondary education who were workers' sons increased from 3 percent to 14 percent between 1936 and 1944 (Peyre, p. 10). Zeldin incorrectly states that peasants' sons first attended secondary schools in numbers after World War I (*France,* p. 51).

APPENDIX:
EXPLANATION OF THE TABLES

The data in the tables for this chapter are derived from the responses to the inquiry of 1864–65 from principals of 234 secondary schools among the 80 lycées and 239 collèges communaux. The grands lycées of Paris are not included in this data, though a comparative reference to a major Parisian lycée, the Lycée Bonaparte, is made in the text.[1] Most of the other schools that are missing are collèges communaux that had been recently established or offered only a partial program of studies and, therefore, had no graduates or students about to be graduated. The 27,711 students and graduates surveyed here made up about 90 percent of the total graduates or graduating students from provincial lycées and collèges communaux. Less than 5 percent are listed as of unknown career preference or occupation, and "unknowns" are excluded from final percentages.

The occupations of fathers of many graduates are missing because the questionnaire did not make clear whether they should be included. Nevertheless, the father's occupation is known for some 9,000 students and some 3,500 graduates. The data are more than sufficient for general conclusions, though there are difficulties for analyses of some particular occupations and geographical areas.

Occupational categories presented a problem. An *inspecteur* and a *vérifacteur* were not of the same social class; yet, both are included in the category of government. A graduate of the École Centrale may have pursued a career within government or become a member of the industrial bourgeoisie, a skilled worker, or an army officer. Here, he is included among professionals, as are all students who entered grandes écoles. Both army officers and teachers are also considered as professionals, although they might also have been included in the category of government. The categories used here overlap, but they seem to me the most reasonable categories from which to begin analysis.

The categories are, of course, the result of my initial occupational coding. I first listed all occupational descriptions that occurred among a random sample of 5 percent of the responses to the questionnaire. I combined some (for example, "financier," "banker," "stockbroker," "ship owner," and "broker"), because of the small numbers involved and added a few more as coding developed, for a total of ninety-six occupational groupings. After an initial printout, these were simplified again to total fifty by regrouping codes that had miniscule percentages (for example, *métayers* and *fermiers* were joined with *agriculteurs* and *cultivateurs;* [2] butchers, bakers, etc., were combined with other petit commerçants). These fifty groups I placed within categories shown in the tables.

There may be opportunity to discuss these groupings or other possible ones in a more detailed study of this evidence. Let me point here only to what strike me as major problems A small percentage of those included among commercial bourgeois were described in the questionnaire simply as in *assurances* or *finances*. A large group whom principals described simply as in *commerce* I have assumed to be petits commerçants. Industrie is a vague category that probably included some bourgeois, some skilled workers, some unskilled ones. It is listed separately, but for fathers' occupations, at least, it probably refers to workers, because principals often employed more specific appellations (e.g., *entrepreneur*). The major problem of definition is probably that of designating skilled and unskilled workers. I have simply listed among skilled workers all those designated as having specific skills—*ebenistes, mécaniciens,* and some thirty others.[3] Unskilled workers include *mineurs, laboreurs, journaliers,* and *ouvriers.* Unfortunately, categories of the nineteenth century are not the same as our own, but the most difficult definitions are for those groups that participated least in secondary education.

Of the five tables which appear in the text, 9.1, 9.2, and 9.4 list eight general occupational categories as well as fourteen more specific ones. Table 9.2 refers only to the program of enseignement spécial, the place of which in secondary education is discussed in the text. This table does not include all students enrolled in the special program. Only a minority of principals listed students by program, and many of them did not distinguish programs for all their students and graduates. Because of the irregular nature of reports specifying enseignment spécial, a sample of schools in departments that had a high percentage of students in the special program was taken. Of 92 schools checked, 37 made some distinction between programs; 25 of these schools were collèges communaux and 12 were lycées. This sample permitted us to assign 7,492 (10.7 percent) of the cases definitely to the program of enseignement spécial; it resulted in a slightly higher percentage (12.3 percent) of identifiable fathers' occupations because principals who took the care to differentiate between programs usually included the occupations of graduates' parents as well.

Neither the sampling nor the available information permits an exact representation of social categories for the program of enseignement spécial. The representation might be refined, with adjustments made for schools missing from national and departmental statistics, but such precision is unnecessary for purposes here. The sample is sufficient to illustrate the major social differences between students in each of the programs.

Extended analysis of enseignement spécial could result in some significant changes within occupational categories for secondary education in general. The subtraction of students now identified as in enseignement spécial, however, would result in a maximum increase or decrease of 2 percent in percentages shown for any category in the present tables. Therefore, I have not included separate tables specifically for enseignement classique. Any increase in precision would be less than the increase in confusion.

The adjusted percentages in Tables 9.1, 9.2, and 9.4 need further explanation. Each of these percentages refer to the relation between absolute figures within each occupational category—between student preferences and graduate careers or between fathers' and graduates' occupations. Absolute numbers are misleading because there are a different number of total cases for those groups. Table 9.4, for example, includes 17,124 graduates but only 12,605 fathers; therefore, the number of graduates in each category there was multiplied by the factor 0.705 before comparing it to the number of fathers. With that adjustment made, one finds that of the adjusted total number of students and graduates planning or following a professional career, 60 percent were students. Thus, one and one-half times (60:40) as many students intended to pursue a professional career as actually did.

NOTES

1. Information for the other grands lycées unfortunately was not included in the archival report. Data for the Lycée Bonaparte has been excluded from the tables because occupations were only estimated by the principal and because it was unique, even among lycées.

2. Those few who were designated as propriétaire/agriculteur were coded as agriculteurs; this was the only dual description encountered, save perhaps for an isolated case. I probably should have distinguished between agriculteurs and cultivateurs. The failure to do so should not affect present arguments, but any differences might be of interest to historians analyzing peasants' attitudes.

3. Cabinet-makers (*ebenistes*) and mechanics (*mécaniciens*) may have had quite different attitudes, and I mention these as an example of diverse groups who are discussed by other historians. See Georges Duveau, *1848: Making of a Revolution* (New York, 1967).

PART V

Elementary and Secondary Education in Early-Twentieth-Century America

The Discovery of the Adolescent by American Educational Reformers, 1900–1920: An Economic Perspective

BY SELWYN K. TROEN

The first two decades of the twentieth century marked an important watershed for public education in the United States. For the first time, educators became concerned with adolescent dropouts and instituted curricular and legislative reforms designed to encourage them to remain in school and to coerce them if they hesitated. This constituted a fundamental break with the largely literary curriculum and voluntary attendance that characterized nineteenth-century education. The popularity of vocational courses and the effectiveness of new compulsory education laws caused the average duration of schooling to double between 1900 and 1920. As formal education came to have an increasingly important place in the lives of children, society placed significantly higher expectations and demands on it.[1]

Interest in teenagers became a widespread phenomenon and contributed to educational reform. Many noneducators sought to improve the social conditions affecting youth through legislative as well as educational programs. As recent scholarship has shown, the discovery of "adolescence" just before the turn of the century, primarily through the work of G. Stanley Hall, generated distinctive institutional responses to deal with the special problems of this stage of personal development. Although it is difficult to weigh the motives of educators, it is probable that psychologists and philanthropists offered additional reasons and rationales for extending and adapting educational institutions to meet the needs of the adolescent.[2] Nevertheless, this essay argues that the attention lavished on youth by educators was not so much a consequence of new psychological insights or of a newly sensitized social conscience as of a recognition of educators' responsibility to prepare future workers for a technological society. An examination of the shift in attitudes toward established patterns of school attendance at the turn of the century suggests that the primary and direct impetus for change derived from an appreciation that the urban economy had developed into a more advanced industrial phase and that, therefore, unschooled teenagers were becoming a liability to society and to themselves.

I

In the second half of the nineteenth century there was a continuum in the patterns of school attendance and a pervasive set of attitudes that sustained them. For example, an analysis of attendance in St. Louis discloses that schooling was nearly universal for children from ages eight through eleven, with an average attendance of three to four years. Children began to drop out around age twelve, so that by age sixteen less than 20 percent were still enrolled. Moreover, those who discontinued their education began their vocational careers immediately, with the exception of some girls who returned to the isolation and dependency of the home.[3]

Although their data revealed that the children of the higher occupational classes stayed in school longer, educators did not lament the failure of children of the poorer classes to remain, since even middle-class children had relatively abbreviated scholastic careers. And when the problems of elimination and retardation were systematically explored in St. Louis and elsewhere around the turn of the century, most investigators concluded that poverty was not the reason children dropped out. Rather, they faulted the curriculum for failing to sustain the attention of older students.

The figures on St. Louis are representative, for the underuse of educational opportunities was a national phenomenon. In 1898, William Harris, the United States commissioner of education, reported that of every one hundred students, ninety-five were in elementary schools, four in high schools, and one in post-secondary institutions. Harris interpreted these figures as a sign of success, for they suggested that public education was fulfilling its mandate to diffuse basic reading, writing, and computational skills. This attitude, which accurately reflected the sentiments of other educators and of the public at large, was based on the conception that the schools' prime responsibility was to impart to students the requisite tools with which to continue their education on their own after leaving school. Belief in the culture of self-help inevitably minimized the relationship between formal education and vocational preparation. Until a greater appreciation for such a relationship occurred, the curriculum was severely circumscribed—at least by present standards—and consequently, attendance was comparatively limited.[4]

What is most impressive as well as suggestive about nineteenth-century attendance is that it was voluntary. Compulsory education laws tended to confirm already existing levels of attendance rather than to bring in older students.[5] These laws, which were widely enacted outside the South in the post–Civil War period, generally stipulated twelve as the legal minimum age for terminating schooling and therefore did not result in increased attendance. Laws directed at those above that age were rendered ineffective because of numerous loopholes—including easily invoked claims of poverty and literacy; meager statutory punishments, especially small fines; and the obligation of the state to prove that infractions were "willingly and knowingly commited."[6] In 1895, for example, a task force established by the state board of education in Massachusetts to investigate compliance with the law reported that parents still regarded the schooling of their children as strictly their own concern and violated the laws without fear of prosecution or fines.[7] In reviewing the efficacy of New York's 1874 legislation, the superintendent of public instruction commented: "It has failed to accomplish anything except subject itself to ridicule." The 1874 law was itself advertised as a reform of New York's fundamental compulsory education law of 1853.[8] Similarly, the Pennsylvania statutes went through periodic revisions without significant impact. The 1897 law permitted children aged thirteen to sixteen to work if they could produce a certificate attesting merely to the literacy expected of a third-grader. In fact, even these examinations were a farce, and for twenty-five cents a child could obtain the certificate enabling him to work.[9]

Child labor laws—which might have resulted in increased attendance, since they were directed at children twelve to fourteen—were also ineffective. A major shortcoming was the fact that the states invested limited resources in their enforcement. For example, Illinois's nationally respected inspector of factories and workshops, Florence Kelley, complained in 1896 that she had only twelve assistants with whom to police thousands of establishments throughout the state. In one year this corps traveled thousands of miles inspecting about 6,700 companies and more than 200,000 workers. The inspections were naturally superficial even in the places they were able to visit. The situation was only slightly better in Massachusetts, which at that time had thirty-three inspectors, and in New York, which had forty-four.[10]

Educators' lack of concern for adolescent dropouts was therefore unexceptional in a society that provided only for their most minimal protection. So long as teenagers were able to find gainful employment—and even unskilled work could be considered a necessary or valuable prelude to future advancement—there was insufficient pressure for change. Complacency was encouraged by the many vocational opportunities available in nineteenth-century cities. Children between twelve and sixteen found many openings in service occupations that required minimum skills and in laboring positions that demanded less than adult strength. Thus, large numbers were employed in factories, stores, and offices as cigar makers, messengers, cash boys or cash girls, delivery boys, stock clerks, wrappers, markers, inspectors, and the like. But the invention of cash registers, pneumatic tubes, paper-folding machines, and telephones—to suggest only the most obvious—necessarily made many of their jobs obsolete. An advancing technology had not only brought about the unemployment of legions of adolescents, but in so doing, had also undermined a basic premise of nineteenth-century education. A complete cataloguing and analysis of the consequences of technological change are beyond the scope of this paper. The examples that follow suggest the significance of the topic and the need for extended treatment.

II

Around 1900, department stores were the single largest employer of youths from ages twelve to sixteen in Chicago and among the most important in other major cities. The need of department stores for adolescent labor grew with the rapid development of these enterprises in the post–Civil War period. Although the jobs paid only about two dollars per week in the 1880s, they were desirable since they offered useful experience for future clerks and entrepreneurs. The most common position was that of cash boy or cash girl, which involved shuttling back and forth between the sales counter, cashier, and wrapping desk, carrying a basket containing the salesbook, money, and purchase. Sitting in tight-fitting uniforms on benches, these boys and girls were expected to respond immediately to the clerk's call of "Cash! Cash!" Their task was to take the money, merchandise, and sales slip from the clerk to an inspector for wrapping and checking, then rush to the departmental cashier to make change, and finally to return the package and the change to the salesclerk. The work was simple, essentially mechanical, and an easy prey to technological innovation.[11]

By the 1870s, one-third of the labor force of Macy's in New York was composed of cash girls; the same proportion worked as cash boys in the dry goods section of Marshall Field's in Chicago in the 1880s. In 1902, first Macy's and then Field's introduced the pneumatic tube, which eliminated a major portion of these employees' function. Macy's installed the most elaborate system, consisting in large fans which moved cash and slips, along with millions of cubic feet of air per hour, through eighteen miles of brass tubing to several hundred stations throughout the store. A network of horizontal and vertical conveyor belts was introduced at the same time for the movement of parcels, further reducing the need for human intermediaries.[12] Finally, the cash register, invented in 1878, had become sufficiently sophisticated by the turn of the century to further reduce need for cash boys by concentrating transactions at the counter where purchases were made.[13] Thus, the cash boys and girls who were members of a flourishing and numerous vocation in 1900 were virtually eliminated from modernizing department stores by 1905.

Although it is difficult to obtain figures for teenage office workers, it is clear that their numbers began to diminish at the same time. The growth of offices, as of department stores, in number and in size was one of the phenomena of a modernizing society. One raw indicator of this growth is the number of bookkeepers in the United States, which rose from 10,000 in 1880 to 250,000 by 1900.[14] Particularly in larger firms, managers attempted to gain greater control over operations and to cut costs by replacing personnel with newly invented machines which folded papers, addressed envelopes, affixed stamps, performed calculations, and assisted in bookkeeping. In addition, there were inventions which facilitated communications—typewriters, dictating machines, pneumatic tubes, and telephones. The result was a demand for a more highly skilled worker who was adaptable to the procedures of the modern office and capable of operating its machines. As a consequence, numerous unskilled teenage workers who ran errands in the late-nineteenth-century office were displaced by personnel trained to utilize the new apparatus.[15]

Further obstacles to workers below the age of sixteen arose in the early 1910s when disciples of Frederick Taylor applied his principles of scientific management to the office. Through the introduction of William Leffingwell's methods of "scientific selection," office workers were expected to pass psychological tests and to have acquired the kinds of skills that entailed attendance in a high school or a vocational secondary school. The application of Taylorism to the operations of the office led also to a scientific rearrangement of apparatus and personnel. The result was that in the early 1910s such companies as Curtis Publishing and Montgomery Ward, which employed hundreds of office workers, cut their staffs by half, with only the most skilled, and therefore the most schooled, remaining.[16]

The reports of factory inspectors in Illinois around the turn of the century demonstrate that numerous other industries steadily lessened their dependence on workers under sixteen. Although the inspectors were willing to assume credit for the diminution of child labor, their reports also indicate that technology and more efficient organization produced the same end. The experience of the communications industry, as represented in telegraph and telephone companies, documents this process. In 1900, Western Union's downtown Chicago offices employed 189 boys between fourteen and sixteen, who composed 50 percent of the total work force. By 1906 there were only 64 boys, or 24 percent of all employees. During the same years, the company's total downtown work force declined from 375 to 267. These declines were precipitated by the rapid development of the telephone industry, which, requiring a higher level of skill, employed virtually no children under sixteen. As telephone wires interlaced the streets of Chicago, both the telegraph industry and the telegram delivery boys suffered, becoming casualties of technological advance.[17]

Children's jobs were especially vulnerable in industries where unskilled operations were taken over by machines. For example, in the tobacco industry many youngsters lost their jobs with the relative decline of cigars and the growth of the cigarette trade, which, beginning in the 1880s, became increasingly efficient through improvements in cigarette-making machines.[18] Occasionally, the inspectors themselves contributed to adolescent unemployment. In 1895, one inspector suggested a rearrangement of furnaces at the Illinois Glass Company in Alton, the single largest employer of children in the state, with the result that large numbers were forced out of work.[19] Indeed, so many advances were made in most types of manufacturing that Edith Abbott and Sophinisba Breckenridge, Chicago social settlement workers and leaders in the national struggle for legislation protecting children, admitted in 1917 that "the most convincing argument for the extension of child labor laws is to be found in the fact that at present there is so little demand for the labor of children under sixteen years of age that it is impossible for more than a small percentage of the children who leave school at the age of fourteen or fifteen to find employment."[20] Unlike the period before the turn of the century, leaving school after third or fourth grade was not the beginning of vocational experience or advancement; it led to unemployment.

III

Some educators had foreseen that literacy and a reliance on self-help were not adequate in a modern industrial society. Beginning in the 1870s, John Runkle, the president of M.I.T., and Calvin Woodward, a professor of engineering at Washington University in St. Louis, advocated instruction in Russian *sloyd,* a form of manual training. They established polytechnic high schools as adjuncts to their universities, with sloyd as a central feature of the curriculum. Amidst considerable debate, in which Calvin Woodward and William Harris were the leading opponents, manual training began to infiltrate the curriculum of the public schools in the 1880s.[21] It quickly gained sufficient backing so that in 1891 the National Education Association, the most important association of educators in the country, established a special unit, the Department of Industrial Education and Manual Training.

The growing acceptance of manual training marked the first step in what became a general movement to increasingly specific, industrially oriented courses. This departure from the traditional literary curriculum of the nineteenth century was directly related to an effort to retain the interest of children who ordinarily dropped out at age twelve. Woodward, in perhaps the first studies that focused on explaining why children did not attend school beyond the third or fourth grade, sought to end the complacency with which most educators viewed the massive exit of twelve to sixteen-year-olds. For Woodward the attendance data was evidence of "a public calamity," and the departure of young teenagers from the schools was all the more lamentable since he felt it could be avoided. In his 1900 survey of major American cities, Woodward claimed that a small portion of this exit could be considered "a reasonable loss," attributable to "a certain death rate, a certain amount of pinching poverty, and a certain amount of incapacity which practically shuts out pupils." Concerned with identifying and correcting the causes for "abnormal withdrawals," he refused to grant that among most healthy and able children there was a genuine need to supplement family income as soon as possible, and labeled the claim of poverty merely an "excuse." The real reasons were that parents did not appreciate the value of more schooling and that children were bored with their classes. Sympathizing with these attitudes, he placed the ultimate blame on the schools. More specifically, he faulted neither teachers nor facilities, which he found good, but the curriculum.[22]

Woodward was not surprised that boys and girls became discontented after age twelve. Biological and psychological changes impelled them to engage in a more active life and made it difficult for them to submit to the sedentary and passive behavior demanded in the usual classroom. This was particularly true of boys, who "long to grasp things with their own hands; they burn to test the strength of materials and the magnitude of forces; to match their cunning with the cunning of nature and of practical men." Inevitably, the energies of these youths found expression in the streets or in the factory, office, and home. Manual training for boys and domestic science for girls was the answer, for these courses were "suited to their tastes." Moreover, Woodward suggested ways for assuaging the discontent of parents by showing them that schools could teach their children skills that would meet their needs as future wage earners. This, too, could be met by a new curriculum of a "more practical character" than the traditional literary one.[23]

Between 1900 and 1920, the problem of "elimination," as the phenomenon of early withdrawal was called, became the subject of numerous reports sponsored by city and state boards of education, the Russell Sage Foundation's Department of Child Hygiene, the National Committee on Vocational Education, and the United States Bureau of Education.[24] The studies generally focused on cities, although there was a widespread feeling that conditions were even worse in rural areas, where there were many pressures as well as opportunities for work and the resources for a more advanced education were limited. These studies were similar to Woodward's initial description of the problem and largely agreed with his findings as to its causes. The most comprehensive report, based on a survey of 318 cities, was produced in 1911 by George Strayer, a professor at Columbia University's Teachers College writing under the auspices of the Bureau of Education. It showed that the public schools lost one-half of their students between the ages of thirteen and fifteen. Strayer suggested that the solution was to create a differentiated curriculum that segregated the college-bound from those who would want or need to find work. He argued that "it is manifestly unfair to provide a rigid curriculum which leads straight to the college or university." To be truly democratic, the schools must offer each student "that training which will best fit him for his life's work." The point of Strayer's study was to make a case for vocational training. Unlike Woodward, who had envisioned manual training as a part of a general curriculum from which all students might benefit, Strayer was typical of a current of opinion that advocated the abandonment of a common curriculum and favored the separation of youths into different tracks which assumed that large numbers of students would enter specialized vocational courses. Strayer had modified Woodward's earlier studies in another significant way. He wanted the schools to include all children, even those whom Woodward put into the category of "reasonable loss." He therefore called for special schools that would accommodate the "unusually deficient either mentally or physically," and applauded the movement to enforced compulsory education. Like most early-twentieth-century educators, Strayer joined reforms that would engender new, positive attitudes toward advanced schooling with legislative reforms that would coerce the unpersuaded.[25]

As with Woodward's studies, Strayer's was based on the assumption that more children would stay in school if the curriculum emphasized more practical studies. A large body of statistics confirmed Woodward's belief that the majority of children used poverty as an "excuse" for withdrawing from the schools. In 1910, for example, the Federal Investigation into the Condition of Woman and Child Wage-Earners offered the following analysis of "elimination":

> Child's help desired though not necessary—27.9%
> Child dissatisfied with school—26.6%
> Child prefers to work—9.8%

Thus, about 65 percent of the children were potential students if parents and children could be persuaded that more schooling was worthwhile. Only 30 percent were in the category "Earnings necessary to family support" and 5.7 percent accounted for by "other causes," which included mental and physical problems.

This commission's figure of 30 percent for children whose earnings were necessary for family support was about average, but higher than the 20 percent reported by the Public Education Association's study of New York in 1912 and the Douglas Commission's 24 percent for Massachusetts in 1906. Furthermore, investigators felt that these genuinely poor children were not necessarily lost to the schools, for they believed that if the value of education were sufficiently demonstrated, then poor families might be willing to make the sacrifices necessary to prolong their children's education. The net effect of these studies on educators was to convince them that with the appropriate reforms they could reach a very substantial number of youths.[26]

The necessity for doing so was buttressed by studies conducted during the 1910s on what children did upon leaving school. The most comprehensive survey, undertaken in Philadelphia, inquired into the vocations of 14,000 children. Of these, only 3 percent were in skilled positions. The same was true in surveys taken in Chicago and in Worcester, Massachusetts. These studies showed that the average wage of a child was $3.00 to $3.50, which was only one-third of that earned by adults. In addition, employment was of a temporary nature. In another series of studies conducted at the same time, it was shown that children tended to work at one job for only a few months. At Swift and Company of Chicago children worked an average of only three and a half months; in Hartford, Connecticut, they averaged two and a quarter jobs per year; and in Maryland, which compiled the best statistics, more than 50 percent of children under sixteen worked for two months or less, and 15 percent for only two weeks. Such investigations showed that children who left school, particularly for unskilled work, held a very insecure place in the job market. This meant that there was little likelihood for a steady, dependable income and—what was of great importance to educators—little opportunity to learn new skills. The career of the early dropout was marked by shiftlessness, unemployment, low skills, and low wages.[27]

Paul Douglas, a reformer and academic who later became senator from Illinois, best summed up in 1920 the work of the previous two decades. He described the experience of many children as drifting ''from job to job, from industry to industry, still unskilled, and exposed to all the social and industrial evils which threaten adolescence.'' Typically, when the child matures to manhood, he finds that his position is vulnerable because of the incessant influx of younger unskilled workers into the labor force. The result is that he ''finds himself one of the class of the permanently unskilled with the attendant low wages and unemployment of his class.'' As a final judgment, Douglas noted: ''He had nothing to sell but his youth; he sold it, and received nothing in return.'' Surely, the press of family circumstances and the dissatisfaction with schooling had to be very great to sustain the willingness of tens of thousands of youths to confront these possibilities.[28]

These studies ultimately served to elaborate and make more precise a problem with which many educators around the turn of the century were concerned—the decline of apprenticeship. Woodward connected it with industrialization: ''The invention of machinery and the use of costly machine tools so far modified and limited apprenticeship as to almost ruin it.''[29] Manual training was his response to the problem. Most educators, however, preferred more specific vocational instruction. During the first decade of the twentieth century, a national movement of educators, businessmen, and organized labor successfully collaborated in such organizations as the National Society for the Promotion of Industrial Education and pressed for the inclusion of vocational courses in the public school curriculum. On a national level, their work resulted in the passage of the Smith-Hughes Act of 1917, which allocated federal funds for the first time on behalf of vocational training.[30]

The movement toward vocationalism is most clearly evidenced in the differences in emphasis of two influential studies commissioned by the National Education Association—the 1892 Report of the Committee of Ten, and the *Cardinal Principles of Secondary Education* of 1918. The 1892 statement, which was formulated by some of the most distinguished educators in the United States, was concerned with defining the curriculum of the high school so that there would be a better correspondence between its work and the uniform entrance requirements to which many of the nation's colleges had recently agreed. Commissioner of Education Harris, who wrote the section on the ideal high school curriculum, not surprisingly emphasized the traditional subjects of English, mathematics, geography, history, and foreign and ancient languages. There was no mention of manual training or vocational courses. Since the high school was thought of primarily as a necessary step leading to college, its course of study was subordinated to the demands of the universities.[31] In 1918, the select committee organized by the National Education Association defined more broadly the function of the high school. Arguing that ''a comprehensive reorganization of secondary education is imperative at this time,'' they stressed the need to readjust the curriculum to what they perceived to be a new social order by providing explicit instruction for work, leisure, home life, and citizenship. The result was the ''comprehensive high school,'' which included a ''differentiated curriculum'' that was a direct repudiation of Harris's model in the Report of the Committee of Ten.[32]

The most radical departures stemmed from the committee's recognition of a public responsibility to offer specialized vocational training, for there had developed ''a more complex economic order'' characterized by ''the substitution of the factory system for the domestic system of industry; the use of machinery in the place of manual labor; the high specialization of processes with a corresponding division of labor; and the breakdown of the apprenticeship system.''[33] In the new order, the patterns of advancement and self-development that had applied in the relatively unschooled society of the nineteenth century no longer applied. By 1918, after a generation of agitation for practical studies and the evidence of numerous analyses on the problems of youth, the committee was ready to recommend that in addition to the usual literary courses, there should be agricultural, business, clerical, industrial, fine arts, and household curricula.

IV

The adoption of the *Cardinal Principles* signified less the setting of guidelines for the future than the ratification of innovations already undertaken in many urban systems and an accomodation to the preferences of teenage students. The diversification of the curriculum and the enactment of effective compulsory education legislation first affected such systems during the first decade of the twentieth century and resulted in a dramatic and immediate increase in the duration of attendance. Including in the work of the classroom that which formerly would have been acquired outside, schools became the surrogate for apprenticeship; and the movement to incorporate the adolescent and broaden the scope of instruction developed a powerful momentum. By 1910, about 90 percent of the children in the nation's five largest cities—Boston, Chicago, New York, Philadelphia, and St. Louis—were enrolled from ages seven through thirteen. By 1920, formal schooling extended to age fourteen, or a minimum of eight years of instruction, and almost 40 percent of the students continued through age sixteen (see Table 10.1). This represented a doubling of the extent of schooling that was usually attained twenty years earlier.[34]

The enlargement of the pool of students finishing the eighth grade also contributed to increased high school enrollments. While the creation of active corps of truant officers assured a large reservoir of potential students, it does not by itself explain the expansion of the high school, since compulsory attendance laws generally stopped short of forcing students to remain in school past the eighth grade. The major stimuli for the growth of the high school were probably the diminution of satisfactory work opportunities for teenagers and the attractiveness of the new courses. Whereas perceptions of vocational opportunities cannot be measured, the impact of the new curricula can be tested through the experience of individual systems.[35]

In St. Louis—which may be taken as representative of large, innovating urban

TABLE 10.1
Percentage of Children Ages 5–20
Attending School in Boston, Chicago, New York,
Philadelphia, and St. Louis, 1910 and 1920

Age	1910	1920	Age	1910	1920
5	—	33.7	13	94.6	95.6
6	55.6	75.9	14	80.1	89.1
7	86.9	89.9	15	56.6	68.2
8	91.6	92.6	16	34.8	38.9
9	93.0	93.5	17	17.9	23.5
10	95.9	95.6	18	13.7	14.6
11	96.0	96.1	19	9.5	10.1
12	95.6	96.2	20	6.0	6.8

Sources: Thirteenth Census of the United States, 1910, 1: 1157–59; *Fourteenth Census of the United States, 1920,* 2: 1131–36.

systems—the high school population increased fivefold between 1800 and 1920. While some of this growth is explained by an expanding population, the real significance of this increase is that proportionately more students were continuing on in the higher grades. Only 3 percent of the total day population of students went on to high school in 1900; 7 percent were enrolled in 1910; and 11 percent in 1920. Further refinement of the schools' statistics shows that between 1900 and 1920 there was an important shift directly related to the new offerings in the distribution of the student body. Analysis of the programs pursued by senior class students reveals a decline in the popularity of classical and scientific courses, the mainstay of the old curriculum, and increased enrollment in the new programs—particularly in general studies, manual training, and the commercial course—which by 1920 attracted 77 percent of the students. The figures indicate that the appeal of the general and vocational courses, which were not necessarily related to college entrance, was very great, and that the curriculum of the previous decades had lost the interest of all but a minority of students.[36]

With the creation of innovative programs it became essential to advertise the new options and explain their values. Thus, vocational guidance followed almost immediately upon the introduction of vocational training. The initiation of such services also satisfied the contention of Woodward and other critics that early withdrawal would be diminished and attendance be improved if students and parents were informed of the kinds of skills necessary for success in an industrial society and of how schools could satisfy those requirements. Between 1900 and 1910, individual systems and state education boards established guidance departments which surveyed the local job market, suggested the kinds of courses necessary to fill local needs, and tried to persuade students to avail themselves of new opportunities. The close relationship between vocational training and vocational guidance was also evident on a national level. Shortly after the establishment in 1907 of the National Society for the Promotion of Industrial Training, members of that group called for a new association, which resulted in the organization in 1915 of the National Vocational Guidance Association.[37]

The schools were decisively transformed by the introduction of vocationally related programs. In order to meet the challenges of a changing economy, they assumed unprecedented responsibilities for the preparation of the young and became an intermediary between the emerging labor force and employers. The complementary strategies of an emphasis on practical instruction and effective compulsory attendance laws successfully overcame the relatively limiting definition of common schooling that had been championed by nineteenth-century educators. The crisis over adolescent attendance and its resolution had produced a far more broadly defined and socially engaged concept of schooling which marked a significant departure in the history of American education.

NOTES

1. Basic studies in the development of secondary and vocational education include Edward A. Krug, *The Shaping of the American High School*, vol. 1, *1880–1920* (New York: Harper and Row, 1964) and

vol. 2, *1920–1941* (Madison: University of Wisconsin Press, 1972); Marvin Lazerson, *Origins of the Urban School: Public Education in Massachusetts, 1870–1915* (Cambridge: Harvard University Press, 1971); and Joel Spring, *Education and the Rise of the Corporate State* (Boston: Beacon Press, 1972). The impact of curricular and legislative reforms on school attendance in a major city can be found in Selwyn K. Troen, "Defining Educational Change through Patterns of School Attendance: The Case of St. Louis, 1850–1920" (Paper delivered at the Joint Meeting of the National History of Education Society and the Midwest History of Education Society, Chicago, 26 October 1973).

2. Dorothy Ross, *G. Stanley Hall: The Psychologist as Prophet* (Chicago: University of Chicago Press, 1972); John Demos and Virginia Demos, "Adolescence in Historical Perspective," *Journal of Marriage and the Family* 31 (1969): 632–33; Anthony M. Platt, *The Child Savers: The Invention of Delinquency* (Chicago: University of Chicago Press, 1969); and Joseph F. Kett, "Adolescence and Youth," in *The Family in History: Interdisciplinary Essays,* eds. Theodore Rabb and Robert Rotberg (New York: Harper and Row, 1971), pp. 95–110.

3. Selwyn K. Troen, "Popular Education in Nineteenth-Century St. Louis," *History of Education Quarterly* 13 (1973): 23–40.

4. William T. Harris, "Elementary Education," in *Education in the United States,* ed. Nicholas M. Butler (New York: American Book Company, 1900), pp. 79–94.

5. William Landes and Lewis Solmon, "Compulsory Schooling Legislation: An Economic Analysis of Law and Social Change in the Nineteenth Century," *Journal of Economic History* 32 (1972): 54–89; Moses Stambler, "The Effect of Compulsory Education and Child Labor Laws on High School Attendance in New York City, 1898–1917," *History of Education Quarterly* 7 (1968): 189–214.

6. Forest C. Ensign, *Compulsory School Attendance and Child Labor* (Iowa City: The Athens Press, 1921), pp. 231–51.

7. Ibid., p. 70.

8. Ibid., p. 121.

9. Ibid., p. 184.

10. *Fourth Annual Report of the Factory Inspectors of Illinois for the Year Ending December 15, 1896* (Springfield, Ill., 1897), p. 3.

11. Robert W. Twyman, *History of Marshall Field and Company, 1852–1906* (Philadelphia: University of Pennsylvania Press, 1954), p. 71; Ralph M. Hower, *History of Macy's of New York, 1858–1919* (Cambridge: Harvard University Press, 1943), pp. 196–98, 452–53.

12. Twyman, *Marshall Field,* p. 200; Hower, *Macy's,* pp. 324–25.

13. Isaac F. Marcosson, *Wherever Men Trade: The Romance of the Cash Register* (New York: Dodd, Mead, 1945), pp. 9, 164–68.

14. William H. Leffingwell, *Office Management: Principles and Practices* (Chicago: A. W. Shaw, 1925), pp. 824–33.

15. Leffingwell, *Office Management,* pp. 434–68.

16. William H. Leffingwell, *Scientific Office Management* (Chicago: A. W. Shaw, 1917), pp. 3–7. A survey conducted in eighteen cities during the 1930s demonstrates in typical job descriptions and requirements the extent to which technological advance had eliminated children under sixteen and those without schooling. See Dorothea de Schweintz, *Occupations in Retail Stores: A Study Sponsored by the National Vocational Guidance Association and the United States Employment Service* (Scranton, Pa.: International Textbook Co., 1937).

17. *Eighth Annual Report of the Factory Inspectors of Illinois for the Year Ending December 15, 1900* (Springfield, Ill., 1901), pp. 171–72; *Fourteenth Annual Report of the Factory Inspectors of Illinois for the Year Ending December 15, 1906* (Springfield, Ill., 1908), pp. 653–55. The figures are based on the records of the Chicago Telephone Company and Western Union, which were the largest in their respective industries. The same pattern held true for the smaller companies.

18. In Chicago, of total employees, the percentage of children under sixteen declined from 14.7 percent to 1.1 percent between 1896 and 1906 (*Fourth Annual Report,* p. 107; *Fourteenth Annual Report,* p. xxiv).

19. *Third Annual Report of the Factory Inspectors of Illinois for the Year Ending December 15, 1895* (Springfield, Ill., 1896), pp. 14–18.

20. Edith Abbott and Sophinisba P. Breckenridge, *Truancy and Non-Attendance in the Chicago Schools: A Study of the Social Aspects of the Compulsory Education and Child Labor Legislation of Illinois* (Chicago: University of Chicago Press, 1917), p. 324.

21. Berenice M. Fisher, *Industrial Education: American Ideals and Institutions* (Madison: University of Wisconsin Press, 1967), pp. 72–84; Arthur G. Wirth, *Education in the Technological Society:*

The Vocational-Liberal Studies Controversy in the Early Twentieth Century (San Francisco: Intext Educational Publishers, 1972), pp. 9–15; Calvin M. Woodward, *Manual Training in Education* (New York: Scribner and Welford, 1890), pp. 2, 41–51, 218–19, 264.

22. *Forty-Sixth Annual Report of the Board of Education of the City of St. Louis, Mo., for the Year Ending June 30, 1900* (St. Louis, 1901), pp. 15–16.

23. Ibid., pp. 27–30.

24. An excellent survey of the literature is found in Paul Douglas, *American Apprenticeship and Industrial Education,* Columbia University Studies in Economics, History and Law, 955, no. 2 (New York: Longmans, Green and Co., 1921), pp. 85–108. Among the more noteworthy studies are *Report of the Commission on National Aid to Vocational Education,* House Document 1004, 63rd Cong. 2d sess.; Luther Gulick and Leonard Ayres, *Why 250,000 Children Leave School: A Study in Retardation and Elimination in City School Systems* (New York: Charities Publications Committee [Russell Sage Foundation], 1909); George D. Strayer, *Age and Grade Census of Schools and Colleges: A Study of Retardation and Elimination,* United States Bureau of Education Bulletin no. 5, 1911 (Washington, D.C.: Government Printing Office, 1911). George S. Counts made major contributions to this field in the 1920s and 1930s; see his *Selective Character of American Secondary Education* (Chicago: University of Chicago Press, 1932).

25. Strayer, *Age and Grade Census,* pp. 11, 139–40.

26. *Report on Conditions of Women and Child Wage-Earners in the United States,* Senate Document 645, 61st Cong., 2d sess. (Washington, D.C.: Government Printing Office, 1910), 1: 46; Douglas, *American Apprenticeship,* pp. 89–90.

27. Douglas, *American Apprenticeship,* pp. 96–105.

28. Ibid., p. 85.

29. Calvin Woodward, "Manual, Industrial, and Technical Education in the United States," *Report of the Commissioner of Education for the Year 1903* (Washington, D.C.: Government Printing Office, 1905), 1: 1021.

30. Wirth, *Education in the Technological Society,* pp. 33–42.

31. "Report of the Committee of Ten on Secondary School Studies," *Report of the Commissioner of Education for the Year 1892–93* (Washington, D.C.: Government Printing Office, 1895), 2, pt. 3: 1457–64. For analysis of the setting and significance of the report, see Theodore R. Sizer, *Secondary Schools at the Turn of the Century* (New Haven: Yale University Press, 1964).

32. Commission on the Reorganization of Secondary Education, *Cardinal Principles of Secondary Education,* Bureau of Education Bulletin no. 35, 1918 (Washington, D.C.: Government Printing Office, 1918), pp. 7–8, 22.

33. Ibid.

34. There are many difficulties in obtaining statistics on attendance prior to the 1910 census, since they are compiled for age spans, such as five through thirteen or five through twenty, rather than by each age. The only means for establishing more complete statistics is to utilize the manuscript census. The results of the most extensive use of this procedure are reported in Troen, "Popular Education in Nineteenth-Century St. Louis."

35. National statistics on the popularity of various curricula are not available or not usable. The difficulties are (*a*) not all schools reported; (*b*) definitions of what constitutes a high school are not standardized; (*c*) not all high schools offered the new courses, thus biasing statistics when available; and (*d*) the modes of grouping courses into a curriculum also varied.

36. The same trend towards vocational courses was found in the evening classes, which underwent a similar expansion. A more complete analysis of student selections can be found in Selwyn K. Troen, "Defining Educational Change through Patterns of School Attendance." For a generalized discussion of the shift in student preferences, see Krug, *The Shaping of the American High School,* 2: 55–59.

37. Wirth, *Education in the Technological Society,* pp. 33–42.

CHAPTER 11

The Failure of Progressive Education, 1920–1940

BY ARTHUR ZILVERSMIT

A progressive educator of the pre–World War II period listening to the current debates about open education may be excused a tolerant smile as he recognizes that many of the issues he hotly debated in his youth are being raised once more. If his smile is tinged with a sad edge, this too is understandable, for the current debaters pay him little heed; to many young educational reformers, the history of progressive education is unknown or irrelevant. Yet if the current discussions of educational innovation are to have any lasting impact, it is important to understand the fate of previous reform efforts; those who do not understand the past are doomed to repeat it.

The progressive educators of the 1920s and 1930s had hoped to transform the shape of American education. Although many of them worked in private schools, their aim was to restructure public education as well as private. How successful were they? What effects did progressivism have on public education in the years before World War II (the period when organized progressivism had reached its peak strength)? Lawrence Cremin, one of the most intelligent historians of American education, has argued that progressivism had a profound effect on the public schools: "The twenties and thirties were an age of reform in American education, as thousands of local districts adopted one or another of the elements in the progressive program."[1] But Cremin devoted only a few pages of his larger study of progressivism to its impact on public schools, and he made little attempt to assess the impact of the ideas of progressive educators at the local, classroom level in typical American schools. Since it concentrated on a few examples of progressive education in outstanding school systems, Cremin's selection of evidence may have led him to exaggerate the impact of progressivism.[2] The fact that so many of the issues raised by the progressives are being considered anew may indicate that progressivism's impact on our schools has been much less than Cremin suggested. Despite a growing literature on educational progressivism we know surprisingly little about its impact at the local classroom level; consequently we know very little about the real impact of progressive education on American schools.

This essay is an effort to estimate the impact of progressive education on American public elementary schools in the interwar period, in the hopes that such an estimate will illuminate an important period in the history of American education, will inform the current debate on educational reform, and will contribute to an understanding of the interface where ideology intersects with popular institutions.[3]

Forming an impression of what was typical of American education at any point in the past is a process that is fraught with difficulty. To begin with there is the sheer size of the American educational enterprise—in 1940 over 18 million children attended 183,000 public elementary schools, housed in buildings ranging from ill-ventilated hovels to exciting architectural monuments.[4] Furthermore, control over American schools was extremely localized. Traditional suspicion of state interference (let alone federal intervention) meant that most decisions affecting the education of American children were made at the local district level, either by one of the approximately 117,000 administrative units responsible for the functioning of public schools, or by local administrators and teachers.[5] Because their roles in matters of curriculum and classroom management have been minimal, federal and state governments have collected few statistics in these areas. Their interest has largely been confined to the financial aspects of education and to certain programs (such as vocational education) that have attracted special support.

Furthermore, in the absence of hard data on what was actually being done in American classrooms, issues have been obscured by much of the rhetoric of educational advocacy. In an effort to persuade schools to adopt innovations, progressives often described educational experiments in glowing terms. Educational journals of the interwar period were filled with descriptions of innovative schools, but few articles attempted to depict what was going on in more typical classrooms. This "Schools of Tomorrow" educational journalism gives a false impression of the degrees of innovation in American education. Similarly, those who favored retrenchment in the face of the fiscal crisis of the 1930s also exaggerated the extent of innovations in the schools as they decried the cost of "fads and frills" that had been added to the curriculum. The cumulative effect of reading these ideologically motivated discussions gives the impression of great ferment in the American classroom—a conclusion that other evidence does not support.

Finally, the degree of educational innovation is obscured by an understandable willingness on the part of educators to head off criticism by giving old practices new labels. If a combined social studies course used the same materials previously taught as separate history, geography, and civics courses, the change was likely to obscure the nature of the school's commitment to educational innovation.

Despite these difficulties, however, there are ways of establishing with some degree of certitude the nature of the impact of progressivism on American public elementary schools in the interwar period. An extended analysis of a limited number of school districts is one way of establishing its impact. Later, I hope to make such a study of the schools in the Chicago area. But another way of getting at the problem—the method used here—is to use the scattered information that is available—being cautious to recognize its limitations.

Before we embark on an examination of the impact of progressive education on the public schools, it will be necessary to deal with one more difficulty. This is the illusive meaning of the term *progressive education*. The word *progressive* is difficult because it is not only identified with a specific historical development in education, but it is also used as a general term of praise describing any movement considered to be in keeping with a perceived trend of which the writer approves. According to this definition any change can be seen as "progressive" if it accords with someone's sense of the direction of historical development, and the term has often been used in this broad sense. Thus, the installation of flush toilets in school buildings is a "progressive" step. Yet the term also has a more definite and restricted meaning. In the 1920s and 1930s a progressive school was usually defined as one that followed a child-centered rather than a subject-centered curriculum. It was a school in which the children played an active role in determining the content of their education. It was a school concerned with meeting the needs of the "whole child"—his emotional and physical needs as well as his intellectual development. Finally, it was a school which believed that its program would allow children to develop in ways that would ultimately make for a better larger society. Although other writers on the history of progressive education (most notably Lawrence Cremin) have used much wider definitions of progressive education, I will use the definition outlined above because I believe that it represents the essential unifying themes of progressive education in the twenties and thirties.[6] Moreover, this definition is in accord with what laymen meant when they discussed progressive schools in the interwar period. The host of stories that began "There was this child who went to a very progressive school . . ." did not refer to schools with industrial education programs or education based on a rigid use of IQ tests: they referred to the child-centered schools that were exaggerated examples of progressive education.

Although it is difficult to measure exactly a concept as illusive as child-centered education, there are indicators that are suggestive of the degree of progressivism in a school system. For example, while the ratio of fixed to portable school desks is not by itself an index of the progressivism of a school system, there is a relationship between the kind of seats a school board chooses to purchase and its attitude towards education: a school system that continued to purchase fixed, bolted-down desks was not interested in a child-centered curriculum. Similarly, although a teacher who received her training in a thoroughly orthodox normal school might still become a dedicated progressive teacher, there is a relationship between the educational philosophies of teacher-training institutions and the views of their graduates. The relationship is not sufficiently direct that we can establish an accurate index of progressivism, yet here is another indicator which is suggestive and which, with other such indicators, will allow us to form some assessment of the progressivism of American public education. Like a scientist, I will try to describe a complex phenomenon on the basis of a limited number of reflections and emissions, recognizing that some of the signals are mere random static but hoping that most are intelligible and bear a fixed relationship to the subject being examined.

II

If the child was to be at the center of progressive education, progressive reformers clearly saw that it would take a highly trained, sensitive teacher to place him there. If rote learning and a rigidly subject-centered curriculum were to be eliminated, the role of the teacher would become absolutely crucial. For progressives, then, there was no such thing as a progressive classroom without a progressive teacher. There is no doubt that there were talented progressive teachers in the 1920s and 1930s—teachers who used the spontaneous enthusiasm of their pupils as an important factor in establishing the setting for significant learning experiences, teachers who were able to differentiate the needs of individual children and who could structure situations that would allow all children to achieve and attain a sense of self-worth. But if such teachers were typical, we would expect to find that teacher-training institutions were at least attempting to foster this kind of education. There is little evidence that they tried.

To begin with, American elementary school teachers were not highly trained. An overwhelming majority of them had no more than two years normal school education, while fully one-quarter of them had even less professional training. Only 10 percent of elementary teachers had sufficient training to earn a B.A.[7] Moreover, they could not claim that professional experience made up for their lack of formal training since public schools "were taught predominantly by young, unmarried women with little teacher experience."[8] Moreover, the training of faculty members of the teacher-training institutions was singularly unimpressive; over 50 percent of the faculty members of state teachers colleges and normal schools had one year or less of graduate work, and most of them had had no personal experience in elementary education.[9]

The typical normal school and teachers college was not a center for progressive education. Even the best of the teachers colleges and normal schools were remarkably traditional in their teaching methods.[10] Moreover, the educational philosophy of faculty members at teacher-training institutions was, in large part, quite traditional. A detailed study of the educational philosophy of teachers of teachers made in the early 1930s reveals that although the majority of faculty members had "acquired the vocabulary of various trends and movements in education," they had "failed to gain a deeper understanding of the philosophy which underlies them." Despite the general impression that "the traditional school" had disappeared, the author of this study found that faculty members of teachers colleges and normal schools "in significant degree . . . hold to those purposes, ideals, and practices which are in basic agreement with the older philosophy underlying the traditions of American education." Faculty members of teacher training institutions, therefore, "seem to represent an influence which makes for the continuance of a large part of the traditional in education rather than a break with it."[11]

Although the progressive teacher would have to be considered the most important factor in establishing a progressive classroom, the course of study, whether developed by individual teachers or by a school system, clearly set parameters for the progressivism of any classroom. On the eve of World War II, an analysis of some 85,000 courses of study by a group from Teachers College, Columbia University, reached conclusions that were clearly disappointing to those who hoped that progressivism had made important inroads in American classrooms. While recognizing a significant trend to find new patterns for organizing materials and experiences—a "trend to find new bottles, if not new wine"—the authors of the study concluded that "in most cases the contents remain more or less the same." Moreover, "the majority of courses still reveal no significant change in organization from the traditional separate subject matter point of view." When activities had been added to course material, "the activities and experiences seem to be merely addenda appended in an effort to rejuvenate a more formal academic outline of content." In most cases new courses of study did not reflect a change in educational philosophy, but represented a superficial change in traditional academic subjects.[12]

Classroom furniture provides another clue to the progressivism of American elementary schools. Progressive education can, of course, take place in the most unlikely setting, but progressive educators favored portable furniture over the older, bolted-down desks, because teachers could rearrange portable desks to suit their needs at any particular moment. Portable desks facilitated dividing a classroom into small groups and informal instructional settings. Although a progressive teacher could obviously function in a room with bolted-down desks, and a traditional school system could use portable furniture as if it were still bolted to the floor, a school system's decision to purchase portable instead of fixed furniture offers some clue to its educational philosophy. According to statistics of the school seating industry, it was not until 1931 that a majority of new desks sold were portable, and as late as 1934 stationary school desks still accounted for almost 40 percent of new desks sold. The single most popular kind of seating sold in 1934 was still the fixed, nonadjustable combination seat and desk.[13] Although the trend in school seating was clearly towards portable furniture, in the mid-1930s many school systems were still purchasing old-fashioned desks suited to the traditional classroom, and as late as 1940 school seating manufacturers were still advertising bolted-down models.[14]

The progressive concern for the well-being of the whole child involved a serious commitment to the mental health of pupils. A concern for promoting mental health was expressed in a model progressive school system, such as that of Winnetka, Illinois, by having a team of psychiatrists, psychologists, and social workers to counsel with children and to aid teachers by making them aware of the psychological needs of their pupils. Although a few other communities provided similar facilities, they were clearly exceptional. The rarity of public school employment of school psychologists and social workers in the twenties and thirties is most clearly evidenced by the almost total lack of statistics on the number

employed. The best available estimates indicate that there were only approximately 250 school social workers in the entire nation in 1940.[15] There are no
estimates of the number of school psychologists employed in this period, but the
fact that New York State had only sixty-seven qualified school psychologists in
1939 is suggestive of the national picture.[16] An extensive commitment to the
provision of psychological services for pupils came only after World War II.

The picture of American educational practice that emerges from the scattered
statistics and studies of the 1930s indicates clearly that American schools had not
made very significant steps towards implementing the child-centered education
that had been advocated for many years by John Dewey and the progressives.
These observations are reinforced by a more detailed examination of one state—
New York—for which an excellent comprehensive survey is available. For the
very reason that New York is not a typical state, it might very well be expected to
be in advance of other states in instituting progressive educational innovations, and
the absence of progressive practices in the elementary schools of New York is an
important clue to the impact of progressivism on the schools of other states.

From 1935 to 1938 a group of educational experts under the direction of Dr.
Luther Gulick undertook an extensive investigation into the ''character and cost of
public education in New York State,'' culminating in over twelve separate volumes and numerous articles. According to Professor Gulick, it was ''the last of the
great surveys.''[17] Although the Regents' Inquiry (as the study was officially
named) was not concerned with the impact of educational ideology, the volumes
and manuscript records of the survey are a rich source for understanding education
in New York in the last of the prewar years and contain valuable information on the
extent of progressive innovations in the state's schools.

The Regents' Inquiry is an unusually useful source for several reasons. First of
all, the study was not done by the state education department, but by educational
experts who came from outside the state, so that those who conducted the study had
few personal axes to grind. Secondly, the Regents' Inquiry was concerned to find
out what was happening in typical schools rather than what was the practice in
exceptional cases. Finally, the inquiry concentrated on an extended analysis of a
limited number of topics and areas, providing a very rich source of data on a
number of important topics. Rather than amassing reams of statistics on the whole
state, the inquiry staff began by making a detailed study of the social and economic
characteristics of the communities of New York and then selected fifty of these
which could be considered typical of the many diverse kinds of communities in the
state.[18] The schools of these communities became the subject of detailed investigation (including classroom observations) and analysis. The thoroughness of the
study was unsurpassed in American education.

The state's elementary schools were the focus of a series of studies under the
direction of Dr. Leo J. Brueckner of the University of Minnesota. The title of this
volume—*The Changing Elementary School*—may perhaps have been ironic, for
the whole thrust of the study was the degree to which elementary education had not
been adapted to current educational theory. Brueckner's staff examined courses of

study, curricula, and teaching methods and in each case noted their failure to conform to the standard of progressive educational theory.[19] They found that the elementary curriculum was dominated by state syllabi (many out of date) and textbooks. "The purpose of instruction," they found, "appears to be largely to get pupils to master organized bodies of formalized, inert subject matter." Generally, the academic subjects were kept in their separate compartments and not linked (as progressive educators had urged). Furthermore, "little is done by many teachers to relate much of what is taught to the experience of every day life."[20] For the most part teaching was frankly old-fashioned: "Most of the teaching observed was very formal and along traditional lines," emphasizing "the acquisition of bodies of materials."[21] According to the investigators, schools were "placing undue stress on the teaching of specific facts and skills with the result that they tend to neglect the development of social understanding, rich interest, effective study habits, and worthy use of leisure time."[22] The elementary schools of New York offered a relatively traditional, subject-centered curriculum and were staffed by teachers who, for the most part, adhered to traditional philosophies of education.

The more detailed studies by subject-matter specialists supported these conclusions. William S. Gray and Bernice Leary examined the reading programs of New York elementary schools, visiting 310 classrooms in 72 schools. They rated reading programs on a five-point scale and found that over 60 percent of the reading programs observed were in the lowest category: "A narrow, formal type of instruction which was provided during the reading period two or three decades ago, and which gave major emphasis to mastery of the mechanics of reading rather than to the broader ends which reading may serve in child life."[23] As an example of the type of instruction offered by a school in the lower part of this category, they described a classroom where the children were required to sit "in position, hands folded, eyes on the blackboard"; their only relaxation from the drill was "through a different kind of formality, when windows were opened and all stood erect breathing 'in-out, in-out' to the teacher's formula."[24] In most classrooms reading period was devoted to oral reading from a basic text; very little time was devoted to "voluntary, independent reading," and adjustment for individual differences was "more frequently hoped for than attained."[25]

Arithmetic instruction was equally motivated by traditional ideas, implemented by old-fashioned methods. Typical arithmetic instruction ignored the social aspects of the subject, its relevance to the world outside the classroom, emphasizing instead computational skills. "In many of the lessons observed pupils merely copied long lists from the blackboard and worked them at their seats, a deadly routine procedure." Fewer than 10 percent of the teachers observed made any attempt to "relate the arithmetic being studied to local situations."[26]

A study of the New York program in English instruction gave further evidence of the absence of progressive educational policies in the elementary schools. Dora V. Smith, the inquiry's expert on English instruction, described one of the classes she observed as follows:

A first grade class sat bolt upright in straight rows and seats nailed to the floor. At a signal from the teacher that the "language" lesson was about to begin, each child clasped his hands on the edge of his desk, set his feet squarely on the floor, and prepared for a ten minute solo performance of *The Three Bears* by a child obviously superior to the rest of them in attainment in language.

Miss Smith acknowledged that such an English lesson seemed "incredible" except to those who had "spent considerable time in the classroom," but, she maintained, "this formula for the development of language power . . . is still the most generally practiced procedure in use."[27] She found that over 60 percent of New York's teachers "still adhere to a program of segregated, non-functional teaching of English skills." Moreover, teachers made very little effort to adjust material in accordance with the individual needs and abilities of students: "No basic philosophy of individual need seemed to prevail, but rather the necessity for coaching certain weak pupils so that they might meet an arbitrary standard set."[28]

In the social studies the inquiry staff found a mixture of progressive and old-fashioned practices. On the one hand, the investigators reported that social studies teachers were, for the most part, quite imaginative and were able to lead discussions in which they asked more "thought questions" than questions designed to elicit factual material. They made extensive use of field trips and conducted relatively democratic classrooms: "The prevailing practices can probably be described as 'guidance without domination.'" The report went on to suggest that "an investigator who knew schools of thirty years ago might well be impressed with the degree of pupil freedom."[29] On the other hand, as in the other subjects, the state syllabi were too rigid, and very few local syllabi were any better. In most cases the social studies were not integrated (as the progressives maintained they should be) but consisted of parallel courses in history and geography, with little reference to the other social sciences. "The curriculum as pupils experience it," the report pointed out, "is largely a matter of acquiring factual information. While such information may be justifiably memorized, the higher objectives of understandings, attitudes and skills are not adequately emphasized."[30] The report did not attempt to reconcile its praise of the quality of teaching with its low estimate of the curriculum as experienced by pupils.

A careful reader of the reports of the Regents' Inquiry would be forced to conclude that the movement for a more child-centered school had failed to make a great impact on New York schools. New York was by no means unique. A study of innovation in Pennsylvania schools concluded that the process of diffusing educational innovations was extremely slow. The report argued that despite the fact that recent controversies in education left "the general impression that the schools, by and large, have adopted the practices that are debated" and despite the charge that the ills of society are the result of "progressive education," schools have not changed a great deal: "In the schools of Pennsylvania today and, the authors venture to say, in the schools of America, we find little manifestation of the practices subject to controversy. As a matter of fact, the succeeding waves of 'reform' which have come and passed in this century have left discouragingly little mark.''[31]

III

Despite the impassioned discussions of progressive education in the 1920s and 1930s and the marked progressivism of a few school districts, it seems clear that by the eve of World War II progressive education had not significantly altered the broad pattern of American education. The call for a child-centered school had, for the most part, been ignored. How do we account for progressive education's lack of impact in most schools and explain its success in a few school districts? I hope that a more detailed examination of the schools of the Chicago area will help me to answer these questions, yet some tentative conclusions are possible at this point.

The role of the depression in discouraging educational innovation was of obvious importance. Many school districts found themselves cutting back on previously adopted programs and in no position to experiment with new approaches and programs. Everywhere music, art, and other "nonessentials" were under fire from irate taxpayers; and school boards were forced to retrench. Under these circumstances widespread adoption of progressive practices was extremely unlikely.

Moreover, the depression exacerbated previous problems. School systems that had been overcrowded in the 1920s found that they had to defer building programs in the 1930s. Schools that were operating on double shifts and concerned with the basic problem of finding enough seats for their pupils could not commit themselves to searching for answers to less immediate problems. For some elementary schools, particularly in rural areas, the problem was to maintain a building that approached the basic standards of health and safety. Thousands of schools (particularly in the South) lacked basic sanitary facilities. For these schools, operating below the standards of the nineteenth century, progressive education was not a relevant concern.[32]

Aside from economic considerations, other factors complicated the transformation of the schools. The philosophy of progressive education had not established itself as the dominant point of view at teacher-training institutions before World War II. I believe, however, that further investigation will reveal that in the 1940s these schools became more and more committed to progressive ideology. As teachers of teachers were forced in the 1930s to go to graduate school and get higher degrees, they were exposed to the tenets of progressive education at such pioneering progressive institutions as Teachers College, Columbia University. This contact with progressive education was probably influential in reorienting the faculty of teacher-training institutions, and in the postwar period more and more teachers who had received their training according to progressive precepts were entering the public schools. By the 1950s a majority of American teachers were probably recruited from those who had had their training in progressively oriented schools of education.

The 1950s also brought a period of great expansion to American education. Just as an economic depression had discouraged educational innovation in the thirties, the period of affluence and expansion in American education produced an atmosphere favorable to change. There may well be a rhythm to patterns of educational innovation which is closely linked to the economic cycle and variation in the size of the school-aged population, with periods of affluence and generous school budgets, favorable to educational change, alternating with periods of contraction when innovation is particularly difficult.[33] In the 1950s a great deal of money was available for building schools and for recruiting teachers and other school personnel. In the atmosphere of largesse for education, there was less questioning of the cost of particular educational practices, and educators had greater freedom to innovate. As more schools were built in the suburbs (which had been friendlier to progressive education all along), progressivism gained strength. It seems quite likely, therefore, that the real impact of progressivism came, not in the 1930s, but in the 1950s, not when the Progressive Education Association was at its height, but when it was on the point of collapse.[34]

If further investigation proves that this was indeed the case, we are left with the observation that the vicious attacks on progressive education which marked the late 1950s was not an attack on a superannuated program of education that had grown lax with age, but rather a systematic effort to destroy a form of education that was still young, relatively untried, and had unrealized potential for American school children. With the destruction of progressive education during the educational crisis of the late 1950s, there was a hiatus in public concern for child-centered education, and it was left for today's advocates of the open classroom to reenunciate many of the principles of progressive education.

NOTES

1. Lawrence Cremin, *The Transformation of the School: Progressivism in American Education, 1896–1957* (New York: Vintage Books, 1961), p. 291. Cremin qualifies this statement by pointing out that reforms proceeded at an uneven pace in different areas.

2. Ibid., pp. 291–308. Cremin does deal with a more or less typical school system, using the Lynds's study of Middletown. He suggests that the "conservative progressivism" of this city's schools "typifies the influence of progressive education on the pedagogical mainstream during the interbellum era" (p. 305). In his bibliographical essay Cremin points out that his use of Middletown "is in many respects a literary device at best" (p. 383).

3. I have chosen to concentrate on elementary schools because the introduction of progressive ideas into secondary schools was complicated by the problem of meeting college admission standards. There was considerably less pressure on elementary schools to meet a uniform standard of preparation. In many cases I have used statistics dealing with the late 1930s in order to represent the degree to which the innovations of the progressives of the 1920s and the 1930s had actually been adopted.

4. U.S. Office of Education, *Biennial Survey of Education in the United States, 1938–1940 and 1940–1942*, 2 vols. (Washington, D.C.: Government Printing Office, 1947), vol. 2, chap. 1, p. 5; chap. 2, p. 3.

5. Ibid., chap. 3, p. 24.

6. For Cremin's definition of progressive education see *Transformation*, esp. pp. viii–ix. Cremin's use of the term "conservative progressivism" (quoted in n. 2 above) indicates the kinds of difficulties inherent in his very broad definition of progressive education.

7. U.S. Office of Education, *National Survey of the Education of Teachers*, Bulletin, 1933, no. 10, 6 vols. (Washington, D.C.: Government Printing Office, 1932–35), 2: 42.

8. Ibid., p. 36.

9. Ibid., pp. 162, 174.

10. Ibid., 3: 136–38.

11. Francis E. Peterson, *Philosophies of Education Current in the Preparation of Teachers in the United States,* Teachers College Contributions to Education, no. 528 (New York: Teachers College Bureau of Publications, 1933), pp. 126–27, 131–32.

12. Herbert B. Bruner et al., *What Our Schools Are Teaching: An Analysis of the Content of Selected Courses of Study with Special Reference to Science, Social Science, and Industrial Arts* (New York: Teachers College Bureau of Publications, 1941), pp. 205, 208, 209.

13. Ray L. Hamon, "Trends in Types of School Seating," *The Nation's Schools* 16, no. 3 (September 1935): 57–58.

14. See advertisements in the *American School Board Journal* of the period.

15. Wilma Walker, "Social and Health Work in the Schools," *Social Work Year Book 1941* (New York: Russell Sage Foundation, 1941), p. 514. The 1935 edition of the *Year Book* reported that there were approximately 175 visiting teachers (an earlier term for school social workers) employed in seventy-one centers but that nowhere did the number of visiting teachers approach the goal set by the White House Conference on Child Health and Protection of one visiting teacher for every 500 pupils (Shirley Leonard, "Visiting Teachers," *Social Work Year Book 1935* [New York: Russell Sage Foundation, 1935], p. 533).

16. Ethel L. Cornell, "The Work of the School Psychologist," University of the State of New York, *Bulletin,* no. 1238 (June 1942), p. 9. In Ohio the state made no provisions for school psychologists until 1945, and it was not until 1949 that 10 percent of school districts in Ohio had approved units in school psychology (S. J. Bonham, Jr., and Edward C. Grover, *The History and Development of School Psychology in Ohio* [Columbus, Ohio: State Department of Education, 1961], pp. 1–3).

17. Interview with Luther Gulick, April 1973.

18. Julius B. Maller, *School and Community: A Study of the Demographic and Economic Background of Education in New York,* The Regents' Inquiry into the Character and Cost of Public Education in the State of New York (New York: McGraw Hill, 1938).

19. Leo J. Brueckner et al., *The Changing Elementary School,* The Regents' Inquiry into the Character and Cost of Public Education in the State of New York (New York: Inor Publishing Co., 1939). Their critique indicates that the members of the inquiry staff generally accepted a moderate version of progressive education: they favored a child-centered curriculum but did not believe that teachers should abdicate their own sense of what was important for children to learn.

20. Ibid., pp. 164–65.

21. Ibid., p. 171.

22. Ibid., p. 47.

23. William S. Gray and Bernice Leary, "Reading Instruction in Elementary Schools," in Brueckner, *Changing Elementary School,* pp. 285–86.

24. William S. Gray and Bernice Leary, *The Teaching of Reading in the Elementary and Secondary Schools of the State of New York,* The Regents' Inquiry into the Character and Cost of Education in the State of New York (New York: The Regents' Inquiry, 1938), p. 24.

25. Ibid., pp. 44–45.

26. C. L. Thiele and Leo J. Brueckner, "Arithmetic Instruction in Elementary Schools," in Brueckner, *Changing Elementary School,* p. 333.

27. Dora V. Smith, *Evaluating English in the Elementary Schools of New York: A Report of the Regents' Inquiry into the Character and Cost of Public Education in New York,* Eighth Research Bulletin of the National Conference on Research in English (Chicago: Scott, Foresman and Company, 1941), p. 64.

28. Ibid., pp. 62, 63.

29. Edgar B. Wesley and Howard E. Wilson, "An Inquiry into Instruction and Achievement in Social Studies," Regents' Inquiry into the Character and Cost of Education in New York State, Elementary Division (Typescript, New York State Library, Albany, N.Y.), p. 57.

30. Ibid., p. 39.

31. Paul R. Mort and Francis G. Cornell, *American Schools in Transition: How Our Schools Adapt Their Practices to Changing Needs: A Study of Pennsylvania* (New York: Teachers College Bureau of Publications, 1941), p. 3.

32. "The Nation's School Building Needs," *Research Bulletin of the National Education Association* 13, no. 1 (January 1935).

33. This point was suggested to me by Robert Lyke, "Suburban School Politics" (Ph.D. diss., Yale University, 1968).

34. The rise and fall of the organization that represented educational progressivism is related in Patricia A. Graham, *Progressive Education: From Arcady to Academe, A History of the Progressive Education Association, 1919–1955* (New York: Teachers College Press, 1967).

Library of Congress Cataloging in Publication Data

Main entry under title:
Schooling and society.

    "Published under the auspices of the Shelby Cullom Davis Center for Historical Studies, Princeton University."
    1. Educational sociology—Addresses, essays, lectures.   2. Community and school—Addresses, essays, lectures.   I. Stone, Lawrence.   II. Shelby Cullom Davis Center for Historical Studies.

LC191.S265   370.19   76–15005
ISBN 0–8018–1749–8